SHOOTERS
THE TOUGHEST MEN IN PROFESSIONAL WRESTLING

JONATHAN SNOWDEN

Copyright © Jonathan Snowden, 2012

Published by ECW Press
2120 Queen Street East, Suite 200, Toronto, Ontario, Canada M4E 1E2
416-694-3348 / info@ecwpress.com

All rights reserved. No part of this publication may be reproduced, stored in a retrieval system, or transmitted in any form by any process — electronic, mechanical, photocopying, recording, or otherwise — without the prior written permission of the copyright owners and ECW Press. The scanning, uploading, and distribution of this book via the Internet or via any other means without the permission of the publisher is illegal and punishable by law. Please purchase only authorized electronic editions, and do not participate in or encourage electronic piracy of copyrighted materials. Your support of the author's rights is appreciated.

LIBRARY AND ARCHIVES CANADA CATALOGUING IN PUBLICATION

Snowden, Jonathan, 1975–
Shooters : the toughest men in professional wrestling / Jonathan Snowden.

ISBN 978-1-77041-040-4
ALSO ISSUED AS: 978-1-77090-220-6 (PDF); 978-1-77090-221-3 (EPUB)

1. Wrestling—History. 2. Mixed martial arts—History.
3. Wrestlers—Anecdotes. I. Title.

GV1195.S66 2012   796.812   C2011-906981-4

Editor for the press: Michael Holmes
Cover and text design: David Gee
Cover images: Special collections of the University Libraries
              of Notre Dame, © George Napolitano
Printing: Webcom   1 2 3 4 5

PRINTED AND BOUND IN CANADA

SHOOTERS

ALSO BY JONATHAN SNOWDEN

Total MMA: Inside Ultimate Fighting
The MMA Encyclopedia (with Kendall Shields)

Intro **1**
1 Muldoon and the Dawn of American Wrestling **3**
2 The Uncivilized Import: Catch-as-Catch-Can **13**
3 "Farmer" Burns **23**
4 Jenkins, The Turk, and the American Title **29**
5 The Russian Lion Roars **37**
6 Old World vs. New World: Gotch vs. Hackenschmidt **47**
7 From the Kodokan to the Count of Combat: Mitsuyo Maeda **59**
8 A World Without Heroes **65**
9 Policemen, Trustbusters, and the Double Cross **78**
10 Thesz **93**
11 The Revolution Will Be Televised **105**
12 The Great Danny Hodge **117**

CONTENTS

13 No One Before Kimura, and No One After **124**
14 Wigan **132**
15 Judo Gene and Bad News **145**
16 The Inoki Legend Born **159**
17 Brisco: The Last of His Kind **168**
18 The UWF and Shoot Style **176**
19 The Next Level: The Shoot-style Revolution **183**
20 UFC: No Holds Barred **196**
21 Fighting for Pride **208**
22 Saku **215**
23 Brawl for All **233**
24 Your Olympic Hero: Kurt Angle **247**
25 The Next Big Thing **254**
26 Wrestling Invasion **267**
27 The Future **285**

Sources **291**
Acknowledgments **309**

Wrestling may be the only universal sport. It transcends culture, race, and creed. The art form has been passed down all over the world, each country doing things just a little differently. The Greeks perfected brutal submission holds. In Switzerland and Iceland, they wrestled with their belts on, concentrating on throwing opponents with this handle rather than grappling on the ground. The Egyptians thought wrestling form important enough to preserve it on pottery. Turks bathed in oil before pushing each other around, accompanied by increasingly frantic music. On the American frontier, rough and tumble grapplers would often wrestle until one of the men had their eye gouged out.

INTRO

Kings wrestled. So did battlefield generals and American presidents. Ivan the Terrible and Peter the Great were both big believers in the art of wrestling. Even the angels wrestled in the Bible. There are many great wrestling stories to be told, but we'll focus on just one — the tale of the sport's true toughmen.

Tales of toughmen, of great fighters, are often tall to begin with. But they tend to grow taller with every subsequent retelling. The odds get longer, the foes grow ever bigger and more dangerous, and contests that lasted mere moments are turned by memory and by legend into epic struggles that lasted hours. We have a shared impulse, a kind of collective desire, to transform even the best among us into even better versions of themselves. It's not enough to have been a strong fighter with a record of fine victories; we demand ever greater heroes with ever greater triumphs, and we get them in the stories we tell.

Shooters traces those stories back to the men behind the myths, following the evolution of a sport that combined art and entertainment, skill and spectacle long before the WWE and UFC. Our story takes us around the world, from Japan to America and back again, and south to Brazil and back again. It all begins in the New York of the 1880s, at the dawn of professional wrestling.

William Muldoon was built like a Greek God. In an era that saw women afraid to reveal even their ankles beneath a long skirt, the "Solid Man" wasn't afraid to show a little skin. Even as far back as the 1880s, at the dawn of professionalism in sports, wrestlers already needed gimmicks to sell bouts to the masses. Muldoon, for his part, was leading the way. He was a gifted wrestler but a better salesman. His gimmick was dressing as a Roman gladiator. Before bouts he was photographed in a loincloth and sandals, often naked from the waist up.

He was a man who knew gimmicks, and with the gladiator getup, he was taking

1 MULDOON
and the Dawn of AMERICAN WRESTLING

iconography to the next level. Donald Mrozek, author of *Sport and American Mentality 1880–1910*, thinks Muldoon was onto something that resonated with his audience. Muldoon's costumes suggested that he was something more than a mere man. His sculpted body was the proof:

> *Closely tailored and spare, Muldoon's costume emphasized his good proportions and well-developed physique. It not only had the practical advantage of freeing him of encumbrances for wrestling; it was a way of calling great attention to the attributes of his body apart from his physical performance. As much as it constituted an aid to Muldoon's performance in the ring by its sparsity and an assist to his image by flattering his impressive physique, Muldoon's costume was the feathering of a peacock, the uninhibited flaunting of the body in general and the male body in particular.*

Muldoon had first learned to use that rock solid body in the Union Army during the Civil War. Just a boy when he enlisted, Muldoon had essentially grown to manhood in raucous Army camps. The Union in particular often whittled away long hours with impromptu as well as organized wrestling contests. It's said that wrestling was such a big part of life in the Army that General Ulysses S. Grant had to apologize to Confederate leader Robert E. Lee when Lee came to Appomatox to surrender. Grant's tent, it seems, was in disarray:

> "Pay no attention to things, Bob," the General said, "me and some of the boys were having a wrestling match in here last night."

Muldoon was one of the very best grapplers in the Union Army and never gave up the sport. Not ready to give up the soldiering life either, he volunteered on the French side during the Franco-Prussian War in 1871. It was there that he was introduced to Greco-Roman wrestling. Developed in France and quickly spreading throughout the European continent, it was a style well suited for a man with Muldoon's physical gifts. Never the quickest or most skilled, what Muldoon did have going for him was size and strength. Greco, which prohibited holds below the waist, was the perfect style for a man of his statuesque proportions.

When he returned to New York in 1876, he settled into a career as a police officer. Even as he progressed to the rank of detective, wrestling was never far from his thoughts. His home base was Harry Hill's saloon, known for comely barmaids, nefarious characters, and equally nefarious prizefights. Muldoon became acquainted with boxing at Harry Hill's, but it was wrestling where he made his mark. The boxing matches were illegal, so it was easier to strip to the waist and grapple — especially for a police officer making a few extra bucks. For a prize between $5 and $10, Muldoon would wrestle anyone who dared.

Muldoon soon took his act on the road, the first step towards wrestling's demise as a legitimate sport. At these vaudeville shows, often contested on the same stages that housed plays and other high art, the goal was to entertain — and to convince the audience into putting their money down on side bets. Professional wrestling's secret isn't that it once featured real contests and later shifted towards entertainment. The real secret is that, from Muldoon's time forward, professional wrestling was never a legitimate sport. Very early on, powerful promoters took hold of the sport, and money became the primary motivator. Even before Muldoon's reign as champion, fans and critics were already decrying a sport that was anything but pure. The *Brooklyn Eagle* contends that wrestling bouts were being scripted all the way back in the 1870s, singling out a match between Frenchman Thiebaud Bauer and "Professor" William Miller:

> There is probably no sport before the public — not even excepting professional billiard playing — in which there has been so much regular "hippodroming" and crookedness practiced as in the wrestling arena within the past two or three years. There has scarcely been an important contest in which the result has not

been known beforehand. A system of humbug has been carried on in the form of creating a supposed bitter rivalry between prominent wrestlers, in order to get up an excitement, and matches have been arranged which have been alleged to be for thousands of dollars a side, when not a dollar has been put up on either side, the contest being one for the gate money alone, and that is equally divided, the betting deciding as to which party should win. The men have been found guilty of it and in one case the knavery was publicly exposed out West. But still the people are being gulled by these so-called championship wrestling matches. The latest contest in the wrestling arena was that between Miller and Bauer at Boston last night, in which Miller was defeated, Bauer winning in one fall. The usual $1,000 challenge followed, and another profitable gate money match will be arranged. Pools were sold at Boston on the match, in which Miller was the favorite with those not behind the scores, he being the strongest man and the best wrestler. The fact is nothing has been such a blight on honest sport as the curse of the pool box. It has almost killed professional billiards in the Metropolis; has broken into the healthy life of baseball; driven professional oarsmen out of the arena, and brought odium upon every sport with which it has been connected. But for the pool rooms of Chicago and St. Louis — encouraged by the local press there — there would have been no such crookedness in the Western baseball nines, which recent developments have disclosed.

Bauer would lose a rematch to Miller, giving up two of three falls for the princely sum of $500. Muldoon, while later becoming a very serious man and the head of the New York State Athletic Commission, wasn't above that kind of tomfoolery in his own nascent wrestling career. He worked closely with the above mentioned Miller in a series of bouts in 1878 and was caught by police detective Thomas Adams and the *New York Times* trying to work a match with Bauer to build up his name:

Muldoon attempted to perpetrate a little dodge on the public by making an arrangement with the wrestler Bauer to appear at the entertainment in a match with him, it being prearranged that Muldoon should throw Bauer, and thus enlarge upon his previous reputation.

Adams belonged to the executive committee of the club, and took great pride in pure athletics. When he discovered Muldoon's scheme he went to him and forced him to drop it, telling him that he would expose him if he attempted to make a false reputation at the expense of the club. This made Muldoon a bitter enemy of Adams.

Despite the questionable legitimacy of his wrestling, Muldoon was a public relations dream. By 1881 his matches were such attractions that the Solid Man, celebrated in song and verse, left his job to become a professional athlete. At the time, this kind of professionalism was unheard of. Athletics were a pastime, a pursuit to build healthy bodies and minds. No one did it as a vocation. No one, that is, until Muldoon.

Even before turning pro, Muldoon had already been crowned Greco-Roman champion of the world. In 1880, the *Spirit of the Times*, an early sports periodical, made a gold medal up for grabs between Muldoon and Bauer. The winner would receive the medal and the title of World Champion. At New York's Gilmore's Garden, the Madison Square Garden of its day, the two wrestlers drew a crowd of 3,000 spectators and more than a handful of photographers and reporters. Muldoon, who outweighed his opponent by more than 20 pounds, took the first fall in 43 minutes, but not before entertaining the assembled crowd with his feats of strength, easily breaking all of Bauer's holds. In the second fall, 20 minutes in, Bauer scored a flash pin, Muldoon's shoulders having touched the mat for just an instant despite controlling most of the action.

In the deciding tumble, Bauer got behind the policeman and looked to have things under control. But it only takes a momentary lapse, a loss of focus, to lose a bout contested at the highest skill levels. When Bauer wiped the sweat from his eyes, Muldoon struck, tossing him to the mat and pinning him in just three minutes.

"THE SOLID MAN" WILLIAM MULDOON

Title lineage was constantly in dispute. Others also claimed to be the world's best, and at different times a handful of men were often listed as the champion. Muldoon, for his part, took on all comers. His first challenger was Professor William Miller, a British strongman who teamed with boxer Jem Mace on a tour of the Americas. The battle raged into the early hours of the next day, neither man able to secure even a single fall. Of course, bouts that ended with a disputed finish led to boffo box office for the inevitable rematch.

It was a pattern that was repeated in Muldoon's first famous bout with Clarence Whistler. The two locked horns for eight hours with no end in sight. Finally the venue owners shut off the gaslights at the Terrace Garden Theatre, sending a crowd of 2,000 home unsatisfied.

It was a brutal match. Whistler was the quicker of the two and spent much of the bout behind Muldoon, once even dragging him to the ground looking to turn him for the pin. The two went at it for seven hours, each hour round separated by a 10-minute rest period. Muldoon's arms and neck were streaked with red, a product of Whistler's fingernails, purposely kept long to wreak havoc on the champion. After hours of wearing away, Muldoon claimed Whistler then doused his head in ammonia, rubbing this new weapon into Muldoon's many wounds and causing excruciating pain. For his part, Whistler had his left ear torn partially from his skull. Certainly no one left that match prettier than they were going in. Still, as the years went on, Muldoon remembered his opponent fondly.

"I am convinced Whistler could not have thrown me," Muldoon said after his foe's 1885 death. "But I must admit that he is one opponent whom I do not think I could have beaten at his best. He was a wonderful wrestler — the greatest I have ever met, and one of the greatest, probably, the world ever knew."

The Whistler bout was Muldoon's last as a city employee. Combining grueling training with a dangerous job was too much for any man. From that point forward, the Solid Man was a full-time athlete. Professional athletics wasn't a realistic goal for most of American history. But changing demographics, including a fast-growing urban population and the development of a national rail system, made both major attractions and touring shows possible. Muldoon, by now becoming a bona fide star, was quick to take advantage.

The *Police Gazette*, a scurrilous weekly magazine known for its scantily clad women and lurid crime reporting, had found an audience rabid for sports content. Perhaps the first American tabloid, there was no account the publication wouldn't run, no story too lurid for an audience looking for the sex and violence traditional daily papers were shielding them from. The story of an illegal prizefight in West Virginia between Paddy Ryan and Joe Goss, the English champion, sold 400,000 copies. The "proprietor" of the *Gazette*, Richard Fox, smelled a hit and the magazine became the sports chronicle of record through the dawn of the 20th century. Muldoon knew Fox well. The two had become close as the wrestler built his reputation in bar room matches and Fox always gave the wrestler plenty of ink. Muldoon's friend and biographer Edward Van Every emphasized, "Almost every week some mention of Muldoon was to be found."

Muldoon was an innovator, always looking for ways to improve his performance. In the North East, dedicated sports fans expected a bout to be a long and drawn-out affair. They were diehards, often with money at stake, and expected a wrestling match to last all night. People gaping at wrestlers on a nationwide tour didn't have the same expectations. Far from it. Seven-hour bouts were certainly not going to be tolerated. Muldoon would soon become the first promoter to institute a time limit.

There was much more to Muldoon's act than mere wrestling. His performance art was generally what onlookers would remember years later. The wrestler called them "plastic poses." He would cover himself in white paint and stand perfectly still, a human representation of a classic Greek statue or a scene from antiquity.

Wrestling was a major part of the act. Along for the ride were familiar former foes like Whistler, Miller, and Edwin Bibby, a British wrestler skilled in the catch-as-catch-can game. Whistler was his most popular foe, and it was said that while "the firm of Muldoon and Whistler coined money, Muldoon was always uncomfortable while the partnership lasted." Whistler, it was whispered, was the better man in a real contest. The troupe traveled around the country, from New Orleans to San Francisco, developing the sport of professional wrestling as they went.

As Gerald W. Morton and Geroge M. O'Brien relate, "All the hoopla of modern professional wrestling as a roadshow attraction was there. The media build up before bouts and challenges issued in the local press, claimants to regional titles, a collection of impressive championship belts, foreign challengers, colorful tights and even costumes were all part of the wrestling scene in the 1880s."

Some of Muldoon's bouts were on the level, others exhibitions staged to please his fans. Crowd challenges were common, with Muldoon offering $200 to any man who could throw him even once. Against legitimate local studs like Ohio's John Theurer, Muldoon would up the ante. Theurer would get $300 if he could toss Muldoon. The champion would collect $100 if he could best the challenger once every 10 minutes for an hour. Future major league baseball president Ban Johnson was on the scene for the *Enquirer*, gushing over Muldoon's impressive physique, "showing plainly the grand development of which the human body is capable." The muscles were for more than show: Muldoon finished off Theurer 10 times in just 23 minutes.

In 1883, Muldoon truly established himself as the top Greco wrestler in the country. He defeated Bibby and Whistler in a second epic match from Clarence's homebase of San Francisco. Foreign challengers followed, men from Germany, France, Spain, England, and even Matsada Sorakichi from Japan. None could best Muldoon.

Traveling for a decade straight, Muldoon remained undefeated, although many of the contests were just for show. Other wrestlers like catch wrestling star Evan Lewis came and went on the tour, as did boxing great John L. Sullivan, who Muldoon had discovered in Boston and brought back to New York to jump start a splendid career; Muldoon was the constant.

BOXING'S ORIGINAL BAD BOY: **JOHN L. SULLIVAN**

It's the famous Sullivan who has carried Muldoon's name alongside his own into history. The two men were polar opposites. Muldoon was a staunch believer in Muscular Christianity, a philosophy that combined religion, masculinity, and physical fitness. As a teetotaler who frowned on alcohol and tobacco, Muldoon was the favorite of respectable society. Future president Teddy Roosevelt trained with him, and he brought a hint of class with him to the otherwise disreputable athletic shows. Even his art, Greco-Roman wrestling, was considered more proper — his scandalous nearly nude modeling dignified by the allusions to classical art. As his career wound down he toured for several acting companies, performing Shakespeare rather than suplexes.

Sullivan was a fat and slovenly drunk. While Muldoon put on airs, putting a humble upbringing and a stint as a bar bouncer behind him, Sullivan never rose above his circumstances. His mother had dreams of the priesthood for him. He preferred drinking and fighting to his year and a half at Boston College. Yet despite what the *New York Tribune* called "his brutality, his coarseness, and his vices" Sullivan's fighting prowess was never in question: "He certainly is not afraid of meeting any living man with his barefists."

He and Muldoon often traveled together in touring troupes but kept separate company. Sullivan had dispatched Paddy Ryan to claim the heavyweight title but struggled with drink and weight issues. The two men were brought back together in part by a mutual distaste for *Police Gazette* owner Richard Fox. Muldoon and Fox had fallen out when the champion defeated Fox's personal find Sorakichi. The newspaperman's enmity for Sullivan was legendary. They were said to dislike each other from their very first encounter. Fox was used to sportsmen kissing up to him, desperate for favorable mentions in the *Gazette*. When he found Sullivan at the same establishment, Fox called the boxer into his esteemed presence. According to boxing lore the legendarily headstrong Sullivan was having none of it:

> "Mr. Fox would like a word with you."
>
> The answer, bellowed to the waiter, was heard by everyone in the establishment.
>
> "You tell Fox that if he's got anything to say to me he can Gahdamn well come over to my table to say it!"

From the day of the insult forward, it was Fox's mission in life to dethrone Sullivan. The dispatched Paddy Ryan was his boy; Fox even presented him with a diamond encrusted title belt. Sullivan's supporters then raised money to buy him an even gaudier belt. "Fox's is like a dog collar compared to mine," the fighter was said to exclaim. Ryan would fall to Sullivan's heavy hands three times, but Fox was hardly through with him. He brought in fighters to challenge Sullivan's crown, men like Tug Wilson and "Maori" Slade who fell short of the goal, each clobbered by Sullivan's prodigious punching power.

Finally Fox unleashed his toughest competitor yet — Jake Kilrain, a rugged former mill worker who was also, in a strange mixture of sports, a former championship-caliber rower. Fox tried for years to get Sullivan, who had made almost a million dollars touring the

BOXING GREAT JOHN L. SULLIVAN
LIBRARY OF CONGRESS

world making boasts and performing exhibitions, into the ring with Kilrain. In 1887, while Sullivan was attracting huge crowds in Britain including the Prince of Wales, Fox declared his protégé to be the heavyweight champion of the world, hoping to raise Sullivan's ire.

When the two were finally set to meet, Sullivan's backers were almost ready to forfeit their $10,000 side bet rather than send John L. into the ring for an inevitable whooping from Kilrain. Sullivan's British debauchery was legendary and his health had never recovered. Enter Muldoon, the proponent of physical fitness who had developed quite a reputation for healing the ills of society's elite.

Muldoon staked his reputation that he could get the grotesquely out-of-shape Sullivan into fighting trim in time to face Kilrain. It wasn't easy. Sullivan was too stubborn to quit and performed all the physical tasks asked of him. It was quitting liquor that was the hardest part. Muldoon kept a watchful eye on the pugilist, once even following him into town and dragging him back as he was just getting started in what would surely be an epic bender. By the end of training the two were sharing a single room but hardly speaking. Recounts historian Arne K. Lang, "Their relationship, cordial at best, became downright hostile as the fight drew near. Toward the end of his stay, Sullivan purportedly stopped talking to Muldoon all together. Although they were literally inseparable, virtually Siamese twins, an entire day would pass with no verbal communication other than Muldoon's terse commands."

The training paid off as Sullivan was able to last 75 rounds before Kilrain's corner finally threw in the towel. It was a strange bout, as the contestants and the crowd all had to evade the law. Louisiana officials were dead set on stopping the fight. Eventually the fighters and 3,000 fans snuck onto a special train and made their way to Richburg, Mississippi. There the town sheriff entered the ring to stop the fight. He was given $200 and stepped right back out. The fight was on!

It was a classic battle between technique and power. Kilrain peppered the champion with punches, but Sullivan landed the harder blows. This was the last championship fight contested under London Prize Ring Rules, which made Muldoon's expertise valuable in more than just physical fitness. The bout included plenty of grappling, with Sullivan throwing Kilrain violently to the ground on multiple occasions, often attempting to land a knee or kick for good measure. As temperatures reached 100 degrees, both men sipped whiskey between rounds. The combination made Sullivan vomit when he took a hard punch to the gut in the 44th round.

One hour became two and still the men fought on. They were barely coherent, struggling for breath and to maintain their feet, when Kilrain's corner threw in the towel. After 75 rounds, Sullivan remained champion. Despite the success, Sullivan and Muldoon would never work together again, with the champion going as far as to say if the two crossed paths again he would punch the wrestler's lights out. Muldoon responded in an open letter in the *New York World*. Translated into today's verbiage, it carried a simple message: bring it on.

Like Sullivan, Muldoon was the last of his kind. Just as the Marquess of Queensberry Rules supplanted the bareknuckled bouts of Sullivan's time, a new form of wrestling was pushing Greco-Roman aside. Muldoon had carried the sport with personal charisma and celebrity. But long and dull clinch-fests couldn't hold spectators' attention the way the fast and action-packed catch wrestling could. A new day was dawning in American wrestling, with Evan "Strangler" Lewis leading the way.

While Muldoon's Greco-Roman impressed dandies and wealthy sportsmen, including President Theodore Roosevelt, Harry Houdini, and other dignitaries, another style of wrestling was slowly overtaking Greco in popularity. It was once again an import, but instead of coming over from France as the misnamed Greco-Roman style had, it was a product of the English countryside.

In Lancashire, England, the wrestling was as hard as the men. A collection of mill workers, miners, and textile workers, the blokes were rough and tumble and fit. Entertainment in the 19th century was primitive — singing, dancing, and scuffling.

2 THE UNCIVILIZED Import: CATCH-AS-CATCH-CAN

Wrestling was a big part of life, and the best men would meet in front of large audiences in challenge matches, with side bets making the result of more than a little interest to the spectators. These open-air bouts, often contested in just underwear, were a staple of Lancashire gatherings well into the modern age.

Sporting aficionados, even other English wrestlers, considered the Lancashire style beyond the pale. It was seen as simply uncivilized — the attacks on the legs and wrestling on the ground just didn't seem appropriate to many Englishmen. Of course even fierce critics like author Walter Armstrong admitted that it might just come in handy when push came to shove came to fisticuffs: "In a rough-and-tumble encounter, when 'all is in,' a knowledge of Lancashire wrestling might be of service; but even in a street fight it is not the fashion for an Englishman to battle on the ground, but to allow his opponent to get up again."

It was this ground wrestling that separated the Lancashire style of catch-as-catch-can from the other British wrestling arts that focused primarily on the throw. In Lancashire the action wasn't over when the bout hit the grass — it was just getting started. Attacks included a variety of pinning holds, head locks, and arm locks. Arms and fingers were often broken in these contests; however, if the referee thought the hold was intended to do permanent damage he would disqualify the offending party. It was an aggressive and attacking style far removed from the kind practiced in the rest of Britain. To first-time viewers it was often an uncomfortable experience, and an 1893 compendium of sports and pastimes notes, "A Lancashire wrestling match is an ugly sight: the fierce animal passions of the men which mark the struggles of maddened bulls, or wild beasts, the savage yelling of their partisans, the wrangling, and finally the clog business which settles all disputes and knotty points, are simply appalling."

It was these "wild beasts" that came to America to spread their style of wrestling throughout the mid to late 1800s. Men like Tom Connors, Jim Parr, Edwin Bibby, Joe Acton, and Tom Cannon toured the country as part of a wrestling troupe. Acton may have been the best of the bunch but was only a middleweight. At around 140 pounds, he could meet all comers in the catch style but struggled in mixed-style competitions, which included Greco-Roman or collar-and-elbow style contests that placed a premium on bulk. The Brits initially dispatched all comers in their free-wheeling style and even had some success in Greco-Roman wrestling, particularly Bibby, who battled the "Western Hercules" Clarence Whistler to a draw in New York. Whistler "shook him like a dog would a rat" but couldn't secure a fall. As good as he was in the French style, Bibby excelled in his own, beating Duncan Ross in a match to crown the first American heavyweight catch wrestling champion in January 1881.

Ross was a *National Police Gazette* favorite, taking on all comers not just as a wrestler, but in foot races, hammer throws, and a variety of athletic endeavors. Among his specialties was a mounted broadsword competition with blunted weapons and a bit of armor. He often signed his correspondence "Duncan Ross, Champion Athlete of America." After meeting Bibby on the mats he could still claim that title, but he was no longer America's champion wrestler.

The Brits controlled the American championship for most of the 1880s, and in the classic American way this Lancashire style was soon assimilated into a melting pot of wrestling techniques called American catch-as-catch-can. At the same time the Lancashire style of wrestling was finding an audience, Japanese jiu-jitsu aces were touring the country sharing their own brand of wrestling. The combination of the two, along with traditional American "rough and tumble" and collar-and-elbow moves, proved nigh unbeatable.

A STRANGLEHOLD ON THE COMPETITION: **EVAN "STRANGLER" LEWIS**

It's fitting that the first true American wrestling champion in the catch-as-catch-can style was a man every bit as hard and ruthless as his English forbearers. A native of Ridgeway, Wisconsin, Evan "Strangler" Lewis was the son of a farmer and butcher. Already a wrestling stalwart in his tiny town, he left to seek his fortune out west in his early twenties.

Lewis made waves first in Montana, where he won a 64-man tournament, returning home in 1883 as the Montana State Champion. Lewis dominated the Midwest scene for several years, often in front of raucous crowds criticized by some as being truly disgraceful.

In 1885 he debuted his famed stranglehold, described by a reporter on the scene as a "peculiar neck-lock." Victims included Charles Moth and the Englishman Tom Cannon. The Moth win was followed by whispers the bout had been staged, or in the parlance of the time, a hippodrome. Those suspicious of a match's validity simply followed the money. Despite losing the first fall to Moth in Moth's favored Greco-Roman style, the bets poured in for Lewis. Sure enough, Moth was disqualified for using a stranglehold and the win went to Lewis. The *Wisconsin State Journal* called the bout fixed and the audience denounced it. Still Lewis's popularity soared in his home state and eventually his reputation demanded he venture out into the wider world to face the country's best wrestlers.

Working with promoter Charles "Parson" Davies, the top "manager of athletic entertainments" in the Midwest, Lewis was groomed for stardom. Davies was a born huckster and controversy followed him wherever he went, starting with organized walking contests (once one of the most popular sports in the country) before graduating to wrestling and finally prize fighting once wrestling had been thoroughly exposed as no longer on the level. Davies, like all the best con men and promoters, was a smooth operator with the media. When he passed through Ogden, Utah, on his way to California, Davies held the local reporters in the palm of his hand. For example, the *Ogden Standard* reported, "The 'Parson' is in good health and looks more like a preacher than a sporting man. He is a very handsome, clean-shaven man of about 35 years of age and dressed in faultless style. He is recognized among the fraternity as being the best living authority in his particular line, and whoever obtains a straight tip from him considers himself lucky indeed. Mr. Davies is a fluent and interesting talker and a prime favorite with the newspaper boys."

Between marquee matchups, Davies and his team of grifters found a foolproof way to pocket a pretty penny. Davies, and other companies like his, crisscrossed the country providing wrestling and boxing exhibitions. In fact, the major matches served as advertisements for these traveling shows. You could make a decent buck with a major event, collecting a few pennies from each spectator to see your show — but you could really become rich by taking bets, building up expectations by making a local performer look unbeatable before fleecing bettors when an unheralded wrestler in the troupe would beat him soundly to close the show.

Of course, the wrestlers on tour had to be double tough as well as sneaky. You never knew when a local kid had real wrestling chops or a ringer would journey to the same town the troupe was performing in to cause trouble. Whether wrestling was on the level in the late 1800s is an open question, especially in high profile bouts between business partners. But there was never a dull day on the road.

"In the 1880s & '90s, the time of Muldoon, and then Evan Lewis, and those who followed, with shrewd promoters like Davies showing the way, headline wrestlers took on 'all comers' via participation in vaudeville revues and other forms of legitimate stage bookings," wrestling historian J. Michael Kenyon wrote. "Like the vaudeville acts, they'd put on afternoon and evening shows, day after day, for weekly engagements, with payoffs to anyone who could 'stay' the prescribed time with the headliner. Often times, the week-long bookings would end in a blow-off bout with a local of some prominence . . . depending on how many suckers they could find to get involved with some betting. This sort of thing provided living expenses for the stars, with the wagering providing their 'bonus' cash."

Before Lewis could headline one of these traveling extravaganzas, he first had to make more than a regional name. His first major test was Japanese strongman Matsada Sorakichi. One of the first wave of Japanese wrestling stars to tour America, Sorakichi was the perfect foil for the homegrown American talent. Promoted by Professor Phil Kirby and the creation of the National Police Gazette's Richard Fox, the Japanese sensation was derisively referred to in the papers simply as "the Jap." Unlike the jiu-jitsu and judo stalwarts who would soon follow him from Asia, Sorakichi wasn't selling science. His style, called simply "the Japanese style," was essentially Sumo mixed with a little bit of thuggery. His most effective move involved plowing his head into his opponent's midsection with all the force of his 160 pounds. Many ribs were broken this way, and plenty of noses bloodied, giving the wrestler a fearsome reputation.

Unfamiliar with the western methods of wrestling, Sorakichi found scant success against the likes of Acton, Bibby, and even Muldoon in a mixed rules match that included Greco-Roman, Japanese, and catch-as-catch-can action. Fox worked hard to set up the Muldoon bout, but four falls took less than 15 minutes and the audience was said to have left "disgusted," believing Muldoon had intentionally thrown the third fall.

It was a rare misfire for Sorakichi, who generally left fans satisfied and would tour the country in 1885, wrestling a who's who of the time including Duncan Ross, Joe Acton, and Germany's Karl Abs. A draw with Ernest Roeber and wins over Andre Christol and the tough collar-and-elbow stylist Jack Gallagher helped build his reputation, and his drawing power, to the point that Muldoon was begging for a rematch. He never failed to entertain, approaching every match with a furious intensity. Win or lose, at the end of a match with Sorakichi, his opponent would know he had been in a battle. The Japanese star was immensely strong. Between matches he would entertain the crowd by twirling 250-pound Indian clubs. It was this strength that made him competitive when wrestling ability and smallish size left him at a disadvantage.

He met Lewis in Chicago in January 1886. Sorakichi would be giving up almost 30 pounds to Lewis but proclaimed himself unconcerned. He told a reporter he wasn't worried — after all he had held his own with the monstrous Karl Abs. Sorakichi was more concerned with Lewis's reputation for finger breaking and choking, but assured his supporters he had a counter for the chokehold.

Unfortunately, that didn't appear to be the case. After winning the first fall by pinfall, Lewis was shoved out of the ring by his Japanese foe. Sorakichi proclaimed it an accident. Nevertheless, after the incident the mean-spirited Lewis head-butted his opponent right off the stage, landing the two men on the same spot the Japanese had deposited him moments before. Lewis was immediately disqualified, losing the fall. In the third and deciding fall, Lewis was able to secure his vaunted chokehold. As he coughed blood, Sorakichi had enough time to cry uncle before passing into unconsciousness. Lewis was the victor, but agreed with Sorakichi's self-proclaimed status as wrestling's strongest man: "Sorakichi is the strongest man from the waist up that ever I came across. When I wrestled Cannon, Leon, 'Greek' George and those fellows, I knew I had the advantage of them in strength, but the Jap has arms like a bar of iron."

Lewis's string of wins brought him the attention of the sports world and Joe Acton, a man who was once loath to battle the Japanese star but eventually took him under his wing and was Sorakichi's trainer for the bout with the Strangler. Acton was also the man considered by most to be the top British catch-as-catch-can wrestler, and he challenged Lewis to a match in either Philadelphia or Chicago. First, however, there was the matter of a little unfinished business with Sorakichi.

A rematch was signed for the very next month in Chicago. Lewis brought 3,000 rabid fans to the Second City for a bout with the stranglehold barred. Debate about the use of the hold would follow Lewis throughout his career and many opponents wouldn't wrestle him without the hold being declared illegal. Cynics could see it as an easy way to work what would later be called a "program" with opponents. One match would be held with the hold legal, a follow up with it barred. That's exactly what happened here. Sorakichi wanted it clear he didn't intend to be choked again, telling Lewis that if he choked him, Lewis would be shot. Lewis vowed to the Japanese that he would instead "screw your leg off."

True to his word, Lewis caught Sorakichi in a vicious leglock, nearly breaking the smaller man's leg. The crowd was riotous when Sorakichi finally rolled over and allowed himself to be pinned. This was commonplace at the time, since tapping out, the universal symbol of submission in modern martial arts, didn't really exist yet. When caught in a painful hold, a wrestler would usually cede defeat by turning to his back and allowing a pinfall.

Not understanding submission locks and considering them unsportsmanlike, some in the crowd called for Lewis's head. Promoter Parson Davies feared the worst and asked newspaperman R.L. Carey to calm the crowd. He explained such potentially dangerous holds were allowed in the catch-as-catch-can style and that both competitors had undertaken the risk of potential injury. Lewis was awarded the first fall, and when Sorakichi couldn't continue, the match.

An article in the *New York Times* claimed the hold broke Sorakichi's leg, but it was actually only badly sprained. Although it swelled up to twice its normal size, the Japanese star was right back on the mats in less than a month. Lewis, too, took right back up where he left off. Now a bad guy in much of the Midwest for what they perceived as cruel treatment of Sorakichi, Lewis was booed the next month in Milwaukee. The local *Sentinel* proclaimed, "His brutal treatment of the Jap will not soon be forgiven."

A week later, Lewis wrestled Edwin Bibby in St. Louis, securing three of five falls against the Brit. The great Muldoon himself challenged him to a match in Minnesota later in the year. In his preferred Greco-Roman style, the Solid Man could only pin the Strangler once within the 60-minute time limit. He had promised two pinfalls in the allotted time, making Lewis the winner of their handicap bout. His opponent's tactics did not amuse Muldoon, who blamed Lewis's manager Davies for the Wisconsinite's evasive strategy.

"Mr. Lewis fully carried out his instructions," Muldoon wrote in an open letter. "And proved to the audience that he could run backwards further in one hour than any man they had ever paid admission to see."

A rematch was scheduled for June in Chicago with the two men splitting falls before Muldoon was too tired to continue. The crowd booed loudly when Muldoon didn't return for a final fall and the great Greco-Roman star would never again agree to meet Lewis in the increasingly popular catch-as-catch-can style, despite the two regularly appearing as part of the same touring group.

THE ORIGINAL "STRANGLER" LEWIS

Part of a growing nationalism, catch was seen as an American style, a homegrown sport founded in the heartland. Greco-Roman, based on its name alone was inherently foreign. Never mind that catch had its roots in England. Sometimes perception is more important than truth — and in this case it helped propel catch wrestling to forefront of the grappling world.

To further Americanize catch wrestling, Lewis would have to dispatch with two long-standing British stars, Joe Acton and Tom Connors. He took his first shot at Acton in February 1887 in front of 4,000 fans in Chicago. He lost the match, but was able to take a fall from the Brit. On April 12 in Chicago, again before a large crowd, he defeated Acton and laid claim to the catch-as-catch-can championship.

Two months later, Lewis would meet Acton's countryman Tom Connors in a wild match in Pittsburgh, Pennsylvania. Lewis was his usual self — ultra aggressive. He had raised the ire of the fans in the Midwest with his use of the chokehold and crippling holds against Sorakichi. With the stakes even higher, and the opponent even more talented, it seemed there were no limits to which Lewis might not sink.

It was a foul-filled affair that included head butts, kicks, and the occasional punch. When Lewis secured his dreaded stranglehold, Connors defended by grabbing the American's fingers, causing the Strangler to cry out in pain. He eventually secured a strangle that caused Connors' brother Jim to call foul, rushing into the ring and punching Lewis.

When order was restored, the match continued on into the night. Lewis continued to kick Connors and attempted to smother him, another example of the kind of poor sportsmanship that made him the most feared man on the grappling circuit. Connors defended with a head butt or three and was disqualified, losing the fall.

Connors rebounded strongly to take the second fall via pinfall and was awarded the match when the referee determined a Lewis stranglehold, using a thumb and finger to grab an opponent's windpipe, was an illegal hold in the third. Connors was proclaimed the champion of America. Parson Davies, for once, was powerless and fumed over the decision. Lewis proclaimed the match was a farce and he couldn't get a fair shake in Connors' homebase of Pennsylvania. The *Pittsburgh Dispatch* report makes it clear Lewis was known for his foul play: "It is a well known fact that Lewis is noted for this, and in every square contest in which he has ever been engaged, there had been kicking and a claim of fouls. Connors knew this and went in to give as good as was sent, consequently the affair descended into a bloody struggle."

While Lewis and Connors would occasionally exchange barbs back and forth, the two never met again on the mats. The negotiations before a Lewis bout were often as contentious as the matches themselves, as Connors learned to his dismay. Lewis insisted that the *Police Gazette* rules that prevented strangleholds didn't apply to his own favored hold — a hold he claimed was legal under the rules. Because there was no single style of wrestling and no agreed upon standard set of rules, there was much to discuss before any significant wrestling bout.

Not only did the men have to settle on rules and a style, but they also had to negotiate how to split the gate receipts and the amount and terms of a side bet. Money was required upfront and the stakes were given over to a third party to await dispensation to the winner. Most prominent wrestlers didn't have to front their own money — rich fans and businessmen often did that for them, sometimes to their detriment if the two wrestlers had their own prearranged idea of how the match would go. In some cases, large side bets were announced to attract a crowd, but in actuality, there was no personal stake of any kind — the wrestlers were just building up a crowd and splitting the gate receipts, letting the betting action decide who won the fixed bout. It was a complicated and often dirty business.

Frustrated with a lack of progress in their negotiations, Connors challenged Lewis to a rough-and-tumble fight, essentially a no-holds-barred contest similar to today's Ultimate Fighting Championship. "I am no fighter of that sort, and do not care to engage in it," Lewis told the *Milwaukee Sentinel*. "But if Mr. Connors insists upon it, all right, I'm his huckleberry."

The proposed match never took place. Lewis became ill before the match could be booked and upon regaining his health went on tour with Muldoon for Davies. It was on these long nationwide tours that mat men made their real money, and Davies knew Lewis could still draw fans to the box office. Despite the Connors loss in 1887, Lewis again claimed the mantle of America's champion. After defeating an overmatched Jack Wannop, a phony claimant to the British title, Lewis was declared world champion.

But some fans had not forgotten Connors. Both men continued to wrestle throughout the Midwest with each accused of faking matches. Lewis accused Connors of hippodroming a match with Jack Carkeek, a Davies and Lewis associate who was later arrested for his part in various scams around the country. Carkeek was once arrested after he and his associates built up his reputation in Chicago as a great runner. They wrangled a saloonkeeper into betting $400 on Carkeek in a race. The wrestler took an early lead but mysteriously came up lame. These kinds of hijinks went on everywhere the wrestlers went. Of course, the Strangler was no choirboy. A typical Lewis match was so questionable the *Sentinel* thought it worth remarking that his match with Charles Green was on the level.

Accusations of fraud weren't unique to wrestling in this era. All professional sports were suspect at the time, including horse racing and boxing. While skepticism was warranted, historian Melvin Adelman believes crowds were likely too quick to call foul. Almost any upset was greeted with howls of derision in the late 1800s and as wrestling historian Lee Casebolt pointed out, wrestling was a particularly hard sport to parse. Two men could work an audience subtly if they did it right, often with no one knowing the difference: "Sham wrestling, though, is a difficult thing for even an experienced observer to detect when practiced by skilled performers, and 'losing a fall was unproblematic when friends could back the winner, and the winner might share the prize money.'"

The same kinds of troubles were plaguing the Greco-Roman scene as well. By this point it was speculated most of Muldoon's matches were more show than contest. He was a star and an attraction. Whether he was a better wrestler than the other members of his troupe was inconsequential. He was the meal ticket for his entire sport and was carefully protected. Even so, credibility could only be stretched so far. As he approached 40,

Muldoon looked for an out. He would still tour some, but would no longer compete for championship honors. Ernest Roeber, Muldoon's handpicked successor when the great man retired in the early 1890s, didn't have Muldoon's personal charisma or steady stream of challengers. As a result, interest waned. Many attribute his initial lack of success at the box office to a problem that would go on to plague Frank Gotch's successors in years to come — Roeber didn't earn his sucession in the field of combat. Roeber bristled at the critique: "He told them he was passing the title on to another, and one whom he knew he could trust to defend it with honesty and sportsmanship and that he knew of no better man to pass it over to. 'The new champion,' [Muldoon] said, 'is Ernest Roeber.' There were some who questioned Muldoon's right to pass his crown to me, but I stood ready at all times to meet all comers."

Roeber was put up against the always-exciting Lewis, but the bout failed to pick business up off the mat. They wrestled in New Orleans, to mild interest. The local paper was skeptical from the get-go, declaring, "Wrestling has fallen into disrepute because it became impossible to distinguish between genuine matches and exhibitions." Despite these admonitions, the two did manage to draw 2,000 fans for the contest that would see the winner take home a $2,000 purse.

Roeber came into the bout in top form. Lewis on the other hand had been ill and also had been mourning his first wife, who had passed away earlier in the year. Despite this, he was willing to give it a go. A coin toss may have decided the best of five falls match. The winner would choose his favored style to lead off, meaning the two would grapple in his chosen art for three of the five falls. The winner was Lewis who, of course, led things off with catch-as-catch-can.

Lewis won the two falls decided by catch rules easily in around 20 minutes total. Roeber also won the Greco-Roman falls, but it was more of a struggle, lasting nearly an hour combined. After 73 minutes on the mat it came down to a final fall contested under catch rules. This time Roeber was only able to stay alive for 62 seconds. Lewis pinned his shoulders to the mat and won an important victory for catch wrestling.

Roeber soldiered on, declaring he was still the Greco-Roman world champion. He continued wrestling and even made a box office resurgence battling a stream of "Terrible Turks" at the turn of the century. But his day and Greco-Roman's hold on the wrestling public were over.

Unfortunately, it seemed Lewis's best days were behind him as well. He was often ill, even suffering from a grueling bout of consumption that almost killed him in 1894. Wrestling needed a new champion and one was on the horizon. Martin "Farmer" Burns spent much of the year demanding a title shot. In April 1895, Lewis agreed, but only if Burns would wrestle with the stranglehold legal. Though giving up 15 pounds, the Farmer was close to his prime. Lewis was "fat as a prize pig," but his legend was so great there were still cries that the fix was in. John Kline, one of Lewis's supporters, told the Chicago-based *Inter Ocean* paper that he was disgusted by his friend's lack of pride: "I am ashamed of Lewis for selling out that match, for I have no use for fakes; but, then, Lewis was square with his personal friends and put them on that they lost no money on that match. . . . I knew before the Lewis-Burns match that Lewis was going to lose it, but he lost it so clumsily I am surprised that any one who saw the alleged contest did not catch on to its being a fake, and he barely missed winning the match even while trying to let Burns have it. The referee did not know that there was a job put up, however."

Lewis would continue wrestling for several more years, taking falls for whoever opened their wallet. He is a legend of the sport and a pioneer for catch wrestling. But Burns, and more importantly his students, would lead wrestling to new heights.

The photograph is iconic, the content unforgettable: Martin "Farmer" Burns hanging by his neck from a noose. A normal man would, of course, never survive the experience. In fact a wrestler who later tried to duplicate the stunt died in the attempt. But Farmer Burns was no ordinary man.

Raised in Iowa by Irish immigrants, Burns seemed born to be a wrestler. His wrestling career started out almost that early. By the tender age of eight he was wrestling friends in the schoolyard — always for money. This much, at least, never changed.

As a teenager he spent his days plowing fields and his nights wrestling at every chance

3 "FARMER" BURNS

he got. By the age of nineteen he was quite well known in the neighborhood of Dennison, Iowa, as a very husky young man with a reputation as a winner.

The Farmer wasn't actually a farmer for long, just four years according to martial arts historian John Gilbey. Farming, after all, was back-breaking all-day labor. It was much more profitable to make a living from wrestling. But before he could turn to wrestling full-time, Burns needed some seasoning. He was a skilled grappler, but not among the world's best, at least not in his youth. Like all amateurs, he needed to learn the tricks experienced professionals used to survive. Some lessons were learned the hard way. In 1886, Burns lost a match to Evan Lewis with the latter's dangerous stranglehold. Vowing to never let that happen again, Burns (who weighed just 160 pounds) developed his neck until it was a gargantuan 20 inches.

According to the legend of Farmer Burns, three years later, on a trip to Chicago to sell some hogs, Burns saw a sign advertising that pro wrestlers were in town. He desperately wanted to give Lewis another go and "The Strangler" was taking on all comers for a $25 prize. Lewis and his partner Jack Carkeek knew Burns was legitimate and wanted no part of him. This was one of the pitfalls of challenge matches. Usually it amounted to beating planted audience members or local toughs. But sometimes, when a man like Martin Burns crossed the threshold, an easy night of fun was no longer an option.

Manager Parson Davies told Burns they had all the challengers they needed that night. But Burns was a patient man; he told them he'd be back every night until they had room. Finally Burns was allowed to take the stage, dressed in his farmer's overalls, a gimmick he would use throughout his career. Taking one look at him, master of ceremonies J.W. Kelly decided to yuck it up:

> "What would you call a man who hoes potatoes and squash and shucks corn?" Kelly asked.
> "A farmer," replied the musician.
> "Well, then," he continued, "if this farmer would get locked up in a house and the house would catch fire, what would happen to the farmer?"
> "I do not know," the musician replied.
> "Farmer Burns," replied Kelly.

It was Burns who would have the last laugh. He faced Carkeek, another tested professional, lasting a full 15 minutes, and held off Lewis in another 15-minute bout to take home $100. It wasn't often that touring wrestlers were beaten at their own game, and Burns, now known as "The Farmer," quickly became a part of their close-knit fraternity. He studied with the best, men like the Englishman Tom Connors, looking to learn every trick in the book. Realizing that skill could only take him so far, like William Muldoon before him, he built his body into a perfect machine, avoiding cigarettes and alcohol.

Traveling the country with Connors, Burns soaked up knowledge. He also put on a great show. Beyond the hangman's noose, Burns had plenty of gimmicks to draw a crowd. A favorite gambit was challenging a town's entire football or baseball team to wrestle. If Burns defeated them all, one after another, he would win and collect a side bet. If one of them were able to beat him, he'd have to pay up. More than any of his other contemporaries, wrestling was life for Burns. For most of his adulthood, it was a singular focus.

Eventually, when he thought he was ready to assume the responsibility of being America's top wrestler, the Farmer took another stab at greatness. Burns had become a crowd favorite, but champion Evan Lewis refused to meet him on the mat. He wanted Burns to earn his title shot; after touring the country for years, Burns believed he had. In 1895, after calling the champion out for more than a year, Burns finally got a shot at Lewis's crown. In an April match at the Savoy Theatre in Chicago, considered by most observers to be an obvious setup, Burns finished the Strangler's career as a serious mat man. The Farmer was the world champion.

Burns was a wrestling machine, seemingly impossible to wear out. He toured often prior to winning the title. Afterwards he was constantly at work. He wrestled in the touring athletic shows and when they were taking a break, worked the fair circuit as well. Starting with Connors & Green's Specialty Show, Burns wrestled for a variety of vaudevillians, including the Tarjee and Conner All-Star Show, the English Gaity Show, and the ubiquitous Parson Davies' Floto Show. Soon he was leading his own troupe for the Richards & O'Donnell Company, putting on a show and developing new talent for the then-gargantuan sum of $300 a week. Burns had an eye for talent, recruiting some of the best and most marketable wrestlers of the era. He also expanded and perfected the time-tested methods of sucking an audience dry.

"Burns became the master of what I — and the old Greek pimps and hustlers who taught me a lot of those tricks — call cross-roading," historian J. Michael Kenyon wrote. "It was the business of sending in 'advance' men and then following up with late-arriving 'challengers.' Burns's troupe, which included most of the great rascals of the pre–World War I era, would work an area for, maybe, four or five months at a time. Then, having robbed the locals of every nickel and dime they could get their hands around, they'd skedaddle — and open up shop in another region."

Harper's Weekly had an interesting tale of exactly how Burns and other professionals would sucker local sportsmen out of their hard-earned money. It was called barnstorming, the practice of traveling the country looking for local wrestling stalwarts and taking them for a ride. Wrestling as McCarthy, a wood sawer, Burns challenged a Scandinavian farmer with a reputation for toughness. After giving up the first fall, a Burns compatriot in the audience bet $100 it wouldn't happen again. The Scandinavian's neighbors, having seen the first fall, were quick to accept the bet. Then Burns took over, winning consecutive falls in less than a minute. Burns turned a cartwheel and revealed his true identity to the crowd, suddenly revealing they had been played for patsies. This kind of thing was repeated across America as wrestlers used local pride to soak fans who vehemently supported their local favorites.

MARTIN "FARMER" BURNS (*right*)

Burns discovered many of the greats who followed him into wrestling history, including "Toots" Mondt, Charles Olsen, and Earl Caddock. His crew also included Emil Klank, John Berg, Billy Sandow (who was later the second Strangler Lewis's manager), and Bob Manoogian (who usually appeared as "The Terrible Turk"). These were among the best wrestlers in the world at the turn of the century.

"FARMER" BURNS   25

Farmer Burns was not just a gifted athlete. He was also a leader of men, the kind of man others wanted to follow. A brilliant teacher who could explain the complicated human chess involved in a wrestling match so it made perfect sense. He opened wrestling schools in Iowa and Nebraska and was soon hawking his teachings nationwide in a mail-in course called *The Lessons in Wrestling and Physical Culture*. Filmmaker John Nash thinks Burns was doing more than selling pamphlets. He was helping create a wrestling resurgence in popular culture:

> *Burns's success can be attributed to an increased interest in amateur wrestling across the country, which in part was fueled by an interest in professionals such as Burns. As the nation's urban centers grew, a movement started to organize sport as recreation for the industrial workers. In 1888 the Amateur Athletic Union sanctioned its first national tournament and soon afterwards became recognized as the governing body for amateur wrestling in the United States. Athletic clubs opened across the nation offering wrestlers a place to train and compete. In the early 20th century colleges began to hold wrestling meets. In a few decades wrestling had gone from a sport where two local toughs challenged each other to one where hundreds of professional athletes supported themselves wrestling and where a vast amateur network gave tens of thousands an opportunity to participate.*

Of course, despite his own accolades and his success as a promoter, Burns has been overshadowed by his protégé, the great Frank Gotch.

THE LEGENDARY FRANK GOTCH

Born on his family's farm in Humbolt, Iowa, in 1876, Frank was the ninth child of Fred and Amelia Gotch. Like many strapping lads from the heartland, he grew up strong from his chores and with a love of wrestling. With his very aggressive style of wrestling, he owned the local scene as a young man, terrorizing anyone who dared match up with him. Young, strong, and unskilled in wrestling science, Gotch was the perfect mark for a man like American heavyweight champion Dan McLeod.

McLeod was traveling the country under an assumed name in 1899, pretending to be a furniture mover from Omaha, Nebraska, named Dan Stewart. Using his real name would have been impossible; McLeod was well known as the man who bested Farmer Burns in 1897 for the American Championship. Under that assumed name he could draw betting action against him when he challenged local stars like Gotch. Not knowing who his opponent was, Gotch was happy to accept the stranger's challenge. His supporters were just as happy to bet on him against "Stewart."

The two engaged in a fierce contest on a cinder track at a Modern Woodmen of America picnic. They battled for more than an hour before McLeod was able to secure a fall. Gotch called it the most difficult contest of his career. "I was picking cinders out of my anatomy for more than a month after that battle ... we went at it like a couple of Turks. Head spins and all sorts of things," the champion recalled in his 1913 biography.

The pain, not just from the cinders, but from tasting defeat, was eventually well worth it. The match with McLeod brought Gotch to the attention of Farmer Burns, the most powerful man in American wrestling. Always on the lookout for new talent, Burns was pleased to put Gotch to the test himself later that year in Fort Dodge. Gotch had come to challenge the wrestlers, and Burns, rather than let one of his troupe potentially fall victim to the talented lad, decided he'd better answer Gotch's challenge himself. Historian George S. Robbins paints the scene: "Burns was offering $25 to anyone who could last 15 minutes without getting pinned. Gotch gave him all he could handle, but the Farmer prevailed after 11 minutes of hard wrestling. The Farmer then addressed the audience and told them, 'Ladies and gentlemen, I have never met an amateur wrestler the like of this fellow in my life. If he will go with me, I will make him champion of America in a few months.'"

From Burns, Gotch learned the art of wrestling. Under the tutelage of Burns's cronies like Jack Carkeek and Joe "Ole Marsh" Carroll, he learned the business of wrestling, warts and all. Touring Iowa and the Midwest, working programs with Burns when other challengers didn't present themselves, Gotch was initiated into the industry's inner workings. Gotch lost a match to a local baker, Oscar Wasem, in 1901 despite outweighing his foe by almost 30 pounds. Two weeks later, Burns came to the rescue, getting revenge for his protégé in straight falls. It was basic storytelling, but it worked. The local crowd was much

FRANK GOTCH

more willing to support their champion with an important win over Gotch under his belt. Interest in the Burns match was much higher than it would have been without building Wasem first. Gotch was learning not just how to win wrestling matches but how to control the audience with the kind of showmanship that separated mere wrestlers from champions.

With a firm understanding of how the business really worked, Gotch was tagged to travel to the Klondike as part of an elaborate scam. Teaming with Ole Marsh and the ancient collar-and-elbow specialist Colonel James McLaughlin, Gotch journeyed to the Klondike to fleece a mining community starved for entertainment. Gotch went by the name Frank Kennedy and joined the camp as an actual miner. McLaughlin and Marsh were the top wrestlers who had come to challenge any who dared.

Soon challenges and money were flowing freely. As Kennedy, Gotch established himself as the toughest man in the camp. Of course he was chosen to face the professionals in their midst, the other miners unaware he was actually in partnership with his opponents. Eventually, the camp began catching on. It was time for the final hurrah — Gotch as Kennedy finally scoring a big win over Marsh. The wrestlers then disappeared from Alaska like smoke in the wind, but not before a final scare — the original ship scheduled to take Gotch back to the mainland sunk with all his worldly goods, but not his money stash, on board. Fortunately, Gotch had stayed behind for a final soiree.

Upon his return Gotch was not just flush with cash — he had also proven his worth to Burns and the powers behind the scenes. He was ready to take a step into the limelight, ready to go beyond being merely champion of Iowa. He was ready to take on the great Tom Jenkins for the championship of America.

Tom Jenkins was a man made of iron. It's little wonder; he built his rock-hard and powerful body working in the steel mills in Newburg, Ohio. Jenkins looked like a wrestler from another era, with callused hands and steel grip to go along with a missing left eye. Unlike wrestlers in the wild and wooly American frontier, Jenkins didn't lose his eye in a grappling match. It was an accident much more innocent than a reckless gouging — a toy cannon exploded on the Fourth of July when he was just eight, taking his eye and breaking his jaw.

Jenkins grew up hard, on the proverbial wrong side of the tracks. His eye injury

4 JENKINS, THE TURK, and the AMERICAN TITLE

slowed him down for a year, when he was confined to a dark room to protect his vision. Soon enough, though, he was running amok in the streets, a petty thief stealing from one street vendor and selling his ill-gotten wares a few blocks down the street to another. By the age of 12 he had been arrested eight times.

Like many professional wrestlers of his time, Jenkins came about his career by happenstance. He had been working full-time since the incredible age of 10, first making tire irons before getting a job at a steel mill in his teens. At 18, he finally got his break. During a benefit for an injured waterboy at the mill, one of the wrestlers scheduled to entertain failed to appear. The mill manager George Patton volunteered Jenkins, who impressed everyone by going to a draw. Sensing real potential, his boss sent Jenkins for wrestling lessons in 1891. Two years later, he was turning professional, a mat natural.

Although not a skilled technician, he made up for it with raw power and willingness to dish out and accept pain of all kinds. Jenkins was immensely strong. His job at the mill involved redirecting red hot 100-pound iron bars with a giant pair of tongs. He did this day after day, hour after hour.

"That job taught me to be quick," Jenkins said. "And it put a neck and arms on me and horny calluses on the heels of my hands. When I got my man on the mat, I ground the calluses into his face. It took the skin off."

Using his hard-earned calluses to his advantage was just one of Jenkins' tricks. He was tenacious and aggressive to the point of being dirty, relying on power moves like body locks to soften opponents up and a stranglehold as his finishing technique. When that hold was banned in most contests, he moved to a jaw lock, which to even the most careful observers looked an awful lot like a stranglehold.

Jenkins became an attraction right away. He must have been quite a sight — before each bout he would remove his glass eye, shocking those not in the know, and wrestle with his socket exposed to the world. It was a fitting image for a no-nonsense athlete who came up the hard way in a hard world.

By 1897, under the management of George Tuohey, Jenkins had worked his way into title contention. He sat ringside along with 1,500 other rabid wrestling fans that October in Indianapolis to witness Dan McLeod take the world championship from Farmer Burns. Immediately after the bout, which McLeod won two falls to one, Jenkins issued a challenge to the new champion.

Instead, a month later in front of the same fans, Jenkins beat Burns in consecutive falls. Both he and McLeod claimed the world championship. It's unclear who had the right to call himself America's best. Jenkins had battled Burns that March and the champion failed to throw him the required two times. But it wasn't reported at the time as a title change. Going forward, both claimed to be the champion. A bout to settle the score seemed logical, but since Jenkins wasn't part of the Burns inner circle, he didn't get a real opportunity to dethrone McLeod for several years. Instead he returned to the Northeast, leaving the Burns troupe to their Midwest stomping grounds.

Between bouts with McLeod, Burns, and other major names of the time, Jenkins stayed plenty busy. Bravely, perhaps foolishly, he boxed with champions like Jim Corbett, risking his one good eye. Corbett won handily but made it clear he didn't think there was a man out there who could take it to Jenkins with a more liberal rule set. In a straight fight, Corbett believed Jenkins was one of the toughest men in the world.

A FOREIGN MENACE

Jenkins was one of the few Americans willing to take the challenge of the enormous Terrible Turks who came to the melting pot of the world to ply their trade against the nation's best wrestlers. Foreign challengers would become a staple of the American mat game, but Youssuf Ishmaelo was a trendsetter, the first real Turkish wrestling star to make the trip to the western world to test his prowess against our mat masters.

That fact seems to have been lost in what was to follow; dozens of "Turks" eventually made their way to America, led by manager Antonio Pierri, described as having a head "shaped like an egg" and being as crooked as they come. The bulk of these were clearly frauds. Some, like the "Turk" who wrestled for Farmer Burns's troupe, were really just swarthy Americans putting on a show.

It's this confusion that may have caused the attack on Youssuf's reputation in the years after his death, a tragic boating accident in 1898 that cost 546 people their lives. By the time Graeme Kent wrote *The Pictorial History of Wrestling* in 1968, Youssuf was being referenced as a French dock worker who wasn't a real wrestler at all.

While there's little doubt that wrestling at the time was filled with chicanery and plenty of gimmicks, it's unlikely Youssuf Ishmaelo was one of them. If you wanted to create a gimmick wrestler to fill the role of "villainous foreigner," why go through the trouble to recruit Koca Yusuf (Ishmaelo's real name), one of the leading Turkish oil wrestlers of his generation? If you didn't need him to actually be able to wrestle, why pursue the real thing when a Parisian dock worker really would have served just as well?

Ishmaelo was brought to France in 1894 where he ran roughshod over the leading European grapplers of the time. He beat Pierri, who would later become his manager, the enormous Frenchman Paul Pons, and the British star Tom Cannon before touring America in 1898.

The Turk immediately made a huge splash in New York. Promoters claimed he had won 115 bouts in Europe and promoter William Brady, an early motion picture and theater producer who knew a good drawing card when he saw one, offered $100 to any man who could last all of 15 minutes with the foreign terror. Veteran catch specialist George Bothner took him up on the challenge, but at 125 pounds was no match for the giant. Youssuf was furious that such a slight man would dare challenge him and knocked Bothner unconscious with a thunderous slam. The smaller man still remembered the bout clearly years later:

> *He was a modern Hercules and he knew how to apply his punishing strength, as he was as quick as a jungle cat and master of all holds. Youssuf came at me like a bull. He rushed me right off the mat into a bunch of chorus girls in the wing. The first thing I knew I found myself helpless. The Turk picked me up as if I was a kitten. Never before have I felt such terrible strength. Before I could give a wiggle or squirm he dashed me down on the boards with terrific force, knocking all the strength and wits out of me.*
>
> *They told me that after I had landed, Youssuf rolled me over with his foot, looked out over the audience, gave a contemptuous snort, and walked off the stage. When I came to, I was a sadder, but wiser young man. Somehow or other I got into my clothes, hobbled out into the street and started to walk up Third Avenue towards my home. Youssuf had given my neck such a wrench that he almost tore it from my shoulders. It was several days before I could look in the direction I was headed.*

Beating Bothner was one thing, he was 125 pounds soaking wet. Taking on a legitimate heavyweight was another thing altogether. But Youssuf was up to the task, challenging Evan "Strangler" Lewis, Ernest Roeber, and other wrestlers of note. Roeber was the first to respond, and the Turk manhandled the Greco-Roman star in front of a standing-room-only crowd at Madison Square Garden. It was a spectacle that intrigued more than just the male sports fans that typically attended wrestling bouts. The *New York Times* was shocked to find as many women as men in the crowd, all howling for the Turk's blood. He entered with pomp, wearing an overcoat over his trunks and a giant plaid turban. He was a monster of a man, 6'2" and nearly 300 pounds. The *Times* noted his muscular back and giant hands. Roeber, a man who relied much on physical strength as most heavyweight Greco-Roman wrestlers do, seemed to be in trouble: "The two men met on a giant open platform open on all sides. This was typical of the time — sports-specific arenas didn't exist yet and performances were often held on the same stages that regularly held stage actors and musicians. Roeber wanted little to do with his enormous opponent. He danced around the edges of the platform, refusing to engage. Eventually Youssuf had seen enough. He pitched Roeber right off the platform. The American champion fell five feet to the ground and couldn't continue."

The crowd was hot for blood, calling for a lynching and surrounding the stage menacingly. The Turk was escorted to the back by a squadron of police officers. Tom Cannon volunteered to take him on in Roeber's place, but officials felt the crowd was too riled up to bring the foreigner back onstage. Fearing for Youssuf's safety, the evening's entertainments were brought to a close.

Promoters, of course, were delighted. A rematch was scheduled for the Metropolitan Opera House a little more than a month later. The crowd packed into the building, and a large contingent of women again turned out to see the bout. If possible, it was even crazier than the first match.

This time the ring was surrounded by ropes, designed to keep the Turk from tossing his opponent out into the crowd again. Instead, Youssuf used them to his advantage by forcefully hurling Roeber into the corner. Fans and critics complained that the Turk was more animal than wrestler, avoiding holds and using brute force instead. This was actually the style of the Turkish wrestlers. When they competed in their home country, both competitors were oiled up to the point holds were impossible. Brute force was their science, but Roeber and the audience failed to appreciate this. The *New York Times* chronicled the chaos that erupted when the two styles clashed:

> *Tiring of the big man's roughhouse tactics, Roeber punched the Turk square in the face twice. Chaos erupted as Youssuf's promoter William Brady hit the ring to try to tackle Roeber but was met in the middle by the wrestler's training*

partner Bob Fitzsimmons. A renowned pugilist and wrestler, Fitzsimmons tossed Brady from the ring like he was a child. Brady landed on the table housing reporters and was prevented by police from reentering the fray.

The ring filled with police, trainers, and sportsmen. When the police restored order, both sides wanted the other disqualified. Instead the bout was declared a no contest. The crowd was furious and after the previous hijinks in Madison Square Garden, believed they were being put on. The bout that was supposed to rescue wrestling from its growing reputation of not being on the level was instead met with cries of "Fake, Fake, Fake" that echoed through the building.

The next month it was Jenkins' turn to meet the Turkish sensation. Wrestling for $1,000 a side, in front of the largest crowd ever to witness a wrestling contest in Cleveland, Jenkins could do nothing with Youssuf. Before the bout Jenkins claimed his opponent downed a whole bottle of olive oil and the liquid was oozing out of his very pores. He tried all the holds he knew above the waist but couldn't move the massive man. When he dove for the legs, the behemoth kicked him. The resulting row ended with the Turk leaving the ring in a fury. Coaxed back in, he made short work of the American champion. The press claimed the foreigner made Jenkins look like a boy in the hands of a monster. Jenkins agreed. "He roared like a bear, picked me up and spun me over his head in an airplane whirl and threw me out of the ring like I was a chip," Jenkins recalled. "I landed in the third row of seats, hurt."

Youssuf had taken the first fall in just over an hour and was awarded a second when Jenkins refused to continue after being tossed off the mat. With the victory, the Turk had a strong argument that he was the best wrestler in the world. After dispatching former champion Evan Lewis in Chicago in June 1898, Youssuf sailed for Europe, certain to return for bouts with other top American stars. Instead, his ship wrecked, his claim to the world championship dying with him in the swirling seas off Nova Scotia. Pierri was forced to bring forward a new slew of Turkish champions, each one a paler copy of the last. But the memory of Youssuf remained strong. Dubuque, Iowa's *Sunday Herald* reported,

Wrestling has been steadily declining for years. But the advent of Yousouf [sic], the Terrible Turk, about whom thousands of yards of "fairy tales" were written by susceptible critics, threatened for a time to cause a rejuvenation of the game. Yousouf was a fat, ignorant, stolid, eccentric, and powerful Mussulman who threw to the winds all sorts of theories about athletics. He was so gross and corpulent that no ordinary mortal, no matter how strong he was in his back and arms, could throw him on the mat.

Yousouf became at once a sort of a fad. But he was in bad hands. The men

who brought him to this country as the "Sultan's Imperial wrestler" challenged any wrestler in the country on behalf of their Turkish wonder. Yousouf perspired and grunted before throngs that spoke a language with which he was not familiar, threw his men sometimes and fouled his rivals whenever it pleased the management to have the Turk lose. Stuffing a few dollars in the pudgy hands of the Turk, his managers would tell him in choice Turkish that "it was all right," and the foreign athlete would return to his room and his several gallons of strong coffee, many pounds of fried chicken, and pounds of rank tobacco, to "train" for another contest.

TRADING THE AMERICAN TITLE: JENKINS VS. MACLEOD

Jenkins' reputation wasn't badly damaged by his loss to the Turk and a subsequent draw with Hadli Adlai in November 1898. The mammoth men were barely considered human at the time, and their tactics weren't considered sporting. Between his major bouts, Jenkins took on all comers in a variety of vaudeville and carnival acts, vowing to throw any man who lived in less than 15 minutes. Only once in hundreds of attempts was he forced to pay out his $50 prize. He beat a succession of boxers, including former champion Tom Sharkey, who took up wrestling when boxing was banned in New York at the turn of the century. But another shot at the title eluded him.

By 1900 it had been years since Jenkins whipped Burns in straight falls, and he was no closer to getting matches with any of the Burns-affiliated mat men who controlled the grappling game through much of the Midwest. Jenkins traveled to Iowa to meet with Burns and took on a young Frank Gotch in a gym match.

As we've seen, many of the bouts in front of the audience were for show. But behind the scenes, with just the other wrestlers watching, the boys went all out. Often the matches were for more than pride — side bets were common. While we don't know if Jenkins took Gotch's money, we do know he pinned the young up-and-comer in less than an hour.

Also unknown is what kind of accommodation Jenkins made with Burns and his crew. What is known is that Jenkins was soon back in the fold, settling all disputes about who the legitimate American champion truly was by beating McLeod in Cleveland in November 1901 in front of 6,000 fans at the Central Armory. Jenkins lost the first fall before coming back to pin the champion in the final two falls. "McLeod is a wonder," he told the press after the bout. "He is certainly the best white man I ever met. Never have I had to work so desperately before."

McLeod got his revenge the next year. After wrestling Jenkins to a draw in June, he took home the title on Christmas day in Worcester, Massachusetts. Jenkins had injured his leg against John Parr and exacerbated it in an exhibition with lightweight Bothner. He had promised to throw the smaller man four times in an hour, but could manage only three. To make matters worse, his injured leg got infected and blood poisoning set in. Jenkins wore a brace with brass buckles to support his injured leg rather than postpone the bout with McLeod. It was a bravura show of guts, but ended up costing Jenkins big time. According to onlookers, the brace fell apart and tore into the champion's skin. Some even say McLeod targeted the vulnerable area. The *Chicago Tribune* account noted,

> *In order to protect the injured leg Jenkins had a leather bandage with a steel strip down the front of the shin fastened with brass buckles. Two of these were broken in the early part of the match and the brass points dug into his flesh until the pain was unbearable and he was afraid of further blood poisoning.*
>
> *He had wrestled 20 minutes in the third bout when he told McLeod the condition he was in and offered to quit and call the match a draw or go on wrestling. McLeod insisted on continuing, but Jenkins' manager refused to let the big fellow go on and forfeited the match.*

The championship changed hands, but McLeod's win rang hollow. To most wrestling fans, Jenkins was still the top hand in the business. He proved it the next February in Cleveland, where he beat Burns's rising star Gotch in straight falls. Gotch, known as a dirty wrestler who liked to hurt people, hit Jenkins in the face several times with the heel of his hand. Jenkins, in turn, roughed Gotch up badly, drawing blood as he indiscriminately threw his arms across Gotch's body, purportedly looking to secure an arm hold, but conveniently whacking the Iowan in the face time after time.

The finishing hold in the deciding fall was Jenkins' patented jaw lock. Many called it a chokehold disguised as a headlock, and it drove Gotch to his knees and then to the mat. The young Iowan later called Jenkins the toughest man he ever met: "Some could not understand why I lost to Jenkins. The headlock defeated me. It will defeat any man when secured by a wrestler as strong as Jenkins. He secured the jaw lock on me while we were standing. I tried in vain to extricate myself. Jenkins applied the twist and I began to think of all the mean things I had ever done. I wanted my head for future use, so I dropped to the mat."

Although some of their later matches would be all about business considerations, this bout had all the signs of being a legitimate contest. It was a long trip back to Humboldt, Iowa, for the future champion. He had come to Cleveland fully expecting to win. Instead, in Jenkins he'd met a man who was willing to go to any lengths to win a wrestling match. Strangely, this realization actually seemed to strengthen Gotch's resolve. Biographer George S. Robbins recounts, "Gotch had suffered terribly from strangleholds and Jenkins' old trick of stabbing across the face for a further arm hold and hitting the nose. Gotch was a sorry sight as he returned to his homefolk . . . bruised and bandaged, his body decorated with plasters and other reminders of battle, but eager for a return encounter."

Jenkins would go on to take the title back from McLeod that April in Buffalo and closed the year with yet another win over his foe. Once again champion, and seemingly at the height of his powers, Jenkins would face Gotch the next January, a turning point in the sport's history. Meanwhile, in the old world, a great champion was being forged in Europe's Greco-Roman wrestling tournaments. George Hackenschmidt was about to join the Americans on the world stage.

While Gotch and Jenkins battled over American supremacy, a new contender to the title of world's best wrestler was being created in the salons and gymnasiums of Europe. The "Russian Lion" George Hackenschmidt took the continent by storm. The son of a German and a Swede, Hackenschmidt was born in Estonia and trained in Russia. He spoke five languages fluently and could be claimed by fans all over Europe as one of their own.

A natural athlete, Hackenschmidt came to the attention of the Russian tsar's physician Dr. von Krajewski, a millionaire bachelor interested in wrestling and physical culture. Von Krajewski, a confirmed bachelor, was a prominent supporter of most of Russia's young

5 THE RUSSIAN Lion ROARS

strong men. An interesting character who did all his own exercising in the nude, von Krajewski often housed promising young athletes, who would gather in his St. Petersburg, Russia, home to wrestle and lift weights.

With nothing to occupy him but exercise and rest, Hackenschmidt quickly developed into one of the strongest men in Europe. He perfected more than just your run-of-the-mill lifts. He could lift a horse onto his shoulders, and it was said he could hold a wrestling bridge while lifting as much as 311 pounds. He was also a gifted gymnast, once jumping over a table from a standing position 100 times in succession to win a bet.

In 1898, with Hackenschmidt a now robust 20 years of age, von Krajewski decided it was time to unleash him on the world. The budding strongman had already beaten the notable Frenchmen Paul Pons in a wrestling match and won several weightlifting competitions when he confronted the legendary strongman Eugen Sandow during a performance in St. Petersburg, questioning the older man's claims that he was the strongest in the world. Sandow was a great showman, the founder in many ways of modern bodybuilding. He didn't just lift for records — he put on an extravaganza, often using a "dumbbell" that was actually a bar with a giant basket on each end. In the baskets he would put real people. It was often less weight that simply pressing iron, but it was quite a show. Hackenschmidt, for his part, wasn't impressed. Wrote biographer David Chapman,

"Sandow went through his usual routine, lifting sausages marked plainly '4,000 lbs.,' snapping crowbars with his bare hands, permitting a dozen men to load themselves on a platform balanced on his chest and then lifting platform and all with one puff of his pneumatic lungs. Then came the challenge. At that moment — such was the careful planning — Hackenschmidt dropped his trousers in the darkness of the box, peeled off his shirt and jumped to the stage in full gymnasium costume. The engagement was brief. Hackenschmidt not only managed all the feats of strength but dusted the floor with Sandow's extremities and then ran him clear into the wings. That finished Sandow and started Hackenschmidt."

By the turn of the century it was clear Hackenschmidt was something to behold in the Greco-Roman style. He won his first tournament in Vienna at the end of 1898, won again in Finland in January 1899, and finished the year as the Russian champion. In France that same year, he earned the nickname "The Russian Lion." In June 1900 he turned professional, earning 2,500 francs a month and immediately proving to backers he was worth it by winning tournaments in Moscow and St. Petersburg.

By then, Hackenschmidt was a star. Crowds gathered to gawk at his physique and watch him perform, not just wrestling, but feats of strength. He traveled to Dresden where he was an attraction, wrestling three to five opponents a night and making a spectacular showing of it. In Budapest he beat the Turk Kara Ahmed after a three-hour struggle, atypical for Hackenschmidt, who often dispatched foes in mere minutes. Hackenschmidt recalls, "The whole audience rose like one man, and thunders of applause echoed through the building. I was seized, carried shoulder high and decked with flowers. For fully a quarter of an hour I was borne like a victorious general through the streets, kissed, embraced . . . I was heartily glad when I at last made my escape to the privacy of the dressing room."

He won tournaments all over Europe, sometimes epic affairs that lasted for more than a month. In 1901 he won the world championship in Vienna, a championship he considered the most significant of his career because of the sheer talent gathered in one place. He repeated the feat later that year in Paris and, having conquered mainland Europe, was off to take on all of Britain.

GEORGE HACKENSCHMIDT

It was a tough go at first. The British had no Greco-Roman tradition and Hackenschmidt's growing reputation meant he attracted little interest from the cautious English mat men. Only an impromptu challenge from Jack Carkeek, a veteran of the mat game who had worked with everyone from William Muldoon to Farmer Burns, rescued Hackenschmidt from a return trip to Europe.

Carkeek was accepting all challengers at the Alhambra Theatre in Leicester Square in London. His cronies, notably smooth-talking C.B. Cochran, took an interest in the Russian wrestler and suddenly Hackenschmidt was off and rolling in England. Cochran organized a tour of the country and his new compatriots taught him how to play to the crowd. His first real success came in Liverpool, beating an aged Tom Cannon, another veteran of the American scene. The most exciting event that night, despite the wrestling action within, came outside the Prince of Wales Theatre. The theater management had second thoughts about the show and tried to stop it by disconnecting the gas supply and announcing the match was cancelled. Eventually a fight broke out between thugs hired by the theatre to tell the crowd the show was off and ruffians hired by the promoter to tell the crowd the show would go on. Locals called the dustup the Battle of Clayton Square.

Despite a complete lack of familiarity with catch-as-catch-can, the scrappier British version of the mat game, Hackenschmidt seemed to thrive. He and Cannon pulled out all the stops. First Hackenschmidt upset the veteran in Septemeber. His reputation in the new style established, the two wrestled to a time limit, before Hackenschmidt won the culminating "match to a finish." It was classic American-style pro wrestling booking, the kind hustlers in the new world had been using to part fools from their money for years.

Hackenschmidt clearly learned plenty from Carkeek, a notorious con man who would later do jail time for his role in the infamous Mabray Gang. When he organized his own tour of Australia a few years later, Hackenschmidt attempted to send a wrestler in his employ named Woods to bolster the local competition and build excitement. When he refused to throw a match, Hackenschmidt fired him: "Woods asked for $5,000 damages because Hackenschmidt discharged him. He told the court that Hackenschmidt requested him to 'go down' to Clarence Weber, a local light, so that when Hackenschmidt came to wrestle Weber there should be some public excitement. Woods refused to do as asked because he reckoned himself immensely superior to Weber. 'Why don't you do it, like Carkeek's men did?' asked Hackenschmidt, in surprise."

Whether his wins were all on the level is arguable. His rising profile in the sport was not. Hackenschmidt soon hooked up with Antonio Pierri. An accomplished wrestler in his own right, Pierri kept a steady stream of Turks headed to New York for an American wrestling fandom that couldn't get enough of them. The gimmick played just as well in Britain.

Pierri pledged to find a Turk who could defeat Hackenschmidt and returned with Ahmed Madrali. While some claim Madrali was really a dockworker from Marseilles in disguise, he was played up big, booked by Pierri in the Old Surrey Music Hall, where he built a reputation of his own.

The two men collided on January 30, 1904, at the Olympia in London. The giant building had housed the circus, dog shows, and was even turned into a gigantic roller skating rink when that fad was at its peak in the 1890s. Nearly 10,000 fans flocked to see the wrestling match there, bringing London traffic to a standstill.

They didn't get much for their money. Hackenschmidt secured a hammerlock, and when he threw the Turk to the mat, a scream of pain was heard throughout the cavernous hall. Hackenschmidt had dislocated his opponent's elbow and was declared the winner in just 44 seconds.

"The victory raised my reputation to its zenith," Hackenschmidt recalled. "And since that time I do not think that I had a wrestling rival in the affections or esteem of the British public." He would not be able to say the same about America.

A RIVARLY ON TWO CONTINENTS: JENKINS, HACKENSCHMIDT, AND GOTCH

Three days earlier, in Bellingham, Washington, a sleepy town just 20 miles from the Canadian border, Frank Gotch won the American title for the first time against Tom Jenkins. It was a brutal bout and the crowd was rabid for the action. The building was packed to the point that some of the 3,000 spectators, most of them gamblers with monetary interest in the bout, were forced to observe from the rafters. Four of them took a long fall into the ring from the ceiling. It was worth it to witness in person a legendarily violent match. Jenkins had made his reputation with a roughhouse style, but Gotch was giving as good as he got. Neil Fleischer gives a play-by-play in *From Milo to Londos*:

> *For 20 minutes the men wrestled head to head without going to the mat. Jenkins was roughing it at every opportunity, rubbing his elbows and fists across Frank's face.*
>
> *Gotch retaliated in kind and both were dripping blood after a few minutes work. Jenkins tripped Gotch after 20 minutes and one second and was behind for a few minutes, but Frank wriggled out of a dangerous wristlock and jumped to his feet. As Jenkins arose Gotch rushed him about the ring, cuffing and rubbing his doubled fists into the Clevelander's midsection.*

And so it continued before Gotch slammed Jenkins four times and pinned him after almost an hour of wrestling. Jenkins had to be carried to his corner, but after a 10-minute rest returned to action like a wild man. He was desperate, going again and again to an illegal stranglehold. Gotch remembered,

> It is the most dangerous grip in wrestling, and yet the old timers used to employ it quite often. In my match with Tom Jenkins at Bellingham, Washington, when I won the American championship, he put a strangle hold on me after I had won the first fall. His powerful arms and great strength made it difficult for me to extricate myself.
>
> Maddened over the loss of the first fall and the peril of losing the championship, which he had held for six years, Jenkins charged at me furiously in the second [fall] and in a mix-up worked himself behind me. He slipped his left forearm under my chin and bore the weight of his right arm against the top of my head, tightening his grip and completing a stranglehold, from which it would have been impossible for a weak man to escape.
>
> There is only one way in which to break this hold, and one cannot linger, as delay may prove fatal. That is to employ both hands in grasping the aggressor's left member below the elbow, and thus lessening the heavy pressure on the Adam's apple. If one possesses great strength it is possible to break the hold. I employed this method in escaping from Jenkins.

Gotch retaliated by any means necessary, leaving the champion bloody around the eyes and mouth. One stranglehold was met by Gotch lifting Jenkins high into the air with a huge slam. A frustrated Jenkins hauled off and punched Gotch in the head, perhaps the last resort of a desperate man. The referee disqualified the champion and awarded the match and the American title to Gotch, as the crowd at ringside, covered in both men's blood, cheered enthusiastically.

"A gent that would gouge out another man's eye ain't no gent," Jenkins said. Titleless, he journeyed for the first time to the shores of England, making it his business to challenge the great Hackenschmidt. The two met in a Greco-Roman match at Albert Hall in front of 6,000 fans. The British public was not initially impressed with Jenkins. He clearly wasn't the physical specimen Hackenschmidt was and was "carrying too much flesh." He won them over with his enthusiastic and clever wrestling. It was a different Jenkins who wrestled the Russian champion. Gone were the roughhouse tactics that had won him such success in America. He was the perfect gentleman while in England, losing in straight falls, but doing it honorably in a combined 35 minutes. *The Sportsman* gave the American challenger due credit:

> When the men got to grips, Hackenschmidt attacked in decisive style, and twice just missed with the flying mare. In less than three minutes he fixed his rival in a cruel body grip and swung him over onto the stage. Jenkins endeavored to spring forward onto his feet, but Hackenschmidt's arms shot out like lightning,

and he pulled his man down with the greatest ease. The American defended very cleverly, and, failing to find an opening for an arm-hold, the Russian picked his opponent up with the intention of pitching him over his back. Jenkins smartly eluded his grip, and after six minutes both were on their feet.

. . . The strength and science which the challenger exhibited were a complete revelation, and he kept his opponent at bay without much difficulty. When a quarter of an hour had gone, Hackenschmidt rushed in and swung Jenkins bodily round the stage, describing three circles before he threw him to the boards, but the American once more eluded his grip like an eel. Then the Russian braced himself for a big effort. Twice he twisted Jenkins over onto one shoulder, and just as promptly did Jenkins, with a mighty contraction of his neck and shoulder muscles, snap the holds. At this point Jenkins mysteriously weakened. Hackenschmidt bore down on him with the power of a Hercules, and with a pedal action similar to a man pushing a heavy roller up a hill, forced his man over on his back, and with an irresistible "half-nelson" gained the first fall in 20 minutes and 37 seconds. The cheer which he received after his defeat was quite as hearty as that accorded Hackenschmidt.

But the matchup with Jenkins was not without controversy. Another Russian wrestler, George Lurich, was looking for his own bout with Hackenschmidt, and when it wasn't offered, he blew the lid off the wrestling business in the London papers. Lurich said he had been all set to wrestle the champion, but the arrival of Jenkins changed everything. Eventually the two Russians met to discuss the issue and Lurich asked Hackenschmidt point blank if and when they might wrestle. Lurich stated,

Hackenschmidt then led me to understand that Jenkins was not only prepared to go down to him in Graeco-Roman, but also in catch-as-catch-can, and that he, Hackenschmidt, would go down in catch-as-catch-can to Jenkins in America, and pretended that he was in a dilemma, adding, "Jenkins is prepared to go down in both styles and what am I to do?"

The only inference to be taken from his language was that he would wish me to wrestle if I would do as Jenkins had promised to do. I, of course, have a reputation to lose, as well as Hackenschmidt, and pretended that I did not understand his meaning. Hackenschmidt afterwards made precisely the same statement to another Russian wrestler in the Artistes Club, and both he and myself are prepared to swear to the truth of these statements.

I was not surprised at what Hackenschmidt had said regarding Jenkins, as a certain wrestling promoter, named Haggarty, who informed me he had come

from Jenkins, called one day and endeavored to obtain my sanction to wrestle Jenkins a mixed match under catch-as-catch-can and Graeco-Roman rules. He said he had Jenkins' permission to say that he, Jenkins, would go down in Graeco-Roman if I would go down in catch-as-catch-can.

I refused these overtures, and the same person repeated his call, this time assuring me that if I would wrestle a match with Jenkins, the American was prepared to go down in both styles, and that there were rich Americans who would back him and the money could be shared. I have witnesses to prove the truth of what I have written regarding this affair. How far Jenkins was connected with these mediums, I cannot say.

No one can say with certainty whether Jenkins really proposed to take a dive for Hackenschmidt. Later in life he would admit to friends that he had lost money in a bad investment and he complained regularly about the lack of money in the wrestling racket. True or not, Hackenschmidt left town to escape the heat of the Lurich exposé, traveling to Australia where he had surgery on the knee that had troubled him for years. With London out of the question, not yet ready for his return after the scandal, Hackenschmidt made his first trip to America, specifically to meet Jenkins. That spring was integral to the history of American wrestling; the three months between March and May 1905 were as action packed as any sports fans had ever seen.

STATESIDE SHOWDOWN

In March, Jenkins upset Gotch, who had beaten him in a return match earlier that year in Cleveland, to win back the American title. Fans in Cleveland didn't respond well to the match, accusing Gotch of losing the first fall on purpose to spur betting on Jenkins. "There never was a prize fight or a wrestling match pulled off that someone did not yell fake," the champion replied.

The *New York Times* reported that Gotch and Jenkins played to a sellout crowd at Madison Square Garden, with hundreds more peering in to get a glimpse of the mat behemoths. Jenkins took the first fall, Gotch returning with a previously unseen vim and vigor to take the second in just six minutes. Looking unstoppable, popular opinion (and the betting) swung towards Gotch to win the match. "The experts in this case were mistaken," the *Times* reporter drolly conceded. Jenkins was again champion, making his upcoming bout with Hackenschmidt more important than ever.

Lurich had already revealed to London sportsmen exactly what would happen in a match between the American and the European. Perhaps the news hadn't crossed the Atlantic with Hackenschmidt, as he was met with great pomp and circumstance in New

York after sailing into San Francisco in April. People came to the Orpheum Theater in the East Village just to look at the man and see him spar.

On May 5, Hackenschmidt dispatched of Jenkins to claim the world championship, just as Lurich said he would. Despite it being, by his own account, his first significant bout in the catch wrestling style, Hackenschmidt was never in danger against a repeat champion in the style. In his efforts to get Jenkins down on all fours he repeatedly sent the American whirling. Once he gave Tom a taste of his prodigious power, grabbing him by the shoulders and tossing him clear off his feet.

Hackenschmidt won the match in straight falls and departed for Britain. Gotch challenged him to a bout before he left, but the new champion declined. He had just beaten Jenkins, who had himself vanquished Gotch a mere two months before. A match with the Iowan seemed a step backwards to the proud champion who went back to London still a star, albeit a diminished one.

When he met Madrali in a rematch the crowd was still large, but not nearly as large as it had been in 1904. "The expensive seats were not a quarter filled, to the profit of the gallery, who climbed down and took possession of all the vacant places," the *Bystander* reported. Even winning a world title hadn't quite scrubbed Hackenschmidt clean from the charges he was a faker.

Two weeks after the Hackenschmidt match, Jenkins defended his American championship against Gotch. The *New York Times* described the bout as sensational, claiming it nearly drove the crowd to riot. Gotch had Jenkins in trouble throughout, nearly pinning him several times with Jenkins scrambling for the ropes whenever he was in trouble. It was a foul-filled affair, with Jenkins resorting to kicking and a stranglehold and Gotch giving it right back. Jenkins claimed Gotch even bit him, showing the referee, an overwhelmed Tim Hurst, the wound on his right forearm.

The match was started and stopped several times as both sides protested various fouls. It started late, at 10:30 p.m. and lasted past the *New York Times* deadline, going well beyond midnight before the second fall even started. Gotch was exhausted by the time it was all over. He had to be carried to the back by his seconds and Jenkins escaped with the title.

By now the writing was on the wall that Jenkins' competitive career was coming to a close. He was 33 and starting to pack on weight, when President of the United States Teddy Roosevelt threw him a lifeline. Roosevelt was a supporter of wrestling, boxing, and the newly discovered Japanese art of jiu-jitsu and thought self-defense was so important that it needed to be taught to future military leaders at West Point.

"I am wrestling with two Japanese wrestlers three times a week," Roosevelt wrote his son Kermit. "I am not the age or the build one would think to be whirled lightly over an opponent's head and batted down on a mattress without damage. But they are so skilful that I have not been hurt at all. My throat is a little sore, because once when one of them had a stranglehold I also got hold of his windpipe and thought I could perhaps choke him off before he could choke me. However, he got ahead."

Despite being enamored with the Japanese style, Roosevelt thought Jenkins would be the perfect man to teach unarmed combats to prospective Army officers. Future students included George Patton amongst a host of other military legends. But before he could retire from the mats, there remained the small matter of the American championship. Jenkins lost the title for the last time to Gotch in Kansas City's Convention Hall on May 26, 1906.

It was a departure from their earlier bouts. Jenkins eschewed his usual roughhouse routine and wrestled Gotch in a straight match. According to wrestling historian Steve Yohe, Gotch's manager Horace Lerch had $3,000 from Gotch supporters in Buffalo. After Jenkins took the first fall in a convincing fashion, Lerch used the money to cover all the bets coming in from the Jenkins fans. Of course, Gotch then proceeded to wipe the mat with Jenkins, winning the next two falls in just over 30 minutes.

After the bout, Jenkins congratulated Gotch, telling the crowd he would be champion for many years to come. That was true, but only after a quick title switch with Fred Beell, like Gotch a Farmer Burns disciple, who beat the champion in a huge upset that December. Gotch hit his head on the ring post and was knocked loopy. The 165-pound Beell took advantage and took the American title.

Many point to this being a worked match, erroneously believing it to be the first of its kind. Others, like Gotch biographer Mike Chapman, believe it was just one of those things that happen in sports, a weird injury that led to a once in a lifetime upset. Gotch took the title back later that month and would never again meet defeat, only ever conceding one more fall in his entire career. Beell would go on to be a regular Gotch foe, also serving as a setup man for future Gotch opponents and even wrestling old mainstays of the Burns trust like Jack Carkeek and the old Farmer himself. Beell went from making $60 a week to clearing $2,829 for the Gotch rematch alone.

In Europe, Hackenschmidt continued to draw respectable crowds, but his body was breaking down, perhaps from his training regimen that included carrying 600 pounds of cement on his back with a 232-pound training partner lounging on top of that, all while the champion did light exercises. He recalled, "In August 1907, my old knee trouble again made its appearance, but this time the water gathered in the joint itself, so that my knee cap stood away from the joint quite a quarter of an inch. By medical advice I now always wore a bandage, and found it practically impossible to do any serious wrestling practice. Even a slow trot caused me such pain that I could only fulfill my ordinary engagements with the utmost difficulty."

By the time he was finally to meet Frank Gotch in 1908, Hackenschmidt was no longer at his best physically. His legs were shot, but money talks — and the $10,000 offered by promoter William Wittig for a single bout with Gotch spoke loudly indeed. In March 1908, Hackenschmidt sailed for the United States. The two best wrestlers in the world were headed for a showdown.

When the two greatest wrestlers of their era finally met in the ring, it was more than a wrestling match — it was an event. Wrestling promoter William Wittig offered up a $10,000 purse, an astronomical sum at the time, and the big Russian sailed once again for America, arriving in March for a bout scheduled on April 3, 1908, in Chicago.

The match was bigger than the two individuals involved. It was billed as a battle between old Europe (represented by the urbane and educated Hackenschmidt) and America (represented by the rough and tumble Iowan farmer Gotch). The bout would also be a battle of styles. Hackenschmidt specialized in the Greco-Roman form, popularized by

6 OLD WORLD vs. NEW WORLD: Gotch vs. Hackenschmidt

Muldoon decades prior in New York, while Gotch was the standard-bearer for America's own style of catch-as-catch-can wrestling.

The match was promoted nationwide, with headlines announcing the bout had been signed and that Hackenschmidt had sailed, and articles detailing the world champion's tune-up bouts on the east coast. Some of the promotion was pretty clever. In January 1908 Hackenschmidt beat the enormous American wrestler Joe Rogers in straight falls, barely breaking a sweat by accomplishing this task in less than 20 minutes. In March that same year, Rogers was back in New York to wrestle Gotch at the New Amsterdam Hall. Gotch struggled mightily with the big man, who weighed more than 250 pounds, and fans couldn't help make comparisons. If Hackenschmidt had dispatched with Rogers so quickly, and Gotch had so much trouble with him, wouldn't the Russian Lion have his way with Gotch as well?

Moments like that helped establish Hackenschmidt as the prohibitive betting favorite. He was the toast of the town, wowing even noted wrestling fan President Teddy Roosevelt. "If I weren't president," Roosevelt said upon meeting the great wrestler at the White House, "I'd want to be George Hackenschmidt."

The champion seemed to be buying into his own hype. He barely trained in Chicago, later claiming the proprietor of the local gym had been rude to him, leaving him to confine his workouts to the hotel. Despite his lack of activity, his opponent couldn't help but be impressed. "Picture the most perfect man, and you've described George Hackenschmidt," Gotch admitted.

But the American was also confident in his abilities. "He thinks I'm a mark," the Iowan told referee Ed Smith. "And he isn't training. I never was better in my life and can stand him off for a half hour easily. Then he will begin to weaken and after that he will quit. He never will let me throw him because he will want to go back to England and say he couldn't be thrown and will have some bad excuse to offer."

The two had met face to face once before, when Gotch challenged the champion in Buffalo, days after Hackenschmidt had secured his claim as the world's best against Jenkins. When they met again at 10:29 p.m. on April 3, 1908, at the Dexter Pavilion in Chicago, it was to shake hands and wrestle. Six thousand fans looked on as the two men battled for supremacy.

"Gotch was a cunning and tricky wrestler, and as strong as a bear," said Hackenschmidt. "I soon found it impossible to get a grip of him, and so was at a great disadvantage. In addition, Gotch was not above probing me in the eye from time to time with his thumb, until I was almost blinded."

Gotch wrestled a very defensive match. As Hackenschmidt chased him around the ring, the Iowan responded with the kind of rough tactics that had become par for the course in American wrestling. Hackenschmidt, already the victim of one knee surgery, was deathly afraid of Gotch's famed toehold. Though it wasn't his bread and butter finishing move, Gotch was known not only to use the hold, but to do serious damage with it.

A PROMOTIONAL POSTER FOR THE GOTCH-HACKENSCHMIDT MATCH AT COMISKEY BALL PARK

Looking back, a *Washington Post* reporter who'd been at the match remembered Gotch's previous gleeful brutality:

> Frank Gotch was first to use a "torture hold" that had nothing to do with wrestling, the object of which always had been to put an opponent on his back. Gotch invented the "toe hold." With it he wrenched an opponent's ankle until he quit. Gotch always seemed to think there was a fine bit of humor concealed somewhere in this performance. I once saw him wrestling a tall young German

in Chicago. The German was no match for Frank as a wrestler, so to put a little pep into the match Frank sat on him, got his toe hold, and very slowly bent his ankle back until it was nearly broken.

The German wrestler, unable even to roll over on his back, screamed. This was before the days of grunt and groan wrestling, and it was a real scream. The crowd piled into the ring and pulled Gotch away. Frank got up and walked around, grinning. The German was carried out. I heard afterward his ankle actually was broken, and six months later he was still partly crippled.

Despite Gotch's crippling holds, the two wrestled for more than two hours without a fall. Hackenschmidt, used to much shorter contests, began to tire quickly. He asked several times for the bout to be declared a draw. Each time, Gotch refused. In the end, Hackenschmidt simply quit. "You can have it, Mr. Gotch," he said, and walked out of the ring. In the immediate aftermath, Hackenschmidt told reporters he had fallen to a superior wrestler. "Gotch is the better man," the former champion said. "I have to acknowledge it." Weeks later, safely back on his home turf in London, Hackenschmidt was more vocal, telling the papers that he had been a victim of foul play. He told the *Lowell Sun & Citizen Leader* that Gotch's dirty tactics, combined with his oil-covered appendages, made victory almost unimagnable. Hackenschmidt claimed it was nearly impossible to grip the slippery American. When he complained to the referee, Hackenschmidt said Ed Smith's answer was terse: "Don't squeal."

It wasn't merely the oil that concerned Hackenschmidt. The toehold seemed ever present on his mind, perhaps due to his history of knee injuries. Hackenschmidt wrote to the *London Daily Mail*:

The people at ringside were all prejudiced against me and unfair, so that I concluded the best thing to do was to keep silent and do my best. Gotch then dug his finger into my eye, and I called out, "Unfair," but he continued, and the referee did not stop him. Then he caught hold of my ear and started to pull it off. In releasing my ear he scratched my face, tearing the skin off. Now happened an unusual thing, which I don't think fair. Gotch grabbed my big toe and tried to sprain it, with the object of crippling me by breaking the bone. Throughout the match he kept pulling and wrenching my toe, and I saw that it was not a wrestling, but a butchery match. After an hour and a half, I was disgusted and ready to quit, but I decided to try again. Gotch seemed to weaken, but, cheered by the crowd, he kept up the "bloody work" on my face, so half an hour later, I said, "I'm done."

Gotch scoffed at the accusations he had cheated to win. "I made Hack reach for me all the time and he never did get a chance to exert his strength close up," the new champion said. "He was forced to use his power at arm's length, which greatly diminished it of course." He also disputed the idea that his toehold was designed to cripple, claiming it was all a matter of science. In *How to Wrestle*, Gotch explained,

> I was asked quite often to explain the toehold. A sporting writer asked me whether I thought it right to use such a painful grip. He said it was against the rules to twist a wrestler's finger and it was certainly just as unfair to twist one of his toes. To have answered that question would have spoiled a good joke, but it expresses the general idea of the toe hold, which is an erroneous one. One day when I had been wrestling in Cincinnati a newspaperman wanted me to show him how I secured the toe hold. I told him to get down on the floor and I would show him a touch of real life.
>
> "Gotch bent over me," said this writer, "toyed a while with one of my feet, then quickly grabbed the other and gave it a twist. I looked for a nice clean spot on which to put my shoulders to keep my leg from snapping off. I wanted the leg for future use. It felt as though Gotch wanted to take it along with him. At that he exerted only a few pounds pressure."
>
> This writer had caught the principal idea of the toehold — the idea of leverage. I made a study of mechanics and it was there that I learned the true value of leverage in wrestling.

Referee Ed Smith also vehemently denied any foul play: "Hackenschmidt subsequently told the most disgraceful stories about Gotch and myself after he got to England, claiming to have been fouled deliberately and in general to have been the victim of a job to down him. Inasmuch as Hackenschmidt was utterly unable at any time to secure one hold of any importance on the wonderful man from Iowa, those who saw the match at once construed his talk as being that of a mighty bad loser and the words that might be expected from a quitter, for that is what Hackenschmidt showed himself to be that night . . . Hackenschmidt's tale about Gotch being greased was the veriest bosh."

With the win over Hackenschmidt, Gotch became an international star. The motion picture of the bout traveled the country and then the world, and he was featured in the play *All About a Bout*, which toured America. Nightly, fans arose from their seats at the beginning of the performance to give the new champion a standing ovation. Gotch toured with the play for 38 weeks, wrestling new manager Emil Klank at each performance, even traveling overseas, taking his act to London. He was a product pitchman as well, shilling everything from whiskey to a Swedish "muscle vibrator" for home massage. He should have sold both to his battered rival.

ENTER JACK CURLEY

PROMOTER JACK CURLEY (*center*)

Boxing at this time was in ill repute, partially due to a series of questionable contests, but also spurred by blatant racism as white fans refused to accept African American champion Jack Johnson. As boxing's heroes became villains, Gotch emerged as the leading light of combat sports. Fascinated with fisticuffs, he got involved in the despicable smear against Johnson, joining Farmer Burns to help train the "Great White Hope" Jim Jeffries for his comeback fight against Johnson.

He and Jeffries toured the country with a troupe of wrestlers, boxers, and baseball stars in a show called "The Band of Champions." Gotch made a fortune on these kinds of tours, wrestling Dr. Benjamin Roller nightly and collecting easy money. A world tour was planned, a tour Johnson derailed by knocking out Jeffries with embarrassing ease. Gotch was suggested as a possible opponent for the boxing champion, but having tasted defeat during a boxing match in his early years in Alaska, he wisely demurred. Retirement was on his mind, but promoter Jack Curley, who managed Gotch on this tour, believed a Hackenschmidt rematch would be worth sticking around for.

Curley, a genius promoter who had booked the speaking tour of William Jennings Bryan and performances by the Vatican choir, had gotten involved in the wrestling game when boxing was banned in many locales in 1909. Curley successfully promoted a Gotch title defense against Yussif Mahmout in April of that year, drawing 10,000 fans in Chicago to see Gotch whip a foreign foe who would later become his training partner and right-hand man.

Curley had connections to seemingly every major wrestler of the era. He had promoted Gotch in several matches and a big money tour, managed Roller in the good doctor's bouts in London, and emerged in 1910 as the manager of George Hackenschmidt as well. Soon Curley, Hackenschmidt, and Roller were touring America, with Roller taking the fall for the Russian night after night. Roller's hometown paper, the *Seattle Times*, wasn't buying it as legitimate competition:

> *Dr. Roller of Seattle was licked again last night. He went to the mat with George Hackenschmidt, the "Russian Lion," in Montreal last night and was beaten in two straight falls — the first in 47 minutes and the second one and the match in 19 minutes . . .*
>
> *Hack is billed to wrestle Jess Westergaard in Chicago in a finish match pretty soon. He will beat Jess, too, and after cleaning up a few more like him, the boards will be swept clean for Gotch. Along about the first of the year the yapping will begin for Gotch to come out of his retirement and clip the whiskers of the Russian Lion, who, by the way, is a German.*

The paper had seen Roller work the crowd in Seattle and simply wasn't believing any contest with the doctor at the forefront as honest. "It is safe to say that 99 percent of all wrestling matches where an admission fee is charged and where professionals take part have been prearranged before the men shake hands. Many have even trained together — those that made any show of training. The hitting and biting in the matches, the kicking, the calling of foul vulgar names, the threats, the falls from the stage, the challenges from the audience — all those things are the little jokers used to stir up the maddened crowd. It does little harm, and it makes the game 'good,' say the wrestlers."

Still, no exposé seemed to slow down rabid wrestling fans. It didn't matter that Curley was managing Hackenschmidt against Roller, a man he had represented mere months before. Fans wanted to buy into the matches and nothing could persuade them to do otherwise. Despite these signs of corruption, not only did fans continue to come to the shows, they continued to bet on matches with abandon. Curley saw dollar signs when he imagined a rematch between Gotch and Hackenschmidt. Gotch, angry over the Russian's post-match accusations, and the American public needed some convincing. The *Saturday Evening Post*'s Milton McKay summed up the situation: "[Gotch] considered himself as important as a United States senator and his manners were very little better. He developed a very personal dislike for Hackenschmidt, and once described him as a 'money-hungry greaseball.' Gotch was convinced that Hack had quit cold in their 1908 engagement, and missed few public opportunities to say so. A large section of the sporting group agreed with Gotch's diagnosis of Hack's competitive temperament."

Gotch retired several times in 1910 and 1911, although they never seemed to stick. He was lured back to the ring for a bout with Hackenschmidt in September 1911. His continued and vehement attacks against the Russian in the press helped fire up the fans, and the former champion himself, for the contest. Hackenschmidt was in peak form for the match. Training extensively with Roller, he was prepared this time, he claimed, for all of Gotch's tricks. In one training session, Hackenschmidt had felt particularly good. Almost done for the day, Hackenschmidt wanted one more tumble with Roller.

"Dr. Roller advised me to stop, but I requested him to hold me down once more, and I should endeavor to get up from the knees," Hackenschmidt told *Health and Strength* magazine. "I jumped up to my feet, but, unfortunately, Dr. Roller had the same movement as myself, and in consequence caught me with my right foot over his knee, and in doing so he tore the sinews from the bone — this only five days before the contest with Gotch was to take place. When it was dark, I was carried home. The following day Dr. Mackenzie, the doctor who extracted the bullet from President McKinley, when the latter was shot, was called in."

Thousands had gathered in Chicago for the rematch, most unaware of the injury that threatened to call the bout off. Hackenschmidt considered it, but promised $11,000, there were plenty of reasons to fight through the pain.

"Curley, my manager, and the promoter of the contest," continued Hack, "was insistent that I should not compete against Gotch unless I felt able to do so. I knew that tickets to the value of over £6,000 had been sold, and a lot of other expenses incurred, but it was the splendid attitude of Curley that finally determined me to go forward."

Wrestling champion Lou Thesz helped spread the rumor that Ad Santel, a noted shooter, had actually injured Hackenschmidt's knee, intentionally hurting the foreign star at the instruction of Farmer Burns. There is no indication that this is true, though Santel was in Hackenschmidt's camp. The principals had a pretty consistent story, with

Hackenschmidt, Curley, and Roller all singing the same song. Hackenschmidt, who spent years complaining about his injured knee, would have certainly leaped at a story as colorful as being intentionally injured by an agent of his opponent.

Whatever the cause, there is some debate about the severity of Hackenschmidt's injury. The wrestler insisted he could barely move. His manager, decades later, disputed this account, explaining that a respected doctor in Chicago "examined Hack's injury and pronounced it trifling but, to satisfy both Hack and myself that his diagnosis was correct, had x-ray photos taken of the knee. They bore out his diagnosis absolutely."

Despite attempts to cover up Hackenschmidt's injury, word soon began to spread that something was fishy. What Curley had marketed as the battle "of the century" was turning into a farce. Tens of thousands planned to attend, packing the new Comiskey Park and setting wrestling attendance records that would stand for years. Reported the *Reno Evening Gazette*:

> *Through personal friends Charles Comiskey was induced to permit the match to be held at the ball park — at grand opera prices — Comiskey to receive scarcely enough to pay the expenses of cleaning the grounds. The match was wonderfully advertised, and on the afternoon of the contest more than 20,000 persons were piled into the stands.*
>
> *But three days prior to the match it became evident that something was wrong. There had been an abortive effort to put across a great betting coup — and the public refused to come in.*
>
> *On the afternoon prior to the match ugly rumors began to pass around and, gradually, toward night, the rumor persisted that Hackenschmidt was suffering from a badly sprained leg and had agreed to wrestle only on condition Gotch did not touch that leg or use the famous toehold. This was angrily denied by friends of the promoters.*
>
> *During the following morning the rumors persisted. One Chicago paper learned so much that it printed a warning to all its readers to avoid the match. The storms of angry comment arose and it was a suspicious and war crowd that gathered. An hour or so before the men were to go on the mat Comiskey held a conference with the wrestlers, promoters and referee. He told them plainly that they could not use his park to stage the robbery of the public. He and some others had taken the matter up with the chief of police, who ordered Referee Smith to call off all bets.*
>
> *Before going onto the mat, Gotch calmly declared it didn't make any difference to him whether it was a fake or not — he was going out to throw Hackenschmidt. The men stepped into the ring, and before the applause subsided, Referee Smith announced that by orders of the chief of police, he declared*

all bets off. An angry roar ran through the crowd followed by a buzz of wonderment as to what it meant.

"In addition to 20 yards of India-rubber bandaging round my right knee," Hackenschmidt said, "I had ordinary bandages from my ankle upwards, and it was in that condition I engaged upon the match. . . . On entering the ring, I requested the referee to call off all the bets. At first he refused, but on my saying that otherwise I should leave immediately, he did as asked."

PRINT FROM THE 1911 GOTCH-HACKENSCHMIDT MATCH FOR WORLD'S CHAMPIONSHIP

Gotch proceeded to wipe the mat with the Russian. He pinned him easily in the first fall, shockingly calling his shot like "Babe" Ruth would in the 1932 World Series:

It was told to Gotch in 1911 that an American wrestler who wished to see him defeated had been tutoring Hackenschmidt against the grapevine hold leading to the half-nelson and crotch. The world's champion laughed at the story. He said the Russian Lion was privileged to practice the maneuver all he pleased, but he would defeat him in one fall by this same ruse. This remarkable prediction actually came to pass.

When Hackenschmidt met Gotch for the second time in Chicago he was coached to the minute to avoid this rapid-fire attack of Gotch. It was the means of his downfall in the first bout. Gotch put Hack off his guard, raised his near

OLD WORLD VS. NEW WORLD: GOTCH VS. HACKENSCHMIDT

leg, grapevined his far one and then reversed it into a half nelson and crotch, with which the "Lion" was pinned for the first fall in the bitterest defeat of his career.

"In the condition I was in, the merest tyro could have beaten me and Frank Gotch is one of the most powerful opponents I ever met," Hackenschmidt told reporters after the match when back on his home turf in London. "I could not put my left knee to the ground, or even bend it, and my left foot was worse than useless, because every lateral movement gave me intense pain. Without his feet the wrestler is helpless."

Whether the match was a worked bout, a work gone wrong with Gotch double-crossing Hackenschmidt, or simply a winning performance by an all-time great is much debated even today between wrestling historians. Gotch biographer Mike Chapman believes that the great champion was beyond reproach. Chapman hangs his hat on the newspapermen of the time, stating, "The dilemma for today's wrestling historians is this: If the newspaper editors of the era considered wrestling to be fixed, why would they give it such tremendous coverage? And conversely, if it was fixed, shouldn't they have known that was the case . . ."

Steve Yohe, another noted historian, believes almost all of Gotch's matches were works. Historians like Yohe would point out that plenty of newspapermen did question wrestling, outright calling it phony. Others, like the newspapermen Chapman relies on, were often part of the promotional machine. For example, Ed Smith, the referee in the first Gotch-Hackenschmidt match, was also a Chicago-area writer. These, some historians say, are hardly unbiased accounts. Yohe believes that big-time shooting matches rarely happened, if they happened at all:

> Everything I've learned from pro wrestling stops me from agreeing with such fantasies. Pro wrestling has always been made up of people interested in making money with sportsmanship and ideas of fair competition left to amateurs. It wasn't the contest or your won/loss percentage that was important. It was the money you brought home to feed your family that decided if you were a success or failure. Pro wrestling, as it is today, was a work. Styles are always changing but the concept of working matches has changed very little over the years. . . .
>
> Now I believe the wrestlers of this period to be just as they were billed. They were shooter/rippers who deserved their reputations and I believe only the best were pushed as the major wrestlers. I also believe that most of what they did were shoots or near shoots. Major wrestlers spent most of their time performing in carnivals or traveling shows taking on all comers who were overmatched. At times special matches were set up with local amateurs with good reputations, who really had little chance versus a true pro. These matches, a good percentage

of the time, were contests, but when a pro stepped into a ring with another skilled professional or amateur, he knew the outcome before he left the dressing room. Some matches may have been shoots if the dominant wrestler was sure of winning, but, for the most part, pros worked matches. Of course, this style of work also had to look completely legitimate, because some very hard people were betting on the outcome, and they were breaking the law. So kayfabe, in those years, was no joke. "Show moves" did not exist.

Gotch's known associates also point to the possibility of deceit. Jack Carkeek was in Gotch's corner for his 1908 match with Hackenschmidt. Just over a year later he was in federal prison, arrested as part of the Mabray gang and accused of putting on fraudulent wrestling bouts. His former manager Joe Carroll, who Gotch fleeced miners with in Alaska in 1901, was also arrested in the same nationwide scam.

Gotch was surrounded by frauds. There remains the possibility that he was an innocent among wolves, but it seems unlikely he was untouched by his cohorts' efforts to fix matches. These weren't random hangers-on. This was one of Gotch's main training partners and his former manager. Gotch's mentor Martin "Farmer" Burns was also often accused of working matches in the latter years of his career.

Finally, the promoter of the match, Jack Curley, was also suspected of masterminding a phony boxing match between Jack Johnson and Jess Willard. Johnson was struggling with the law and racist law enforcement agents, and had to flee America to escape an arrest warrant. Johnson's biographer Geoffrey Ward writes that Curley had a solution to the champ's problems: "According to Johnson, Curley had a ready answer. If Johnson would lie down to Willard and give up his championship, he could have a sizable off-the-record payment, in addition to which Curley promised to use his personal connections to see that he was allowed to go home again without fear of prison."

Many Americans had already figured out wrestling wasn't on the level. Not every performer was as talented as Gotch, and some hippodromes were easier to spot than others. Gotch's wrestling seemed real; ironically, despite this legitimacy, the second Hackenschmidt match did more to damage wrestling in America than 100 newspaper exposés. Historian Scott Beekman believes it was the end of the golden age of wrestling. The poor performance in the match exposed the sport to ridicule nationwide, especially when film of the bout became widely available: "The Gotch-Hackenschmidt rematch fiasco did irreparable harm to professional wrestling. Already reeling from more than a decade of concerns over the legitimacy of matches, the Chicago debacle, occurring in a highly touted world championship bout, destroyed much of the remaining public faith in wrestling."

The Gotch match was the last of Hackenschmidt's career. He returned to Europe where he lived a long, full life outside the ring. Gotch, despite periodic retirements, defended his title on and off until his death in 1917. He spent much of his time working the carnival circuit, wrestling friends and business partners and eschewing competitors he did not already have an established relationship with. In 1916 he went on a 30-week tour of America with the Sells-Floto Circus. Accompanied by Jess Willard and manager Curley, Gotch took home a cool $1,100 a week.

With his inactive schedule, Gotch had essentially taken the wrestling business hostage. Promoters wanted to match the old champion up with rising star Joe Stecher, but Gotch made such unreasonable financial demands that the match never happened. In the end, a freak injury to his leg did what no opponent ever could — cause the great Gotch to collapse to the mat in pain. His leg was caught between two mats and his fibula was fractured during an exhibition with Bob Managoff in July 1916.

Gotch declared himself done, but as usual his retirement only lasted a few months. In August he filmed a match specifically for Selig Polyscope for use in the theaters. He was offered $85,000 to film two more matches, but he demurred. Again, though, Gotch found it was hard to stay on the farm. He wrestled a final bout against Leo Pardello at the Chicago Coliseum on May 1, 1917.

By the end of the year, Gotch was dead. There would be no comeback. Wrestling would have to find a new standard bearer. Two men were up for the job. Joe Stecher and Ed "Strangler" Lewis would battle for wrestling supremacy for much of the next two decades. While the two catch wrestlers met on the mats in America, a new generation of Japanese matmen was also preparing to take the world by storm. As American wrestling was finding a style of its own, across the Pacific judo stars were ready to shine in Japan and beyond.

Mitsuyo Maeda — judoka, catch wrestler, and key figure in the founding of what would come to be known as Brazilian Jiu-Jitsu — is a man around whom wild stories have swirled for more than a century. With Maeda, the tall tales take us back even further than the globe-spanning professional contests that would earn him the title Conde Koma ("The Count of Combat"), all the way back to the circumstances surrounding his earliest training, his first days at Jigoro Kano's Kodokan, the very center of Japan's grappling revolution. The tallest tales have been told by Maeda's most famous students.

Brazil's great Gracie family has undoubtedly given more than most to the martial arts

7 From the KODOKAN to the COUNT of COMBAT: Mitsuyo Maeda

world. From the days of Carlos and Helio, that first generation of Gracie grappling innovators, to the family's current champion Roger, who shows the beauty of his family's art every time he steps onto the mat or into the ring or cage, there can be no doubt of the efficacy of what has become the world's foremost school of submission grappling. But one curious part of the Gracie package, part of what has sometimes been called "The Gracie Myth," surrounds the origins of their art, and the supposed origins of Maeda, the instructor from whom all follows. In his excellent book co-authored with John Danaher, Renzo Gracie describes Maeda as "a highly regarded student of classical jiu-jitsu [who] eventually switched to Kodokan judo." Crosley Gracie tells the same story, but in much more detail: Maeda, the story goes, overwhelmed his first five opponents at the Kodokan using skills honed by years of classical jiu-jitsu training and was awarded the rank of purple belt on the spot, in recognition of this considerable feat. That Maeda could burst onto the scene as Gracie describes it is unlikely but certainly possible; that he was awarded a purple belt — despite the fact that the introduction of coloured belts other than black, brown, and white did not occur until decades later under Mikonosuke Kawaishi in France — is an impossibility and shows the cracks in the Gracie version of who Mitsuyo Maeda was.

The most meticulously researched and documented accounts of Maeda's life paint a different picture of his origins as a martial artist. Born in 1878 in remote Aomori prefecture,

Maeda came of age at a time when many of the classical, old-school koryu jiu-jiutsu schools were dying out. The relative few that remained suffered from poor reputations and were losing both high-profile challenges and promising students to Jigoro Kano's Kodokan judo, founded in 1882 at Eishoji Temple. Kano had artfully synthesized the teachings of several koryu branches, notably Tenjin Shinyō-oryū and Kitō-ryū, and added to them the guiding principles of seiryoku zenyo (maximum efficiency) and jita kyoei (mutual welfare). Kano focused his judo — literally "the gentle way," a self-consciously philosophical take on "the gentle technique" of jiu-jiutsu — on a relatively small number of techniques that could be drilled safely at full resistance, and discarded the more fearsome maneuvers of the old schools, which, while deadly in theory, were impossible to practice safely, or at all.

The emphasis at the Kodokan was on vigorous randori, live sparring that put a premium on throws, trips, pins, chokes, and joint locks that were both combat effective and safe — indeed, combat effective precisely *because* they were safe — and could be trained regularly and intensely. This, the best evidence suggests, is the crucible that forged Mitsuyo Maeda: not an unspecified, unnamed, unknown classical jiu-jiutsu school, but the Kodokan itself. After a youthful false start in the world of sumo — a sport which offered few possibilities for a diminutive man whose height and weight, variously reported, never exceeded 5'6" and 155 pounds — Maeda entered the Kodokan at the age of 18 while a university student. At the Kodokan, Maeda came under the tutelage of Tsunejirō Tomita, one of Kano's original pupils, and one of the famed "Four Heavenly Kings of the Kodokan," a now legendary group of judo's earliest champions, veterans of the challenge matches that helped earn judo its place of prominence in the Japanese martial arts world. After four years of study under the guidance of Tomita, Maeda earned the fourth-degree black belt rank of yondan with a dynamic performance at a Kodokan tournament that saw him defeat no fewer than eight consecutive opponents.

Maeda was thriving. So too was judo on the whole: having firmly established itself as the preeminent grappling art in Japan by the turn of the century, Kodokan judo began its inexorable spread around the globe, fulfilling Kano's international aspirations for his creation. Yoshiaki Yamashita, another "Heavenly King" of the early Kodokan, was one of judo's most successful ambassadors in this period, taking up a teaching position at the U.S. Naval Academy and once instructing President Theodore Roosevelt, an avid boxer, in the fundamentals of judo at the White House. A year after Yamashita had set out on his tremendously successful visit to America, Tomita decided to follow suit, and brought with him two assistants: Soishiro Satake and the 26-year-old Mitsuyo Maeda. The three arrived in New York December 4, 1904, and straight away began a series of demonstrations at Columbia, Princeton, West Point, and various YMCAs throughout New York and New England. Tomita and Maeda would perform various kata — prearranged give-and-take exhibitions of judo techniques and principles — before taking on challengers from the crowd: wrestlers, football players, tough young athletes of whatever stripe. In order to make wins even more impressive, and to mitigate the impact of a loss or draw, Maeda and Tomita would generally solicit challenges from people larger than themselves (which wasn't hard). Tomita and Maeda continued with these sorts of public demonstrations, extolling the virtues of their judo way for the better part of a year, establishing a modest judo club in New York City along the way.

But it wasn't until Maeda parted ways with Tomita later that year that the shape of things to come would come into focus. A November 6, 1905, article in the Asheville, North Carolina, *Gazette News* reported that Maeda had been in contact with Akitaro Ono, a judoka who had come to America in hopes of securing a teaching position and turned to professional wrestling to make ends meet when those hopes were dashed. Ono would eventually go on to teach in military academies in Berlin and Gross Lichterfelde and would come to be seen as a pioneer of German judo, but when Maeda came upon him in North Carolina, he was in somewhat rougher shape: less than two months earlier, Ono had been battered in a bout against Charley Olson, a much smaller wrestler who is thought to have made off with the better part of $10,000 in side bets for his efforts. Not long after this encounter with Ono, Maeda was taking pro wrestling bouts in Georgia, and, according to the *Atlanta Journal*, living out of a YMCA in Selma, Alabama. This was not exactly what Kano had in mind when he encouraged his students to take his judo abroad. "With judo," Kano said, "We have no professionals in the same sense as other sports. No one is allowed to take part in public entertainment for personal gain. Teachers certainly receive remuneration for their services, but that is in no way degrading. The professional is held in high regard like the officers of a religious organization or a professor in the educational world. Judo itself is held by us all in a position at the high altar."

There can be no doubt that Maeda, making the leap into the world professional wrestling, was, out of necessity or otherwise, turning his back on at least part of the lofty educational ideal of Kodokan judo. But Selma, Alabama, was a long way from the Kodokan.

It was also just the beginning. For much of the next 20 years, Maeda would travel the world, joined variously by Soishiro Satake, Akitaro Ono, and Tokugoro Ito, a rough-and-tumble judo champion turned professional wrestler who, according to martial arts historian Joseph Svinth, might well have been originally brought overseas by the Seattle Japanese Association "to intimidate union organizers and patrons of Chinese-owned gambling houses and brothels." First, they went to Cuba, where they would come to be known as "The Four Kings of Cuba," then in quick succession England, Scotland, Belgium, and England again where, most notably, Maeda competed in the 1908 Alhambra tournament and impressed many with strong performances against much bigger men. Later, he came up short in a 1909 bout against heavyweight boxing great Sam McVey. In Spain, Maeda performed under the name "Komaru Maeda," or "Troubled Maeda," in an "ironic allusion to his financial troubles," but it was another name bestowed upon him during his time in Spain that would stick with him for the rest of his days: "Conde Koma," The Count of Combat. We know that throughout his many travels, Maeda taught judo whenever he could, and we know that he wrestled and fought almost constantly to make a living; what we don't know, exactly, is when he was working and when he was shooting. There was, in all probability, more of the latter than the former.

The oft-repeated claim that Maeda won no less than 2,000 professional fights in his day is complete speculation and does not bear scrutiny. Maeda and his comrades were all tough, skilled martial artists, with strong, verifiable backgrounds and achievements in a physically demanding discipline before they began their careers as professional wrestlers. There was nothing ambiguous about their skill. But there is, understandably, a great deal of ambiguity surrounding the legitimacy of the bouts they took part in regularly to pay the rent.

Other times, the game was entirely clear. After Spain came Havana, and after Havana came Mexico City, where Maeda took up residence at the Principal Theatre in 1909 and made his mark with a simple proposition: if any man could throw him, that man would walk away 500 pesos richer. If it turned out you couldn't budge Maeda, but Maeda couldn't throw you either, you would earn the more modest but not inconsiderable sum of 100 pesos. There is no record of anyone ever collecting either sum, although we are probably within our rights to wonder whether or not these encounters were entirely on the up-and-up. What happened next, we can be sure was pure theater: a mysterious Japanese by the name of Nobu Taka emerged as a challenger to Maeda in a bout that was billed as the World Jiu-Jitsu Championship. In front of a stunned audience, Taka won the match, only to drop the entirely fictitious title of World Jiu-Jitsu Champion back to Maeda a mere four days later. History records that "Nobu Taka" was in fact Maeda's old friend Soishiro Satake; it does not record how, exactly, their impressive little stunt was viewed by Mexican bookmakers.

Despite theatrics like these, Maeda was somewhat controversially promoted to the Kodokan rank of fifth degree black belt for his considerable work popularizing judo, particularly in Cuba, even if his methods were rarely in keeping with the founder's vision. He would ultimately attain the rank of seventh degree. Through all the stunts and the shenanigans, the real challenge matches and the staged wrestling bouts — and who knows where his contest against a knife-wielding Capoeirista falls on that spectrum? — Maeda was always a man of judo. After he married and settled in Brazil, the pro wrestling matches and the fights dwindled, but his commitment to the art he studied under the watchful eye of Tomita those many years ago never wavered. Maeda, with his chief partner in crime, Satake, are celebrated as key figures in the history of judo in Brazil, a country where judo has positively thrived. Clube Remo, a judo club Maeda founded in 1921, still operates to this day.

But despite those considerable contributions to the sport of judo and to his adopted home of Brazil, Mitsuyo Maeda would have almost certainly remained little more than an obscure footnote in the history of professional wrestling and the martial arts were it not for a chance encounter with a young Carlos Gracie. Had the 14-year-old Gracie not been in the audience at the Teatro da Paz in Belem that night in 1917, had he not been fascinated by the grace and efficiency of Maeda's peculiar judo, a judo shaped by contests against all comers from all over the world, would we, today, know the name of either man?

Here, again, the Gracie myth, that curious and unfortunate part of the Gracie package, rears its head. Carlson Gracie, describing his father's brief but vital period of study under Maeda, inexplicably suggests that "at the time, it was considered a crime against the nation for a Japanese national to teach jiu-jitsu to a non-Japanese." As we've seen, nothing could be further from the truth: Yamashita, Tomita, Maeda, and others like them traveled the world over with the explicit aim of spreading Kano's art, and were in fact commended for their efforts by the Kodokan itself, the very heart of judo.

Nor should we be confused by the Gracie insistence on referring to Maeda as a practitioner of jiu-jitsu: in this first wave of judo's internationalization, the relatively new term "judo" was used interchangeably with "jiu-jitsu"; early texts even make reference to "Kano jiu-jitsu." What Maeda taught Carlos in their few short years together, and what Carlos and his frail brother Helio brilliantly transformed into the foremost submission grappling style on the planet, wasn't unique because it was some ancient, secret strain of jiu-jitsu, a mysterious vestige of the feudal past, passed on to them by an exile committing a crime against his country. No, it was judo that Maeda taught, because that was all he had to teach, but it was, crucially, a judo twisted into new shapes and contortions by the demands of a life spent in the rough-and-ready world of professional wrestling.

AD SANTEL: JUDO CONQUERER?

While Maeda was bringing judo to converts in North and South America, another important exchange was taking place at the Kodokan. Adolph Ernst, a wrestling world titleholder at lightweight as Ad Santel, brought the techniques and strategies of catch-as-catch-can wrestling to fellow grapplers in Japan.

Santel's name has survived what otherwise might have been a long forgotten wrestling career because of his role in the early development of future champion Lou Thesz. Santel was a legend in Thesz's eyes, and contemporaries say a legitimate tough guy, a real handful for even the best wrestlers despite weighing just 175 pounds. Santel's epic feud with the judoka of his era started simply enough — with a professional wrestling match in his hometown of San Francisco. His opponent was Ito, Maeda's former running buddy who had returned to America when Maeda settled in Brazil. Santel dispatched with Ito by slamming his head into the ground for a TKO win in February 1916.

Knowing a good gimmick when he saw one, Santel proclaimed himself the "world judo champion." Wrestling, at the time, was a local and regional sport for the most part. While its popularity ebbed and flowed nationally based on the heavyweight champion, local areas could do brisk business with the right wrestlers as headliners. The world champion might, for example, visit Santel's California stomping grounds just a few times a year, if that. The rest of the year it was up to him, and wrestlers like him all over the country, to draw a crowd. A gimmick like this just made it easier for Santel to keep food on the table for wrestlers in California.

Four months later, Ito got his win back: "Ito threw Santel around the ring like a bag of sawdust. . . . When Ad gasped for air, the Japanese pounced upon him like a leopard and applied the stranglehold. Santel gave a couple of gurgles, turned black in the face and thumped the floor, signifying he had enough."

Santel's loss was easily forgotten when the German made the trip to Ito's adopted hometown of Seattle, Washington. Ito had beaten all comers there and established himself as a legitimate tough guy. A win over Ito carried weight in Seattle and Santel used his notoriety to challenge local judokas, beating two tough grapplers in 1917, slamming one so hard he was dizzy for some time.

The Japanese judo establishment was aghast. They claimed Ito's 10-year absence from the motherland might have weakened his judo foundation. He hadn't been able to train with the very best. Thus, they claimed the losses did little to show wrestling's superiority over their art. It merely showed a weakness in individual athletes.

Santel decided to see for himself, traveling to Japan in March 1921 and challenging all comers at the Kodokan itself. While the venerable Japanese institution allowed mixed matches for research purposes, it did not approve of professionalism and refused to sanction matches for money. This didn't stop some judoka from answering Santel's challenge. Santel wrestled two men to a draw and won one match, a contest with a Japanese star who was part of Santel's touring group.

While Santel's status as "judo conqueror" seems overstated, he and others who traveled to the land of the rising sun to try their hand at the Japanese style, like Russian wrestler Karl Pojello, had a lasting impact on those they grappled with. One of Santel's opponents, Hikoo Shoji, became a pioneering if ultimately unsuccessful wrestling promoter in Japan. But even over in America, pro wrestling's popularity slumped as the industry faced a promotional challenge of its own — what to do without its biggest stars.

By 1913, Gotch had worn down. His final official title defense was in April of that year against Russian strongman George Lurich. In the immediate aftermath, chaos reigned. Gotch hadn't taken a fall for a successor, still wanting to tour the country alongside boxing champions Jim Jeffries and Jess Willard with the Sells-Floto Circus. It was important to Gotch that he remain "The Unbeatable Frank Gotch" and so he left competitive wrestling with his reputation intact.

Feeling some loyalty to his cartel and the industry he had helped create, Gotch attempted to use his influence to proclaim Charles Cutler as his rightful successor. Cutler

8 A WORLD Without HEROES

was another Farmer Burns protégé and a fairly good wrestler and boxer. He had barnstormed with the great John L. Sullivan and even boxed the legendary champion Jack Johnson, who knocked him out in the first round. But Cutler met his match in Omaha, Nebraska, on July 5, 1915, against a gangly youth named Joe Stecher, the first of many double crosses that would shake the wrestling industry throughout the first half of the 20th century.

Stecher had slowly built his reputation in Nebraska, making his professional debut in 1912 after seeing Dr. Benjamin Roller in action. The usual group of hustlers had come to Nebraska to fleece him and his supporters. Men like Burns protégé Yussif Hussane and Ad Santel, who hid behind the moniker "Otto Carpenter," challenged the young Nebraskan, only revealing their true identities after the match had been agreed to. It didn't matter what they called themselves, Stecher pinned them both with his leg scissors, taking advantage of a pair of tree trunk legs that looked odd underneath his lanky upper body. Although the leg scissors was not a new hold, historian Nate Fleischer explained no one had ever used it quite like Stecher:

> *The climb from obscurity to fame, in any of the more strenuous sports, is usually tortuous and attended by pain and sorrow, but Stecher accomplished it*

almost overnight by the discovery of the body-scissors hold, the first really new trick devised in this form of athletics in a century.

Marlene Dietrich's limbs made her a million dollars. For a young lady to make a fortune by reason of her legs is natural to understand. But when a man makes a half a million dollars with his underpinnings, then there's a good reason for climbing to the rooftops and telling the world all about it.

Yet that's exactly what Stecher did. His trick legs, sturdy as an oak, brought fame and fortune to the gladiator from the Middle West.

The top wrestlers from around the world didn't quite buy the developing Stecher myth, flocking to Nebraska to challenge him, confident they would solve the mystery of the scissorshold. With the "ringers" came plenty of gamblers, looking to take advantage of the locals who had invested so much in the hometown hero. This time the joke was on the hustlers. Joe and his brother Tony, a middleweight who took on the best smaller wrestlers in the country, always cleaned house.

"Joe and I beat every 'ringer' the smart boys sent at us," Tony later recalled. "And our farmer friends really cleaned up the gamblers."

Cutler was supposed to be the one to finally beat Stecher. Chicago-based gambling interests were counting on it. An all-star team was assembled to train him, including future world champions Ed "Strangler" Lewis and Earl Caddock. The gambling was fast and furious and literally hundreds of thousands of dollars were wagered on the bout, despite an earlier Stecher contest being canceled when Omaha police had gotten word it might not be on the up and up. Evidence of duplicity never seemed to stop the betting, which is many cases was more about figuring out what the hucksters would decide outside the ring than what was happening inside it.

This match, contested in July 1915, appears to have been on the level. Cutler simply believed he would be able to beat the wunderkind — but he failed. Stecher took the first fall in 18 minutes and Cutler took his time getting to his feet, his insides crushed by the leg scissors Stecher had used to pin him. The second fall went even faster, the powerful

LEG SCISSORS INNOVATOR JOE STECHER

scissors pinning Cutler to the mat in just 10 minutes. Cutler wasn't just beaten, he was humbled.

"We were a bunch of boobs," Cutler told the local *Fremont Herald*. "We had the idea that another 'farmer wonder' had been courageous enough to announce himself in the heavyweight class and we came out here with the feeling that it would be like taking candy from a baby. . . . Stecher is a better man than I am. He can throw any man in the world. Frank Gotch cannot throw him, nor can anyone else."

Gotch was sitting ringside for the bout and for most wrestling fans was still the real world champion. There was money in a match between the old champion and his 23-year-old successor, and wrestling historian Steve Yohe believes it's a match that was essential because "Gotch's shadow hung over any claim Stecher had."

The match was tentatively set for Omaha when Gotch broke his leg in training, shattering his fibula and Stecher's chances of being a transcendent star in a single mishap. Gotch died a year later of uremic poisoning, and an era died with him. Mac Davis described a whole state in mourning: "In Humboldt, his hometown, every store closed down, the schoolhouse was shuttered and empty, on the day of his funeral. Thousands of weeping mourners, gathered from many parts of the land, trudged the icy path to the rural cemetery on a cold December day to bid a final farewell to the farm boy who had been the greatest wrestling champion in history."

With Gotch and his mentor Farmer Burns out of the picture, a new collection of schemers and mat men had to carry the business forward. Gotch and Burns never ended up giving back to the burgeoning industry that had made them rich, failing to crown a new champion and leaving nothing but scorched earth behind them, the business falling into disrepute wherever they set foot. Stecher and his compatriots would have to build wrestling from the ashes of its former glory.

THE BIG FOUR

While Stecher took on all comers, his main rival was the burly Ed "Strangler" Lewis. Canonized by sportswriters and his protégé Lou Thesz as one of the toughest men of all time, Lewis was born Robert Fredericks in Wisconsin in 1890. He took his name from the original Strangler, Evan Lewis, and came to prominence with a win over Dr. Benjamin Roller in Lexington, Kentucky, for the American title in 1913.

Soon after, Lewis met Billy Sandow, a former middleweight wrestler who had a flair for promotion. Together with a Burns protégé named Joseph "Toots" Mondt, the two would form the Gold Dust Trio, one of the most notorious and successful wrestling conglomerates in the sport's history. When he first met Stecher, however, Lewis was just making his name nationally.

The two wrestled to a draw in Evansville, Indiana, in October 1915, a dull affair that saw Lewis mainly on the defensive. Of course, only the few in that town knew how boring the match had been — the result was what mattered, and Stecher's inability to pin Lewis was a feather in his cap that Lewis and Sandow used to promote Lewis throughout the country.

A return match was booked in Stecher's homebase of Omaha where 18,000 people watched the two grapple for almost five hours on July 4, 1916. When darkness claimed the last of the daylight, the mat was illuminated by car headlights. The two eventually had to settle on a draw. Many have used this match to demonstrate the turning point for the wrestling business. The theory proclaims that shooting contests were too slow and ponderous for fans to enjoy. It was matches like this one that led to creation of worked bouts to keep things interesting for paying spectators.

It's possible, however, that wrestling history is wrong — this match pointed at so often as the turning point between real and phony wrestling may have actually been far from a contest. Historian Steve Yohe believes the five-hour tilt between Stecher and Lewis was a product of gamblers betting on when the match would end. The longer the match went, the more fools were parted from their money, sure a winner would eventually come forward: "It wasn't just a bad match, the people of Nebraska lost thousands of dollars betting on Stecher. Before and after the match, no one felt Lewis had a chance of beating or pinning Stecher, so the real bet was on the length of the match. Joe won all his matches in short time and straight falls, so the farmer types thought it was a safe bet to put their money on 'Stecher under 60 minutes' or even under 30 minutes. As the match continued, they kept raising their bets with each half hour. A small fortune was made by the Lewis bettors and big city gamblers all over the country. Lewis was willing to stall and ruin the contest because the money was in the gambling, not winning a match or a title. Stecher, himself, was probably in on it and made money. The word 'mark' was a gambling term long before it was used by the wrestling world."

While this famous example of a shoot may have indeed been a work, there's no doubt that the wrestling business was transforming quickly. Fifteen thousand people had seen Stecher beat Cutler and 18,000 had been in attendance for the Lewis match, a dramatic increase in attendance compared to most bouts at the turn of the century. It was easier than ever to travel from town to town and urban areas were exploding all over the country. Money at the gate was becoming significant, and newspaper exposés of con men made betting less of a factor than ever, with potential marks leery of being suckered by professional con men.

Curley was the leader in changing the business to reflect a rapidly declining attention span and the increased competition for entertainment dollars. It was no longer enough to come into a town and put on wrestling matches. They had to be entertaining or no one would come. Historian Scott Beekman makes the case for Curley as a transformative figure in the sport's history: "The excitement engendered by boxing knockouts, motion pictures, and the startling home run power of Babe Ruth demonstrated to Curley that professional wrestling required a dramatic overhaul to stay competitive in the box office market. Curley and the other promoters, therefore, agreed to a variety of rule changes, including the adoption of time limits, referee's decisions (to alleviate the public anger over time limit draws), and the increasing usage of one-fall matches. Most important, they recognized that through cooperative effort promoters could dominate the sport and effectively eliminate the power of independent-minded wrestlers."

Curley's main opposition were Western promoters led by Gene Melady, a former football star who had made his money in the livestock business and then promoted many of the biggest matches of his era. He had been the man behind Stecher's matches with Cutler and Lewis and controlled Earl Caddock as well. Dubbed the "Man of 1,000 Holds," Earl was one of the top amateurs in the country, an AAU champion at both light heavyweight and heavyweight. Caddock was without a doubt a skilled wrestler, using the head scissors as his finisher in most matches; Melady took him to Farmer Burns and Frank Gotch for extra seasoning, making him even more dangerous. He trained with Gotch throughout 1916 as the legend prepared for a match with Stecher. Instead, with Gotch dropping out with an injury, promoters turned their attention to a Caddock-Stecher match, building both men into seemingly unstoppable juggernauts.

When the two finally met in 1917, it was an extravaganza, packing an arena in Omaha full of more than 7,500 spectators paying $14,000 for the pleasure. Stecher had been known as wrestling's last honest man, but let down his fans in a controversial contest. After splitting falls with Caddock, the first time either man had his shoulders pinned to the mat, Stecher refused to return for a third fall. In the seminal exposé *Fall Guys*, Marcus Griffin calls the bout nothing more than an opportunity to take Stecher's fans for all they were worth:

> *Again the unsuspecting friends and supporters of a wrestling king were taken into camp by the sharpers. Ranch men and farmers who had seen Stecher apply his famed scissors hold to luckless opponents were convinced that not a living man had a chance to beat their Nebraska pride and joy. Imagine their consternation when Stecher lost.*
>
> *The Stecher-Caddock bout has always remained one of the unexplained matdom mysteries. Joe won the first fall and Caddock the second after nearly an hour and 40 minutes of tugging. Then it was that Stecher threw down the many friends who had been betting on him by refusing to come out of his dressing room for the third and deciding fall. Caddock was named victor by "default."*

While Caddock, Lewis, and Stecher dominated the scene in the Midwest, a fourth major star was created by in the Northeast. Wladek Zbyszko, younger brother of Polish wrestling sensation Stanislaus Zbyszko, became a player with a strong performance in a Greco-Roman tournament and a win over Lewis, both in New York. A big man with bulging muscles, Zbyszko looked the part — and unlike his brother had learned some hooks to go along with his classical wrestling acumen.

Wladek, Stecher, Caddock, and Ed Lewis main-evented cards across the country for Curley and his partners, becoming the four biggest wrestling stars in America. Historian Steve Yohe calls it a golden era of wrestling, one often overlooked in the rush to move the narrative from the dominance of Frank Gotch to that of Lou Thesz in the 1950s.

Gotch's success was golden for Gotch and his friends, not the wrestling business as a whole. Gotch became rich and famous but at a great cost to the industry. There weren't any other stars of his caliber, he had made sure of that, and when he walked away it left a huge hole.

Wrestling promoters like Jack Curley were determined not to let this happen again. In the teens and 1920s, there wasn't a single champion standing head and shoulders above the rest of the business. Instead, four men drew big money all over the country — Wladek Zbyszko, Joe Stecher, Ed "The Strangler" Lewis, and Earl Caddock. The big four took turns losing to each other and each remained strong. Complex and intricate booking made sure there was a steady stream of challengers for the champion du jour. Gotch may have been a bigger star than anyone who followed him — but the business as a whole was in a stronger place without him.

When the Great War broke out most wrestlers did all they could to avoid substantive military service. Caddock, the champion, was different. To his credit, he served honorably in World War I, a true blue patriot. He didn't just hang around Army bases in the States, wrestling every weekend like the other stars of the day. In 1918, Caddock actually went to Europe with his unit, fighting the good fight. Zbyszko was the opposite extreme — he took his appeal to avoid wartime service all the way to President Woodrow Wilson, and when he was finally assigned to a unit in Maine was almost immediately discharged, claiming his cauliflower ears prevented him from hearing.

Wrestling insiders wanted Caddock to drop the title before he left for Europe, but his manager Melady refused. He wanted to keep his hand in the wrestling racket and was afraid that losing to any of the top contenders would lead to a business centered on the East Coast, where he had no sway and his great rival Jack Curley held all the power. Curley, the Stecher brothers, and Lewis signed written agreements to work together in the major cities on the East Coast. Caddock and Melady were left out in the cold. When Caddock left for the war, he took the title with him.

Caddock's wartime service further muddled an already unclear title picture and the stakes were raised when rumors spread that he would have to retire after being poisoned by gas in the killing fields of France. Zbyszko and Stecher both made claims to the title. Win or lose, Lewis always seemed to bill himself as the rightful champion. A tournament was scheduled in 1919 to settle the score, and Caddock announced he was fit enough to take on the winner upon his return from active duty.

In a double elimination tournament, Stecher beat both of his rivals and then pinned Caddock in a thrilling bout at Madison Square Garden in 1920. The match drew more than 10,000 fans and $80,000 and there were seven cameras on hand filming the bout for the theater. The *New York Times* reported tickets ringside were $22. The cheap seats went for just $2.20. All of New York society was there, including the Wall Street elite. It was roundly considered a huge success, defensive and exciting all at once. The two wrestlers made $30,000 for the film rights, and it's one of the earliest wrestling matches to survive on video.

The four continued to tour the country, in opposition to each other in various pairings. It was a big money enterprise, brought down by greed. Lewis, in the booking, was clearly the lesser of the four men. This rankled him, as he felt no man was his master when it came to actual wrestling. He had done jobs for all three while getting mostly draws and indecisive wins in return. When he finally got the chance to hold the world title at the end of 1920, he wasn't inclined to give it back.

THE SECOND STRANGLER

Though he had competition from Zbyszko, Stecher, and Caddock, Lewis eventually distinguished himself as the biggest star of his era, remaining at the top of the business until he was in his 40s, and only finally retiring for good in 1948 as he approached 60. The Strangler was one of the toughest wrestlers in the world, a defensive grappler who was big and strong enough to stifle even the very best opponents. When he wanted to make things difficult, Lewis could make matches ponderous affairs, simply outlasting his opponents.

Lewis was one of many promising young wrestlers when he met Billy Sandow in 1914 in the wrestling hotbed of Kentucky. Sandow was a veteran wrestler and promoter who was a key figure in taking the Strangler to the next level. He helped invent a back story for Lewis, as a University of Kentucky instructor, a clean-cut and educated kid. Lewis, in reality, had worked at a paper mill and in a warehouse.

He built his legend with a single hold, the stranglehold from which he took his name. But that was a hold he couldn't rely on as his bread and butter — it was illegal in most states at a time when wrestling was still thought to be legitimate, and thus regulated by many athletic and boxing commissions as if it were real sport. As an alternate hold, he used a "neck yoke" in which he pressed his opponent's chin into their chest with a front facelock, cutting off their air supply and making them easy prey.

Sandow did more than just create a legend for Lewis; he had the power to help him make it to the top of the game: "Before 1918, most of the power in pro wrestling was in the hands of managers. To be a major star in the sport, you needed a strong manager. Managers didn't just manage bookings and money, they provided training for their performers and probably booked the actual matches. The manager with the biggest star, who could draw the most money, would control who won or lost. Most of the time that meant his wrestler won, and if another manager didn't like the situation, he didn't have to take the big money match. Sometimes the dominant manager would pull a switch, if there was more money to be made losing. Even Gotch did big money losses to Jenkins and Beell. The manager also made bets and made sure his grappler got his cut from gamblers. A good manager might have meant more to a wrestler than great wrestling ability."

Sandow also helped Lewis get over his finishing hold, one of the most legendary in wrestling history. Today, the headlock takeover is a move you see in almost every wrestling match, often in the beginning of the bout before things really get going. In Lewis's day, the headlock into a takedown was a thrilling finisher. He would often apply the hold multiple times before finally getting the pinfall. It was dramatic and exciting — but it was also a clear sign that wrestling matches might not be on the level. The side headlock wasn't a real hold — to apply it you had to give your opponent your back, something unthinkable for any wrestler worth his salt. "Strangler" Lewis may have been a great legitimate wrestler, but his patented hold was far from real.

Lewis's penchant for drawn out battles necessitated a change in the way business was done. His refusal to lock up with opponents was bad for business, so a points system was put into place. It was a time of innovation, with no idea too outlandish. These bouts were given a time limit and a wrestler would be awarded points for activity. Promoters hoped this might encourage defensive wrestlers like the Strangler to open up more. As it stood, many didn't like having him on their cards. He drew a good crowd, but his style often ruined long-term business.

"The refusal to meet the Strangler is not based on any belief that he is not a good wrestler, but simply on the fact that so many of his contests have proved unsatisfactory," Caddock's manager Gene Melady said, explaining why his fighter preferred to meet Zbyszko. "Lewis and his manager have succeeded in killing the game nearly everywhere they have appeared, because Lewis whenever he meets a man of ability has shown a penchant for playing on the defensive alone. His most notable offense was in Omaha when he wrestled Joe Stecher five hours without once trying to take the offensive."

Lewis was behind Stecher and Caddock in the pecking order for several years before

ONE OF THE TOUGHEST OF ALL TIME: ED "STRANGLER" LEWIS
SPECIAL COLLECTIONS OF THE UNIVERSITY LIBRARIES OF NOTRE DAME

finally moving to the fore. He became the first man to actually pin Stecher twice in a single match, winning a 1919 bout in Chicago, but put over Zbyszko and Stecher in big matches in New York. The idea was to convince fans anything could happen when these evenly matched competitors did battle — and it worked. When Lewis met Zbyszko in March 1919, thousands had to be turned away from a sold out Madison Square Garden.

He finally got the big win from Stecher on December 13, 1920, taking the world title for the first time at the 71st Regiment Armory in New York. In front of a packed house, the two had a fast-paced and exciting bout, a far cry from their first two contests that had bored the socks off fans in Nebraska. The bout finally came to an end after Lewis kicked free of Stecher's famous scissorshold and looked to finish his opponent. Nate Fleischer described the match in *From Milo to Londos*:

> As soon as Stecher, who was weary from his own efforts, reached his feet, Lewis sprang like a panther and circled the champion's head with his left arm. Down went Stecher and it was nearly a minute before he succeeded in getting his head out of the lock. That was the beginning of the end as the champion was weak when he got on his pins.
>
> Seven times more in quick succession the Strangler put the headlock on his weakened opponent and on the eighth time Stecher was unable to escape and was pinned to the mat.
>
> When Lewis released his victim, Stecher, nearly blind from the severity of the clutch, staggered around the ring and his seconds were compelled to lead him to a chair till he recovered.

Although Lewis told people for years that the match was a shoot, the description above sounds like anything but. The *New York Times* raved about the match, saying Stecher and Lewis provided more action in the final seven minutes than in the preceding hour plus: "In fact, there was more lively, uninterrupted work by both grapplers in this space than is provided in the ordinary boxing match."

Lewis started his reign strong with a sellout win over Caddock but still wasn't a popular attraction in his own right. His match with John Pesek in April 1921 only drew 4,000 fans, half of what he and Caddock drew earlier in the year. His headlock was also becoming controversial, especially in New York where the athletic commission, run by former wrestler William Muldoon, couldn't seem to make up its mind about which holds should be barred. Many thought the headlock was just a chokehold in disguise, with Lewis slipping his arm under the chin and onto the throat whenever possible. Against Pesek the hold was disallowed.

Lewis dropped the title to the ancient Stanislaus Zbyszko in May 1921, but in a shocking turn of events, a return match that November at Madison Square Garden was promoted not by Curley, but by his rival, boxing promoter Tex Rickard. Curly was on the outs and Sandow and Lewis were effectively running the wrestling racket. On March 3, 1922, Lewis won the title back from Zbyszko. As usual, money was the motivation.

Boxing champion Jack Dempsey had issued a challenge to Zbyszko for a mixed match that February. "I'll knock out Zbyszko and a half dozen other champion wrestlers the same night," the boxer proclaimed. Lewis and Sandow salivated at the idea. Dempsey was the biggest draw in sports. His last fight, against Frenchman Georges Carpentier, had drawn almost $2 million at the box office. To put that in context, no wrestling show had ever drawn as much as $100,000. A match with Dempsey would be big, and he seemed up for the idea. Sandow became obsessed by the idea but wanted Lewis in the match, not the older, less capable Zbyszko.

In March 1922, after Lewis took the title, Sandow made a challenge to Dempsey and his manager Jack Kearns. "I mean business," said Sandow. "Let [Kearns] deposit a check for $5,000 as I have done on the behalf of Lewis and the match will most assuredly be staged. Our money is up and we stand ready to deposit another $5,000 when Kearns puts up the money for Dempsey. And my personal wager of $5,000 still stands that Lewis can beat Dempsey inside of 20 minutes in any ring in the world."

Instead, Dempsey toured Europe with a series of exhibitions. Sandow refused to let the idea die and allies in the press continued to push the idea. Walter Eckersall, a sportswriter for the *Chicago Tribune*, even wrote up a fictional account of the match, one he saw Lewis winning. Dempsey seemed to be seriously considering it.

"If the match ever went through, I think I'd be mighty tempted to try to beat that wrestler at his own game," the boxer said. "I've done a lot of wrestling as part of my preliminary training and I think I've got the old toehold and headlock down close to perfection. If I can win the first fall from him, I'll begin to use my fists. But I've got a funny little hunch that maybe I can dump him without rapping him on the chin."

For his part, Lewis told the press he could "throw myself feet forward at least 15 feet. In doing so, I believe I could break the leg of a man like Dempsey. . . . I could cover up long enough to get hold of him, and once I got hold, he would not have a chance, because he does not know how to break wrestling holds and I am stronger than he is. Of course there is one chance in a thousand that he might hit me with a punch hard enough to knock me out before I could get hold of him, but that is only one chance."

Tom Law, a promoter in Kansas, offered to build a stadium and provide a purse of $300,000 for Dempsey. Suddenly things were looking serious. The match seemed like a possibility when Lewis ended up costing himself potentially the biggest payday of his career. He was scheduled to meet with Dempsey and Kearns to discuss terms and shoot some publicity photos. But Lewis had been arrested the night before in Tijuana, Mexico, after an assault at a party. He missed the meeting and possibly the biggest match of his career. The incident was hushed up and never made the press, but the damage was done. The match was suddenly on Dempsey's backburner.

The publicity continued throughout the year. According to the Associated Press, Dempsey accepted an offer from promoter Al Woods for the bout with Lewis to be held in New York, part of a three-fight deal that would pay him a cool million. That too fell through. Later in life, Sandow would blame Kearns for the match never happening. The boxing promoter had dabbled in wrestling and knew the characters well enough to be sure that a double cross was likely and that Lewis would shoot on Dempsey no matter what they had agreed the outcome would be. Both men continued on as champion in their respective sports, the world never knowing who was the better man.

Lewis's second title reign was much more successful than his first. He was becoming a star thanks to national radio and had learned how to work crowd-pleasing matches. According to Griffin, it was hardly business as usual. Lewis and his cronies changed the way the business worked, moving events from smaller venues to the "finest auditoriums in America" and bringing an unprecedented level of organization to the matches, making sure the results made sense and that they were always building up contenders for the title. They also changed the way wrestling looked in the ring, led in this effort by their new partner Joe "Toots" Mondt. "We'll take the best features of boxing and the holds from Graeco-Roman, combine these with the old time lumber camp style of fighting and call it 'Slam Bang Western Style Wrestling,'" Mondt said.

STRANGLER LEWIS LOCKS UP WITH THE COSSACK GIANT IVAN LINOW WITH A DEADLY HEADLOCK AT THE INTERNATIONAL CHAMPIONSHIP WRESTLING TOURNAMENT

LIBRARY OF CONGRESS

76   SHOOTERS: THE TOUGHEST MEN IN PROFESSIONAL WRESTLING

Sandow and Lewis acquiesced and with the help of other mat men who saw the possibilities, the new trio of Sandow, Mondt, and Lewis sped up wrestling, changed the public taste, and within a few months wrestling gates soared to new heights and the old guard was brought to its knees and forced to work with the new trust. According to *Fall Guys*,

> *Sandow signed wrestlers to contracts, and it is said that he had as many as five hundred hulking bonecrushers under his banner at one time. Thus was Sandow in control, not only of wrestlers, but wrestling clubs too, for without mat men, independent grappling promoters couldn't operate, and via contract, Sandow had every worthwhile attraction under his thumb.*
>
> *Practically overnight Billy Sandow became the coast-to-coast wrestling Czar, and he cracked the whip over meat tossers and promoters alike in the style expected of royal rulers. In the basement of his California home, Sandow built a gymnasium, which he called "The Bullpen." In the enclosure, from early morning until late in the afternoon, his behemoths tugged and hauled, working out "finishes," testing each other's hearts and ability, and giving the "Boss" a general line on the workers he had under contract.*

Sandow, of course, wasn't working in a vacuum. He got lots of input from Lewis, who had seen it all, and Mondt, a tough shooter and a mainstay of the New York wrestling scene.

"Toots was responsible for adding another wrinkle to the game still in existence today — wrestling as a packaged show. In fact, it was probably his greatest contribution," Lou Thesz wrote in *Hooker*. "Up to that point, wrestlers moved around a lot, like the old barnstormers, getting bookings for themselves wherever they could, usually no more than a date or two in any town, and promoters acted as little more than matchmakers. Toots's idea was that it made a lot more sense economically to handle wrestling much like a vaudeville show — maintain a stable of wrestlers and stage the bout as a package, replacing some of the talent every so often to keep things fresh."

It was an idea that gave the group tremendous power over wrestlers nationwide. They weren't just offering the occasional match — they were offering cooperative wrestlers a real livelihood. Having burned their bridges in New York, the Gold Dust Trio of Sandow, Mondt, and Lewis concentrated their efforts in the Midwest. Under their leadership the wrestling business was better organized and more coherent than it had ever been. But danger still lurked on the margins. The trio had the business locked up, controlling money and bookings for the nation's mat men — but they still feared a growing collection of wrestlers working outside their system. While they ran the industry with their trust, trustbusters sprang up around the country.

Ed "Strangler" Lewis was one of the toughest legitimate wrestlers of his day. His protégé Lou Thesz observed, "His stamina was absolutely amazing for a man so bulky . . . he could and literally did wrestle for hours without noticeably tiring. When he saw his opponent was starting to weaken, that's when he turned things on."

When outsiders challenged his supremacy, claiming wrestling was fake and that Lewis and the other top wrestlers were scared to face them, the Strangler was game to confront them in the ring. Normally he was talked down — there was too much at risk. Anything could happen in a legitimate contest. Worse yet, the referee or state officials could be on

9 POLICEMEN, TRUSTBUSTERS, and the Double Cross

the take. Wrestling against an opponent without a predetermined outcome could cost wrestling promoters dearly.

Instead, the wrestling trust came up with a more elegant solution. To tame the trustbusters, the trust needed their own shooters, policemen who could keep a territory safe for the wrestling industry. Foremost among the Gold Dust Trio's policemen was John Pesek, the feared "Tigerman."

The Nebraska-based grappler only weighed 185 pounds, but that never stopped him, even against the heavyweight division's biggest behemoths. Pesek had a brutal double wristlock and combined the hold with a head scissors to pin many opponents. Pesek was as vicious as he was eager, often doing more than just beat the promotion's foes. He was out to hurt people, and he did so frequently.

A policeman also tested wrestlers new on the scene to see what they were made of. When Armas Laitinen came from Finland, Pesek put him through his paces, attacking him with a fury that astounded the *New York Times*, cranking on a hammerlock until the Finn "indicated an injury" and had to withdraw.

Laitinen could consider himself lucky — he could have been Marin Plestina. A hulking Serb, Plestina had been trained since he was a teenager by Farmer Burns. Under the leadership of J.C. Marsh, the same huckster and con man who had guided Frank Gotch's early career, Plestina made his reputation challenging the syndicate's champion and proclaiming to anyone who would listen that the fix was in, the matches fake, the champions nothing but cowards. Bernarr MacFadden, publisher of *Physical Culture* magazine, took the bait, as did promoter Tex Rickard, and the American Legion, believing Marsh's claims that the top stars were all afraid of Plestina: "Marsh placarded the country from coast to coast with broadsides proclaiming the crooked and double dealings of Sandow, Lewis, and Mondt. Though the three had never so much as taken a penny unlawfully from any man, Marsh began to make his allegations felt in many quarters. Some of the best towns fell off in wrestling gates."

After a meeting of promoters, Plestina was matched with Pesek. If he could win a "shooting" match, Plestina would get bouts with the top stars of the day on his terms. "It is understood that some of the wrestlers who were charged with avoiding him in the past have agreed to meet him in a tournament of elimination at the Garden," the *New York Times* declared. Of course, if he failed, his opportunity to claim he was being ducked by the trust was over and done with.

Promoted by Tex Rickard at Madison Square Garden, the match attracted wrestling royalty: Sandow, Lewis, Tom Jenkins, Benjamin Roller, and even former Greco-Roman star Ernest Roeber were all in attendance, eager to see a real contest. What they saw was a massacre. Pesek wasn't there to wrestle — he was there to teach Plestina a lesson. The *Times* reports, "Pesek resorted to his foul work soon after the match started. His favorite trick was gouging. The Nebraskan had a penchant for digging the thumb of his left hand into the right eye of Plestina."

Pesek continued fouling throughout the contest, catching Plestina with head butts, gouges, and even a punch or two. Plestina was heard to cry, "God, don't kill me." The crowd was boiling hot, with several members of the audience charging the ring, and a riot seemed imminent. Pesek was eventually disqualified. The next day, Plestina could only leave his room to visit the hospital where he was found to be suffering from serious injuries to both eyes.

Pesek and his manager Larney Lichtenstein were both banned for life by former Greco-Roman wrestling champion and then New York State Athletic Commissioner William Muldoon from ever competing in the Empire State and his purse was withheld. It may have come at a heavy price, but Plestina had been taught an important lesson. Pesek was repaid with a spot in Sandow's group — his new manager was Sandow's brother Max Baumann, who bought Pesek's contract for $22,000.

His reputation now established, Pesek became the shooter of choice when a promoter needed a problem solved. In 1922 former pro wrestler Paul Bowser moved to Boston where, working closely with Sandow and his crew, Bowser replaced former *Boston Post* sports editor George Tuohey as the leading promoter in the city. He also drew some unwelcome attention from Jack Curley, the wrestling king of New York.

Curley, who had once been the leading wrestling promoter in the world, had signed former Olympic silver medalist Nat Pendleton to be his new standard bearer. But Curley was on the outs with the Lewis/Sandow promotion, which meant Pendleton couldn't get matches with any of the era's top stars like Stecher and Lewis.

Curley didn't go down without a fight. He called out his opposition. He had a real shooter on his hands, thinking Pendleton was the toughest guy around, and was willing to flaunt it a bit, challenging Bowser's best. Pendelton's manager made a claim that Nat could beat Bowser, George Calza (a big Boston-based star) and Ed Lewis in one night. A feud in Boston was one thing. Bringing Lewis's name into things was something else entirely. Lewis and his partner Sandow had to act.

After much bickering, Bowser and Curley settled on a bout for $2,000 a side, winner takes all. Bowser's unknown, the only stipulation being that he weigh no more than 190 pounds, was to take on Pendleton and beat him twice in just 75 minutes. Many suspected Bowser himself, still a top star, would be the opponent. He had other plans. Despite the steep odds, Bowser was so confident that he offered to cover all bets up to $25,000. Days before the bout, Pesek was announced as Bowser's man.

It was a tangled web for sure, with everyone involved having more than money at stake. Sandow and Lewis wanted Pendleton to go away — they didn't want a charismatic, legitimately skilled wrestler challenging their champion, Lewis, for supremacy. Curley, in turn, wanted not just to see Pendleton thrive — he wanted Pesek humbled. Pesek was hovering in New York, looking for matches with the Zbyszko brothers, Curley's remaining big stars after the defection of Lewis. Curley wanted Pesek out of the picture so he could promote his big stars in peace. Bowser wanted to control Boston, without the threat of Curley gaining a foothold in his city.

On January 25, 1923, Bowser packed 3,000 fans into the Grand Opera House in Boston for the showdown. Pesek immediately took the Olympian down and almost finished it early with a double wristlock. Pendleton valiantly held on and weathered the storm. He didn't need to win — Pendleton just needed not to lose twice in the 75-minute time limit. After 35 minutes, however, Pesek caught Pendleton with a toehold. The Olympian attempted a leglock of his own, but exchanging foot holds with a master hooker is a bad idea. A snap was heard as Pendleton's ligaments were torn. He submitted and the first fall went to the "Tigerman."

When the match resumed, Pesek showed no mercy. He went right after the injured foot and forced a submission in just a few minutes. Pesek had done the impossible — he had beaten the Olympian twice in less than 75 minutes, winning two falls in a combined 41 minutes. The win helped both Bowser and Pesek make it big within the Sandow group, which was appreciative of the two removing Pendleton from the picture. Bowser went on to be one of the most successful promoters in wrestling history, and Pesek earned title shots against Lewis and a series of big money matches.

In 1924, Joe Stecher returned to action. He had missed most of 1922 and 1923 with a variety of ailments and a turn as a baseball professional, but was back in force and looking for a big match with Lewis. He was ringside for Lewis's December 13, 1923, title defense against Josef Gurkeweicz in St. Louis. Originally barred from the ring, Stecher made his way before the people in between falls and challenged Lewis to a title match, offering $15,000 to Lewis to take the bout.

The Strangler wanted no part of Stecher, and fearing a double cross, he and Sandow demanded Stecher first defeat Stanislaus Zbyszko and Pesek before earning his match with Lewis. This despite Stecher having won his last match with Lewis in San Francisco all the way back in 1921. When Stecher renewed his challenge in Kansas City later that month, Joe "Toots" Mondt, another tough policeman, was added to the list of men Stecher had to conquer to earn his title shot.

Instead of backing down, Stecher plowed forward. Lots of money was at stake — a legitimate claim to the world title was valuable and Stecher was willing to spend money to make money. He beat Zbyszko in St. Louis in January 1924, paying him $10,000 to lose two falls. The wrestlers' cut of the gate proceeds was just $6,600, so Stecher paid out of pocket, actually losing money to get the win over the big Pole. But it was building to a big match with Lewis and Stecher in a wrestling hotbed, a match that could be worth a small fortune.

A match with Mondt followed, but negotiations for the eventual Lewis match were faltering. Stecher, perhaps, wanted a run with the title. Lewis, historian Steve Yohe suggests, may have only been willing to wrestle to a draw. Tempers were high and no decision could be reached. Mondt punched Stecher in their February bout in Kansas City. The cheap shot ended the match and the negotiations for a Lewis bout.

CHANGING GEARS

With Stecher out as an opponent, Lewis, who held the title for almost three years, was running out of competition. Now in his mid-30s, Lewis was getting fat, was constantly booed by fans all over the country, and trachoma, a bacterial infection of the eye, had cost him much of his vision. Wrestling need a change and Sandow had an idea to shake things up that revolutionized the sport's history — and spelled the beginning of the end for the Gold Dust Trio. In *Ringside*, Scott Beekman writes, "With a wrestler's grappling skills no longer the determining factor in match decisions, Sandow recognized that a charismatic individual, with little or no actual wrestling ability, could be built into a champion. He solved the dilemma of a dearth of marketable title challengers by orchestrating the rise of Wayne 'Big' Munn."

Munn was a football player who had attracted a lot of attention at the University of Nebraska. He stood a whopping 6'6" and weighed 260 pounds. Sandow was intrigued by the idea of promoting a champion who had never wrestled at all — it was taking the con to the next level. According to Lewis student Lou Thesz, the champion and Mondt were both game: "Ed and Toots agreed that it was a compelling idea — bring in a mainstream sports hero who was already popular with the sports fans and turn him into a wrestler — so they went along with the plan. Sandow persuaded Munn to give professional wrestling a try, Ed and Toots taught him how to perform a match, and off they went, with Ed and Toots protecting Munn all the way from getting into a match with someone who couldn't be controlled."

Munn took the title from Lewis in Kansas City in front of a huge crowd. The plan was working perfectly. *Time* magazine even did a write-up of the match, drawing attention to the kind of hijinks that characterized the new brand of wrestling that Sandow and Mondt had innovated. *Time* picks up the action after Munn had won the first fall with a slam and then thrown Lewis over the top rope in the second fall:

> *Meantime, Billy Sandow, Lewis' manager, had jumped into the ring. "It's a foul!" cried he. "A dirty foul! You've got to award us the match!" The swarthy Munn peered querulously across the mat, tore off his bathrobe, assumed a bellicose attitude, confronted the irate manager. Munn's manager likewise grew threatening; but for all that the referee gave the fall to Lewis on a foul, allowing the latter 15 minutes to get back into the ring. The crowd was indignant, stormed about the ringside, hooting, booing.*
>
> *The last fall was quickly decided. Lewis appeared, his back well bandaged; soon he was lying limp on those bandages. The heavyweight title had passed to Wayne Munn. The crowd went "mad-dog," scrambled on its seats, shook the rafters of Convention Hall as it screeched, boomed, barked salvos of shouts for the victor. Many sportsmen caterwauled at the dejected figure with the bowed head in the centre of the ring.*

The Munn experiment, like many things tried for the first time, was a noble failure. He won the title on January 8, 1925, but before he could establish whether or not he was going to be a big draw (and before he could drop the title back to Lewis) disaster struck the Gold Dust Trio in the form of Stanislaus Zbyszko. Known as "The Old Man" in the press, Zbyszko was a long time associate of Jack Curley, a rival of the Sandow group. Lewis, Sandow, and Mondt thought they had control of the enormous Pole, providing him a living and a series of major matches. They were wrong. He had been wrestling for them since 1921, but harboring grudges, getting more and more angry every time he lost a match. And he lost a lot in 1924, more times than he had in the previous decade combined. When Curley and rival promoter Tony Stecher came calling, Zbyszko was quick to respond.

Munn met Zbyszko on April 15, 1925. No one suspected a double cross. They had met that February in Kansas City and Zbyszko took a fall as planned. This was to be just another night at the matches in Philadelphia — until things took a turn for the worse for "Big" Munn.

Zbyszko decided he wanted to win the match and no one had bothered to teach Munn much in the way of wrestling. After eight minutes, Zbyszko slammed him to the mat and almost immediately pinned his shoulders to the ground. Between falls, Sandow got in the ring and got right in Zbyszko's face. The former champion was unyielding however — he was going to finish what he started. The second fall was even quicker, lasting just four minutes and 53 seconds, despite a Sandow-friendly referee doing all he could to refuse a fair count. Zbyszko was so dominant the official had to count the fall to avoid a riot. Despite the best laid plans, Zbyszko was the new champion.

A few weeks later, Zbyszko played his cards, dropping the title to Joe Stecher in St. Louis. A new gang was making a play for the wrestling business, with Stecher's brother Tony, Curley, and St. Louis's Tom Packs leading the way. Zbyszko lost the title to Stecher on May 30, the same date of the Lewis-Munn rematch in Michigan City, Indiana.

The balance of power had officially shifted when Pesek left the Sandow conglomerate to work with the new Curley-Stecher-Packs trust. Another top star, Jim Londos, soon followed. Stecher toured the country as champion for almost three years, defending his new title against many of the top names of the day — all the while Lewis was on the outs. Stecher wrestled frequently on the West Coast; his family had moved to Long Beach, California, and the Los Angeles area was becoming a wrestling hotbed, setting attendance records at the new Olympic Auditorium.

Despite Munn's loss, actual wrestling skill meant less than ever. So did the world title. Sandow and Lewis all but ignored Stecher's title, proclaiming Lewis champion. For years the two groups did battle in the press instead of the ring, with both Stecher and Lewis proclaiming their superiority. They went head to head in Chicago in March 1926, with Lewis drawing the bigger crowd. But Stecher was a hit almost everywhere he went — in New York for Curley, in St. Louis for Packs, and in Los Angleles for Lou Daro.

While Thesz claims Stecher refused to defend the title, afraid of Lewis showing up to challenge him, newspaper reports show that Joe accepted Lewis's challenges on at least two occasions. The Strangler wanted no part of Stecher, it seems, in a legitimate contest. Both times, in Chicago and Los Angeles, he left town rather than wrestle the champion.

Lewis canceling one of these proposed Stecher matches in Los Angeles in 1926 led to a bout that many consider one of wrestling's last great shoots. Stecher had already wrestled the formidable John Pesek twice that year, but this time was different. After splitting the first two falls, the Tigerman began shooting in the deciding third fall, trying to take the world title for real. Reports say Pesek had Stecher beat several times, with the referee, a Stecher man, refusing to count any of the pinfalls. Historian Mark Hewitt writes that Stecher asked Pesek in Czech, a language shared by the two, what was going on. "Shoot match," the emotionless Pesek was said to reply.

Pesek eventually made Stecher submit to a head scissors and wristlock combination but the referee again broke the hold. Finally another wristlock ended the contest, a concession hold so obvious that not even a Stecher-friendly referee could deny Pesek had won the bout. Pesek left the building quickly, looking to escape the wrath of Stecher supporters, a tactical mistake. The decision was overturned in his absence. It was said his head scissors was a choke and that using the hold had disqualified him.

Pesek not only missed out on the title, he wasn't given another match anywhere in the country for the rest of 1926, punishment from the promotional powerhouses he had betrayed. But the damage to Stecher was dire too: the most lasting blow received was the one to his ego. He had really believed for years that he was the best wrestler in the world, and the Pesek battle left him with second thoughts that many believed killed his enthusiasm for wrestling.

That and a change in the industry led to his retirement in 1928. Stecher was growing tired of the wrestling grind, including a new schedule that had the champion wrestling more than ever all over the country. The days of coming into a town and training for a week while hobnobbing with the local media were over. The champion was wrestling several times a week and Stecher was wearing down.

Finally he agreed to meet Lewis for a tenth time, again changing the course of wrestling history. The two sides came to a working agreement after meetings in Philadelphia and Kansas City. Tom Packs was the man who brought the Lewis and Stecher camps together, and he got the match for his St. Louis promotion. Lewis was built up for his big match with Stecher by beating John Pesek in St. Louis, Lewis's first time back in the city in years. Pesek then proceeded to do jobs from coast to coast, still being punished for shooting on Stecher the year before.

After building for much of the decade, the Stecher-Lewis match on February 20, 1928, did a respectable, but disappointing, $65,000 at the box office. Wrestling had taken its lumps in 1927, especially in the Midwest where Chicago authorities had investigated the sport's legitimacy to lurid headlines in the local papers. Still, despite the hullaballoo, they attracted 7,500 people, including the mayor, assorted politicians, and dozens of writers from all over the country who reported the next day that Lewis had taken the title from Stecher, winning two of three falls in a match that went on until almost 1:30 in the morning.

The match wasn't without controversy. When Lewis scored the final pinfall, Stecher's legs were both entangled in the ropes. It was a major point of contention, a screwjob finish if there ever was one, but word of it was largely confined to St. Louis: the Associated Press report, distributed nationwide, makes no mention of the ropes at all, saying, "[Lewis] won fairly and decisively, never leaving a doubt as to the outcome." Still, Stecher was able to leave the sport with his head held high. Lewis, for his part, ignored the controversy and proceeded to defend his title exclusively against his own clique of wrestlers controlled by Boston-based promoter Paul Bowser.

DYNAMITE

Weeks before Lewis finally beat Stecher, Gus Sonnenberg made his professional wrestling debut in Providence, Rhode Island, where he was a football star. Sonnenberg had made his reputation nationally at Dartmouth, but football wasn't paying the bills on the professional level. Giving wrestling a try, Sonnenberg was an immediate sensation. He made his debut in Boston for Bowser a week later, and in just a few short months amassed an impressive winning streak, even beating Wayne "Big" Munn, the original footballer turned wrestling star.

Unlike Munn, Sonnenberg was "Dynamite" in the ring, earning that nickname thanks to an exciting style and explosive tactics. There was no veneer of wrestling in Sonnenberg's performance. It was all show, including powerful open-hand slaps to the head and a flying football tackle that laid opponents out. A 1936 *Time* magazine article credits his appearance with spicing up and changing the wrestling game forever: "An upturn was provided in 1928 by Gus Sonnenberg and the flying tackle he used as a Dartmouth footballer. His first opponent, no halfback, was unable to dodge, was carted unconscious from the mat. The success of this new tactic quickly boosted the sport. With addicts neither so naive nor so particular as before, refinement soon disappeared entirely. Eye-gouging, hair-pulling, and kicking became common practice. Assault & battery on the referee proved a popular diversion. Lately one wrestler introduced the new fad of trying to garrote his opponent with three feet of chicken wire. Though even the most bloodthirsty addicts frown on its use, chloroform has been employed on several occasions to down an adversary."

Lewis defended his title against Sonnenberg for the first time on June 29, 1928. The football star had been wrestling for barely six months, but was one of the most popular stars in the game — 14,000 fans packed the Boston Arena for the confrontation. Lewis kept Dynamite Gus strong, giving the 5'7" 205-pound new star the first fall, losing to his patented football tackle despite having six inches, 30 pounds, and decades of wrestling knowledge on his opponent. In the second fall Lewis ducked a Sonnenberg tackle and the footballer went sailing out of the ring, right over the heads of amazed reporters ringside.

He couldn't continue and Lewis was awarded the match — but Sonnenberg hadn't really lost, victim of his own enthusiasm more than anything Lewis had done.

The rematch in January 1929 drew 20,000 fans to the Boston Garden. Sonnenberg had been busy in the meantime, not just winning wrestling matches, but helping lead the Providence Steam Rollers to an NFL title. More than just a tackle, he also played running back, threw for a touchdown pass, and was the team's kicker. Against Lewis in a bout for the title, it was only his tackling that mattered. Sonnenberg rammed his head into the champion's midsection again and again. Fans would compare him to a goat for all the butting he did, but it worked.

It was the end of an era for Lewis, who had been among the sport's top stars for more than a decade. It was the last time the Strangler would ever be the undisputed champion of the world. For $70,000 Bowser bought one clean fall and one countout. Lewis wouldn't allow his shoulders to be pinned twice. In the second fall, the flying tackle knocked him out of the ring seven times.

After the seventh pratfall Lewis couldn't make it back into the ring to answer the referee's count. Sonnenberg's hand was raised and the Boston crowd exploded with joy. Educational Film Exchanges captured the bout on 1,000 feet of film and the match was shown all over the United States and Europe, giving wrestling fans across the country a taste of the action that had made Sonnenberg such a hit in the Northeast.

For nearly two years he defended the title in front of solid crowds, but the specter of a shooter hung over his head. Sonnenberg would only wrestle a handful of carefully selected opponents. With zero real wrestling ability, almost any legitimate contender would be too much for him to handle if someone decided to double-cross him. The restrictions rankled some promoters. Tom Packs refused to use him in St. Louis, and in Pennsylvania he was suspended by the athletic commission for refusing challenges from worthy opponents.

Sonnenberg traveled with a contingent of shooters, ready to take on any challengers who looked like they might threaten the champion. They were also his regular opponents on his barnstorming tour, a fact exposed by the media. One of his policemen, Dan Koloff, wrestled Sonnenberg under five different names.

Of course, none of this stopped him from attracting huge crowds. Fans didn't care whether he was a legitimate shooter. They just wanted to be entertained. A third match with Lewis set a new pro wrestling gate record by drawing $90,000. Held in the gargantuan Fenway Park, the 25,000 who were in attendance there saw what was described as one of the best matches in Boston's history. Lewis won the initial fall, becoming the first to pin the champion, reversing his tackle and sending Sonnenberg crashing to the mat. The champion won the following two with his trademark tackle.

On a west coast swing, Sonnenberg drew well against a returning Stecher, Lewis for a fourth time, and rising star Everett Marshall in a match that drew 25,000 to Los Angeles's

"DYNAMITE" GUS SONNENBERG
SPECIAL COLLECTIONS OF THE UNIVERSITY LIBRARIES OF NOTRE DAME

Wrigley Field, a miniature version of the venerable Chicago institution, for a California record-breaking gate.

Meanwhile, other title claimants began to pop up in droves, including Jim Londos on the East Coast. A Greek immigrant, Londos was a solid wrestler and one of the most popular drawing cards in the country. He had expected the championship reign that was given to Sonnenberg, and when it was denied him, went his own way, teaming with Toots Mondt and drawing big money in his own right. Twenty thousand fans turned up in Philadelphia to see him beat Dick Shikat for their version of the world title.

The promotional rivalry was intense. Londos and his crew even took the trouble to book a fake Sonnenberg in a tour of the south, losing most of his matches. Then, according to Lou Thesz, things got even uglier: "Londos arranged for a friend of his, an accomplished middleweight wrestler, to confront Sonnenberg on a crowded street in downtown Los Angeles and eye gouge him, then give him a thorough beating."

The beating did happen as described, with wrestler Pete Ladjone head-butting Sonnenberg in the face and straddling him, yelling that he had whipped the champion. Sonnenberg went to a police station and pressed charges. His assailant was given 30 days in jail, but the damage to the champion's reputation was done. Damage to his body was piling up too — his aggressive style of wrestling, hard drinking, and numerous auto accidents were taking their toll on him after only a few years in the wrestling game.

DOUBLE CROSSES

While many historians pinpoint this attack as the beginning of the end for Sonnenberg's championship reign, in reality he actually ruled the mats for more than a year after the street fight gone wrong. When the end did come it came at the hands of another newcomer, 1928 Olympian Ed Don George from the University of Michigan. George took the title from Sonnenberg in December 1930, leaving the popular football crossover to travel the country and simply make money for his partners, no longer having to worry about shooters gunning for a world title he didn't actually need to draw a crowd. George was obviously legitimate and didn't present any of the problems Sonnenberg did as champion, but promoter Bowser didn't consult his partners Lewis and Sandow before making the decision to go with the new star. George was the one who paid the price.

Just four months later on April 14, 1931, George lost the title unexpectedly to old man Ed Lewis. The former great, by then barely a month shy of his 40th birthday, wanted to prove a point to promoters and wrestlers in the business. In the weeks leading up to his title match he had been pushed hard, winning straight falls against serious contenders like Everett Marshall. When he decided to take the title from George, he told the young star that he could do it "the easy way or the hard way."

"We were supposed to wrestle a three fall match, and I was going to win of course," George said. "We came out to the center of the ring for the referee's instructions and Ed says to me, really casually and friendly, 'Well, Don, tonight's the night.' I knew immediately what he was saying — that he was going to take back the title — and all I could think of to say was 'Oh no.' Ed smiled and said, 'Oh yes.'"

Lewis himself was supposedly double crossed in a match three weeks later against Henri Deglane in Montreal, Canada, a town promoted by Bowser. Deglane, a 1924 Greco-Roman Olympic gold medalist, wasn't a match for Lewis, even a 40-year-old Lewis, on the mat. Instead, according to the Strangler, Deglane bit himself between falls in the dressing room, then pretended Lewis bit him. Local reports confirm there was a biting incident. The *Arena* magazine reported:

> *There was nothing eventful about the first fall of the match, which came in 33:15, save that Deglane surprised everyone, and especially Lewis, absorbing two devastating headlocks just prior to the end and coming back to side-step Lewis's third rush, clamped on a wicked head and arm lock from which there could be no escape, and pinned the big one solidly. The contender then retired to his dressing room for the rest period, while Lewis remained in the ring, listening to his manager "ragging" the referee in an attempt to get that official excited into doing something like losing his head, but his success was not in evidence.*
>
> *In the meantime, DeGlane used the time to good advantage, returning to the ring in fine fettle and stepped in the lead by applying two or three headlocks that did the headlock king no good at all. Lewis started weakening, all of which might have had much to do with his following maneuver, and as they milled around on the ropes action got brisk fast. DeGlane, behind the champion, reached for a headlock to pull the big fellow to the center of the ring, only to let go in a hurry and fall to the mat beneath Lewis, nearly pinned. The referee, who had been making for the ropes, called the fall for Lewis, only to note the tooth marks and broken flesh on DeGlane's right forearm. Thereupon he quite properly reversed the decision, giving the fall, the match, and the title to DeGlane on a foul.*

The champion was disqualified and Deglane awarded the title. At least that's what Lewis and Lewis supporters like Lou Thesz wanted fans to believe. And it makes a great story — but more likely this was a way to get a championship belt on two different men at the same time. The screwjob loss allowed Lewis to advertise himself as champion in cities where he still drew well, while Deglane and later Don George were also able to represent themselves as the best in the world with yet another version of the world title. The championship was good for business — and the Deglane-Lewis match allowed two men to claim a title instead of one.

They all played second fiddle, however, to Jim Londos, who was drawing huge crowds in New York's Madison Square Garden. Soon Londos replaced Deglane and Lewis as the top stars in Los Angeles as well.

Lewis struck back by challenging Londos in his New York base. Londos had broken free from Jack Curley and booker Toots Mondt, who were no longer getting a percentage of all his checks. They wanted Londos out, but he refused to meet anyone he felt he couldn't trust, and they couldn't find a way to get the title off of him. Plain old skullduggery had to do.

Londos was tricked into signing a contract to face the winner of a Sammy Stein–Dick Shikat match — Londos was expecting the popular Stein to win. Instead, Shikat had his hand raised and Londos was in a pickle. Londos quit the promotion rather than wrestle Shikat in a straight match, and when Shikat did a job for Strangler Lewis, things went from bad to worse for Londos.

Mondt manipulated the Athletic Commission into ordering a match between the two title claimants (Lewis and Londos), and when Londos refused, he was stripped of the title in New York in September 1932. The dashing Greek was fine — he just defended his title in California and elsewhere in front of packed houses. It was New York promoters and fans that suffered with a 40-plus Lewis headlining increasingly empty arenas.

Eventually the commission ordered Lewis to wrestle Ray Steele to determine a rightful champion. Steele, a legitimate shooter, was one of Londos's right-hand men. In a match thought to be a shoot by insiders, Lewis (representing Jack Curley's interests) battled Steele (representing Londos) in a heated match at Madison Square Garden on December 5, 1932. Steele was disqualified for a series of elbows to Lewis's head, allowing Lewis to lay claim to the world title in New York. It was a weird decision in a weird match. Elbows would normally be legal in a wrestling match in this era, seeing as wrestling was a full-on show. In fact they were used without incident on the undercard. But the officials treated this purported shoot differently — a tacit admission that most wrestling matches were not on the level.

The match finish set off an uproar in the crowd. Londos fans and Lewis fans were fighting in the stands. In the ring, Steele's second knocked out Curley with a single punch "that would have made a dent in a brick wall." *Time* magazine claimed the crowd booed the match for 20 minutes straight: "The bout had not ended in a fall. Instead, after stumbling about the ring with their heads locked like two foolishly embattled elks, Lewis and Steele separated, glared, grunted. Steele whacked Lewis on the face with the back of his hand. Referee Forbes warned him to refrain. Steele whacked Lewis three times more. Instead of disqualifying Steele, Referee Forbes warned him again. A wrestler who had helped Lewis train for the match, lop-eared John Evko, climbed into the ring in his bathrobe, whacked Challenger Steele. Referee Forbes tried unsuccessfully to push Wrestler Evko out of the ring, then awarded the bout to Lewis on a foul. A disgruntled spectator slapped Promoter Jack Curley on the nose. Members of the New York State Athletic Commission prepared to investigate the bout."

In the end, peace was reached in a settlement that brought wrestling under the same management coast to coast. Lewis bombing at the box office played a big part in the decision. By 1933 he was drawing just 5,000 fans to Madison Square Garden and dropped the title to journeyman Jim Browning. Londos, a money-drawing star, was better for business and was soon reinstated as the world champion. Icing on the cake for Londos was a September 20, 1934, win over Lewis that set a new record, drawing $96,000 at Chicago's Wrigley Field.

Peace never seems to last long in wrestling and lessons learned are soon forgotten. Londos was replaced by a new hot box office attraction, Irishman Danno O'Mahony. A shot-putter, O'Mahony didn't know a thing about wrestling — but under the tutelage of Boston's Paul Bowser, who had guided the equally clueless Sonnenberg, that hardly mattered.

O'Mahony was thrown right into the fire with a match against Lewis in London. His first match in America drew 14,000 to the Boston Garden for a bout with Ernie Dusek. Irish fans were rabid for the new star, sight unseen. Two weeks later, 16,000 came out to see O'Mahony dispatch Ernie's brother Rudy Dusek. Two consecutive wins made O'Mahony a huge name right out of the gates.

In just his fourth match in America, O'Mahony was main-eventing Madison Square Garden against Ray Steele. He prevailed with his "Irish whip" quickly being established as one of the most devastating finishing holds in all of wrestling. O'Mahony won a reported 49 matches in a row — his 50th win was for the world title over Londos in front of 25,000 at Fenway Park in Boston on June 27, 1935. It was a momentous occasion — no one could recall the last time Londos had lost a clean match. He rarely even lost falls in two of three fall title bouts. He was guaranteed $50,000 for losing and received $20,000 from the gate receipts.

A month later O'Mahony unified the title, beating Ed Don George at Braves Field in Boston. Forty thousand fans packed the stadium to see Danno become the undisputed champion. It was a wild scene as the special guest referee, former boxing great James Braddock, punched out George's cornermen after the bout when they came charging into the ring after Braddock counted George out. An old-fashioned donnybrook erupted in the ring, setting up a rematch, to take place in front of 20,000 at Fenway Park.

The good times came to an end when an angry Dick Shikat shot on O'Mahony during a match at Madison Square Garden in March 1936. Shikat, a real wrestler, was upset he had been passed over for an opportunity at the world title years earlier, when Jim Browning got the nod instead. Feeling mistreated, and doing more jobs than ever, Shikat took his career into his own hands. To get the title back, the wrestling trust actually took Shikat to court. They had a promotional contract with Shikat's name on it and claimed he was in violation when he didn't show up at bookings he knew nothing about. He ended up suspended in many states. The wrestling elite did everything in its power to make Shikat pay for his treachery.

Shikat wanted to drop the title quickly to an outside promoter. The wrestling trust wanted to keep a hold of the belt and sued. It was a risky move, one that could have backfired if wrestling's secrets were exposed to the world. Newspapers in New York reported on the trial, as did *Time* magazine: "One Joe Alvarez, who claimed to be [Shikat's] manager, sought an injunction to keep Shikat from wrestling Baba in Detroit. Shikat frankly admitted that before three recent bouts, a man had pushed his way into his dressing room, instructed him to 'lay down,' lose the match. These orders he had faithfully executed until last March. Then, indignant at having to lose all the time, he disobeyed his dressing room order by pinning Champion Danno O'Mahony in a world championship match. At this testimony Promoter Jack Curley, who with five others rules the wrestling world today, exploded. Such a thing as a 'fixed' match, he yelped, was unknown to him."

The trial became moot when Shikat dropped the title to gimmick wrestler Ali Baba in Detroit, Michigan. To satisfy the New York Commission, he repeated the spectacle a couple of weeks later in Madison Square Garden. Soon half a dozen men were once again claiming to be world champion. It would take a special performer to reunite the fractured wrestling world — luckily one was being groomed by Tom Packs in St. Louis, waiting for his opportunity to shine.

The greatest professional wrestling champion in history was the son of a Hungarian shoemaker, from St. Louis, Missouri. His father, Martin, schooled Aloysius "Lou" Thesz in the fundamentals of wrestling. Thesz was no schoolboy star. The Theszes were immigrants with traditional values. Where they came from in Hungary, a man worked, so when Lou was just 14 he dropped out of school to start full-time in his father's shop. But he dreamed of wrestling, of being one of the greats he and his father watched at the St. Louis Coliseum every week. In the evenings Thesz worked out with the local high school wrestling team, eventually catching the eye of one of the city's wrestling stalwarts. Soon young Thesz was living his dream.

10 THESZ

Tom Packs, the wrestling promoter in St. Louis, liked what he saw in Thesz. Good looking and tall with a muscular physique, Thesz had the makings of a good young wrestler. Packs sent him to George Tragos for seasoning. A former Olympian who competed for Greece, Tragos was one of the most feared men of his time. He was a ripper, a wrestler who wouldn't just beat you, he'd look to hurt you. In the gym they called him "Icewater," thinking that must be what ran in his veins for him to cruelly end so many careers. But Tragos took a liking to Thesz, respecting the boy's willingness to work hard and follow instruction. For two years Thesz learned from the veteran, not just strategies to succeed on the mats but also some carny tricks to make a few bucks.

As a young wrestler, Thesz was making his way in the business, advancing to the main event in his hometown of St. Louis. It was there he would make a connection that would change his life. When Ed Lewis, the legendary former champion, was in town on his way to a booking in the Midwest, Thesz was encouraged to challenge him to a friendly contest. Thesz was fast, young, and a strong 220 pounds. Lewis, despite his formidable reputation, was 46 years old, fat, and nearly blind. The "boys" convinced Thesz it wouldn't be close — and it wasn't, only not in the way young Lou had imagined.

"It was the longest 15 minutes of my life. . . . I was absolutely humiliated," Thesz remembered. "I shouldn't have been, of course, because this was Ed Lewis, but I didn't see it that way at the time. I was so discouraged and embarrassed that I packed my gear immediately after the workout and headed home to brood. The next day I dropped by promoter Tom Packs' office and told him I was quitting."

It was Lewis who called the Thesz house and spoke to Lou's father, telling the elder Thesz that Lou had a real future as a wrestler. Recalled Thesz, "He called my father, which would be like the President of the United States calling you to say 'Hello' because my father had never talked with him. Anyway he said to my father, 'Tell that guy to get back up here.' He said, 'Tell the boy to come back, he did very, very well.' He said, 'But he forgot that he was wrestling me, and I've traveled the world and learned to take care of myself and that's what we were trying to teach him to do.' So I mulled that over a day or two and when I looked at the shoe repair shop again, compared to the fantastic hype you get with the wrestling, I said, 'I think I'm going back to the gym.'"

Lewis would mentor Thesz throughout his career, often traveling with him as a manager. The other great influence on Lou's career was Ad Santel, the tough German wrestler and "judo conquerer" of the early 1920s who contemporaries say gave even heavyweights fits despite weighing just 175 pounds. Thesz already knew some hooks thanks to his early training with George Tragos. But it was Santel who really let him in on the trade, making Thesz one of the most dangerous grapplers in the world.

Thesz explains in *Hooker*, "Once he'd become satisfied that I was serious about my wrestling, Ad decided to induct me into the club. That's exactly how I thought of it too, like an initiation into a very small fraternity, and I was honored this wonderful old man thought enough of me to pass along his secrets. What can I tell you about hooking? Well, all I can say is that no matter where I put my hands on

THE LEGENDARY NWA WORLD HEAVYWEIGHT CHAMPION LOU THESZ

him, Ad could hurt me. And I mean hurt me too. Once, when Joe Malcewicz had dropped by and was watching one of our workouts, I had Ad face down on he mat and was behind him hovering over him; I reached between his legs, trying to turn him over for a possible pin, and he hooked me so quickly and forcefully that he almost broke my arm. 'What are you doing?' Joe screamed at Ad, rushing onto the mat. 'I finally get a boy that I can make some money with and here you go trying to cripple him.'"

The summer he spent with Santel was priceless. Wrestling had changed, and an ability to actually wrestle was barely on the list of necessary skills to make it in the business. But for Thesz, a reputation as a tough guy, as he called it a "dangerous gunslinger," meant everything. It meant promoters could trust him as champion, sending him to foreign lands and all over North America, confident he would come home with the belt if push came to shove.

It also allowed Thesz leverage — the bottom line was, if he didn't want to lose, very few men were going to be able to force him to. And that meant something in the fierce political battles behind the scenes. In an era when most promoters were pushing charismatic characters, Thesz was a firm believer in promoting real wrestlers.

"I never had any illusions that it was anything but a business," Thesz wrote at WrestlingClassics.com. "As I said in my book, any time you sell tickets, it is a business. However, I preferred to see professional wrestling as it was in the gym and in public workouts. I was naive enough to believe it could be that exciting and still involve the audience . . . and still sell tickets."

He often refused to put over showmen on principle, instead making several careers by agreeing to do strategic jobs, turning midcard wrestlers with real credentials into stars overnight. Wrote Dave Meltzer, "Thesz, at least during the prime when he had that power, only waved the magic wand of stardom on occasion and for those who he personally believed deserved it. A believer in wrestling ability as paramount . . . he refused when he was champion to make what he considered subpar wrestlers look good, even if they were drawing big money at the time."

Thesz didn't just refuse to put non-wrestlers over, he would embarrass them in the ring. Thesz held grudges for years, often for reasons known only to him. A run-in with promoter Toots Mondt infuriated Thesz early in his career and it was something Thesz never forgot. He didn't just take it out on Mondt — he took it out on anyone Mondt was associated with, including Antonino Rocca. Rocca was one of the biggest stars in the industry, but Thesz wouldn't work cooperatively with him in the 1950s, costing promoters around the country big bucks.

Angry that Rocca had left the Houston territory for big money in New York, skipping out on dates in the process, Thesz made the Argentinean pay in the ring. Rocca was scared out of his wits when Thesz informed his manager that "tonight, we're wrestling." Refusing to lock up, Rocca tried to escape to the back for a count-out loss. Thesz grabbed him by the throat and forced him back in the ring where he knocked him unconscious with a back suplex.

"Rocca was Toots' property," Thesz wrote in his autobiography *Hooker*. "And I wasn't about to help put money in his pocket. Beating Rocca was my way of paying Toots back for the way he had treated us years earlier."

Today Thesz is most associated with the National Wrestling Alliance and rightfully so — he was the world champion for the promotion for more than 10 years. But before he was the promotion's flag bearer, Thesz had been its fierce rival. Like many top wrestlers, he realized that the big money was in promoting, buying Tom Packs' St. Louis territory with a group of Canadian promoters and fellow wrestler Bill Longson in 1946.

Together, the two men did big business for the territory they owned. Longson was Thesz's opposite — Thesz was clean cut and a scientific wrestler, Longson was one of wrestling's first wild brawlers. The two went head to head as the top stars of their own show for more than a year before Thesz won the National Wrestling Association title in Indianapolis. But it was the other NWA, the Alliance, which would end up ruling the wrestling world.

The Alliance leader was Sam Muchnick. A former newspaper reporter in St. Louis, Muchnick was the publicist for Packs' wrestling promotion. He got bit by the wrestling bug and was running opposition to Lou in St. Louis. Worse for Thesz and his partners, Muchnick was also instrumental in the formation of the NWA, a loose collection of promoters who looked to work together cooperatively. No one thought a national promotion was even possible. The previous decades had seen attempts to organize and work as teams fail when greed got the best of greedy men. But against the odds, Muchnick was making things work with the NWA.

Eventually the two sides merged, with both men doing what they did best; Muchnick was wrestling to control his fellow promoters while Thesz wrestled challengers to his grappling supremacy all over the country. Working three or four nights a week, Thesz wrestled in 32 NWA territories in those early days. In an era of gimmicks, Muchnick and promoters liked having the steady Thesz at the helm. A clean-cut and imposing figure, he demanded respect and got it, even from skeptical promoters. He wasn't the biggest star in wrestling but was solid enough at the box office. And he was a real shooter, capable of protecting himself in the event of a double cross and of coming into cities and challenging the champions of unaffiliated promotions.

Although some old-timers dismiss Thesz's legitimate credentials, pointing out his lack of any real competitive success, perceptions matter. And Thesz was thought to be a tough guy. No one wanted to meet Thesz head on in a real match, so he was able to make rival groups look weak. In *National Wrestling Alliance*, Tim Hornbaker explains, "The core of the Alliance understood that they needed to reestablish faith in a single titleholder among the wrestling fan base. Thesz ascended the throne, and from the moment the membership endorsed him as champion, until the day he lost the strap in March 1956, he brought honor to the title. Thesz led the NWA over innumerable hurdles with his hard work and dedication. He wasn't a huge crowd favorite, but he easily set a high standard for a touring world champion. In a universe governed by gimmicks and scoundrels, Thesz was a principled man playing a dirty game. He faced them all on the mat and in the dressing room, exposed the weaknesses of those trying to test him, and protected the coveted championship internationally. He raised the NWA world heavyweight title onto a distinguished plateau and was admired by peers, promoters, and fans."

Thesz became the standard for all champions to follow, holding the title in his first reign for more than seven consecutive years. "He could enter a room and have an aura around him you knew he was somebody without having to say a word," Terry Funk said. "He carried himself as a champion. He could walk into a room full of sportswriters or dignitaries and every one of them would say, 'That son of a bitch is somebody.'"

But by 1956, Thesz was wearing down. What had been three days a week had morphed into five matches a week, all over the country. The champion was supposed to have a week off every month to recover physically from the grueling matches and the grind of the road. More and more, however, Muchnick was booking the champion on his off week as well. Thesz and the NWA also disagreed about travel expenses, telling Muchnick in a 1956 letter that "a champion representing a sport needed to do it properly," flying first class rather than coach. Thesz was placated, but he was nearing a breaking point, increasingly frustrated with the NWA's promoters, men he had taken to calling "thieves."

THE SEARCH FOR AN HEIR

After a bad ankle injury suffered skiing, Thesz's seven-and-a-half year title reign was ended by "Whipper" Billy Watson in Toronto on March 15, 1956. While Thesz's title run had been nearly eight years, Watson didn't even make it eight months. Always a stopgap, he lost the title back to Thesz in November. The champion was looking for a more permanent heir apparent to turn the title over to, someone who represented his style of wrestling. He settled on George Gordienko, a Canadian wrestler considered by many to be the toughest man in the industry. Gordienko was one of the most intersting men in the grappling business, becoming a painter of note and eventually moving to Europe where he wrestled part time all over the continent. On rare occasions, he was able to combine his two passions. In Paris, he recounts,

> There were a couple of boys there who were into painting and had personal showings. They knew Picasso, since he watched wrestling on television and was said to be an avid fan. He would not be disturbed when the bouts were on.

> *Eventually, and to my very good fortune, while I was in the company of the lads who painted we encountered Picasso, and had coffee together. What a polite, well-mannered person. He even insisted on paying. This was truly a high spot in my life.*

More than an artist, he was also a tough guy's tough guy. "Cowboy" Dan Kroffat recalls a story of Gordienko's rare strength and his flair for drawing attention, describing how the wrestler once walked into a gym with a full suit and top hat on: "He took 300-pound weights off the rack, these guys were doing them. Gordienko just picked the weights up, right off the rack, threw them up in the air over his head, put them down. He had his topcoat on, and quietly walked out the door. Everyone's mouths were wide open."

Despite his strength and showmanship, Gordienko wasn't the clear choice to be the mat champion. There was a catch — as a card-carrying communist, there was significant fear that George would bring wrestling negative attention it could ill afford. Stories varied, some claiming George had only had a dalliance with communism in his college days, his son later saying he was a lifelong Stalinist. Either way, in the heart of the McCarthy anticommunist crusade, it was clear Gordienko was dead in the water.

The NWA put forward Buddy Rogers as the new face of wrestling, but Rogers was a Thesz nemesis from way back. Thesz steadfastly refused. Rogers had once insulted Ed Lewis in Thesz's presence on the way to a match in Louisville in 1948. Nine years later, Thesz still refused the put Rogers over. Buddy, the original "Nature Boy," was the biggest star in the country, and the NWA had high hopes for a Rogers title run.

"I done more for wrestling than anyone," Rogers said in a 1981 interview. "I'd say there's two of us, Lou Thesz and myself. We were the top two wrestlers of the last 25 or 30 years. A lot of things I see in wrestling today are things I invented. I'm constantly being emulated."

He was also the kind of wrestler Thesz despised, a pure performer, a former police officer from Camden, New Jersey, who didn't have any legitimate wrestling experience. "The shooters hated him because here was Buddy, no wrestling ability, yet he's in the main event and they're not. It all comes down to performance," former three-time NCAA Champion Dick Hutton said, calling Rogers the best crowd manipulator he ever worked with. Wherever Rogers worked, he held the people in the palm of his hands. Thesz didn't care about that at all — he wasn't giving his title to a performer. "Get me a wrestler," he told Muchnick, and the St. Louis promoter delivered. The three finalists were Hutton, rising star Verne Gagne, and respected New Zealand–born star Pat O'Connor. *Wrestling Observer* explains the debate:

> *Thesz was gung-ho on Hutton as his replacement. He believed Hutton to be the best real wrestler in the industry at the time, since Thesz's other pick, George*

> Gordienko, couldn't get into the United States because of McCarthyism since Gordienko was at one point in his life a communist. Thesz often remarked he believed Hutton was the best heavyweight wrestler he had ever seen . . .
>
> Gagne was a far bigger and more marketable pro star than the quiet Hutton. While many would argue O'Connor was a superior performer and worker than Gagne, Gagne was a far bigger national name, a better promo and a more established drawing card than the New Zealander. He also had the better "real sports" qualifications and legitimate ability that most of the promoters liked the NWA champion to have. O'Connor's strength was that he was far more unselfish in the ring, as Gagne always had a reputation among the wrestlers for always wanting to look good in the match, sometimes at the expense of the match.

A NOBLE FAILURE

Hutton was the eventual choice, a great amateur Thesz respected a lot. Two years earlier, the men had a match in Pittsburgh, Pennsylvania, that had fallen under the watchful eye of an athletic commissioner bound and determined to prove wrestling was fake. But Hutton and Thesz were able to deliver a convincing performance, and Hutton earned Thesz's esteem.

Hutton remembered, "Before the match, the commissioner called me in and said, 'If this match isn't on the level, I'm going to have both of you suspended and banned in the rest of the country.' That seemed to spook Lou a little because he didn't know me from Adam, so he asked me to come up to his hotel room so we could talk a little," Hutton said. "I guess he was trying to find out who I was, what I could do, and whatever else. We had our match. The commissioner invited people in to watch the match. They were people who were supposed to have knowledge of amateur wrestling. When we finished, they told people that it was the greatest wrestling match they had ever seen. Lou came over and told me, 'Dick, don't let anybody ever tell you that you can't work.'"

Hutton was a three-time NCAA champion at heavyweight, losing an opportunity to win an unheard-of fourth title when he fell victim to future wrestling promoter Verne Gagne in the 1949 NCAA Tournament in Fort Collins, Colorado. The two were so evenly matched that the bout came down to a referee's decision that denied Hutton the record-breaking fourth title. Hutton was seeded first; Gagne, despite an undefeated record, was only considered the second-best heavyweight coming into the tournament. After all, the two had met in 1947 with Hutton coming out on top. The next year Gagne dropped to 191 pounds and both won titles. Now back at heavyweight, they seem destined to meet again.

At 245 pounds, Hutton had 30 pounds on the Minnesotan, but Gagne was deceptively strong and smart. Hutton actually managed a takedown in the closing seconds, but officials decided he hadn't controlled Gagne before time expired. That meant the score was still 1–1; and thanks to a small advantage in riding time Gagne was awarded a referee's decision, denying Hutton his fourth title.

"Verne was an outstanding wrestler," Hutton said. "Not only on the mat but how he sized up an opponent. He knew if he came into me I would beat him decisively. He also knew in matches where my opponent stayed away from me, I would win maybe three to two or two to one. And that's just what he did. In all honesty, I truly believe I won that match. I don't blame Verne. He came out to win and that's just what he did. I believe they should have started him down for not being aggressive. I shot in and caught him in the last few seconds and that put me up three to two. Some kid comes out on the mat from the timekeeper's table and tells the official that the time ran out before he gave me the two points. He took the two points away and walked over and raised Verne's hand. The entire crowd became unglued. The coach of Nebraska was head of the tournament committee at the time. He told me that if coach Griffith would make a formal protest they would reverse the decision. I went to my coach but he wouldn't protest. So I came in second."

After fulfilling his obligations to the U.S. Army, Hutton soon joined the ranks of the professionals. He saw his old nemesis Gagne was making six figures and figured he was at least as good. Trained by Ed "Strangler" Lewis and Leroy McGuirk, complete with Lewis's famed headlock as his first finishing hold, Hutton's first real supporter in the industry was promoter Al Haft in Ohio. Haft loved working with accomplished amateurs and took Hutton under his wing.

Hutton remembered, "Al had this promotional gimmick where one of the boys takes on all comers. . . . The fan gets a dollar a minute and if he beats me $1,000 . . . I took on all kinds. The oddest I ever had was this truck driver. He gets a headlock on me and then he freezes. I swear, for the life of me I couldn't get that sucker off. So I pick him up and drop him backward on his head. That surprised him and he finally let go. Al used these kinds of matches to toughen us up."

Hutton may have been an excellent legitimate wrestler, but his work in and out of the ring was bland. Thesz insisted on passing on the championship to him, wanting a real wrestler, but he was the product of another era. Unlike Thesz, his wrestling excellence didn't translate in a professional context. As champion he was a bust.

With less than five years of experience and no real presence on television, Hutton wasn't a national attraction. His unimaginative style did him no favors when he was introduced in new towns either, nor did his growing waistline. After a title defense against Dory Funk in Odessa, Texas, the local paper speculated he had gained 40 pounds in the four months since he had debuted as champion in the town and declared Hutton "had developed a shape like a collection of overstuffed watermelons. Maybe getting the title swelled him up!"

To make matters even worse, Thesz had lost a controversial match to Canadian

Édouard Carpentier just before losing the title to Hutton, and in many key cities the promoters recognized the acrobatic French-Canadian as champion. It was a throwback to Ed Lewis's loss to Henri DeGlane, allowing wrestling promoters to recognize two world champions. With Hutton failing to draw, it seemed like a good decision in retrospect. NWA President Sam Muchnick battled hard for Hutton with fellow promoters, but according to Tim Hornbaker, the writing was on the wall: "Various promoters had complained about Lou's lack of color, but even more grumbled about the stoic Hutton. He offered a high degree of credibility, but there were promoters who didn't want that. They wanted drama, and if necessary, flying chairs and blood. . . . A fraction of the country now recognized Édouard as titleholder, and rejected Dick's claim all together. More than half of the 28 members still welcomed Hutton into their territories, and he did what he could to maintain the prestige of the title at a low point in Alliance history. His tenure was lackluster in terms of excitement and fan support, and Carpentier was generally regarded as a more electrifying performer."

Hutton was such a lame duck that the Alliance never even issued him a title belt. Thesz owned the belt he used as champion and refused to give it up, so Hutton traveled the country, either not carrying a belt at all or using a strap he had won as an amateur in college. After just 13 months, the Hutton experiment was over. In January 1959, the decision was made to take the belt off of the former college star.

Said Hutton, "Muchnick, the promoter there in St. Louis, and Wild Bill Longson, who was his booker, came into the locker room, came straight up to me, and said, 'Dick we want two straight' and headed out. I said, 'You dumb sonofabitches, come and get it then.' They turned around and said, 'How do you want to do it?' And Pat O'Connor, he's sitting right there and he didn't dare say a word. He had tried me on already in Canada . . . he decided to hook me in one of our matches. Of course, it didn't work and he was trying to get out of the ring because he thought I was going to get mad."

O'Connor did a better job at the box office than Hutton had, but the business was slumping generally. Television, once a primary revenue driver, had overexposed the audience to wrestling shenanigans. It was hard to motivate people to take in a match at the arena when so much wrestling was available on TV.

A LEGEND GROWS

Thesz hadn't been vacationing from the business during the Hutton and O'Connor reigns. He had made major money working with Japanese wrestling pioneer Rikidozan in Japan, drawing an astounding 87.5 television rating for an October 1957 match in Tokyo. Thesz also worked his way through Europe, where he had an altercation that bothered him for the rest of his life.

Lou had arrived in London on the S.S. *United States*, the fastest luxury cruise liner in the world. It made the trip in less than four days, and upon arrival he went right to work. He still had his world title belt in his possession, and despite losses to Carpentier and Hutton, represented himself in England as the world champion. He opened a three-month British tour against Indian star Dara Singh at the Royal Albert Hall in London. While waiting to take the ring, Thesz noticed a commotion. Noted British grappler Bert Assirati was attempting to make his way through security to issue both Thesz and Singh a challenge. He never made it, leaving wrestling fans with a major "what if."

Assirati was notorious in England, well respected by the wrestlers as the top mat man in the country. His strength was legendary. He could clean and jerk 380 pounds, deadlift 800 pounds, and was built like a fireplug — but Assirati could also do a one-handed handstand and a standing back flip. This rare athleticism made him a handful in the wrestling room. Not only that, but like Thesz, he knew all the hooks too: "No one has ever questioned Bert Assirati's skill, agility, strength, or recognition as one of Britain's greatest heavyweights. Open to question has been exactly why Assirati was feared and avoided by many heavyweights of his day. Was it because of the qualities we list above, or was it because of a penchant for hurting opponents and inflicting unnecessary pain?"

In his autobiography wrestler Rene Lasartesse recounts getting a huge pay raise: extra money not for his performance, but for the inconvenience of working with Assirati. In 15 matches together, Assirati broke his nose three times. Lasartesse wasn't alone. The shooter was famous for abusing younger wrestlers, sometimes even going so far as to break bones.

In addition to his penchant for inflicting pain, a refusal to lose upon request had gotten him blacklisted from Joint Promotions, the top wrestling organization in the U.K., leaving him on the outside looking in. Thesz, then in his early 40s, had an interesting opportunity. His reputation as a shooter was mostly just that — a reputation. He had some training shoots and workouts, but no actual competition as either an amateur or a professional to hang his hat on. Opinions on Thesz's ability among old timers varies.

"Lou could wrestle some," former carnival wrestler Dick Cardinal said. "Very quick fellow, but I don't think he was the best wrestler during his time. . . . He was a great performer and looked like a great wrestler . . . Don't get me wrong, Lou could wrestle some too. I mean, some guy off the street wasn't going to beat him, but he wasn't the best hooker or the best wrestler around. Lou told me one time that Ed Lewis beat him in less than a minute."

"Judo" Gene LeBell, himself a martial arts expert and notorious toughman, remembered,

> *I saw him work with a bunch of amateur wrestling champions, national champions, and just play with them. We were in, I guess it was Omaha, Nebraska,*

and there were a couple of guys that supposedly were national champions . . . Lou was working out with these guys, and he's meeting them, really, like, playing with them. You just get very casual. And then, he said, "Okay," to this big guy, and I said, "He's going to have one hell of a rough time. How is he going to get him?" I mean, this guy's big and he's strong. He had me in the air a bunch of times, not finishing, but he's got me up there.

And, he picked Lou up, threw him down, and the next thing I knew — this is all in about a minute — Lou had him in an anklelock, and the guy is screaming for help. And I said, "Oh, fuck." And he got up slowly and was limping off, and he said, "That's great, but it's illegal." What are you going to say? Of course, it's illegal, but you don't play a guy at his own game.

Billy Robinson shared his opinions about Thesz in his autobiography *Physical Chess*: "I'm going to say this about Lou. Lou was probably the greatest of all professional world champions for one reason: he conducted himself professionally inside the ring, in the gym, outside the ring, in business world and with your gentry (royal families) around the world. Everybody respected professional wrestling because of Lou Thesz. He may not have been the best competitive catch wrestler but he was very good in his time."

A legitimate shoot with Assirati would have proved plenty for Thesz, but promoters in England were steadfastly against it. Explains Dave Meltzer, "Word rarely travelled fast in those days about things overseas, but because it was Thesz, quickly the word got to the States that Assirati's reputation was so fierce that even Thesz had backed down from his challenge . . . When Thesz left Europe, Assirati stayed, and proclaimed for the rest of his life that he had made Thesz back down, even though it was clearly a grandstand challenge and the promoters Thesz was working for wanted nothing to do with Assirati anyway. That stuck in Thesz's craw for years."

Thesz wrote in *Hooker*, "Does Assirati deserve to be remembered as one of the greatest of all time? I'm not in any position to say, because I never saw him wrestle. . . . But I've talked with wrestlers who worked out with Assirati and had little or no trouble with him. These same wrestlers say he earned his reputation as a dangerous wrestler by doing things like 'accidentally' head-butting on the break or knocking some teeth loose with an 'accidental' elbow. I do know, too, that he was notorious for hooking opponents when they were supposed to be performing and hurting them. . . . It's one thing to be a great gymnasium wrestler, though, and another thing altogether to make money at it. He may have succeeded at the one, but he was a flop at the other."

Thesz's cavalier dismissal of Assirati infuriated some British wrestling fans and some of his contemporaries. Thesz had made enemies over the years, but there was an unspoken detente amongst wrestling's elder statesmen. Even Thesz and Buddy Rogers had come to terms before Rogers' death. But the publication of *Hooker* opened some old wounds, and wrestlers felt the need to stand up for those dismissed by the NWA icon.

"Bert Assirati, everybody that I've known including Karl Gotch said the guy was an animal when it came to the ring," former WWWF champion and fellow *Hooker* victim Bruno Sammartino said. "Thesz makes him out to be a guy he could have mopped up the floor with. Karl Gotch told me . . . when he went to England to wrestle Assirati, he got an inferiority complex. Assirati was a great submission wrestler. He went to Wigan, England . . . because he was so devastated at how this guy had handled him so he wanted to be good at submission wrestling. Here comes Thesz making this guy, who's also dead, out to be like he wasn't really anything. I've never met a human being who met Bert Assirati who wasn't in awe of him as to how ridiculously tough he was."

No one can say how a contest between the two men would have turned out. Assirati was near the end of his career, while Thesz, also an old man, seemed like he might wrestle forever. He had one final run as NWA champion, returning as the industry's standard-bearer for three years. He won the title at 46, taking it from his arch nemesis Buddy Rogers, which gave him no small pleasure, finally losing the gold belt to Gene Kiniski in 1966 at the age of 49. Thesz continued to wrestle on and off for years, wrestling his final match against Masahiro Chono in Japan in 1990 at the age of 74. He was the last of his kind.

Although wrestlers like Thesz had populated the sport for decades, no wrestler had the impact of a cathode ray tube connected to a fluorescent screen — a scientific marvel changed wrestling forever.

Television changed everything for the wrestling industry in America. The effect of television on the nation, let alone American sports, seems obvious now in retrospect. At the time it was anything but. In 1946, when RCA introduced its first set using wartime technology with an improved picture, only 10,000 sold nationwide at the exorbitant cost of $350. Television was far from a staple in middle-class homes — instead they were found in bars, complete with low brow programming designed for the working class to enjoy while having a drink or three at their neighborhood pub. "Television in 1946 was primarily a 'live' medium just like radio," Albert Abramson explains in *The History of Television*,

11 THE REVOLUTION Will Be TELEVISED

"Programming consisted mainly of 'live' programs of minor character, mainly sporting events (wrestling, boxing, etc.), second-rate motion pictures (usually old Westerns), some newscasts, and demonstrations and discussion programs. While these were not very good, it was the novelty of the experience that made television grow. . . . Just seeing a picture in a store window was a new, exciting experience. Crowds would gather in bars and restaurants to watch sporting events and the new variety shows that were springing up."

Boxing and wrestling in particular took advantage of early television's limitations. The cameras were heavy and tough to move around, and without proper lighting, images were difficult to make out. Wrestling was filmed in a studio under bright lights and offered the kind of action that allowed performers to locate the camera and focus their activity where it could be easily filmed. Not only that, but the rounds in boxing and different matches in wrestling were a perfect spot for commercial breaks.

Televised sports were an enormous success. It was the ideal programming for groups of people, and wrestling in particular was popular with female viewers. Much of the airtime in the New York area was devoted to sports in the late 1940s. According to *The Complete Directory to Prime-Time Network and Cable TV Shows*, three of the top 10 programs in Chicago were wrestling shows:

Professional wrestling was a regular and popular form of entertainment on early, live network television, particularly on ABC and DuMont. The two longest-running wrestling shows originated from Chicago — Jack Brickhouse doing the play-by-play from Marigold Garden every Saturday night on DuMont for almost six years, and Wayne Griffin announcing from Rainbow Arena for ABC for roughly the same length of time. DuMont's other long-running wrestling show originated from various arenas around the New York City area (Jerome Arena, Jamaica Arena, Sunnyside Gardens, and Columbia Park Arena) with Dennis James at the mike.

The most famous of these early wrestling announcers was probably DuMont's Dennis James, whose simplified explanations and infectious enthusiasm made the sport palatable even to little old ladies. His oft-repeated phrase "Okay, Mother" became so identified with him that it was later used for the title of one of his numerous daytime game shows. That a game-show emcee like James could become wrestling's most famous commentator was perhaps symbolic of the fact that on TV, wrestling was more show business than sport.

Wrestling had a place at the table on all the television networks, but it was DuMont in particular that concentrated on the sport. NBC, ABC, and CBS were all profitable and popular radio networks. They had the money to invest in dramas and other higher-class programs. DuMont was a start-up business. They needed to make money off of their television programs — and more importantly, the actual televisions they were selling across the country. Wrestling was cheap programming. There were no sets to build, actors to pay, no expensive writing staff. They simply showed up and rolled the cameras. Announcer James was a big part of the program. He talked directly to the females in the audience, making sure everyone at home knew exactly what was going on.

"If I tried to tell these guys in the bar what a step-over toehold was, they would resent me and say, 'Who the hell is he?' So I would tell it to 'Mother,'" James explained. "And if Mother was watching she would say, 'John, is that a hammerlock?' And John would say, 'Of course,' and it would make him into a hero."

The demands of television changed wrestling dramatically, taking an already over-the-top spectacle to the next level. Characters like "Gorgeous" George became the stars. With his curly blond locks, elaborate robes, and preening manner, George was the perfect villain. "I don't think I am gorgeous," he told the audience at home. "But what is my opinion against millions of others?"

George was just one of many new stars created for the medium. Chicago-area promoter Fred Kohler became, arguably, the most important man in the industry thanks to his control of wrestling on the DuMont network. Wrestlers seen nationwide on television became stars — and Kohler controlled them with exclusive contracts. If other promoters wanted his talent, they had to go through him. *Sports Illustrated* took note in 1955, remarking that there were 5–10 million fans of televised wrestling, almost 4,000 active professionals, and six world champions when decades prior there was merely one. In the heyday of televised professional wrestling, one of those world champions was a talented amateur from Minnesota who would outwit them all in the end.

DUMONT'S RISING STAR

There was room for the occasional "real" wrestler to gain fame under the Kohler regime. Verne Gagne, a clean-cut amateur champion from the University of Minnesota, became a star with his smooth wrestling and good looks.

"He started on the DuMont Network in 1951," Verne's son Greg Gagne said at his father's WWE Hall of Fame induction. "He was kind of the first wrestling star who was made on national TV — him along with Pat O'Connor, Hans Schmidt, Roy McClarty — people like that. It's funny, it seems like wherever we go in the country, people recognize my father from way back then. The people are a little bit older, of course, but they still recognize him and they recognize that that's when wrestling first hit the networks. And he was a major, major part of that."

With Kohler's backing, Gagne toured the entire country, becoming a star nationwide, but particularly in the Midwest where his United States championship was considered the most prestigious wrestling title to local fans. Gagne became NWA World champion Lou Thesz's professional rival. Though the two men only competed a handful of times, they vied for the attention of wrestling promotions throughout the United States.

Gagne had the bigger name thanks to Kohler and charged just 10 percent of the gate, less than Thesz who also collected a percentage for his manager Ed "Strangler" Lewis and NWA booker Sam Muchnick. Gagne was one of wrestling's first crossover stars and an excellent worker in the ring. Unlike many amateur stars who never really understood how to get the audience going, Verne was the perfect babyface, making fans believe when he screamed out in pain and believe again when it was time for him to make his comeback.

"With Verne, I believe it was a genuine competitiveness," Lou Thesz's biographer Kit Bauman said. "I was with the two of them a couple of times, and it was vivid, even long after they'd quit the ring. I've mentioned before that when I asked Lou about the guys who gave him trouble in the ring (or, especially, in the gym), he would go vague on me, for reasons I had a hard time understanding; I came to believe that it was mostly a matter of Lou being stingy with praise. Over time, he loosened up and would talk it, and he said his feelings toward Verne were colored by the behind-the-scenes activities in the early to mid-'50s to put the title on Verne. 'We worked for different people, so there was a lot of pressure on both of us,' he once said to me. Lou also said, however, that their matches were among some of the best of his career, in terms of credibility."

Gagne appeared on the variety and talk shows of the day and had endorsement contracts to hawk vitamins and other products to wrestling fans. He was a big enough star, and Kohler an aggressive enough promoter, that the NWA feared giving him their world title. Gagne was overlooked in the late 1950s when the NWA title passed from Thesz to Gagne's old college rival Dick Hutton. When he was passed over a second time in favor of Pat O'Connor, it was the last straw.

"Lou Thesz was the champion. I wrestled him three times. We had two draws and in the third one he got disqualified," Gagne remembered. "Then I couldn't get another match with him. The last time I wrestled him I said, 'The next time we wrestle, I will beat you.' I never got him to wrestle after that. So we got into promotion here and I bought the Stechers out."

In 1960, Gagne and Wally Karbo, long time consigliere to Minnesota wrestling promoter Tony Stecher, went into business for themselves. In June, Gagne challenged O'Connor to a title match, giving him 90 days to comply. If the NWA champion refused, Karbo insisted Gagne should be recognized as the rightful champion. Of course, this was all for the fans' benefit. Gagne and his partners didn't actually request an appearance by O'Connor as part of the NWA champ's nationwide tour. That didn't stop them from calling him yellow and stripping him of his title in favor of Gagne, then breaking away from the NWA to form the American Wrestling Alliance.

A YOUNG VERNE GAGNE

"Verne made a legitimate effort to meet O'Connor and Pat refused to answer," Karbo said at the time. "Gagne deserved the title shot more than any other wrestler in the game today, but O'Connor didn't even have the common courtesy to send a reply. Other promoters all over the nation are now regarding Verne as champion of the world."

Gagne was in the business of selling Gagne — and for decades it was a good business to be in. He was one of wrestling's most enduring stars and he held the world title he had struggled for so mightily for most of his 21 years on top of the AWA promotion. Gagne was the prototypical wrestling babyface. He used a dropkick to knock opponents down and

108 SHOOTERS: THE TOUGHEST MEN IN PROFESSIONAL WRESTLING finished them off with a sleeperhold. Fans in the Midwest seemingly never tired of seeing Gagne with his hand raised at the end of the night.

"We ran from Chicago to San Francisco with the AWA, and all of those cities in between the major cities," Gagne said. "We were drawing sellout crowds most of the time, 17–18,000, 15,000, whatever the arena held. But we were doing very good business. . . . It was fun. I liked it, enjoyed it . . . I was doing everything at one time — wrestling and promoting and match-making and all that."

Gagne went out of his way to help fellow amateur stars find their way in the business. He helped make Maurice "Mad Dog" Vachon one of the biggest stars in the sport. The diminutive grappler who had once represented Canada in the Olympic Games became one of wrestling's fiercest heels. He was a wild man — in and out of the ring. Vachon, despite being just 5'7", was considered by many of his contemporaries to be the toughest man in the business. Anyone who challenged him in the bar after the matches found out the hard way that the little dog had quite a bite.

"I could beat the shit out of them. And most of the time I did!" Vachon remembered. "That's eventually when Don Owen called me the Mad Dog. So I carried it inside and outside of the ring. I must have had hundreds of street fights. Why I'm not in jail today is a surprise to me."

Other legitimate wrestlers in the AWA included "Red" Bastien, Dr. Bill Miller, Billy Robinson, and Jim "Baron Von" Raschke. Raschke was a two-time All-American at the University of Nebraska, so he had the skills, but Raschke admits, "Verne Gagne actually taught me the difference between amateur wrestling and professional wrestling."

The AWA was full of foreign menaces, with Gagne eventually conquering them all. Raschke was quiet and shy until Vachon got his hands on him, turning him into a Nazi villain and making him a star. From AAU and Army amateur to goose-stepping Nazi was quite a leap, especially for a wrestler who had envisioned himself as a potential successor to Gagne as a big time babyface. But the act worked for Raschke, and he and Vachon made blood boil wherever they wrestled.

Says Raschke, "Once I became the Baron all those inhibitions I had, all those deep psychological restrictions that I put on myself as Jim Raschke were completely wiped out . . . the Baron could say and do about anything he wanted."

TELEVISION'S SIDESHOW: THE CARNIVAL CIRCUIT CONTINUES

For the most part, you'd have never recognized that Vachon or Raschke had legitimate wrestling talents. It just wasn't an important part of the product being presented to fans. But while actual wrestling had all but disappeared from television with its increasing reliance on flashy moves and choreographed pratfalls, real wrestlers still roamed the land.

They could be found with traveling circuses and carnivals, part of the athletic shows (AT shows) that competed with the bearded lady and thrill rides for the audience's attention. It was a tradition that went back to the middle ages, but in colorful modern America it included more than just your typical tough guys. Attractions would include female competitors and midgets, but carnival sideshow expert Ward Hall says the competitors were mostly local farm boys from the Midwest looking to escape a humdrum life, joining the veteran wrestlers in the athletic tent: a simple and Spartan structure, 30 by 30 feet, that contained a 16-foot ring with mattresses underneath, where the wrestlers slept at night.

It wasn't just the facilities that were spartan — so was the pay. Despite being stars of a popular attraction, the handful of wrestlers with each carnival weren't well compensated. Taking home just a few dollars a day, wrestlers often drove the big trucks and helped set up the tents for extra cash. Once the shows were open for business, the wrestlers were responsible not just for drawing a paying crowd, but for winning at all cost. Signs hanging from the tents advertised they would take on all comers. Anyone who could best them took home a cash prize. Locals were often awarded a dollar for each minute they could last with the carnival mat man — wrestlers who couldn't finish the match quickly or lost more than a handful of matches were replaced with those who could win regularly. Historian Mark Hewitt argues this pressure to win created a very hard-nosed brand of wrestler:

> *In its heyday, the athletic show produced a hardy breed of grappler; rough, ready, and able to dispose of any challenger who stepped up from the spectators. The challenger or "mark," as he was known in the business, could be anything from a husky farmer to the local bully. George Drake, who worked "AT shows" out West in the 1940s, remembers his challengers as being "cowboys, wiseguys, drunks, college wrestlers, and football players."*
>
> *"AT show" bouts were time-limit handicap matches, with the "comer" attempting to stay for usually five minutes of wrestling or three rounds of boxing. Often, as part of the show, one of the carnival wrestlers, referred to as a "stick," would be planted out among the crowd. The stick would be worked into the program as all the "marks" were met and defeated in the beginning of the week. Athletic show grapplers faced from two to a dozen or more challengers a day! As the "marks" were weeded out, the stick would stay the limit with a couple of "AT show" men. Then the big end of the week match would be the stick versus the carnival mat star in an exciting finish contest. Other times, a local wrestler or amateur champion would be built up as a worthy contender.*

Martial arts historian Robert Smith wrote about the scam, noting that just like regular pro wrestling the promoter controlled both wrestlers. But eventually they would have to accept a challenge from a tough local. And that's when Smith and others like him would strike: "I'd con the con artists. I would stand up close and holler and stumble awkwardly toward the platform. I was young, skinny, and babyfaced, and hung my head a lot in those days and this would help the deception. They would invariably accept me — once. Because when we got inside and the crowd had paid its dollar or so I'd pin the house man without ceremony. The house guy wasn't usually good enough to be dirty. But he'd try. He would elbow and jab me in close with his palm, try to strangle me, and pretend to throw me while getting into my gonads with an errant 'accidental' foot."

Many carnival and AT show wrestlers were ordinary talents, but most troupes included at least one supremely talented grappler. Known as hookers, these were the men who knew the holds that would make men cry out in pain. The worst of them were known as rippers. They didn't just know how to hurt people — they actually enjoyed it. It was these wrestlers who would be called upon to take on anyone who seemed like a serious challenge, often surprising college standouts and solid technical wrestlers who didn't know enough dirty tricks. Carnivals were a seasonal attraction in many parts of the country, allowing some of the best pro wresters in the world to compete on the circuit in between pro bouts.

"My carnival schedule was: Fridays, Saturdays, and Sundays, from April to September. This was the carnival time of the year," wrestling veteran Billy Wicks said. Wicks was trained by Farmer Burns disciple Henry Kolln and knew all the hooks. He'd needed them. Carnival wrestlers often took on multiple opponents on a single night. If a bested opponent wanted to give it another go, an immediate rematch was granted.

"We wrestled a 300–400 mile radius of St. Paul, Minnesota, for Dubson United Shows. Their carnival tour had the 'whole ball of wax,' that a traditional carnival offered. Our wrestling tent was 40x40 with a platform outside where the barker would talk to the people in the midway. Dirty Dick Evans was the barker getting people in. He would challenge them, 'Ladies and Gentlemen! Come see Free Pro Wrestling! Where we will show you holds.' He would also call out, 'Where are all you tough guys that slap your wife or your cow around? Come see if you can take on my champion!' I wore a mask a lot of time to give it a mysterious feel. We had a 'stick' (one of our guys) out in the crowd to create a show. My stick was Greg Peterson. He was a little guy, he would give them confidence to get up the nerve to give it a try. The sticks were the toughest guys, many times."

Frankie Cain, a street kid who grew up hustling and fighting in the streets of Columbus, Ohio, remembers his time on the carnival circuit fondly. Although he went on to great career as one of the Masked Infernos and as "The Great Mephisto" in traditional pro wrestling, it is the carnival life he finds himself recalling in his later years. A wrestler and boxer, Cain was trained by Frank Wolf, a wily veteran who once served as a policeman for wrestling promoters in Ohio, taking on tough locals and new talent to gauge their skill. Cain admits that much of what went on in the carnival tent was worked, especially when ex-wrestlers from the local area were involved. Many times former wrestlers would become part of the show, building for a final match with a local with lots of side bets on the line.

They were "big, old cauliflowered ear guys," Cain recalled. "They'd say, 'I've wrestled around here for years and I'll take you on!' The people would cheer. You'd go in and, of course, they would work. On the other hand, the old middleweights were really tough. They'd come around to the AT shows and try to knock the AT show boys off for the money. But we'd love to get a shoot with a local guy that looked tough. I read where John Buff made the comment that shoots killed the show. That might have been true in certain parts of the country, but it certainly wasn't true in the AT Shows that I knew. You'd get some of the marks you'd wrestle who were half smart. We'd ask 'em, 'Do you want to shoot, or do you want to show?' On the other hand, we had a lot of challenges from guys who thought they were tough, and they wanted to prove it. Even with the shoots, though . . . we'd sometimes let them go through. We'd put them over a little . . . let them think they could win. Then we'd come back the next night in a return match and you'd beat them."

Future world champion Harley Race, a notorious tough guy who fought his way from coast to coast, scaring even fellow wrestlers with his fistic prowess, got his start in the business as a 16-year-old carnival wrestler. Working for Gus Karras, the young Race was usually planted in the crowd as a "local" challenger. He would volunteer to face the house champion and was usually beaten. Sometimes, if the crowd was especially riled up, he'd get to win to calm them down and prevent a riot. The toughest nights were when Race had to meet a real local in a challenge match: "When we wrestled each other, we watched out for each other in the ring, just like pro wrestlers continue to do today. But wrestling a local was more dangerous, usually to him. If you got hold of a finger, and the guy didn't give up, you broke the finger. In this pre-lawsuit crazy era, arms and legs were fair game too. . . . I often wound up facing some legitimately tough old farmers . . . There were times some of those mean old bastards had me on the ropes for real. I knew if I lost the match, the farmer would get paid and I wouldn't. But if I got disqualified, I got paid and he didn't. So I quickly learned to throw my head into their noses if it looked like they were getting the upper hand. A well-placed head butt preserved my pay many days."

While the carnivals died out, the practice of having wrestlers who could handle challenges from marks in the crowd remained part of professional wrestling, especially in rural areas. That too came to an end with the cautionary tale of Tim Woods. Performing as "Mr. Wrestling" in the Georgia territory, Woods was a great amateur who had finished second twice in NCAA tournaments in the late 1950s. Decked out in all white, Woods was one of the first masked babyfaces in wrestling history.

Georgia booker Leo Garibaldi had pushed Woods hard. He was a mainstay in the arena programs before he ever appeared in the territory and in his early matches proved he had dozens of finishing holds that he could hit you with from all angles. The coup de grace was a $1,000 open challenge. Any fan that could last 10 minutes against Mr. Wrestling would collect — big time.

In 1967, despite wrestling clearly not being above board, some fans were still desperate to prove it was all "fake." That it was all entertainment was evident to anyone with a functioning cortex — but that didn't stop some fans from pursuing the issue aggressively with wrestlers during and after the shows. It was likely the leading cause of fights between wrestlers and fans in bars after the matches — the boys felt obligated to protect their industry.

A group of aggressive fans began attending the shows in Columbus, Georgia, eager to get a shot at Mr. Wrestling. Leading the charge was biker Arnold Spurling, a 280-pound street fighter looking for trouble. Against all reason, Woods proceeded with the challenge, despite knowing trouble was brewing.

"The head of the security police at the City Auditorium warned [promoter] Fred Ward that this guy was trouble. When both men entered the middle of the ring, that Wednesday night for their showdown, Spurling sucker punched the mild-mannered Tim Woods, ripped his mask off and threw it to the audience," wrestler Dickie Steinborn stated on the Wrestling Classics message board. "Everyone was stunned. Tim sat up and buried his face between his knees. Spurling did something no other wrestler was capable of doing for over a year. The mask was thrown back into the ring and the referee handed it to Tim. Now Woods realized what he was in for."

Woods asserted his wrestling dominance from there on out, taking Spurling down easily several times and riding him, wearing his opponent out. He quickly went behind Spurling and took him down amateur style. Spurling was out of shape and Woods seemed to have things under control. Sensing that Spurling was flagging, Woods went for a cross face the third time he took him to the mat. That's when the biker bit an entire joint of his finger off.

"Spurling bit as hard as he could," Steinborn remembered, "to dislodge the tip of Woods' finger from his hand. Tim said, 'What pissed me off, he stood up and disgustedly spit that finger onto the mat.' Tim charged him for a double-leg takedown, which sent Spurling out of the ring and onto the floor. Woods then stepped through the ropes and jumped down onto Spurling's body, sprawled on the cement floor. Spurling's henchmen came out of the audience, which then emptied the dressing rooms to end the melee."

PUNISHING THE MARKS

For the most part, that ended the challenge matches in America, although in Britain wrestlers like William Regal often paid their dues in a carnival setting before making it in the business. In America removing the challenge match limited the ability of wrestlers and promoters to defend the honor of the business. But sadists like Florida promoter Eddie Graham were not easily assuaged. Graham was by all accounts a solid citizen in Florida, well respected in the community and a generous supporter of amateur sports.

Perhaps because of that reputation he felt the need to make sure wrestlers were considered legitimate. Marks still needed to be taught a lesson, both the ones who thought wrestling was fake and the ones who thought they were good enough to be wrestlers themselves. Former Olympian Bob Roop often worked over a steady stream of victims for Graham.

"These guys had to sign a contract that said, 'I will not sue even in the case of serious injury, permanent injury, or death.' Or death! And these guys would sign that," Roop said. "Does that give you a clue that maybe this is a little more than a workout here? A little more than pushups and situps? Of course then they come back there and say, 'Bob, kill the guy.'"

Roop came from an amateur background and didn't feel comfortable hurting people. Pinning them? Sure. Using painful holds like the guillotine (today known in MMA circles as "the twister")? No problem. But doing permanent damage wasn't his style. Yet to promoters like Graham or long-time veterans like Terry Funk, it was crucial that anyone who came to challenge the wrestlers paid a price.

Roop remembers a time he tried to help one prospective wrestler who had bitten off more than he could chew. The man's girlfriend was ringside and it was an ugly scene. The man was out of it and Roop encouraged her to take him out the back door. But because they were parked out front they went out that way — right past Eddie Graham.

Recalled Roop,

> Eddie pops the guy on the eyebrow, busting him wide open. Blood everywhere and they're screaming and yelling. It was sickening. Years later I told Terry Funk about it and he explained something to me. Now Terry grew up in the business and had a much harder mindset than me. Terry and Senior used to fight in bars and things to draw money and show that they were tough.
>
> Terry said when you do wrestle with a mark, someone who has told everybody in his circle of friends, everybody in the bar or wherever he hangs out, that he's going to try out with a pro wrestler — even if you stretch the guy to the point he has to lay in bed for four or five days because he's so sore . . . four or five days later he goes back in the bar and says, "Oh, I kicked his butt. That stuff's fake." But he doesn't have any marks on him. Nothing's broken, nothing's busted. It's possible what he's saying is true. Terry said, 'That's why you've got to mark them.' Put in that context? Makes sense.

While many men doled out beatings for Graham in Florida, the most brutal administer of punishment was an average-looking Japanese man named Hiro Matsuda, a former baseball player who had been one of Danny Hodge's key rivals as light heavyweight champion. Matsuda didn't look dangerous, but that's part of what made him so deadly.

"He was the franchise wrestling backbone of the Florida territory as a heel before Jack Brisco," said former NWA world champion Dory Funk Jr. "But he was also the Florida policeman — the policeman at the gate. If anyone wanted to get into the business, they had to go through Hiro Matsuda first. We'd turn them loose with Matty and find out if they really wanted to be wrestlers. Consequently, we didn't have a lot of guys come into the business at that time."

Matsuda didn't just eliminate the dredges of society and overweight truckers. Legitimate prospects like Hulk Hogan had to pay their dues too — even if they looked like a million bucks and had "future star" written all over them. Matsuda worked Hogan until the big man could barely stand. Then the fun really began. Hogan remembers,

> I told Matsuda I was liable to go down at any second.
> "All right," he said. "Now it's time to wrestle."
> Before I knew it, Matsuda was sitting down between my legs and putting his elbow in the middle of my shin. Then he grabbed the end of my toe and twisted my foot until — crack! — my shinbone broke in half. The whole thing took about two seconds.
> I had barely gotten into the ring and my damn leg was broken.

Florida wasn't the only territory that punished men looking to get into the business. Graham might not have even been the most brutal gatekeeper. In Canada, Stu Hart had his famous dungeon where hearing screams was commonplace for the Hart children growing up. Hart had a sadistic streak; not always looking to teach people the art of catch wrestling, he'd often punish weight lifters and others who made the mistake of coming into his domain.

In the Carolinas, the rugged Anderson brothers were especially aggressive. Like in Florida they liked to work prospects until they were virtually immobile. That's when the beatings began. Ole Anderson would apply a "sugar hold," a half nelson variation that could quickly render a foe unconscious — especially if he had allowed you to demonstrate it on him.

"There were big holes in the low ceilings made by the heads and feet of wrestlers," Stu's son Bret Hart wrote in his autobiography, *Hitman*. "Stu trained and broke in his wrestlers down there, hooking on like an octopus, squeezing hard enough that the screams of his victims would echo eerily through the rest of the house."

"Once I applied the sugar hold, I would really work it," Anderson remembered. "The most effective thing I did with it was to take a mark to the edge of passing out, then bring him back. In other words, as he started to go under, I'd ease up on the pressure and let him relax for a second. Just as he began take a quick breath, I'd clamp down on the hold and push him forward again. It's the most miserable feeling you could ever have because you get panicky. The worst thing about it is, you can't do a thing about it. You can kick or do whatever you want to do, but you just can't do anything to get out of it."

Wrestling had come a long way since the days of Farmer Burns. Burns at least had the intention to actually train the men he stretched. The brutality in later years was an overreaction. Few in the audience believed wrestling was real — perhaps the backroom bouts just compensated for those feelings of inadequacy by showing skeptical fans and wannabe rasslers just how real it could get.

The divide between amateur and professional wrestling had never been greater than it was in the 1960s and 1970s. Verne Gagne was able to sign Olympian Chris Taylor to an AWA contract, but for the most part the top amateurs avoided pro mats like the plague. One exception came, like many of amateur wrestling greats, from the state of Oklahoma. Danny Hodge was no ordinary amateur — he might have been the greatest wrestler in America's history.

It's one thing to see all the accolades on paper. NCAA champion, Olympian, legend. Dan Hodge was all those things. But seeing his power for yourself — that's something else entirely. Hodge, well into his 70s, could take an apple in each hand and squeeze them to pieces. In his prime, he could rip a phone book in half with his bare hands. Typical strong man stuff to be sure — until you remember Hodge weighed just 177 pounds.

"He's a strong man," college teammate and sparring partner Gene White said. "Strong as maybe three men in fact."

"He had big paws and grip strength to die for," two-time NCAA champion Wade

12 THE GREAT DANNY HODGE

Schalles said. "He'd go into hardware stores and say, 'My dad sent me in for some pliers. Give me the very best one's you've got.' Then he'd break the pliers with his hands."

In collegiate wrestling the best wrestler every year is given the Hodge Trophy. That's not by coincidence. Simply put, there is a strong argument Hodge is the greatest wrestler America ever produced. He was a legend before he ever entered NCAA competition, actually representing America in the Olympic Games right out of high school. At 19 he finished fifth in the 1952 Olympics in Helsinki, losing by pinfall to Russia's David Cimakuridze.

Former WWE announcer Jim Ross explained, "He was a hero to small town youth in our state. He came from Perry [Oklahoma], and Perry is like the Williamsport of wrestling. Where Williamsport is known nationally as the capital of little league baseball, Perry was a wrestling Mecca where kids started wrestling at four or five years old. It's a rite of passage there. Hodge, coming out of high school, goes to the '52 Olympics without any international experience. He'd never been on an airplane, never been on a boat. . . . That's pretty phenomenal. He was a hero, and he became a star. His work and his work ethic and the results he got made him a star."

After the Olympics, college wrestling seemed easy. Ineligible his freshman year, Hodge won every match for the next three years running, taking home three NCAA championships for the University of Oklahoma. But that doesn't do his dominance justice.

"He's too good for college boys," opposing coach Rex Peery once said. "He's head and shoulders above what we got."

Hodge was an unstoppable monster, winning nearly 80 percent of his matches by pinfall and never once being taken off his feet in competition. Prior to the Big Seven finals in 1957, Hodge had finished 19 opponents in a row by pinfall — a feat as unthinkable then as it is now. He went on to pin all four opponents in the national finals, finishing with 23 pinfalls in a row.

"Do you know what the average time was in my matches during the Big Seven tournament?" Hodge asks any one who will listen. "Less than two minutes. One minute, 33 seconds. Some were a little longer, some were a little shorter. But nobody lasted too long. I wasn't there to play. I was there to pin you. It's easier to pin you than to beat you."

Prior to his senior year in college, Hodge once again represented the United States in the 1956 Olympics. In the midst of his unprecedented success in the collegiate ranks, he wasn't quite ready for freestyle wrestling's modified rules. On his way to the gold medal against Bulgaria's Nikola Stanchev, ahead 8–1, a momentary lapse led to Hodge's shoulder briefly touching the mat.

"He missed winning the 174-pound gold medal by two seconds," Hodge's college coach Port Robertson said.

"They weren't even touching at the time," Hodge biographer Mike Chapman said in an interview. "I talked to the Australian mat judge, who didn't even know I knew Dan Hodge, and he said it was the worst call he'd ever seen in international wrestling. . . . The people of that era just shake their heads in wonderment. . . . To this day he has to live with the fact that he didn't win the Olympic gold medal when most people could see he was the best wrestler in the world."

Hodge would have been just 28 for the 1960 Olympics and the odds-on favorite to win. But it was a different time and the Olympics held firm — only amateur athletes could compete. Hodge, who grew up working with his father 100 feet in the air on oil rigs, needed to make a living.

"I thought I was going to coach and teach for a while but I went to work for a mud company in the oil fields in Wichita, Kansas," recalled Hodge. "They told me as strong as you are you'd be a good boxer. I started going to the gym in the afternoons and hitting the heavy bag, and the first thing you know they're getting me two or three fights a week."

Hodge gave boxing a try and was undefeated in amateur competition, mainly relying on his superlative athleticism to win the National Golden Gloves tournament in Madison Square Garden as a heavyweight. He looked a bit clumsy at times and was prone to shoving his opponent around the ring — he was warned by the referee several times to "stop wrestling." But Hodge felt good about his chances, confident in his toughness and natural power.

"In wrestling," he said at the time, "you keep your muscles tight and tense; in boxing you keep them loose and agile. That's what I've been doing, loosening up my muscles — jabbing long, working on my combinations, not pulling with my muscles like I would be in wrestling."

He was knocked down early in the finals by Charles Hood — Hodge was still committing some major technical mistakes, dropping his left hand every time he threw a powerful overhand right. Hood did what no wrestler had managed in years — he took Hodge off his feet. The Oklahoman recovered at the count of eight and returned the favor twice in the second round before the referee stopped the fight. The 12,000 fans in Madison Square Garden roared and some were comparing the wrestler to a young Rocky Marciano.

"The crowd was roaring. You can't imagine the noise," Hodge remembered 50 years later. Visions of enormous wealth in his head, Hodge signed on Sugar Ray Robinson's manager George Gainford as his advisor and gave boxing a go. Not everyone felt as good about his chances.

In New York, veteran trainer Charley Goldman was a little less enthusiastic than some fans. "I ain't seen the kid yet, of course, but I ain't excited," he told *Sports Illustrated*. "Everybody thinks they got a heavyweight champion just because they got a big strong kid. Right now, he'd get killed by a pro. He don't know enough about boxing. Of course, Rocky didn't start fighting amateur until he was 25. I understand Hodge is the same age. Rocky didn't turn pro until he was 28 either. If this kid is as big and strong as they say, you could teach him an awful lot in three years. But like I say, I got to see him first."

A YOUNG DANNY HODGE.

Goldman, ultimately, was correct. Although promoters considered matching him with champion Floyd Patterson, Hodge was never a skilled craftsman as a boxer. His final fight was against fringe contender Nino Valdes. Best known for beating former world champion Ezzard Charles and going the distance with the great Archie Moore, Valdes had an up and down career. But he was way too much boxer for a young Dan Hodge, beating him mercilessly in 1959.

"I saw him two weeks after the fight and I'd never seen anyone with that much damage and trauma to his face and eyes," Hodge's friend "Cowboy" Bill Watts wrote. "Danny had such great heart and was one of the greatest athletes I've ever seen, but that doesn't make

THE GREAT DANNY HODGE

you a boxer. He just had so much courage he'd let opponents hit him, and he'd eventually wade through them."

In addition, like many young men entering the fight game, he ran into some clever hucksters who took him for a ride. It's one thing to go through the car crash that is a professional boxing match. It's another to do it for free — yet Hodge says he eventually went home empty-handed.

"I won eight of my ten fights but I never got paid a cent," Hodge admitted. "I told them I could fight all day in Perry, Oklahoma, if I was going to be fighting for free. That's when I decided to call up Leroy McGuirk and give professional wrestling a try."

McGuirk, like Hodge, was a former NCAA champion, taking home the top prize in 1931 at Oklahoma State. McGuirk had been the top junior heavyweight wrestler of his era and the territory he owned, later called Mid-South, was one of the few willing to put a smaller wrestler on top.

Mid-South was the perfect fit for Hodge. It helped that he was a legend in Oklahoma already, so the fans were willing to buy into him as a credible star. Jim Ross says a humble personality may have held Hodge back in the business, because the amateur star was not a natural showman. Wrestling legend Terry Funk writes that as great as he was, Hodge would have had trouble getting over big in other areas of the country:

> *Danny was world junior heavyweight champion for years and was a perfect fit as a legend in Oklahoma and other parts of the South and Midwest. The rest of the country had no idea what they were missing. . . .*
>
> *. . . if you dropped him into New York as the world junior heavyweight champion, the people there would look at him and say, "Oh come on! Who are you trying to bullshit?"*
>
> *They would have prejudged him based on his size and appearance, because he didn't have a musclebound physique, and I don't know how his southern talk, peppered with "dadgums," and "gollys," would have gone over.*

As the right man, in the right place, at the right time, Hodge took to the business right away. He was the world champion within a year taking the title from Angelo Savoldi in front of 6,000 fans at the Stockyards Coliseum in Oklahoma City. The feud was given a boost by Hodge's father, Billy. No one clued the elder Hodge into wrestling's worked nature and he went after Savoldi one night with a penknife. Wrestling historian Tim Hornbaker recounts, "Savoldi bled excessively from injuries on his arm and back, requiring 70 stitches at a local hospital, while Danny's father was arrested. In what appeared to be a complete lack of awareness of the dramatics of wrestling, Bill attacked the heel pummeling his son with blind anger. The unscripted moment was captured in the minds of all who witnessed it, and, of course, played perfectly into the promoter's cashbox."

Hodge would hold the title for four years unbeaten, well short of McGuirk's 11-year reign, but impressive none the less. He also fit into the free-wheeling lifestyle like a hand in a glove. He was a ribber, playing jokes on his fellow wrestlers, mostly involving his enormous grip strength. Hodge would go into the locker room and rip off all the hot water handles in the showers, leaving the boys to freeze. Fans who tried to get cute were also in for a rude awakening. Hodge would offer to diffuse any tension with a handshake. When the fan would try to impress him with a hand-crushing grip, Hodge would turn up the pressure, driving the man to his knees, literally making him beg for mercy with a simple handshake.

He also took matches that others might consider an indignity and turned them into a challenge. One night, Hodge and Watts ended up booked to wrestle a real live bear. A staple of the southern wrestling scene, matches with a bear could leave you permanently scarred if you weren't careful. Watts had a plan for an easy night with the bear, then a match to send the crowd home. Hodge, in turn, wanted to see if he could actually beat the bear.

"Danny was so strong and agile that he was making the bear nervous," wrote Watts. "The bear came to the center of the ring, stood up, and came forward to wrestle, just like a human on two legs. Danny got behind the bear, put a scissors hold on and squeezed hard. The bear squealed and was getting scared and angry."

Hodge was also the perfect man to teach rabid fans a lesson when they wanted to test one of the wrestlers. He was always up for a challenge, and if it turned into a fight, well, that was okay too. Hodge had learned his hooks early in his career from the great Ed "Strangler" Lewis. Combine his knowledge of crippling holds with his unmatched wrestling and strong boxing, and you had a dangerous customer on your hands.

"I remember wrestling one boy, I took him down and he scratched me. I reached up, felt the blood on my face and said, 'Something's got to give.' So I turned him over and started pushing his elbows up past his head," Hodge recalled. "The arm that scratched me? Well, I broke it. That was the only time it went that far, but I needed to show the people that I wasn't somebody they could just run over."

Hodge's most memorable rivalries with two-legged opponents were with Angelo Savoldi, Hiro Matsuda, and Sputnik Monroe, all for the junior heavyweight title, but his Olympic credibility opened up main-event possibilities with top heavyweights all over the country like Verne Gagne, Lou Thesz, Jack Brisco, and the Funk brothers. He made almost $100,000 a year, a monstrous sum in the 1960s and '70s.

Hodge was so revered in the business that all the tough guys wanted to test him.

Florida, especially, was well known for its back room matches, mostly due to promoter Eddie Graham's obsession with shooting.

"Hiro Matsuda spent about 10,000 bucks with Karl Gotch to learn all the shooting holds, the wrestling holds," wrestler Ox Baker remembered. "He wanted to try Danny Hodge out. After about five minutes with Danny, Matsuda looked up and said, 'I just wasted $10,000.'"

In another famous shoot, Hodge ran through Khosrow Vaziri, the future Iron Sheik and a legitimate Greco-Roman standout, like a knife through butter. But shooting matches were few and far between. What mattered was what happened in the ring, in front of the fans, and there Hodge excelled, main-eventing for most of his 17-year career, bringing credibility with him to the ring nightly, even if he wasn't the most exciting worker.

Hodge spent the majority of his time as a babyface and was furious whenever anyone booed him. Bill Watts remembers Monroe getting cheered in Mississippi when Hodge was supposed to be the good guy. Danny made him pay for the indignity. Remembers Watts, "Danny got really hot when they booed him and cheered Sputnik, so Hodge killed him — he tied Sputnik in knots and was so stiff with him that poor Sputnik didn't get a single inch of any match with him. Sputnik could barely drag himself to the back after their last match, but he made it to Leroy's office, where he dumped the belt at Leroy's feet and said, 'Fuck you! Here's the belt! I'm outta here!'"

Wrestling Hodge was no picnic for his opponents. Not only did he demand a credible and hard match, his gas tank was unrivaled. A program with Hodge often involved doing a series of grueling 60-minute matches that ended in a draw. Those matches would be followed with a match that went 90 minutes — Hodge was one of the few who could go an hour and a half and make it interesting. His opponents, quite often, weren't prepared.

"I always stayed in pretty good shape," Hodge says with a wink. "That helped me out quite a bit over my career."

It was a career cut short by tragedy. On March 15, 1976, Hodge became one of many wrestling victims of America's roadways, breaking his neck in an automobile accident.

"It got cold and I turned the heater up and I fell asleep. I hit this bridge and turned upside down. My car was on its rooftop going along the rock banisters and every time it hit one I could feel my teeth and neck break. My first thought was 'God, how much more can I take.'

"I'm waiting for the car to come to a stop and hoping I don't hit anybody," continued Hodge. "It's like 3 a.m. and then all of a sudden my car went off the east edge of the bridge down into the water and the water covered it. As I lay there I felt this water gush over me. I said to myself this was an awful way to go. I got out through the dash window, although my car was bent down to the dash and the seat, you can't imagine what little space there was but I got out through there and swam to the shore."

Holding his own broken neck in place, he knocked out the car window and made his way to safety. Hodge, through force of will, survived his accident. His career wasn't as fortunate. His broken neck forced him to retire, and his days on the mat were over. In his prime, Hodge was as good as any man had ever been. Across the Pacific there was another man who could make the same claim — a judoka who humbled a Gracie and almost everyone else who ever dared compete against him.

Given the Gracie family's well-known antipathy towards professional wrestling, it's perhaps surprising that Mitsuya Maeda is the crucial figure in their story. It was the first time, but certainly not the last, that a professional wrestler would figure prominently in the history of the first family of mixed martial arts. Some of these encounters would be celebrated, others played down lest they upset the Gracie family's carefully crafted narrative, a story they carried with them into the Octagon at the very first Ultimate Fighting Championship, Rorion Gracie's carefully stage-managed tournament designed to bring Gracie Jiu-Jitsu to the broadest audience it could reach. "When Royce Gracie steps into

13 NO ONE BEFORE KIMURA, and No One After

the Octagon," the announcers reverently intoned, "he brings 65 years of tradition with him. That's how long the Gracie family has been undefeated in no-holds-barred competition." This statement, of course, doesn't bear the least scrutiny. Was the skinny, unathletic Royce Gracie a revelation? Absolutely. Was the Gracie Jiu-Jitsu he used to dominate bigger, stronger opponents, for real? Undeniably. Did the Gracie family possess a proud fighting history? Without question. But for all their accomplishments, for all the genuine achievements of their art, they were not undefeated, and hadn't been for decades. That's because Helio Gracie, to his credit, had the guts to step onto the mat against Masahiko Kimura, judoka and professional wrestler.

Kimura was a Japanese judo legend, a four-time winner of the open-weight All-Japan Judo Championship, easily the world's most prestigious judo tournament before the establishment of regular world championships and the sport's eventual inclusion in the Olympic Games. Kimura stood only 5'6", but built a solid, imposing 187-pound physique atop that frame; he was famed not only for his technical mastery, but for his uncommon power for a man of his size.

After defeating eight consecutive opponents at the Kodokan in 1935, Kimura was awarded his fifth-degree black belt at the age of 18; this feat, like so much of what the great champion accomplished, was unprecedented. Although Kimura's name is perhaps most closely associated with a particular submission hold — the entangled double wristlock, or reverse keylock, that now bears his name — in his own time he was most celebrated for his mastery of o soto gari, an outside trip that he honed both in intense sparring and in solitary practice, slamming his body against tree trunks in endless repetition. After suffering four defeats in 1935, Kimura never lost another match in a judo career that ended with an All-Japan title shared with Takahiko Ishikawa in 1949. "No one before Kimura," the saying goes, "and no one after."

At the conclusion of his competitive career, Kimura fell out of favor with the Kodokan and the rest of the Japanese judo establishment. He turned down an instructorship with the Tokyo Metropolitan Police, a position that offered more prestige than financial remuneration, and turned his attention instead to a nascent professional judo organization, which failed not long after its founding in 1950. Kimura, whose wife was sick with tuberculosis, needed money urgently, and in the end, judo didn't pay — but professional wrestling did.

Kimura took up with promoters staging events in the Hawaiian Islands, and later Brazil, putting on judo exhibitions, wrestling, and taking on all comers much in the same way Mitsuyo Maeda had done a generation before.

Helio Gracie was not the first member of mixed martial arts' leading family to test the family art of Gracie Jitsu. Older brothers George and Gastao were the initial Gracies to represent the family honor in competition, accepting all challengers to their supremacy.

"Many of these fights happened at gyms and schools," jiu-jitsu historian Pedro Valente said. "Many times the Gracie brothers invaded other schools, took the press, and challenged the teachers, especially the judo schools. There was already a rivalry between the jiu-jitsu taught by the Gracies and judo schools. The judo people tried to claim jiu-jitsu was old and outdated and that agitated the rivalry." It was this rivalry with judo players that Valente, who trained closely with Gracie for years, thinks inspired Helio to take his most famous bout.

More than a decade earlier, in the 1930s, Helio had made a name for himself with a series of highly publicized fights in Rio de Janeiro. Often competing with pro wrestlers, Gracie showed a unique ability to combat men who outweighed him by as much as 100 pounds. The glory days ended with no-holds-barred fights, called vale tudo in Brazil, banned and Gracie out of work.

It was the return of pro wrestling to Brazil that gave Gracie a second chance at stardom. Kimura and company were the best thing that could have possibly happened for Gracie Jiu-Jitsu. Keen to prove his family's combat style against the visiting Japanese pros, Gracie challenged and defeated Kimura's understudy Kato, choking him unconscious, and demanded a match against the great champion himself. In 1951, in front of a crowd of 20,000 in Rio's Estádio do Maracanã, he got his wish.

Decades later, Gracie would admit that he knew he was doomed from the outset. "I myself thought nobody in the world could defeat Kimura," he told Yoshinori Nishi in 1994. "For me," Gracie said, "fear was surpassed by desire to know what on earth such a strong man like Kimura would do in the fight — he might open the door to an unknown world for me."

But if Gracie truly lacked confidence going into the bout, he did his best to create a different impression entirely: "When I entered the stadium," Kimura recollected in his autobiography, "I found a coffin. I asked what it was. I was told, 'This is for Kimura. Helio brought this in.' It was so funny that I almost burst into laughter."

The Rio crowd, worked into a frenzy of anticipation, threw eggs as Kimura made his way to the mat. But that aerial assault was the greatest threat Kimura would face that day. "Helio grabbed me in both lapels," Kimura remembered, "and attacked me with o soto gari and kouchi gari. But they did not move me at all. Now it's my turn." He made the most of it. "I blew him away up in the air by ouchi gari, harai goshi, uchimata ippon seoi. At about the 10-minute mark, I threw him by O-soto-gari. I intended to cause a concussion." It would not be the first time the famously rough Kimura had sought to end a bout by rattling his opponent's brain, but this proved impossible, since, accourding to Kimura, "the mat was so soft that it did not have much impact on him." Clearly, another strategy was called for.

"While continuing to throw him," Kimura said, "I was thinking of a finishing method. I threw him by o soto gari again. As soon as Helio fell, I pinned him by kuzure kami shiho gatame. I held still for two or three minutes, and then tried to smother him by belly. Helio shook his head trying to breathe." Kimura didn't know it, but Gracie was out. "If Kimura had continued to choke me," Gracie told Nishi in 1994, "I would have died for sure. But since I didn't give up, Kimura let go of the choke and went into the next technique. Being released from the choke and the pain from the next technique revived me and I continued to fight. Kimura went to his grave without ever knowing the fact that I was finished." Indeed, Gracie's lapse into unconsciousness plays no part in the story as Kimura tells it. "[Helio] could not take it any longer," Kimura remembered, "and tried to push up my body extending his left arm. That moment, I grabbed his left wrist with my right hand, and twisted up his arm. I applied ude garami" — or, as it would come to be known, the Kimura. "I thought he would surrender immediately," he continued. "But Helio would not tap the mat. I had no choice but to keep on twisting the arm. The stadium became quiet. The bone of his arm was coming close to the breaking point. Finally, the sound of bone breaking echoed throughout the stadium. Helio still did not surrender. His left arm was already powerless. Under this rule, I had no choice but twist the arm again. There was plenty of time left. I twisted the left arm again. Another bone was broken. Helio still did not tap. When I tried to twist the arm once more, a white towel was thrown in. I won by TKO. My hand was raised high. Japanese Brazilians rushed into the ring and tossed me up in the air. On the other hand, Helio let his left arm hang and looked very sad withstanding the pain."

The Gracie clan would understandably claim this loss as a kind of moral victory. Certainly, Helio's courage in even stepping onto the mat against the bigger, stronger, younger, better grappler is to be applauded, as is the stoicism with which he faced defeat. But the contest itself could not have ended more decisively. Kimura lived up to every bit of his reputation. He may have been traveling the world as a professional wrestler, with his true competitive days behind him, but Masahiko Kimura was still every bit the shooter.

RIKIDOZAN AND THE BIRTH OF PURORESU

In Japan Mitsuhiro Momota was more than a wrestler. He was "Rikidozan," a cultural icon and hero. In the wake of World War II, he restored Japanese pride, doing battle with countless giant Americans, doing what the nation as a whole could never do: winning. With television in its infancy, he became wrestling's defining figure in Japan. Matches with partner Kimura against the enormous Sharp brothers sent Japanese fans scurrying to the department stores, some to gawk at the spectacle, many others to buy their first television set.

Matches with the foreign villains ended up being the most lucrative, but high-profile bouts between Japanese stars also occurred, like his infamous December 22, 1954, bout with Kimura for the first Japanese heavyweight title, in which Riki's double cross of the popular star made him a target for the Yakuza.

Part of the long-standing lore of professional wrestling is that putting a championship belt on a shooter helps create an aura of credibility around a promotion's title. Perhaps just as importantly, having a champion who can defend himself for real could prove invaluable should a challenger suddenly decide to go into business for himself and turn a work into a shoot — a prospect much more likely in wrestling's shady past than in its glossy, sports entertainment present. But wrestling history shows us that even the most skilled and battle-tested shooter can be double-crossed. If it can happen to Masahiko Kimura, it can happen to anybody. And December 22, 1954, at Tokyo's Sumo Hall, it happened.

Kimura entered his match against Rikidozan thinking he knew what to expect. It had all been laid out beforehand: "The first bout was going to be a draw," Kimura wrote in *My Judo*. "The winner of the second will be determined by the winner of a paper-scissors-stone. After the second match, we will repeat this process. We came to an agreement on this condition." It wasn't just the overall structure of their program that had been worked out together; the blow-by-blow details of the match were laid out ahead of time too: "As for the content of the match, Rikidozan will let me throw him, and I will let him strike me with a chop. We then rehearsed karate chop and throws." But what happened in the ring, in the end, looked anything but rehearsed.

Their match started out conventionally enough, as the two grapplers exchanged takedowns, throws, and holds with the kind of methodical, deliberate pace one would expect of a bout of that era. After the opening minutes, however, things began to look slightly off. Rikidozan resisted an ippon seoi nage, a classic judo shoulder throw, in a way that seemed to surprise Kimura, and made both wrestlers look sloppy. Was this all part of the act? Was this a simple miscommunication, a blown spot? Or was Rikidozan feeling Kimura out for real? From that point on, Kimura looked cautious and uncomfortable as the two exchanged only the most basic holds. Gone were the throws and takedowns of the opening minutes, replaced with exchanges of simple and safe positions.

Kimura seemed particularly on edge as Rikidozan began to threaten with his famous karate chops. Maybe Kimura was still only acting the part; this may not have been caution itself, but a performance of caution. Maybe he was still working. But Rikidozan was not. After Kimura ducked under Rikidozan's attempt at a collar-and-elbow tie-up, Rikidozan let fly with a stiff right hand to the jaw that staggered Kimura. Even by the rough standards of Japanese pro wrestling, in which strong blows are routinely exchanged to heighten the apparent realism of a contest, this didn't look right. Kimura covered and backed into a corner as Rikidozan pursued behind a whirlwind of open hand chops and strikes to the head. Kimura tied him up, and seemed to want to take his opponent down for real this time, but when Rikidozan hooked his arm over the top rope, and the referee intervened, Kimura broke.

A WRESTLING PIONEER: RIKIDOZAN

What was Kimura's mindset in this moment? Was he still working? Did he think Rikidozan was simply getting a little carried away with his strikes as part of an honest effort to put on a good show, or did he sense that there could be real danger there? The referee and Kimura exchanged words briefly after the break, and Rikidozan seized this lapse in Kimura's attention to begin his assault anew, connecting with strong, stiff rights and lefts. Kimura again looked towards the referee, clearly unsure how to handle this situation, and Rikidozan connected with a swinging slap to the ear that put Kimura to a knee. Then, in a vicious attack that would be extreme even by the later standards of the soccer-kick-friendly Pride FC, Rikidozan connected with a completely unprotected knee to the face, a kick to the face, and a stomp to the base of the neck. Kimura regained his feet and stumbled into the corner as the referee approached and, after a cursory inspection of the obvious trauma to Kimura's face, told him to continue. But Kimura just stood there in apparent disbelief, one hand on the ropes to steady himself. A few more swinging, clubbing blows sent Kimura slumping to the canvas, lying face down and immobile while the referee counted to ten. Rikidozan's hand was raised in victory while the battered Kimura's cornermen rushed to his aid.

"Rikidozan became taken by greed for big money and fame," was all Kimura could make of the situation, decades later. "He lost his mind and became a mad man. When I saw him raise his hand, I opened my arms to invite the chop. He delivered the chop, not to my chest, but to my neck with full force. I fell to the mat. He then kicked me. Neck arteries are so vulnerable that it did not need to be Rikidozan to cause a knock down. A junior high school kid could inflict a knock down this way. I could not forgive his treachery. That night, I received a phone call informing me that ten yakuza are on their way to Tokyo to kill Rikidozan." It didn't happen that night, and it's doubtful that between December 22, 1954, and December 8, 1963, the night Rikidozan was fatally stabbed by a urine-soaked yakuza blade, that the gangsters were nursing a grudge. There's no clear line connecting the yakuza outrage over Rikidozan's betrayal of Kimura's trust and his eventual untimely death. But the night it happened, the night Rikidozan decided to shoot on the shooter, it was enough to raise the yakuza's ire.

Kimura called off the gangsters who respected him so much, but this may have been real life foreshadowing. Rikidozan liked to play with fire in his personal life. He knew no fear and would treat people he didn't like with horrifying disrespect, even going so far as to pull down his pants and masturbate in public if he thought someone was wasting his time. Still, despite his personal foibles, the match with Kimura bolstered Rikidozan's tough guy reputation and the crowds he attracted continued to grow. His stardom is mind boggling in retrospect. An October 6, 1957, match with NWA World Champion Lou Thesz drew 27,000 fans to the Korakuen baseball stadium in Tokyo. More importantly it drew an 87.0 rating for a live broadcast. Thesz, who had wrestled all over the world, was impressed: "I discovered very quickly that Riki was no fool. I'd already figured out for myself he had built a money-making machine, but I had no idea of its magnitude until he mentioned, almost off-handedly, that he'd gotten a quarter-million dollars — a fortune in those days, especially in yen, from his television network for the rights to televise our Tokyo match. He'd used the money shrewdly, buying advertising and doing heavy promotion, so interest in our match was actually front-page news."

Soon Rikidozan was expanding his business empire. He already owned a thriving wrestling promotion. Condominiums and nightclubs followed, as did an increasingly complicated relationship with the Japanese mafia. On December 8, 1963, it all came to a head in the bathroom of a Tokyo nightclub.

It was there Rikidozan, dependent on drugs and alcohol and living the high life, ran into Katsushi Murata. The gangster had been part of a group supplying vending services at professional wrestling and other entertainment events all over Japan. They had lost big money when a rival took over their business. The mega mob Yamaguchi-gumi had bought exclusive rights to wrestling matches nationwide, leaving Murata and his crew out in the cold. As the two men crossed paths, words were exchanged and Rikidozan punched the smaller man in the face, knocking him to the marble floor. After that, Murata said he could do nothing but fight for his life against the 240-pound wrestler. Historian Robert Whiting recounts, "As he lay flat on his back dazed, Rikidozan then leapt atop him and, crazy with anger and alcohol, began raining blows onto his face. Murata said he grabbed for the six-inch hunting knife he kept fixed to his belt and thrust the blade into his attacker's belly. As Riki rolled over in pain, Murata clambered to his feet and fled."

Rikidozan died a week after the stabbing on December 15, 1963. His passing was treated like a state funeral. Thousands came to pay respects at Tokyo's Ikegami Honmonji Temple, where wreaths lined the walls. He was 39 years old.

RETURN TO BRAZIL

Kimura, undaunted by the Rikidozan double cross, spent the rest of the 1950s traveling, wrestling, and, on occasion, fighting, most notably in two contests against Valdemar Santana, a young Helio Gracie–trained Brazilian who had fallen out of the Gracie fold and publically challenged his teacher. Santana had defeated the much older, smaller Gracie in a grueling contest that had lasted hours. Against Kimura, he would not fare so well: their first, grappling-only bout ended when Kimura once again used ude garami; the second, under the anything-goes rules of vale tudo, ended in mutual exhaustion and a draw after 40 minutes.

After these hard years, Kimura quietly settled into a coaching position at Takushoku University in 1960, where he produced such champions as All-Japan winner Kaneo Iwatsuri and Olympic silver medalist Doug Rogers. Despite his return to the amateur roots of judo, however, Kimura's rank was never advanced beyond the seventh-degree black belt he had been awarded in 1947 at age 30.

When Mitsuyo Maeda traveled the world, spreading Kano's judo while wrestling to make ends meet, he was celebrated by the Kodokan. When Kimura did much the same, he was shunned. Exactly why is not exactly clear; transparency and openness are not necessarily among the Kodokan's principal qualities. But regardless of Kimura's status in the hallowed halls of the Kodokan, it's clear where he ranks in the worlds of competitive judo and professional wrestling, as well as a key competitor in the early contests that helped shape what would become mixed martial arts.

Kimura, of course, was not alone in preparing the next generation of Japanese martial artists for combat. Another man also played a pivotal role. But before we can tell his story, we first must journey across the planet to a small mining town in England where catch wrestling, long forgotten in most of the world, still had a small band of ardent practitioners teaching and competing in the ancient art.

The roof of the gym was corrugated tin. Inside there were no weight machines, no treadmills, no modern comforts of any kind, not even a toilet. In the winter it was heated by a coal stove, noxious fumes filling the room as the wrestlers tried to keep up with the old men who ran the place. Nothing was soft in Wigan, England — least of all its men.

Broken noses and cauliflower ears were part of the uniform. At Billy Riley's famous Snake Pit, wrestlers learned their trade on a rough mat. Brick walls about knee high served as the boundaries. Riley, even as an older man, wouldn't hesitate to get into the thick of things to demonstrate techniques. It was, to be frank, a brutal place.

14 WIGAN

Riley didn't bring his hardscrabble form of catch-as-catch-can wrestling to Wigan, a mining town in Lancashire, England. Instead, it was a product of the environment. In Wigan, two sports mattered — rugby and wrestling. Both were diversions for hardworking miners after a long day at work. Both were just violent enough to satiate a very physical working class. Wrestling was in the blood of Wigan, England, and Riley was just one of many to follow its siren call.

"Wrestling's been handed down in Wigan from generation to generation. I used to hear my mother talk about wrestlers," Riley said. He was the British middleweight champion in the 1920s, taking the skills he learned from local miners and putting them to good use.

"His mother used to back him wrestling," Riley's student Roy Wood said. "They'd fix a match up and even when Billy was 15 he was fighting all the top men. And the top miners. They'd put a lot of money down. Hundreds of pounds, which in them days was a fortune. They say when Billy won, his mother would buy a row of houses. They owned a lot of property."

By the time he opened his own wrestling gym, Riley had retired from the sport. His goal was to train a new generation of wrestling stars and men came from all over, often by invitation, to learn real wrestling from the Wigan masters. Wearing a suit and hat even when he demonstrated techniques on the mat, the dapper Riley was a hard-driving taskmaster. There were two rules in the gym: "Billy is always right" and "You can never train too hard." Luckily the men of Lancashire and Northern England were used to hard work.

"I was in the quarries. And the money was very little really. Shifting 50 or 60 ton a day. Five P a ton. Five pence a ton! You cannot believe it," said Lancashire wrestler Jimmy Niblett, who wrestled as "The Man of Granite" Bob Sherry. "It's the same with wrestling. You've got to do more. I always seemed to be that bit ahead. By doing more."

Riley and his gym, since fallen to the ground, would be lost to history if not for his famous pupils who took the Wigan style to America and, most successfully, Japan. With his right-hand men Joe Robinson and Bob Robinson (who wrestled as Billy Joyce in Britain), Riley trained two students, Billy Robinson and Karl Gotch, who would go on to spread his legend worldwide. Although Joyce was the best wrestler of the bunch ("He used to toy with Karl," Billy Robinson remembers) his career was spent primarily in England. It was Gotch and Robinson who took the Wigan style to the world.

THE OTHER GOTCH

Gotch, who represented Belgium in the Olympics in 1948 as Karl Istaz, did more than anyone in a century to spread the art of catch wrestling to a new generation. A survivor of German prison camps during World War II, Gotch was tough and proud, but not too proud to admit he needed the knowledge he could get only from Riley and the wrestlers at the Snake Pit.

Gotch told Eugene Robinson in *Fight: Everything You Ever Wanted to Know about Ass-Kicking But Were Afraid to Ask*, "I started doing pro matches and then someone casually told me about these fellows up in Wigan, run by Billy Riley, and said I should stay away from them because they would tear me a new asshole. Well, I needed a new asshole, so off I went. . . . These guys in there were like a pack of hungry wolves. So I pick the biggest guy in there and I take him down like I would in amateur wrestling, and once we're down, he grabs my ankle, and I'm screaming, 'What the hell are you doing?' And he says, 'Wrestling.' So I say, 'Oh, that's how you wrestle, eh?' and we go again and I head-butt him and try to run him into the wall."

After barnstorming Europe for a few years, Gotch was brought to North America on the word of Édouard Carpentier, the Canadian star whom he had met in Germany. From there, Al Haft, a promoter who loved to mentor legitimate tough guys, brought him in to wrestle in his Ohio territory, changing his last name to "Gotch" in honor of the great Frank Gotch. Although Gotch would later say Riley wasn't even the best man in his own gym (which wasn't surprising considering he was in his 50s by the time he trained Gotch), early in his career in America Gotch was quick to credit his old teacher for his success in the ring.

"Well, you know what a snakepit is . . . a dangerous place! And that's just what Wigan is if you can't take care of yourself. Billy Riley has no time for a man with no guts, to put it bluntly, so his training is on a 'kill or be killed' basis. In other words, you smarten up fast at Wigan and learn to defend yourself against any attack on the mat," Gotch said. "I give any credit for success to Billy Riley, the 'Old Master' at Wigan. What a fantastic man. When Riley trained you, you learned to wrestle in the strictest sense of the word. You learned the basic moves first — really learned them — and then refined them. Nothing was neglected! When a man left Wigan, he took with him the imparted knowledge of Riley's thousands of matches and years of training."

Many promoters tried to work with Gotch, to turn his fearsome back room reputation into a championship reign. It wasn't easy. He'd adapted the attitude of his mentor Billy Joyce, considered by most who trained with him to be the best of the Wigan heavyweights, who refused to put over less talented wrestlers, saying, "If I can lick 'em, I'll lick 'em." Even a talented wrestler like world champion Lou Thesz wasn't above Gotch's hazing. Once when he saw Thesz torturing a non-wrestler during a match, not letting him off the mat and embarrassing him, Gotch delivered a warning to the promoter. "If he tries that with me," Gotch said. "I'll break both his arms."

The two men had a complicated relationship. Thesz embraced Gotch like a brother, taking him home to meet his parents, recognizing a kindred spirit and countryman, both being Hungarians. But Gotch was resistant to taking Thesz's professional advice. He feuded with wrestlers and promoters alike, seemingly unable to get along with anyone. Later, the two would drift apart over the wrestling business, to the point Gotch refused to cooperate with Thesz when Thesz was writing his autobiography.

KLONDIKE BILL COLLECTS A KARL GOTCH ELBOW STRIKE RIGHT BETWEEN THE EYES

"That relationship was an especially disappointing one for Lou," Thesz's biographer Kit Bauman wrote at WrestlingClassics.com. "It's true that there was genuine heat between them . . . He said Karl was always full of himself and very difficult to deal with; he also said, for the first of what would be many times, that Karl blew his chance at being a major star in this country by refusing to listen to others (namely Lou) about how to best handle himself. Lou had enormous respect for Karl as a wrestler, but he didn't care for the individual; he said Karl was arrogant and stubborn and, ultimately, in the sense of understanding wrestling as a business, a poor businessman."

Lou's widow Charlie Thesz added her own insight:

> Lou wanted Karl to have great success because Lou had his own vision of pro wrestling, and Karl definitely fit the profile. Karl had his own concept and his own definition of success. When two German Hungarians are at odds in their ideas it is not pretty! Lou felt Karl had the same potential for being a champion and Lou wanted to share his formula for success with Karl. Karl did not want it, but I do honestly feel he resented Lou in some way for his success and probably felt Lou "sold out" to get it.
>
> . . . Lou had a tremendous amount of respect for Karl as a wrestler. His disappointment came from Karl not taking his advice and having a different career, instead of being a champion in every sense for professional wrestling at its best. Lou succeeded in distancing his pride from his payday. As Ray Steele once counseled him — it was not a hobby!

Thesz, by then 48 years old, took Gotch on in a series of bouts for Haft in the Ohio territory. Thesz had come out of retirement for a sixth title run as NWA champion and was reclaiming local championships, like the American Wrestling Association version of the title Gotch held in Ohio. The two met five times in the territory in 1963 and 1964, with the men wrestling to a draw or Thesz winning by disqualification each time, until a fateful May night in Detroit. Thesz, looking for his trademark back suplex, was blocked by Gotch. The counter to his suplex did more than make Thesz look foolish — it also succeeded in breaking his ribs. Panicked, believing Gotch to be shooting on him, Thesz immediately went for a hook, catching Gotch with a double wristlock and ending the match.

Gotch's top student Joe Malenko remembered many conversations with Karl about his issues with Thesz. "Thesz used to pick people up for the [back suplex]. When you do that, you're going to do it right. You're going to lay a guy down in the proper manner. If you do that, it's very difficult for him to hurt himself. You're going to lay a guy down flat," Malenko said. "Thesz wasn't always so careful about that. His attitude was 'This is my hold, I'm going to make it look good and you'll land however you land. If you hurt yourself, fuck you.' So Karl said, 'Okay.' And this isn't just Karl talking, I've had a lot of people tell me this — Karl blocked the hold and ended up landing on top of Thesz . . . Karl was very strong willed about this stuff. He was a black and white guy. And a tough guy."

Kit Bauman explained things from Thesz's angle: "He always was alert to the possibility of a double cross, but he trusted Karl enough, once they'd started working, to lower his guard. When Karl blocked him, it hit Lou immediately that something was up, and he ended things immediately. 'I made him howl' is how Lou put it. So yes, Lou believed it was an attempted double cross. And he was mad at himself for almost allowing it to happen. He once said to me, long after that initial conversation, that Karl was an excellent choice to do it, because he was a good wrestler and probably could have pulled it off if Lou hadn't been so quick to snatch him and end the match."

Those who knew Gotch don't believe that this match was a shoot at all, believing the double wristlock submission was the scripted ending of the match. Wrestlers who worked out with both men simply doubt that Thesz would have so easily submitted a wrestler as skilled as Gotch.

But the injury to Thesz wasn't anything unusual for the hard-charging Gotch, who had problems seemingly everywhere he traveled. Wrestler Abe Jacobs told reporter Mike Mooneyham, "I once said to him, 'Karl, you haven't got any friends left.' He looked at me and said, 'Yeah, you're the only one I've got.' Like I said, he was a hard guy to get along with. He had a quick temper and could get madder and madder by the minute."

His most famous incident backstage occurred, once again, in Haft's territory. Buddy Rogers, then the world champion, refused to meet either Gotch or Dr. Bill Miller in a title match. Rogers was the biggest star in the industry, but not a legitimate wrestler. To most everyone in the business this was meaningless — after all, wrestling hadn't been about legitimacy in decades by this point. But to men like Gotch, Thesz, and Miller (a two-time Big Ten wrestling champion in the 1940s) it was paramount. Rogers, perhaps rightfully so, feared a double cross and didn't think either man was worth the risk, neither being a huge draw in his mind. But for the two shooters, Rogers' refusal to fight them was a hit to the pocketbook. A title match with Buddy Rogers meant a big house and a big payday.

Gotch and Miller cornered Rogers backstage at a show in Columbus in 1962. What happened next is shrouded in mystery. Ed "The Phantom of the Ring" Garea, a prominent wrestling historian, tells the tale this way:

> Buddy Rogers was the reigning NWA champion and if there was one person Buddy didn't like, it was Karl Gotch. Rogers often compared Gotch with Lou Thesz, whom he also distrusted, and let anyone within earshot know his feelings. Gotch, for his part, hated gimmicks and performers, feeling them inferior to a skilled shooter such as himself. When Gotch got word of Buddy's feelings toward giving him a title shot, he confronted Rogers in the dressing room. Rogers told him straight out that not only didn't he trust Gotch not to double-cross him, but that there was no money to be made in a match with Gotch. Gotch suggested that they have it out right there and then. Buddy demurred and began to leave the locker room only to find his way blocked by Bill Miller, Gotch's friend and another wrestler snubbed by Buddy. Gotch began to pummel

Rogers with his fists, and Miller, for his part, played the part of goalkeeper, in that he kept Buddy in play when the champ tried to run.

When it was all said and done, Buddy was bloody but unbowed, except for a broken hand, which limited his appearances for the next couple of months. He filed assault charges against the pair, who turned themselves in the next day to the Franklin County (Ohio) Sheriff's Office, where they were released after posting a $25 bond each. Haft was livid, but managed to smooth things over with the authorities, using the old "boys will be boys" canard. The real damage, however, was done in the eyes of other promoters, who quickly listed Gotch as Trouble Personified, one reason why he mainly kept to Haft's promotion until 1965, with only a stop or two in Japan.

Miller, a 6'6" 290-pound giant of a man, admitted they roughed Rogers up a bit, but claims Rogers left relatively unscathed. Rogers' hand, according to Miller's interview with radio host Mike Lano, wasn't broken. "We got him in the dressing room and I stood in front of the opening," Miller said. "Gotch slapped him. Then I slapped him. He ran right past me, pushing me out of the way to get out of there. . . . We never slammed, or crushed, or broke his hand in the doorway."

Whatever happened in the locker room that day, it was the end of the line for Gotch. It was bad enough to be difficult to work with, temperamental, and capable of serious violence. Taking out your frustrations on a money draw was a step too far, especially when you weren't a money-making star in your own right. Miller, a great wrestler and a star, survived the tumult. Gotch was essentially persona non grata everywhere but in Haft's territory for the second half of the 1960s.

Luckily with Miller's help he was able to catch on in Japan, eventually becoming a star there. Things calmed down in the States, as time seems to heal all wounds, and eventually Gotch settled into life as a show wrestler. Gotch and Rene Goulet were even tag team champions for Vince McMahon Sr. in the WWWF. Gotch and Goulet still held the titles when wrestler Antonio Inoki, looking for an opponent for New Japan Pro-Wrestling's debut in 1972, made Gotch an offer he couldn't refuse. With next to no notice Gotch left McMahon and American wrestling behind, taking the title belt he had kept when he was AWA champion to Japan with him — it was the perfect prop for the "Real World Title" Inoki won from Gotch to establish himself as the real deal. In Japan, Gotch finally found a home.

He was too old to be an active wrestler for long, but found work not only helping Inoki book the matches, but as a trainer for the young wrestlers as well. It was here Gotch shined, teaching the up-and-coming stars real wrestling holds and strategies to go along with their pro theatrics.

Shunned and blacklisted in America, Gotch was embraced by the Japanese as the "God of Wrestling." The matches in the ring were still as fixed as ever, but in the dojo Gotch taught the next generation of Japanese stars to wrestle for real. Gotch brought the grappling techniques and teaching methods he learned in Wigan with him to Inoki's New Japan Pro-Wrestling. There, Gotch found students willing to work hard, shut their mouths, and listen.

"He was made for Japan. And Japan was made for him," Malenko said. "Karl had two things going for him in Japan. First, they respect talent. . . . Here in the States we were 'rasslers.' But over there we were wrestlers. Over here it was 'You're one of those jabronis that do that fake shit.' Over there they look at you and actually appreciate your abilities and your talent. . . . And second, he was an older guy by the time he went there to train them and they respect their elders. It's part of their culture."

Things were different in Florida where Gotch settled between tours of Japan and after retiring. He often responded to requests from wrestlers in America to teach them his shooting style with a gruff indifference. Gotch had a firm belief that knowledge had to be earned. The cost he demanded was in sweat and time. He demanded prospective wrestlers be in exquisite physical shape before he would take them under his wing. Otherwise, someone asking to learn would get the Gotch version of the blow off.

"Karl could be very rude," says Malenko. "His social skills were not the best. For somebody who had been in the limelight like he had, he was somewhat socially inept. He felt awkward around people to begin with. And if you were a person who was anything less than respectful and understanding of his skill level, you didn't stand a chance with him. You probably wouldn't even end up on the mat with him — or if you did you'd end up leaving quickly of your own accord. Or on a stretcher. He did not suffer fools gladly."

"Karl used to go over to [pro wrestler Boris] Malenko's and some poor pro wrestler that wanted to learn to shoot would ask Karl to show some holds," Gotch protégé Tom Puckett wrote. "At that point he would run through about 250 submissions in about 10 minutes, then get up and say, 'So now you got it?' The poor bastard would then say, 'Yeah I think so' to which Gotch would go, 'No you don't, you've seen it.'"

With the Japanese, it was different. In their rigid dojo environment, he was in complete control and could demand from his students whatever physical tolls he desired.

Malenko remembers Gotch's brutal training regimen like it was yesterday. "He would crossface me and I would literally just have to take it for minutes at a time. I wasn't allowed to say anything. I wasn't allowed to squeal or move. I just had to take. Many nights I went home and I couldn't even eat. . . . Karl would place me in a bridge and then he would sit on me. Eventually I got to the point where I'd have three or four guys, a thousand pounds, sitting on me. In hindsight, that wasn't good for you. But back then, when Karl said, 'Do it,' you didn't say no."

Gotch's philosophy created a very aggressive brand of submission fighter. He didn't believe in defensive positions like the guard, describing the jiu-jitsu artists who used it as "old whores waiting for a customer." Students of Gotch's, instead, continued to attack until the match was over.

"Karl used to talk about 'rocking the boat.' You had to know a ton of submissions and you'd use holds based on how your opponent responded. You would go from submission to submission and kind of screw with their mind," Malenko said. "They'd think, 'Holy shit, no matter what I do, this guy's getting a hold and it hurts. No matter what I do, he's hurting me.' Mentally you wear them down and wait for that time when something is really available and you can lock and load it and there is no recovery. Karl called that rocking the boat, keeping them off balance until they fall right out of the boat. Because they've lost their equilibrium."

It took years to perfect the skills needed to "rock the boat" the way Gotch preferred. Few were willing to put the time and effort into learning such a specialized art. Those who did tended to succeed. Some, like Yoshiaki Fujiwara, Masakatsu Funaki, and Minoru Suzuki became legends in their own right.

"He cared about the people he was training. He really wanted you to get better," Malenko said. "His goal as a coach was to make you better than him. He wanted pupils that could walk away and kick his ass. He didn't hold back. He'd teach you what you needed to know to beat him."

Malenko adds, "He set the tone for everything I've ever done. Wrestling is a builder of your soul, your morals, your ethics. It's a powerful sport. . . . When you get past the hardness of Karl, which was honed from years of rough times, especially during the war, you have a guy who really loved the sport of wrestling. Did he know he was called the 'God of Wrestling' in Japan? Yes. Did he appreciate it? Yes. Did he have some nights when he asked his lovely wife to call him the God of Wrestling again? Maybe. But that wasn't what drove him. It wasn't his fame. It was taking young guys and creating good wrestlers. Good men."

"I never took one cent from a boy to show him how to wrestle, all I asked for is guts," Gotch once said. "I can make you strong, fast, agile, and train you for endurance and reflex, but guts you get when you are born."

"THE BRITISH LION": BILLY ROBINSON

One of Gotch's training partners at Wigan found more success than he did in America, but like the prickly Gotch, had trouble navigating wrestling politics. Billy Robinson had been a light heavyweight British amateur champion. Like many amateurs, however, he found he still had a lot to learn about wrestling. He found what he was looking for with Billy Riley and the lads in Wigan.

BILLY ROBINSON THROWS ON A DOUBLE ARM SUPLEX
COURTESY BILLY ROBINSON

Robinson described his start in the Snake Pit to Jake Shannon:

> At Wigan, initially, you're not shown too much, and you are used as a sparring partner, but the coach watches you. Like in my case, it was close to four months before he said, "Okay. We'll start to teach this kid." They wanted to make sure I would stay, stick it out, no matter what happened to me. And that's what they did. Not just for me. With everybody . . . Once you do that, like the old-timers you practice with, guys you could learn how to beat, they still like it when they beat you. "He's a piece of shit" or "He's no good," that never happened. You respected them by just getting on the mat. And later on, when you're that much better, they're going to hope you would help them out. The respect is there with anybody, no matter how low or how high, because you know that nobody will say, 'I am this. I am that.' That will never happen because there's always somebody that will knock the shit out of you. . . .
>
> But the old-timers used to come down to the gym because of the atmosphere. And if they see you do something wrong, after your training session, they'd pull you to one side, explain to you, show you, get you back on the mat with a different sparring partner, and make you do it. And the thing was, I used to wake up with [my] head up, screaming, because I'd hear this voice, Billy Riley's voice, Karl Gotch's, God . . . screaming at me, "Do it again. Do it again." And I'd wake up with ringing in my ears, "Do it again. Do it again."

Robinson had the benefit of more than Riley's knowledge. He was sent to Hungary to learn upper body throws from the best Greco-Roman wrestlers in Europe. He soaked in more knowledge in Sweden and Germany. By the time he left Wigan after almost a decade, he had developed into a very well-rounded and capable wrestler. Sometimes he'd return to Wigan between trips and show off his new moves.

"Riley would have a smile on his face. 'I'll show you how to beat that,' he'd say. 'I just wanted you to know what it was in case somebody tried to beat you with it,'" Robinson said. "I got a lot of experience because of Billy Riley sending me to all these different gyms. And in Wigan, I could find five, six, seven sparring partners every time I went to the gym . . . I'd stay on the mat for two hours straight and these five or six guys would come in every few minutes. As soon as he started to get tired, or I was beating him too easily, Riley would send somebody else. That's how we got stamina for long wrestling matches."

In 1970, Robinson followed Gotch to America, but found significantly more success there. He became a main event star in the American Wrestling Alliance, wrestling the promotion's owner and top star Verne Gagne dozens of times. Robinson, like Gotch, also found his calling as a trainer. In a barn, often in the dead of the Minnesota winter, Robinson broke in new recruits for Gagne, including men who would go on to become some marquee wrestlers in the 1980s. *Wrestling Observer* editor Dave Meltzer says Robinson earned a reputation in the Minnesota-based promotion — as a worker, a shooter, a trainer, and a bully: "Gagne used him as his head trainer and shooter when guys in Minnesota would want to be wrestlers. Robinson tortured the guys, and his rep in those camps was very different from the person he portrayed on television. Many call him a bully. But many of the great wrestlers of the era, like Ricky Steamboat, Ric Flair, Jim Brunzell, Curt Hennig, Iron Sheik, Sgt. Slaughter, Ken Patera, and Buddy Rose came out of those camps, all with stories of nightmarish things that they saw, and in some cases experienced. His rep was such that in the mid-'80s, when Randy Savage, who was a wildman who was quick to fight and one of the biggest stars in the business, was confronted, playfully as it was, by a well past his prime Robinson, it was described that he froze in deathly fear and nearly soiled himself."

"I hold him in the highest esteem as a wrestler," Verne Gagne said. "He was a technical genius with the way he would put on submission holds . . . We never did that in collegiate or high school wrestling. We didn't do submission holds. After you turn pro you had to learn them . . . and that's how you became a good wrestler."

Gagne may have respected Robinson's ability, but unlike the other wrestlers on the roster he was mostly immune to the British wrestler's mean streak. After all, Gagne signed the checks. Others weren't always as lucky with the finicky shooter. Robinson didn't like doing jobs, especially for non-wrestlers, and would often take liberties with wrestlers in the ring when he was in a bad mood.

Said "Superstar" Billy Graham, "He was a mean man and would hurt you for no reason. Robinson especially didn't like three types of people — football players, bodybuilders, and bouncers. Obviously, I kept my distance from him. Finally got booked to face each other. I told Verne I thought it was a bad idea, but he wanted the match. I made a point to go by Robinson's dressing room before our match. I showed him where I had taped a razor blade with half the blade sticking on one of my fingers. I told him, 'If you try to hurt me in any way, I won't hesitate to cut you up.' He was a perfect gentleman in our match, lighter than he had every been with anyone before or since."

"Robinson was a prick," fellow wrestler Ken Patera remembered. "That's why he had trouble in different places where he wrestled. Sailor White punched him out in Montreal, then pissed in his wounds. The Rock's grandfather, Peter Maivia, nearly dug out his eye in another fight. Verne and Robinson were close, but outside the AWA, nobody wanted to work with Billy. They were afraid he'd fuck them up with cheap shots. And chances were that he would."

Patera was one of the stars in Robinson's 1972 training camp. A powerlifter, Patera was a natural target for Robinson. The sessions were brutal — Ric Flair quit twice and had to be talked back by Gagne himself. To Robinson, it was just the way things were done. And, in the Wigan style, he didn't ask anything of his students he wouldn't do himself.

"If I asked for 500 squats, I did it with them. They really couldn't complain that much, although it was tough," Robinson remembered. "When I went to Wigan, I wasn't allowed to submit or tap out unless Billy Riley said, 'That's enough.' If I complained, I'd get kicked out of the gym. They wouldn't show me any more. Yes they were good, but they all worked hard. I was going to make those guys work hard too."

Robinson was hard on everyone, but the brunt of his attention went to Khosrow Vasiri, an Iranian wrestler fresh off of a 1971 AAU Greco-Roman championship at 180.5 pounds. Vasiri, who would later go on to fame and fortune as the "Iron Sheik," still had a wrestler's mentality and wasn't humble enough for Robinson's liking. When Vasiri speculated he could outwrestle the professional, Robinson put him to the test.

He put Vasiri in the down position, on all fours, but couldn't turn him over. Vasiri thought he had proven a point until Robinson drove a knee into his hip and quickly turned him over and pinned him. In a pure wrestling competition Vasiri was getting the best of him — but Robinson changed the rules midstream and taught an important lesson or two — most important likely being "Never trust Billy Robinson."

"He thought any amateur could beat a professional wrestler. Because that's what he'd been brought up to believe . . . He said, 'I can beat anybody at anything.' So we started and 15 seconds later he had to go to the hospital," Robinson said, recalling a different version of events. "We got a call from his amateur friends later, asking if we could take him back — just don't hurt him. He was a great amateur wrestler."

Robinson was involved in several out-of-the-ring scuffles that have become a part of wrestling lore. He and Jack Brisco destroyed a hotel room with an impromptu wrestling match in Australia, putting Brisco's NCAA championship credentials up against Wigan's submission style. Both ended the night with newfound respect for each other.

A street fight with Peter Maivia is also a thing of legend. Robinson didn't lose an eye in the confrontation, although that is a popular telling of the story, he did quickly learn the difference between a wrestling match and a fight.

"They are both drunk and they get in this fight, and Billy goes to hook some suplex move, and he throws Maivia down on the ground and lands on top of him," Larry Zbyszko recalled. "Maivia, who was now under Robinson, started biting Billy in the chest through his shirt. Billy did the great wrestling move, but he's getting eaten alive. Soon Billy's screaming, 'My bloody God, my bloody God. Get bloody off me.'"

For his part, Robinson remembers Maivia as out of control and disrespectful to their Japanese hosts. The two had words and the "High Chief" swung on him, missed, and Robinson grabbed him around the waist. Before he could make his next move, Robinson says Maivia bit him on the cheek. Robinson proceeded to throw him down and kick the crap out of him — literally. "It was the only time I ever kicked a man when he was down," Robinson admits.

Wrestling lore also tells of Robinson being egged on by his fellow wrestlers when talking trash about Gagne back stage. The boys wanted to know if Robinson could take his boss, an Olympian and one of the toughest guys in the business. Gagne had outwrestled the best of the best and had punched out the tough bar brawler Dick the Bruiser to boot. Knowing Verne's office door was open, Robinson loudly proclaimed that "Verne can be done at any time."

Despite being in his 40s Gagne's blood was up and he came storming out of the office, saying, 'How about now?' The two locked up and Gagne quickly got the upper hand, locking Robinson in a front facelock and having the entire locker room come by to give him a spanking. The story smells of hyperbole, but the distinction between truth and fiction in the world of wrestling is often hard to determine.

"Verne was a tough amateur but without the submission repetoire of a Wigan guy," catch wrestling expert Jake Shannon said. "I wasn't there so I don't know, but if I were a betting man, I'd find it unlikely Verne did anything except pay Billy."

Robinson, like many of the great technical wrestlers of the 1970s, was in high demand in Japan. He had great matches with Antonio Inoki as well as Giant Baba and "Jumbo" Tsuruta. His Snake Pit pedigree helped get him over with the fans almost as much as his smooth in ring work.

"When I first came into Japan, the guy that had been teaching them was Karl Gotch . . . his style is Wigan-style wrestling," Robinson said. "So, when I got to Japan all the Japanese were wrestling a style that I was probably the best at in the world. . . . They asked me to stay and coach and they named the gym "The Snake Pit" after the Wigan gym. They got Lou Thesz, Danny Hodge, and myself to do the opening ceremonies. I stayed there to coach for 10 years."

Between them, Gotch and Robinson taught a generation of wrestling stars who went on to revolutionize the industry in Japan. Students like Yoshiaki Fujiwara, Masakatsu Funaki, Satoru Sayama, and Kazushi Sakuraba would change pro wrestling in Japan forever. But the most important man in the Japanese wrestling industry, the man who helped grease the wheels for a mixed martial arts explosion, was a Brazil-based track and field star with the ambition and drive to become a leading light. Simply put, without Antonio Inoki, mixed martial arts in Japan might have never taken hold and fans might have missed out on some of the top martial artists of his era — including two judo masters who had turns as professional wrestling stars.

If there's something that gets adrenaline pumping, Gene LeBell has done it. He's fought and wrestled his way around the world; won amateur championships in Judo; and trained martial arts movie legends, showing them how to fight and then letting them beat him up in his role as a movie stuntman. He's wrecked cars, leapt out of buildings, been a motorcycle stunt rider, and choked actor Steven Seagal until the action star defecated on himself. He was allegedly even part of a murder. But today, "Judo" Gene LeBell is best known for a televised bout aganst a pro boxer, a fight that answered many of the questions that would be asked by the Ultimate Fighting Championship three decades later.

15 JUDO GENE and Bad News

When LeBell met Milo Savage in a famous "boxer versus judo" match on a pro wrestling card in December 1963, two worlds came together for the California-based grappler. His mother, the legendary "Redhead" Aileen Eaton, was Los Angeles's leading boxing and wrestling promoter. At the famed Grand Olympic Auditorium, she called the shots, holding more than 10,000 boxing matches in a decades-long career that ended with her enshrined as the first woman in the International Boxing Hall of Fame. According to *Sports Illustrated*, Eaton, despite her diminutive size, was a powerhouse in the city of angels, in sport and politics: "Do not think of her as a delicately declining lady on the brink of warm milk and a shawl and nice long drives in the country. For one thing, no one takes Aileen Eaton for a ride. She does the driving, in the longest Cadillac in southern California, and usually to a place where you pick up cards and dice. The Lady moves, that is, when she has time. Politically lethal, she has been a forceful figure in at least two campaigns, in one of which Attorney General Thomas Lynch won and Pierre Salinger lost. She once ran for the city council and lost, too, but that was the exception. Do not try to beat her on her own turf."

While LeBell once sparred with legendary boxer "Sugar" Ray Robinson and loved the sweet science, his family forbade him to box. Instead, it was the colorful wrestlers who really took him under their wing, making him one of their own. *Sports Illustrated* details his early training:

Lacking a father figure, Gene LeBell was enthralled by the larger-than-life figures who worked for his mother. He got his first wrestling lesson at seven when he asked former professional heavyweight champion Ed (Strangler) Lewis for instruction. The 300-pound Lewis obviously had a soft spot for children. "He slapped a Deadlock on me, and I felt like the room was spinning for 10 minutes," says LeBell.

It was these wrestling chops that helped LeBell win the AAU National Judo championships in both 1954 and 1955. LeBell came out of nowhere to win as a 21-year-old kid, pinning John Osako, an American judo legend who ruled the scene in the Midwest and was considered the top heavyweight in the country, in his very first match. LeBell credits much of his early judo success to wrestling basics.

"A lot of people won't admit it, but judo is wrestling with handles," LeBell said. "If you want to do a 'whizzer' throw in wrestling, it's the same as an uchimata in judo. An ogashi (hip throw) in judo is the same as a hip lock in wrestling . . . the only thing that is different is that judo has strangleholds, which aren't done in wrestling."

That's not to say LeBell didn't respect judo or its practitioners. His earliest experience with the sport saw him get thrown repeatedly by a judo black belt. He was powerless to stop him and decided then and there he would work on the sport until he could defend against it.

"The exotic writing and the sight of people in white pajamas throwing each other around inside intrigued me," said LeBell. "I was very confident in my wrestling and boxing ability and I went to a legitimate dojo. I went against a very short man who threw me high in the air. I jumped up and said, 'I bet you couldn't do it again' and he did. Then I decided I had to learn this stuff. And I wanted to beat this older man. It took me about a year, but then I was hooked. . . . In judo or any other sport, the harder you work the luckier you get."

It was only after winning two judo championships that LeBell really started to get serious about the sport. He traveled to Japan, spending time at the Kodokan, learning from the greats. Like many serious students, he often ran the gauntlet, what he calls "the slaughter line." Victims would be lined up, some of the Kodokan's top players, and LeBell would take them on one by one, until he was finally bested. He often handled 20 or more highly skilled grapplers before someone could stop him.

Japan was also where LeBell first started wearing a pink judogi. What would become his trademark started as an accident — he inadvertently threw in a bright red garment with his whites when doing the laundry. What emerged was the famous pink gi. While some might have cringed, LeBell embraced it — especially when it empowered potential victims to talk a little trash in the gym. LeBell was all too happy to use a pink gi to attract opponents he would then stretch until they cried uncle.

But there was no money in the martial arts, especially judo, so LeBell joined the family business. "I had won more than 100 trophies in judo, but even melting all of them down wouldn't make a single house payment," LeBell said. "There was no money back then in the martial arts. So I turned to wrestling."

LeBell, by most accounts, was a horrible professional wrestler from a technical perspective. Despite being a tough guy, nothing he did was believable. Somehow, one of the world's toughest men looked soft in the ring. Even though he was the brother of promoter Mike LeBell, Gene rarely moved up from the undercard. But the family did find some use for him.

"Not only was he one of the top martial artists in the country, he'd trained for wrestling with some of the most vicious shooters in the business," Fred Blassie wrote in his book *Listen, You Pencil Neck Geeks*. "When the family needed an enforcer to step into the ring with a wrestler who didn't want to go along with the program, all they had to do was open Gene's bedroom door and tell him to get into his wrestling gear."

Family connections, so important in getting him started in the industry, may have ended up hurting LeBell in the long run. His brother Mike, the promoter in Los Angeles, was not well liked in the business and some of that had to have rolled downhill. Gene hit the road, wrestling both under his own name and under a mask as "The Hangman." Friends say as the business became more about ringside antics and less about in-ring wrestling, LeBell tuned out.

GENE LEBELL

"Gene is one of the greatest guys in the industry and it wasn't easy being a great guy," Lou Thesz wrote. " He had to overcome his family ties and a world that was slowly phasing out the sport of wrestling. He had too much ability for pro wrestling and no passion for what it was becoming."

LeBell often thinks about the wrestling business he missed out on, coming up, as he did, in the era of television and heavy gimmicks. "You have to have show business now. You look at Lou Thesz — he never over-acted and he always went for the finishing holds — and they *believed* it. When I first went to Japan and saw some of the superstars from over here clowning around, the audience said 'no way.' We want something that we can believe."

BOXING VS. JUDO

There had been plenty of wrestler-boxer confrontations before LeBell's famous match, including Jack Dempsey's destruction of wrestler "Cowboy" Clarence Luttrell. But while not the first of its kind, the mixed fight with Milo Savage was pretty unique, a chance for LeBell to put himself to the test.

In the August 1963 issue of *Rogue Magazine*, a less classy version of *Playboy*, writer Jim Beck not only called all judo and karate men "bums," he challenged them to a match against a professional boxer with $1,000 of Beck's cash on the line: "Judo bums hear me one and all! It is one thing to fracture pin boards, bricks, and assorted inanimate objects, but quite another to climb in the ring with a trained and less cooperative target. My money is ready."

Not everyone in the martial arts community was amused by Beck's ignorance, confusing judo's grappling-based approach with karate style kicks and board breaking. Ed Parker, the founder of American Kenpo Karate, wanted to take him up on his challenge — and he knew just the man for the job. LeBell says he hadn't seen the story until Parker came charging into his judo dojo around the corner from Paramount Studios in Los Angeles:

> *Ed Parker showed me the story and said, "I want you to fight this guy."*
> *"Why me?" I asked.*
> *"Because you're the most sadistic bastard I know," he replied.*
> *Of course, for a thousand dollars I said I would fight my grandmother but then again she could whip me. A thousand dollars was a lot of money back then and with side bets that I placed on myself, I could come out of this thing with a good chunk of change.*

The story of this interesting bout changes every time it's told. With Gene LeBell it's never easy to seperate fact from fiction. When you talk to Gene, you don't interview him as much as listen to his schtick. And the man is full of interesting stories. But, more often than not, those stories are partially the product of his very clever imagination.

Take, for example, the boxing pedigree of his opponent Milo Savage. In his book, LeBell makes the claim that Savage was the number five–ranked light heavyweight in the world at the time of the bout. In fact, he was 39 years old with a pedestrian record of 49–45–9. He was also a career middleweight, not a light heavyweight — none of which stopped outlets as prestigious as *Sports Illustrated* from repeating this fiction as late as 2010. A cursory internet search would show a journeyman fighter who lost two fights in his first year of competition and never got better, losing bouts on the regular during a career that lasted almost two decades. It's unlikely Savage was ever ranked in the top five — he never won more than six fights in a row in his entire career.

Savage, in short, was a never-was, worse, an old never-was who was on his way out of the boxing business. He was a sparring partner for Gene Fullmer, not a legitimate star in his own right. Claims that he was in line for a title shot are absurd. That was Fullmer, who indeed fought Dick Tiger for the title twice in 1963. Savage had never even approached the summit, let alone climbed the mountain. Months before, he had fought on the undercard in Salt Lake City, Utah, in front of barely more than 100 fans. You can't get much further away from title contention than that.

The rules of the bout are also in dispute. LeBell claims they were settled on the night of the fight in the locker room. Dewey Falcone, a lawyer who represented LeBell, wrote an article in *Black Belt* magazine that makes it clear the rules were determined in advance and approved by both parties. LeBell's book says the fight would have gone on until a finish. *Black Belt*'s account details a fight with five rounds. Both accounts agree LeBell was allowed to use what Savage's manager called "all that judo crap." He was forbidden the karate kick, which wasn't a major part of his arsenal anway.

Savage wasn't constrained by any traditional boxing rules. He could punch from the clinch and wasn't required to wear standard gloves. LeBell's team did insist the boxer also be outfitted in a gi. When Savage came to the ring he had on a small karate gi and speed bag gloves. LeBell would later claim the gloves were even more dangerous than they appeared:

> *He was wearing brass knuckles covered in leather. It looked like they tried to disguise the brass knucks as a leather glove but you could see what they were. I mean the guy wasn't taking any chances.*
>
> *My lawyer said, "You're not going to fight him with these irons on his hands are you!?!"*
>
> *I said, "He'll need the brass knuckles because when I hit him there'll be two sounds: one when I hit him and two when he hits the ground."*

Considering the other tall tales in LeBell's recounting of the bout, it's worth taking that claim with a grain of salt. Either way, when Savage hit LeBell, his hand would hardly be protected at all — LeBell would be hit hard by a professional boxer with 24 knockouts on his resume.

There was significant debate at the time about whether a boxer could beat a grappler or a traditional martial artist, and 1,500 fans came out to the Fair Grounds Coliseum in

Salt Lake City, Utah, to see the spectacle — well short of a sell out, but respectable enough. Fans hadn't yet learned one of the key lessons of mixed martial arts — that a grappler will beat a striker almost every time. But LeBell, who had been around both sports, was confident.

Footage of the fight shows LeBell towering over Savage. LeBell was in the midst of his pro wrestling career and was much larger than he had been as an amateur judo ace. Savage was a true middleweight but showed uncanny strength and balance for his size. Both men appeared terrified of each other in the first round, each cautiously circling, neither willing to make the first move. The restless crowd rained down boos as LeBell grabbed, but was unable to throw Savage. Apparently, LeBell had reinjured his left shoulder in pro wrestling competition. The bum arm left LeBell limited and he focused on a single technique he could pull off — the front choke.

Savage proved hard to get to the mat. He had obviously studied some judo and fought like a tiger every time LeBell got a grip on him. At the time, LeBell's bad shoulder and Savage's karate gi top, smaller and more slippery than a traditional judo gi, were blamed for LeBell's struggles. In the decades to follow, LeBell's litany of excuses grew.

According to LeBell, "The idea, to beat a boxer, is to tackle him below the waist, because he has no defense below his waist. . . . But at the last moment, they told me tackles are illegal. . . . When I got in close to him, he had grease all over him. He had great training — he was not only a boxer, he was also a wrestler. So when I threw him down, he grapevined my leg, which a boxer wouldn't do but a wrestler would."

Savage didn't land many hard punches — LeBell was wary. But the wrestler would admit to friends after the bout that the boxer had him worried for a time. "It was a good thing the guy didn't follow up on that first jab," LeBell told his friend Jess O'Brien after the fight. "If he had followed through, I would've been down."

LeBell was able to get the mount in round two, but Savage escaped. LeBell told friends he likely could have finished it with an armlock but was afraid the crowd might not understand. Everybody understood unconscious.

In the fourth round the judo ace pushed Savage into the ropes and used harai goshi, a hip throw, to toss the boxer to the mat. From there, LeBell secured a gi choke to finish the bout. Savage considered biting him as a defense, but the wrestler threatened to gouge his eye out if he did. The boxing referee in charge of the bout didn't recognize the danger Savage was facing. Instead of breaking the hold, he wandered around the two fighters, checking Savage's limp arm before finally stopping the fight.

A jubilant LeBell stepped on a limp Savage as he celebrated the win. The crowd was furious, throwing chairs and bottles. People weren't used to seeing a fighter choked unconscious and it just felt wrong for many in attendance. It took time for the medical personnel to wake Savage up and some in the crowd feared the boxer had been killed. On his way to the locker room a fan even tried to stab LeBell. It was a tough night, but "Judo" Gene had defended the honor of his sport against the boxer.

A HARD-KNOCK LIFE

LeBell eventually left the wrestling business for a life in the movies. He became one of the most respected stuntmen in Hollywood, even landing a number of bit roles in classic films like *Raging Bull*. Only Gene LeBell could leave one dangerous job for something even more lethal.

"The hardest stunt is a stunt that goes wrong, because you're investing your body, and that can be expensive if it goes bad," LeBell said. "Contrary to my mother's belief, I'm not perfect. I lost my concentration when jumping a car and looked away just to see how much air I was getting in the jump. The second I hit the ground I got whiplash so hard I couldn't walk straight for a week. I've been burned, cut, and suffered broken bones."

LeBell never stopped training and learning, he was just in the gym with progressively more famous partners. With his new Hollywood contacts, LeBell was soon training not just wrestlers like "Rowdy" Roddy Piper, but martial arts movie stars like Chuck Norris and even the great Bruce Lee.

"I was a stuntman on *The Green Hornet*," LeBell recalls. "Bruce was a hard guy to get to know, always actin' kinda sophisticated. So, when I got tired of it, I'd pick him up, sling him over my shoulder, and run all around the set with him. He'd scream, 'Put me down, put me down.' I reckon I teased him so much I eventually got him to loosen up a little. He got to where he took jokes pretty good — 'specially if ya'd grabbed him 'round the neck."

Lee, like LeBell, had an insatiable thirst for the martial arts. Soon the two were exchanging techniques. Lee loved judo and saw the efficacy of the throws and holds, but he didn't think they were capable of wowing an audience. Americans, Lee thought, wanted the flashy action he gave them in the films:

> "Bruce loved to learn grappling, he ate it up," LeBell said. "He said that people would never go for it in movies or TV because the fights are over too fast and most of the good stuff was hidden from view. He said they wanted to see fancy kicking, acrobatics, and weapons — he was a savvy showman who knew how to give 'em exactly what they wanted. I wish he could be around now to see how well grappling is doing these days. I remember one time he kicked me really hard. I remember thinking it was a good thing he only wore a size six shoe instead of a 14 like me, otherwise that kick would have sent me to China! He was strong for his size, lemme tell ya."

MURDER WAS THE CASE

In 1976, LeBell's life started to look a little like a movie in its own right. Months after being the third man in the ring for the Muhammad Ali–Antonio Inoki match, LeBell found himself in a tangled web of deceit, chaos, and murder.

On July 22, 1976, private investigator Robert Hall was shot through a kitchen window of his Burbank, California, home as he rummaged through the refrigerator for a midnight snack. Hall died with a fresh cherry in his mouth and four more in his hand. Pornographer Jack Ginsburgs was charged with the crime; LeBell was a co-defendant, accused of driving his friend to Hall's house and then taking him from the scene of the crime to LeBell's house to lie low.

The three men had all been friends and business partners in a detective agency and a pharmacy, until, according to police, a business dispute led to a parting of ways — and a vicious feud.

"Mostly it was crazy stuff like having my phone cut off or calling the utilities companies and canceling my water and power. Once [Hall] even had a big bag of garbage delivered to me," LeBell told the *Los Angeles Times*. "I'd also get phone calls at all hours of the night. He would know that I had stunt work, so he'd call me at 3 a.m. . . . But it was Jack's life that Hall had turned into a nightmare with a lot of the same sort of stuff, plus constant threats to kill him."

Tension between business partners had escalated when someone set LeBell's truck on fire the month before the murder. LeBell blamed Hall and violence seemed imminent. LeBell blamed these pranks on Hall's drug use.

Police Captain Jack Egger, a friend of all three men and a frequent guest of LeBell's at the Olympic Auditorium for the wrestling matches, was central in bringing the accused killers to justice. Ginsburgs had actually called Egger to tell him they were going to take care of Hall, then called him again from LeBell's house to tell him the job was done. Egger didn't believe his friend was serious until Hall's widow called him, crying hysterically.

Egger threatened to turn the two men in for the shooting. Ginsburgs in turn threatened the life of Egger's son, and the police officer initially caved in to the pressure, providing LeBell an alibi and keeping the truth hidden. Eventually, wearing a hidden wire, he was able to get both men to confess.

According to court documents, LeBell told Egger, "The man did not deserve to live because he was on the earth the last couple of years to do harm to whomever he touched. . . . How do you say, 'Get off my back' without going out and risking beating the shit out of him and ending up in jail or something like that? I have thought a million times of getting him alone, but not to kill him, to giving him a permanent injury where there was no witnesses . . . . I always picture killing him by breaking his neck, you know, making him quiver."

LeBell, allegedly knowing what Ginsburgs intended, drove to Hall's home and parked a half a block from the house. He waited there until Ginsburgs returned and told the wrestler, "I did it. I shot the son of a bitch." With confessions recorded, both men were looking to do serious time. Ginsburgs was convicted and sentenced to life. A six-man, six-woman jury acquitted LeBell of the murder charges but convicted him as an accessory after the fact. LeBell was sentenced to a year in county jail, but was free on $3,500 bail while his appeal was processed. His sentence was overturned in 1979 when an appeals court ruling cost the prosecution all the statements LeBell had made about the Hall murder. LeBell was a free man.

SEAGAL SAGA

Through the murder charges and legal battles, LeBell continued to work in Hollywood. The week before his sentencing, he was still serving as Henry Winkler's wrestling coach on *The One and Only* movie set. His career never missed a beat.

Today, everyone in the movie business knows Gene LeBell. LeBell is still doing stunts, recently falling out of a casket on the ABC detective show *Castle*. According to coworkers he's gregarious and fun to work with — unless you're a bully like action star Steven Seagal.

Seagal is well known for throwing his weight around on set. He is rough with stunt men and tries to physically intimidate them with a bizarre habit of randomly kicking them in the balls. Former Pride announcer Stephen Quadros, one of the fight trainers on Seagal's movie *Exit Wounds*, describes one memorable occasion when Seagal had him in his sights:

> *I kind of steered clear of him for the most part. But one time he came on the set and started walking right towards me. I thought, "Shit, I don't have my cup on!" So he walks close to me and my radar was up. Then he grabbed my wrist. I am not an aikido guy and I'm not saying I am better than Seagal at wristlocks but my first instructor was Korean and had taught us hapkido, which included many techniques that were similar to aikido. So I reversed his grab to where my hand was on his wrist.*
>
> *He grabbed the same wrist with his other hand. I reversed him again. This little game went on for about a minute. I was really trying not to upstage the guy because on a movie set it's a no-win situation to do that to the star, especially him. But I for sure was not going to let him get me into a compromising position physically. I know guys he has hurt to the point of having to have surgery. He suddenly stopped and pointed at me and said, "You're good." I didn't know what to say so I just smiled. He walked away.*

Seagal's legend in Hollywood as a legitimate tough guy grew as his movies found an audience. Seagal told anyone who would listen about his work for the Central Intelligence Agency when he lived in Japan, and his mastery of aikido and sundry weapons. The press and the studios ate it up. Even his ex-wife refuting the story didn't stop the legend of Steven Seagal, according to a scathing article in *Vanity Fair*.

> *Seagal's not-so-secret history, it must be said, was a PR masterstroke, the beauty of it being that the CIA never comments on personnel matters — if Tori Spelling claimed to be an agency assassin, no one could disprove her. So on Seagal went, self-mythologizing in the grand Hollywood tradition."*

When LeBell met Seagal on the set of *Out for Justice*, things didn't go well for the actor. Like much of the LeBell myth, the story varies depending on who's telling it. Some say LeBell was standing up for the battered and embattled stuntmen on the set. In *Blood in the Cage*, reporter Jon Wertheim writes that Seagal was incredulous the 50-something LeBell could choke him out. Seagal didn't believe anyone could get close enough to him to execute a choke:

> *Seagal joked to him, "Old man, these guys are saying you could choke me out."*
> *"I've been around since the Last Supper," LeBell is said to have responded. "I'm so old, my first movie was* Birth of a Nation. *But I could choke you out? Yeah."*
> *With that, he grabbed Seagal, threw him to the ground and choked him out.*

Seagal, who claimed he wasn't ready, wanted another go. This time, when LeBell choked him out, Seagal is rumored to have defecated himself. LeBell won't talk in detail about the incident on the record — it doesn't look professional and Seagal has a reputation of harassing people who embarrass him. But that doesn't mean LeBell won't talk about the incident off the record to anyone who will listen — including UFC announcer and comedian Joe Rogan, who shared his LeBell encounter with his podcast audience.

"Gene never really tells you the whole story," Rogan said, shifting into a pitch perfect imitation of LeBell. "Steven was saying no one could choke him out, you can't choke him out. He had this move that would stop you from choking him out. So I said, 'All right, Steven, let's try it.' I get him in the headlock there, the rear naked, and [he] takes his free hand and karate chops me right in the old sisters. . . . Well, I guess he got tired after doing that and he just fell asleep. And I guess maybe he forgot to go to the bathroom, so he went to the bathroom then."

LeBell is still active on the mat to this day. His students, like Karo Parisyan, have competed in the UFC, and another student, Neil Melanson, is training the next generation of fighters. "There's one Gene LeBell and there's only one you can claim," Parisyan said. "He's an amazing person. He's a great guy. And he had that style, that catch wrestling style. . . . He helped us out with those techniques but at the same time he was more of a mental coach too. Never say never. There was no die in the guy. So that's what really helped us out in our careers."

Most assume that a young Gene LeBell, transported into the modern world, would excel in the sport. He's not so sure he would have even pursued it.

"Maybe not. I do stunt work, and when you're making $200,000 or $300,000 a year doing stunts and collecting residuals, why the heck should you get beat up? There's only 1 in 1,000 MMA fighters who make money," LeBell told BlackBelt.com. "Same in boxing. A lot of fighters are broke. The only thing I have against MMA is they don't have a retirement plan. In the stunt world, I get a pretty doggone good retirement from SAG and AFTRA — and I can still work."

BAD NEWS

A decade after LeBell was in his judo prime, a young star exploded onto the scene, stunning observers and opponents alike with his physical prowess and knack for "the gentle way." Allen Coage grew up hard in Harlem in the 1960s. Just going to and from school was a daily struggle. Fighting was part of his life when he saw a sign in concert pianist Jerome Mackey's dojo that read, "Don't Let the Hood Beat You Up and Take Your Money."

Coage was soon as hooked by judo as he had been by that sign, ascending the ranks with shocking speed and ease. Something about judo just clicked with Coage. He hadn't been a natural athlete, describing himself in high school as a kid with two left feet. He was a baker and worked nights, covered in flour. The days he spent on the mat. *Black Belt* magainze reported,

> An Allen Coage comes along once in every generation. He has climbed from white belt to black belt in two-and-a-half years, winning some local tournaments along the way, and in five years of grudging practice at Mackey's luxurious dojo has been promoted to san (third) dan. . . .
>
> . . . Many others saw Mackey's posters, but unlike most people who might have observed them, perhaps taken a lesson or two and waited for God to strike them with black belts (which has never happened) and then gave up, Coage was different. He immediately set for himself an intensive training schedule of three hours daily, four days a week.

In 1966 Coage won the heavyweight AAU championship. A year later, he brought Pan Am gold back to Harlem. In 1970 he traveled to Tokyo to study judo full time at Nihon University, a prelude to making a serious run on the world stage. He hurt his knee at the 1972 Olympic Trials, eventually necessitating surgery, and in 1976, internal politics almost cost him another opportunity at the games. When organizers changed the structure of the trials mid-event, Coage and his opponent bowed to each other and simply walked off the mat, refusing to compete even with television cameras rolling.

It took a lawsuit to get him another shot at that Olympics, but he made the most of the opportunity, becoming just the second American to medal in the sport, when he fell just a fraction of a point short of the silver. It was the end of the line for his judo career — the world of pro wrestling was beckoning.

But even a historic bronze medal didn't pay the bills. "I was always broke," he said. "I came home from the Olympics with 60 cents in my pocket. [As a pro wrestler] I was getting paid. So I was happy."

The fighter took to wrestling even quicker than he took to judo, earning him a spot with New Japan Pro-Wrestling. "Training for wrestling was a breeze compared to my judo training. Wrestling was very easy for me. New Japan Pro-Wrestling took care of me and booked me at various venues. I listened to advice given to me from the veterans. Most young guys out there have had six matches and think they know it all: you never stop learning and asking questions if you want to be good at what you do."

MR. HITO SCRAMBLES FOR SAFETY, BUT BAD NEWS'S DIVE FROM THE TOP TURNBUCKLE LANDS RIGHT ON TARGET

While Coage was famous in wrestling circles for his judo accolades, his real claim to fame was a confrontation with Andre the Giant on a tour bus in New Japan. Andre had been making racist jokes and Coage, an African American, demanded they stop the bus. He got out and challenged the Giant to come and settle things man to man. "The Giant looked out the window and never made a move," Bret Hart wrote in his autobiography *Hitman: My Real Life in the Cartoon World of Wrestling*. The next day at the hotel, Coage renewed his challenge. Finally, the Giant backed down and apologized.

Hart's family would become all too familiar with "Bad News" Allen Coage in the years to come. He was the lead heel in Bret's father Stu Hart's Stampede promotion for years. His propensity for in-ring savagery was legendary. Even Tom Billington, the reckless

"Dynamite Kid" who helped popularize the ladder match and took enormous risks in the ring, often thought his matches with Coage were out of control:

> *It was as if he didn't know you. I've had a lot of hard matches in my career, most of them in Japan because that's how they like their wrestling, but the matches I had with Bad News were something else.*
>
> *Violence was a main feature of all our matches, and I could guarantee we'd both end up hurt. If Bad News picked up something to hit you with, a plank of wood, a chair, a bottle, you had to move fast because he would hit you. He didn't care.*

Announcer Ed Whalen was so put off by Bad News's violent matches and interviews that he briefly quit the promotion. The athletic commission in Calgary also suspended Coage. Fake or not, the matches were brutal. Coage hit Billington with fire extinguishers and chairs, and once even took a swing at him with a real axe.

To Coage, this didn't seem extreme. "That's the way Tommy and I approached it. He'd lay in with the chops and the punches and I would do the same. When the audience saw it, they thought, 'This is the real thing.'"

By the time Bad News hit the big time, in Vince McMahon's WWF, it was 1988 and the Olympian was 45 years old. McMahon changed the wrestler's name to Bad News Brown, allowing McMahon to control the intellectual property, and inserted Coage into his circus-like promotion.

Bad News Brown was a succesful midcard heel, but never really got a big run on top of the promotion. He wrestled Randy Savage and Hulk Hogan for the world title on a number of occasions, but his highest profile match was probably a *WrestleMania VI* bout with Roddy Piper. It's also one of Coage's least favorite bouts. Piper painted himself half black for the match, a move Coage strongly objected to.

After two years in the WWF, Coage was fed up and ready to move on. The money was good, but everything else associated with the business was driving him crazy. Coage calls McMahon a "back-stabbing egomaniac who wants to put himself over and screw the rest of the world," and explained, "Vince lied to me constantly. When I would confront him he always told me what he thought I wanted to hear and the second I turned my back he stuck the knife in it. There wasn't a day that went by during my contract with him that I didn't want to kick his scrawny, lying ass."

Though Coage walked away from the WWF, he never completely left wrestling behind. He went back to Japan to work shoot style for the UWFi, but age and injuries limited him. He stayed a part of the scene and loved the UFC, even helping train young Canadian wrestlers, including UFC fighter Krzysztof Soszyński.

"I met him after he had two hip replacement surgeries," Soszyński said. "He was still on the floor in his 50s, still grappling with the kids he was teaching. I could definitely imagine how tough he was back then and how well he would have done if [MMA] had been around. He traveled extensively to Japan as well, learning aikido and jiu-jitsu. I had the privilege of meeting him during one of my circuits across Canada. He invited me out for a two-week camp at his place in Calgary and that's where he showed me a Kimura and an arm bar. I was hooked. Immediately after that two week training camp, I came back to Winnipeg, quit wrestling, and took up Brazilian Jiu-Jitsu. Six months later I had my first fight. So, he was very instrumental to me turning into a mixed martial arts fighter. If it weren't for him, I wouldn't be here. I'd be doing something else."

While Coage proudly represented an Eastern art in the heart of North America, the Japanese were embracing the western tradition of professional wrestling. An icon was being created in Tokyo by master gameplanners — and the ultimate chess piece was the most famous athlete in the world.

The stabbing death of Rikidozan, Japan's most popular wrestler and a cultural icon, was a blow to Japan's wrestling industry the country almost never recovered from. Only two supremely gifted protégés held the business together. Shohei "Giant" Baba and Antonio Inoki were the two top titans of Japanese wrestling after Riki's death. They had trained together in the early part of 1960 and made their debuts on the same September 30, 1960, card at Daito Ku Gymnasium in Tokyo. Baba, a former baseball pitcher and a giant at 6'9", soon overshadowed Inoki. Despite Inoki's athleticism and natural charisma, no matter how special the performance, he would always remain in Baba's shadow.

16 THE INOKI LEGEND BORN

Inoki may have been the better performer, but Baba, towering over a foot above the average Japanese male, was a spectacle unto himself. Baba didn't excel in just Japan: he was an almost immediate main-eventer in the United States as well. During one memorable tour of the United States in 1964, Baba challenged Lou Thesz for the NWA title in Detroit, Bruno Sammartino for the WWWF title in New York, and Freddie Blassie for the WWA title in Los Angeles. Inoki, by contrast, never made a big splash in the States.

With Baba in the lead role, the two men became tag team partners and took the Japanese Wrestling Association to new heights between 1967 and 1971. In *The Top 100 Pro Wrestlers of All Time*, John Molinaro explains, "Baba's straightforward, clean living persona sanitized the corrupt image of the industry that Rikidozan had left behind, opening the doors of Japan's major venues to pro wrestling once more. With Baba as its top drawing-card, the JWA enjoyed a renaissance, successfully renewing the archetypal Japan vs. America morality play first made famous by Rikidozan."

As the JWA prospered, Inoki and Baba became less satisfied by their paychecks. Perhaps outgrowing their roles as mere wrestlers, the two attempted a coup in 1971. When they were sniffed out and crushed, Baba was welcomed back. Inoki was taught a lesson. He was fired in December, but landed on his feet, forming New Japan Pro-Wrestling in

1972 with old friend Hisashi Shinma. Baba would end up leaving the JWA later that year, forming his own All Japan Pro Wrestling promotion in October.

A fierce battle brewed between the two men behind the scenes. Baba was a known quantity and received the backing of the National Wrestling Alliance. Inoki had to settle for scraps, his top star a journeyman Belgian shooter named Karl Gotch who he pushed as the top "real" wrestler in the world. Gotch had helped train many of the Japanese wrestlers, including Inoki, and was regarded behind the scenes as the toughest man in Japan. The two headlined the first New Japan card with Gotch pinning Inoki to set up the chase. That October, when Inoki pinned Gotch to win the "real" title, it was the crowning moment of his career. Finally, he stood on top of a promotion as the world champion. It was the beginning of a lifelong obsession for Inoki to be the most legitimate wrestling star on the planet.

New Japan scored a coup when Seiji Sakaguchi, a judo player who was the third biggest star in the country, went with Inoki over Baba. Inoki needed the star power more. With access to top NWA stars like the Funks, Harley Race, and Jack Brisco, Baba had no shortage of opponents. Inoki had to be more creative. After inventing a title to take from Gotch, he bought his next world title. New Japan invested in the National Wrestling Federation, a struggling promotion out of Buffalo and Cleveland, to allow Inoki to fulfill two dreams — winning a world title and becoming a star in America.

BABA LOCKS KARL VON STEIGER IN A TIGHT ARM-WRINGER.

The dream turned into a nightmare shortly after the big title win. Inoki couldn't attract an audience and they had to close the American promotion. With his supply of foreign talent dried up, Inoki instead took on fellow Japanese star "Strong" Kobayashi, champion of Japan's distant third promotion, the IWE. The two drew a big crowd, but not one to be outshined, Baba countered with his own holy grail win — a run with the NWA title. By paying champion Jack Brisco for a one-week title reign, Baba became the first Japanese star ever to win the wrestling industry's top title.

The NWA title was wrestling's crown jewel and solidified Baba as one of the business's top players. Matching this accomplishment was no easy task. Inoki and Shinma, to their credit, came up with an idea that was designed to shake the business to its core, an idea that was conceived to make Inoki a bigger star than Baba could ever dream of being.

Inoki wanted the world to believe he was a top flight martial artist. He signed Wilhelm Ruska, an Olympic judo gold medalist, for a match in February 1976. But beating Ruska was just the appetizer. Inoki and Shinma had already made a deal for the biggest wrestling match of all time — Inoki vs. Muhammad Ali in Tokyo's Budokan Hall.

THE CHIN VS. THE LIP

Before the match Ali was at the height of his powers. He was set to earn more than $17.4 million in 1976, causing *Jet* magazine to call him one of the most successful black businesses in the country. Mego made a special Ali toy, he had dinner in the White House with President Gerald Ford, the Smithsonian declared his gloves to be monuments of American history, Dean Martin roasted him on national television, and ABC's *Wide World of Sports* gave him his own television special, essentially to talk about himself.

The fame had come at a great price. A year removed from the "Thrilla in Manila," his third and final bout with archrival Joe Frazier, Ali wasn't the boxer he had been a few years before. There were already rumblings he should retire — and it was universally agreed that a match with a professional wrestler would be a disgrace. Red Smith, the nation's leading sports columnist, wrote: "Perhaps it is naive to feel that a world champion ought to comport himself like a champion. After all, boxing is show business, more so than ever now that every performance by the champion is a multimillion-dollar production. Maybe it is unrealistic to expect more of a champion than a succession of pratfalls on the burlesque circuit. Nevertheless, some do mourn the Sweet Science."

The match went forward despite the protests from the boxing hoi polloi. There were six million reasons for the show to go on — the six million dollars Ali would take home for the bout, the biggest paycheck of his long career. Top Rank promoter Bob Arum, who masterminded the event, didn't have to work too hard to keep Ali interested. The champ was a long-time pro wrestling fan, often crediting wrestler "Gorgeous George" Wagner as one of the inspirations for his own bombastic pre-fight interviews.

Originally he believed the match would be all in fun — a night of wrestling action that would make him rich and make Inoki's career. The plan was to finish the evening's contest with some classic pro wrestling role-play: "Ali would pound on Inoki for six or seven rounds. Inoki would be pouring blood. Apparently, he was crazy enough that he was actually going to cut himself with a razor blade. Ali would appeal to the referee to stop the fight. And right when he was in the middle of this humanitarian gesture, Inoki would jump him from behind and pin him. Pearl Harbor all over again."

What Ali didn't count on was the vehemence of the public's response to the potential bout. As the two toured the country with the legendary wrestling bad guy Freddie Blassie, chosen for the role because he was a well-known heel in both America and Japan and had the gift of gab, they were met by a skeptical press. Ali was feeling the heat. The martial arts community was equally skeptical of Inoki. For years they had wanted to test a boxer against an Eastern martial artist. Having that opportunity wasted on a fake wrestler stuck in their craw. Donn Draeger, probably the foremost martial arts historian of the time, told friends the bout was sure to be a setup:

> *Inoki can't wrestle, but looked fierce and could be taught to roll around. . . . Inoki, like Baba, is not world champ except in his own billing.*
>
> *Inoki's recent "defeat" of Wilhem Ruska was a farce. Ruska could murtilize him if he was allowed to do so; so could Anton Geesink. The whole thing with Ali is a promotion gimmick.*

Still, Inoki and Ali continued to hype the match, tearing each other down in the media at every opportunity. Ali dubbed Inoki "the Pelican" in reference to his large chin. The Japanese wrestler told American reporters he had a unique method of preparing his now famous jaw for Ali's power — having martial artists step on his face with their heels 100 times a day to strengthen it. "When I was young I was very embarrassed by my chin and I went to a plastic surgeon to have it changed," Inoki said. "He said it would be a good trademark. So I kept it. And he was right."

The plan to make more money was relatively simple. Each major city would feature the match on closed circuit, showing Ali on a big screen after a night of local action. Ali and Inoki were touring the whole country to drum up interest, but in the wrestling world, only Vince McMahon Sr. took a real interest in promoting the event. The NWA, initially scheduled to play a big role with champion Terry Funk taking on boxer Henry Clark in a mixed match, ended up having little to do with the spectacle. Ali was getting plenty of attention on local news outlets throughout the country. On wrestling programming in most territories, however, the bout wasn't heavily pushed.

But in New York, where the press set the trends, the show was a hot topic, getting lots of play in the local media. McMahon planned a big show to take advantage of the interest and get the crowd ready for the main event on closed circuit television. His top star Bruno Sammartino would be looking for revenge against Stan Hansen, a rising prospect who had broken Sammartino's neck in a storyline and in real life. Underneath the title bout was wrestling's top attraction Andre the Giant taking on Chuck Wepner, a tough boxer who had gone the distance with Ali the year prior. With that amazing lineup, McMahon hardly needed Ali and Inoki to put 32,000 in Shea Stadium. The boxer versus wrestler matchup was just icing on the cake.

In the weeks leading up to the fight, Ali made the talk show circuit and even did some pro wrestling. He did a run in during a Gorilla Monsoon match on WWWF television and the former amateur standout, by then a bloated 400 pounds, put Ali on his shoulders with an airplane spin and dropped him on the mat like a sack of potatoes. On ABC's *Wide World of Sports*, a disgusted Howard Cosell called the action for what was purportedly an Ali training session with two wrestlers, but what in actuality was some obvious pro wrestling tomfoolery. Ali took a back breaker, a jobber bladed, causing guest referee Verne Gagne to stop the action, and bad guy manager Bobby Heenan took an outrageous pratfall for an Ali punch that missed by at least a foot. Cosell was beside himself. "The thing is, in all this nonsense," the announcer who had rode Ali's coattails to fame and fortune said, "Ali could get hurt."

Heenan remembers Ali as a savvy guy, hip to the wrestling business and how they made their magic:

> Before he met with Ali, Verne Gagne told us not to "smarten up" Ali to the wrestling business. The plan was that he was going to knock off Kenny Jay real quick. Verne told Ali to be careful when he was boxing Buddy Wolfe because he opened up easily over the eyes.
>
> Ali said, "OK, I'll hit him a couple of times so he can back away and cut himself."
>
> Ali was "smart."

Despite themselves, members of the media were sucked into the "boxer versus wrestler" debate. It was an argument that had raged for centuries. Some recalled William Muldoon throwing the legendary John L. Sullivan to the ground. Others remembered champion boxer Jack Dempsey beating the hell out of wrestler "Cowboy" Luttrell. Everyone had an opinion, and wrestlers around the country, never shy about getting some free press, sounded off with theirs. "It would last less than a minute. I'd immediately go to the floor," Pat Patterson said. "Ali would try to dance, but he'd have no chance. I'd get him somewhere in the legs and bring him to the mat. After that, God help him."

Everything changed when Ali actually made it to Japan. Either the boxer, or more likely someone in his camp, had second thoughts about going through with the wrestling match. It wasn't losing that bothered them — it was being associated with something designed to con the world. Ali had started playing the game, going corporate. Being involved in a scandal was bad for his long-term interests. Behind the scenes, according to Meltzer, he was also making the Japanese contingent very angry. Operating from the "plush Keio Plaza Hotel" where New Japan was footing a $2,166 nightly bill, Ali was letting Inoki have it in the press. Reported the *Wrestling Observer*:

> When Ali arrived in Japan ten days before the fight, the media was following him everywhere. Ali and Inoki were doing press conferences constantly, with Ali

breaking up the house with his jokes about Inoki, calling him "The Pelican" and saying how nobody knew Inoki and he was making Inoki famous. In Ali's mind, he was telling the truth, because nobody in the U.S. did know Inoki, but in Japan, it was an insult, equivalent to an arrogant foreign soccer star coming to the U.S. and claiming that nobody in the world had ever heard of Tom Brady, Peyton Manning, or LeBron James. Every press conference ended with mock pull-aparts, with Blassie, 58 at the time and only a few years past the days he was selling out arenas on his own due to his mouth, surprisingly low-key. Even he recognized he couldn't match the kid who grew up watching him and copying him, when it came to promoting a fight, with his main role being to hold the champ back when Ali would pretend to want to go after Inoki.

Chaos reigned behind the scenes as Ali let it be known that plans had to change. It looked for a time like the bout might be canceled. Inoki couldn't afford that — they had spent a fortune promoting the bout around the world. Canceling it would be an epic disaster. Ali's people knew they had the Japanese in a tough place and weren't afraid to take advantage of them. It was decided the two men would compete in a real contest instead of a wrestling match.

The rules they negotiated were draconian. Inoki would be allowed almost no offensive techniques. He wasn't allowed takedowns below the waist. Without gloves, he couldn't throw a closed fist punch. He wasn't allowed to kick to the head or body. Although Greco-Roman throws were allowed, Inoki's famous back suplex was explicitly banned. On the ground, no submissions or ground and pound would be legal. Worse still, Ali could get the fight back to the standing position by grabbing the ropes. Essentially, Inoki's main tool to win the fight was a karate chop. They were rules that seemed to inevitably lead to a cautious performance from the Japanese star — what other option did he have but to survive?

Ali almost backing out changed the tone of the event in the final days leading into the match. What had been a laid-back affair took on a different demeanor entirely. The press covering the bout seemed to note the change. In the *New York Times* on the day of the fight, reporter Andrew Malcolm quoted no less than four people talking about how serious the bout had become. Interest in Tokyo was fierce. Ringside seats were going for $1,000. Tickets just to see Ali work out were $175. Sparring partner Jimmy Ellis crystallized what most were thinking. "Ali's been in combat so many times and they've been for real," Ellis said. "A lot of Inoki's have been fake."

What followed was an amazing 15-round affair. Inoki devised an extraordinary strategy, dropping immediately to the ground in a crab-like position and spending 45 minutes pot-shotting the boxer's legs. Ali landed only five punches the whole fight. By contrast, Inoki scored with 64 kicks to the leg, some of them hard and stinging, even knocking the

INOKI'S FEARSOME KNEEDROP, PAUNCHED FROM THE TOP TURNBUCKLE ON STAN HANSEN

© BOB LEONARD

boxer down on several occasions. Although no one outside the kickboxing community really understood the power of leg kicks in 1976, the effects on Ali were obvious. He was limping by the end of the bout and had no idea how to defend against the technique.

Fans in 37 countries wished they could have joined the crowd at Budokan in booing the display. The boos started as early as the second round and by the end of the night the crowd was furious. *Sports Illustrated*, on the scene for the bout, noted it wasn't phony. But that was the only nice thing they had to say:

> *It was more like a tea ceremony, or watching a man getting a haircut, than a fight.*
>
> *Inoki turned out to be a fraud of the first rank — not even a good illusionist, as some are in his trade. He was just an ordinary wrestler with a good pair of legs and a lot of money with which to accommodate his strange whims, one of which was to challenge Ali. For 15 rounds he moved around the ring on his back — like a crab with his belly up. For his part, Ali clowned, sticking his tongue out and gesturing to Inoki to stand up and punch with him, meanwhile staying close to the safety of the ropes. The rules said Ali could stop the action — action? — by grabbing the ropes. The scene left one to meditate on his own sanity and the Japanese word wakarimasen, which means "I can't understand."*

Throughout the match Ali taunted Inoki to no avail. "Inoki sissy . . . Inoki fight like a girl," the champ roared. But over and over again Inoki flopped to the mat and made mincemeat of Ali's legs. Ali's legs were so bruised and battered that his personal doctor Ferdie Pacheco was concerned the bruises could easily become blood clots. His match with Inoki, supposed to be a farce of an evening and the easiest $6 million a man had ever made, had lasting effects on his career.

"I wouldn't have done this fight," Ali told reporters in his dressing room after the fight, "if I'd known he was going to do that. Nobody knew this was going to happen. So we had a dead show. It all proved boxers are so superior to wrestlers. He didn't stand up and fight like a man. If he'd gotten in range, I'd have burned him but good."

The match had immediate effects on both men's careers. Ali was more injured from Inoki's assault than anyone knew at the time. He left Tokyo to go on a USO tour entertaining troops in South Korea. It was a mistake. When he returned to Santa Monica, California, he was forced to check into St. John's Hospital with blood clots in his legs. His boxing career, already on a downhill slide, was never the same.

For Inoki, the effects of the match were more financial than physical. He had wanted to ride the wave of the bout to worldwide fame and fortune. Instead, he was a laughingstock. Although in the immediate aftermath he announced he was satisfied with his performance, after several months of weak box office gates for his New Japan Pro-Wrestling promotion he began to have second thoughts.

"I think perhaps last summer I was too serious," Inoki said. "I was doing my best to win. It wasn't a fake fight or it would have been more interesting. I think I should have stood up more and taken a beating from Ali even if it led to my defeat. Then, at least, that way the audience would have enjoyed it more."

In 1977 Inoki went public, blaming the ridiculous rules for the dull match and suing Ali in Tokyo District court, seeking $743,333 for financial losses. Inoki proposed an out-of-court settlement: one more match. But despite offering to meet any wrestler in the world in the immediate aftermath of the Inoki fight, Ali had moved on. Inoki, it seems, wasn't the only one who suffered financially from the whole debacle. Ali, who had been promised $6 million, only ended up collecting $2.1 million due to a strange contract that paid in tiers. Ali was guaranteed $3 million by New Japan Pro-Wrestling and their Lincoln National Productions partners. Some of that money, the Japanese contingent explained, was paid in the form of a tax credit. Ali was also promised the first $3 million Top Rank collected for the closed circuit broadcast in America. With a net of just $1 million, that wasn't going to be easy. It was a mess, one that Ali's manager Herbert Muhammad said had an easy solution going forward: "It confirms my principle of getting all the money in the bank ahead of time. I didn't do it this time."

While the match wasn't a financial boon for anyone, despite drawing $2.5 million at the gate and an amazing 46.0 rating on Japanese television, it did receive worldwide attention. Even royalty knew about the bout, as witnesssed by Ali's trip to England later in the year. According to *Time* magazine, Queen Elizabeth herself was familiar with the details of the contest: "After a dinner . . . at the British Embassy that night, the Queen displayed a rather thorough knowledge of the sporting world during a reception for 1,400 guests. 'How are you feeling?' she asked boxer Muhammad Ali, who was still limping from Japanese Wrestler Antonio Inoki's bruising kicks in their recent bout. 'Which leg was hurt the worst?' It was his left, and it was getting better."

For Inoki, time healed all wounds. What was once a legendary debacle became a legendary triumph. He had faced the best boxer in the world with his hands essentially tied behind his back — and survived. With his manager Shinma's help he rebuilt his tough guy reputation with a series of mixed matches with other martial arts stars like "Monster Man" Everett Eddy, Willie Williams, boxer Chuck Wepner, "Bad News" Allen Coage and a host of others. Eventually Inoki was as popular as ever and he even came full circle with Ali, who made the long journey to Japan for Inoki's wrestling retirement in 1998. Just as importantly, he influenced a new generation of wrestlers, one that would take Inoki's desire for legitimacy to a whole new level. Back in America the real wrestlers were almost entirely absent from the scene. But at least one remained — and unlike most of his amateur peers, Jack Brisco had dreamed his whole life of being a pro wrestling champion.

Young men grow up with a lot of different dreams: to be a cowboy, an astronaut, even president of the United States. For Jack Brisco, the dream was always to be the world heavyweight champion.

"I wanted to be a pro wrestler since I was in high school. I followed Danny Hodge very closely of course, having grown up in Oklahoma and I wanted to be just like Danny," Brisco said. "A lot of amateurs didn't like it, but I was a huge wrestling fan. We used to go to the corner drug store every Saturday to look at the wrestling magazines. My favorite was

17 BRISCO: The Last of His Kind

Lou Thesz. I always liked reading about Lou and his travels around the world. It made it seem like an exciting business to be in. I owe my career to those two guys."

Brisco went to Oklahoma State where his career got off to a bang — and then fell completely off the tracks. After winning the freshman title, he had gotten married and had a child. He took two years off to find work and save money, eventually returning as a junior. He lost only once in two years of amateur wrestling competition, falling short in the 1964 NCAA Finals against Harry Houska at 191 pounds. In 1965, he went undefeated and scored three consecutive pinfalls to win the NCAA title.

After that, there was another title on Brisco's mind. He had idolized Thesz, and despite wrestling at just 191 pounds in college, it was the heavyweight gold he had on his mind, not the junior title. Like most Oklahomans, Brisco got his start in the wrestling business in what would later be called the Mid-South territory.

"Within just a few months of being broken into the business by Leroy McGuirk, I was wrestling my hero Danny Hodge all over the Oklahoma territory," Brisco said. "Danny treated me like I was a veteran professional and everything went real good. We even made some money even though I didn't know much about that yet. McGuirk's was a great territory to start in because it was all old timers, guys Leroy remembered from before he lost his vision. It helped me learn a lot real quickly."

Early in his career Brisco felt untouchable. He was cocky around the other boys according to some, because he knew no one could touch him. Danny Hodge quickly showed him otherwise, pulling him out of the car they were traveling in together and walloping him, teaching the young wrestling star that as tough as you are, there's always someone tougher. For Brisco, that man was Hodge and years later Bill Watts says the world champion was still wary of the junior heavyweight star:

> "Bill," he said, "if he hurts me, I'm walking out of the ring."
> I said, "Jack, you've been telling people for years that you can beat him."
> "Yeah," he said, "but you know that's bullshit."

Before 1965 was over he was already a champion, winning the NWA Missouri junior heavyweight title from Don Kent that October. Brisco was another wrestling natural and his flowing black hair, good looks, and amateur background made for a perfect babyface.

Despite his rapid climb, Brisco wasn't an overnight success on the national level. He struggled in Tennessee for Nick Gulas and only had mixed success in Texas for Fritz Von Erich. Despite his amateur credentials he was a glorified job guy for Dory Funk Sr. in Amarillo, the beginning of bad blood between Brisco and the Funks that broiled for years.

"I thought about quitting, I really did," Brisco said. "Old man Funk just had it out for me. They spent weeks building me up, talking about my credentials. Then he had Junior beat me all over the territory in about two minutes. Then I went around the circuit with Terry and it was the same results. Then it got worse. I was NCAA champion and he wanted me to be a referee instead of a wrestler. He just didn't care for me I guess. He didn't think he owed me any explanation."

Even after being taken under the wing of former world champion Lou Thesz, it wasn't until he went to Florida for Eddie Graham that things really fell into place for Brisco. Graham was one of the most respected promoters in wrestling and took a liking to Brisco immediately.

JACK BRISCO, NWA WORLD HEAVYWEIGHT CHAMPION

BRISCO: THE LAST OF HIS KIND

"Eddie was great. Eddie was probably more instrumental in helping my career than anybody. Eddie taught me the figure-four leglock," Brisco said in an interview with the *Wrestling Perspective* newsletter. "That's the hold Eddie used for his finish. Before TV one day, Eddie got me down on the floor in the dressing room and taught me how to do the figure-four.... I used it in that TV match. It was onwards and upwards from there."

With Graham behind him, the future was suddenly awfully bright for Brisco. Terry Funk wrote that Brisco owes much to his powerful benefactor: "While Jack was a great worker, it was Eddie Graham who made him what he was. Eddie, Jack's biggest supporter, was the great manipulator, and he groomed Jack to where Jack had to be a star. Eddie was the right mind to get behind Jack's push. Eddie was capable of seeing Jack's potential and knowing how to get the most out of him."

Bill Watts agreed: "Brisco was a middle-of-the-road guy at best on the cards he wrestled before meeting Eddie. His talent hadn't been developed, and he was very limited in exposure when Eddie found him, brought him into Florida, and started grooming him. Eddie was the one who saw his talent."

FAMILY FEUD: **FUNKS VS. BRISCOS**

The Funks were also a huge part of Brisco's rise to prominence. In Florida, Brisco challenged Dory Funk Jr. for his world title for the first time in 1969. The two would become Florida's hottest attraction, soon taking their act all over the country. As Dave Meltzer explained, being a part of wrestling families (Jack's brother Gerry joined the business that year) made booking compelling programs a snap:

> *The advantage of Funk Jr. being world champion and being part of a wrestling family was established at this point. After Brisco followed it up with his first win over Funk Jr., in a non-title match, as well as pinning Jr. in a tag team match, and being on the verge of beating him in another 60:00 draw, both his father, Dory Sr., billed as the undefeated king of the Texas death matches, and his younger brother, Terry, came into Florida numerous times. The storyline was that Sr. put up a $10,000 bounty for anyone who could cleanly defeat Brisco in a match, and thus knock him out of the No. 1 contender spot. Sr. himself came in, for Texas death matches, and Brisco got over as not only being a great technical wrestler, but as a tough brawler to the local fans, by beating the king of the Texas death matches at his own game.*
>
> *Terry really established himself as a big-time player during this run, as he was the key opponent during a period where Brisco headlined 13 straight weeks of selling out the 5,500-seat Armory in Tampa. Terry would continually try, without*

success, to get the win that would enable Dory Jr. to avoid Brisco in a rematch. Or Brisco would beat other top stars with the same goal in mind, pinning Brisco to knocking him off the No. 1 contender perch, or injuring him, to collect Sr.'s bounty. The matches also frequently sold out the rest of the territory. It was the most successful run in the history of the territory up to that point in time.

While the two Funk brothers were both world champion-level stars, Jack was the clear standout in his wrestling family. "My brother was a tremendous influence on my career and my life," Gerald Brisco said. "Jack was sort of my father figure and my brother figure at the same time. He got into amateur wrestling then I got involved in amateur wrestling. He got into professional wrestling and then I came along in professional wrestling. . . . Of course the feud with the Funk brothers was a natural tie-in. Them being from Texas and us being from Oklahoma — there was always that natural rivalry."

The wrestling world took notice of this compelling program and soon it was being repeated all over the Southeast. It was also Brisco's ticket to the next level, making him a national star.

"I was starting to get name recognition all over the country, [especially] up the southeastern coast," Jack Brisco remembered. "The Florida Championship Wrestling tape was real popular. It went through the Carolinas, Florida, up and down the coast. I was getting quite a name for myself without really realizing it. Sometimes the tapes were going further up north. They were also going into St. Louis. I ended up going to St. Louis to work for a month. After working a couple of matches there, I began selling out the Kiel Auditorium."

Brisco spent years chasing Dory Funk Jr. for the title. The two wrestled hundreds of times, often to 60-minute time limit draws. Finally, in 1973 it was Brisco's turn to pin Funk's shoulders to the mat. But suddenly, according to wrestling historian Ed "Phantom of the Ring" Garea, the Funks were having second thoughts about putting Jack over. The NWA board chose Brisco over Harley Race to be the next world champion. The match was scheduled for March 2, 1973, in Houston, where promoter Paul Boesch spent weeks pushing Brisco strong on television. But Dory Jr. no-showed the match at the last minute, claiming an injured shoulder suffered at his ranch in Texas. When Funk returned to action, he dropped the belt to Race instead of Brisco and all hell broke loose behind the scenes.

Funk Sr. had been one of two promoters who voted against Brisco being given the strap. In Brisco's mind, this was Senior's way of sending a message to the National Wrestling Alliance. Brisco might end up with the title, but he wouldn't be winning it from a Funk. Senior was very protective of his sons and didn't want Dory losing to a fellow technician like Brisco. That would be tantamount to admitting someone else was the better wrestler — something the Funks didn't intend to do, no matter how long Jack had chased Dory for the title. When he lost, it would be to a heel and there would be chicanery involved.

Brisco eventually beat Race that July to claim a brand new world title belt to replace the tattered classic, but he still held a grudge over the four months he spent without the title. To prepare for his reign, he had traveled to all the major territories and lost matches to their big stars. That, the NWA felt, would provide hot matches for his first swing through each territory. When he didn't win the belt, those carefully laid out plans went to waste.

Many in the business were skeptical of the Funks, and in St. Louis they remembered Dory Sr. using a car accident at the ranch as an excuse for missing an important match in 1965. But in his autobiography, Terry Funk makes clear there was an accident, while not shying away from the fact that there was a lot going on behind the scenes as well:

WORLD CHAMPIONS: DORY FUNK JR. AND TERRY FUNK

First, there was a wreck. I saw the truck. The hood ornament was slightly twisted, and there was a little dent in the right front bumper. Junior even had to comb his hair, because it had gotten mussed!

No, I'm just being silly, but that's what the Briscos seemed to assume. The truth is, the truck was totally torn up, and Junior was hurt. . . .

Second, has anybody thought that the Briscos might have been trying to maneuver the Funks out of the picture through Eddie Graham? We had guys biting at our asses — they wanted us out. There's no one-way street in the business, and there never was. But that's the business. Someone didn't just decide one day to make Dory Funk or Jack Brisco world champion, and it suddenly happened. Someone had to push for them — it was a promotional thing, and there was a lot of politicking, on all sides, before votes were cast.

. . . So yes, there were some political struggles between Eddie and Jack and the Funks, but I don't have a single complaint about it. Geez, that's the stuff that makes the past worth talking about.

As far as the Funks were concerned, the way things went down ended up being great for all concerned. It may have hurt Jack temporarily in cities around the country, and they may not have struck when the iron was hottest, but it kept the program with Dory fresh and exciting for years to come.

"That was fantastic for business," said Funk Jr. "Jack beat Harley Race for the belt. He didn't win it from me. When we brought the match into the Amarillo territory, everywhere we did capacity business. It was unfortunate the pick-up truck accident took place, but it was good for him."

Brisco controlled the title for almost three years. He had developed into a fantastic worker, full of fire on his comebacks, and carried himself in a manner that really emphasized his legitimate athletic background. When announcer Gordon Solie ran down Brisco's athletic achievements, fans believed him — because Brisco looked the part. Business wasn't at its best with Jack as champion, but his reign came in the middle of the 1970s gas crisis. Fans were struggling and wrestling wasn't always the first thing on their minds. It's a credit to Brisco that the business stayed relatively strong in a period of economic turmoil.

In December 1974, Brisco, a sharp business man, innovated a new way to get paid. Shohei "Giant" Baba was in the midst of a brutal promotional war with rival Antonio Inoki. To the Japanese fans the NWA world title, carried for so long by the great Lou Thesz, had real meaning. For Baba to carry the belt, even for a short time, would mean the world. Brisco was willing to do the favor for the Japanese star, but it was going to cost him. He negotiated a pay off of $25,000 for a one-week reign. By the standards of the time it was a huge payday — Brisco's previous best for one night had been $2,600.

In the end, the schedule wore Brisco down just like it had Funk Jr., Kiniski, Thesz, and every touring champion before or since. Finally it was time to drop the belt. Brisco was so exhausted he was even willing to lose to a Funk, just to get rid of the belt. The champion recalls, "I couldn't do it anymore. I was mentally and physically drained. The schedule was just more than you can imagine. I spent years on the road with no break. I wrestled every day all over the country, sometimes twice. I was ready to get out and they would tell me, 'Soon Jack. We'll do it soon.' And it went on and on. Finally I just refused to go to their yearly meeting. That riled them up and they finally did something about it. I tried to put that stuff with old man Funk and Junior behind me. I didn't want to waste time being bitter or mad. I liked Terry fine. We had a lot of fun together, but I didn't think he'd be a good champion. I would have dropped the thing to anybody though. I was just ready to have it off my waist."

SHOOTING

Brisco was long considered one of the toughest men in the business. Like most of the tough guys in Florida, he spent time hurting people who wanted to get into the wrestling business, twisting limbs and smashing faces mostly to satisfy promoter Eddie Graham. Graham loved the carnage and always had someone on the roster to stretch the marks. Sometimes it was Buddy Colt teaching them lessons, sometimes Olympian Bob Roop, and sometimes, according to fellow wrestler Jim Wilson, it was Jack Brisco:

> *Jack got in with a young guy with a nice body [who] didn't know anything about wrestling. Jack got him in a full nelson and dragged him down to the mat. With the guy's arms hanging upward, Jack pushed his face into the mat. BLUUP. He mashed the guy's face farther into the canvas, as the blood flowed across the ring. He broke his nose.*
>
> *It was the first time in my life I witnessed deliberate, sadistic breakage of human bones, legs, arms, jaws and noses. As my stomach turned, Eddie Graham experienced near orgasmic excitement as he stood nearby, sweating a little and giggling. It was a weekly ritual that appealed to Graham's perverse sadism and functioned as bizarre public relations for Championship Wrestling from Florida. When guys who were beaten up got back on the street, they told their friends, "Hey, that shit is real."*

But Brisco took the rare thumping too. "Big Cat" Ernie Ladd allegedly laid out both Briscos with a tire iron when they paid him a visit courtesy of Graham. Ladd had been scheduled to drop the Florida title and agreed to do so — but only if the match wasn't taped for television. When he saw the camera running, Ladd left the ring and took off. When the Briscos showed up to teach him a lesson, at the direction of Graham, Ladd was ready, dropping both and putting them in the trunk of his car. Their final destination? Eddie Graham's front lawn.

In the beginning stages of his career, Brisco was tested by another of wrestling's toughest men. Billy Robinson had been trained at the famed Wigan Snakepit and was tough as they come. Brisco, true to form, admitted Robinson was a man to be reckoned with — while making it clear he felt he was still the better man in the ring. The two were working together for Jim Barnett in Australia when things got out of hand one night back at the hotel.

"We had a lot of discussions about which style of wrestling was best," said Brisco. "Billy was a lot like me. He had come from nothing and fought for everything he got. And he was a real tough wrestler. The style he had, the hooking style, it worked with a lot of guys. But I had never met anyone who could get me in the positions to make me vulnerable with it and I told him so. We got to drinking a little beer and we moved all the furniture out of the room. Just me and him, we decided to find out. We would wrestle some, then drink some more beer. Then wrestle some more. We did this for hours. I broke fingers on his hand and his thumb. He had me in some spots too. He really could apply his holds in a real match. We ended up missing our flight, but I proved no one was tougher than an American catch-as-catch-can wrestler."

Later in his career, Brisco was best known for his behind-the-scenes maneuvering. He discovered Hulk Hogan at a Florida nightclub, altering wrestling history forever. He also helped pour gasoline on the 1980s wrestling war, selling his share of the Georgia promotion to Vince McMahon Jr., allowing the New York promoter to control the nation's premiere wrestling outlet, WTBS in Atlanta. That power play led to a final run in Vince's WWF, but Brisco had tired of the wrestling business and didn't have much left to give. Unlike all of his contemporaries, when he called it quits, it was for good.

"I worked for Vince and it was just like being champion again," Brisco said. "He was pushing hard and we were traveling nationwide. Seven days a week. It was a hard grind. I was with my brother Gerry in Pittsburgh. It was winter and I was tired, cold and worn out. We were lost in the parking lot in the snow looking for a car to drive to Philadelphia and I told Gerry, 'I'm getting on a plane south and I'm not coming back.'"

Brisco was among the last of a dying breed in America. Wrestling had become so comical, so over the top, that the amateur community turned on the sport in a major way. The NCAA contenders who were once the backbone of the industry were now few and far between. It was only in Japan that wrestling stuck close to its roots, with real competitors who could handle themselves if things went awry.

Riding his famous fight with Ali, Antonio Inoki became Japan's standout wrestling star. While Shohei Baba had the NWA and its biggest stars in his corner, Inoki had the backing of Vince McMahon Sr. and the WWWF in New York. The relationship gave Inoki's New Japan Pro-Wrestling access to McMahon's roster of stars, including Andre the Giant, champion Bob Backlund, and later a young Hulk Hogan.

New Japan's success led Baba to attempt co-promotion with his rival, but after a single show in 1979, the two groups parted ways. Inoki's promotion was just too hot. It was more than just McMahon's stars and Inoki's reputation from winning matches with martial arts

18 THE UWF and Shoot Style

champions. Inoki and his booker Hisashi Shinma were innovating professional wrestling with a number of great ideas.

In addition to the martial arts matches, Inoki and Shinma created the "interpromotional" angle that would also spark record business in America when Eric Bischoff borrowed the idea for his WCW vs. nWo program in the 1990s. Inoki had noticed that cards featuring matchups with wrestlers from the defunct IWE promotion in Japan drew better crowds than matchups featuring New Japan wrestlers against New Japan wrestlers. With no other promotions to do business with (except the hated Baba) Inoki and Shinma created their own rival promotions. Former Olympian Riki Chōshū turned to the dark side and attacked Inoki's protégé Tatsumi Fujinami. The two men picked their squads and Chōshū's Ishingun, billed as a rival promotion, did battle with Seikigun, led by Fujinami.

The idea led to a box office bonanza in 1982–1983, selling out 90 percent of the shows during the year, an unprecedented level of success. When Inoki went out with an injury in June, business continued to flourish. Suddenly it became obvious that stars like Chōshū and Fujinami, alongside junior heavyweight sensation Satoru "Tiger Mask" Sayama, were just as important to New Japan's success as Inoki had been.

While their popularity was rising, their paychecks weren't. In fact, some wrestlers received pay cuts as Inoki and Shinma allegedly funneled money into some of their failing side ventures. The wrestlers rebelled, with Sayama leaving the company in a fury. Inoki was forced to resign as New Japan's president, but it was Shinma who took the real heat. New Japan's booker and Inoki's right-hand man for years, he was fired from the company he had helped build.

Shinma wasn't done with wrestling though. He created the Universal Wrestling Federation (UWF) in 1984. The idea was for Inoki to leave with him, starting fresh again on their own. When Inoki opted to stay with New Japan, Shinma looked to create a new Inoki with a young prospect named Akira Maeda. Shinma had discovered Maeda in the New Japan years at a karate tournament in 1977 and with his ideal size (6'3", 240 pounds) and a natural athleticism, Maeda was being groomed for big things.

Maeda wasn't the only New Japan wrestler to jump ship. Another top prospect, Nobuhiko Takada also left the company, as did Yoshiaki Fujiwara, a Karl Gotch disciple who was one of the first graduates of Inoki's wrestling school back in 1972. Fujiwara had never been a huge star for New Japan, but his influence was felt keenly behind the scenes.

Fujiwara, a top judoka in college, where the sport is heaviliy focused on the ground game, was one of Gotch's first students and his best. He brought the submission holds of Judo with him and combined them with Gotch's catch-wrestling teachings to create a particularly effective style. When Inoki needed a tough guy to corner him in the Ali fight, he chose Fujiwara.

The UWF wrestlers proclaimed themselves the strongest martial artists in Japan and were open to any challengers looking to contest that claim. When martial artists came calling, they would send them to Fujiwara, who always cleaned house. Fujiwara credited all of his victories to his teacher, Gotch, who he loved and respected for his single-mindedness.

Recalls Fujiwara, "One time during training Mr. Gotch got a very bad toothache. His toothache was interfering with his training. So he went to the hospital, or maybe dentist, and asked them to pull all his teeth out. They said it's dangerous. He said, 'That's OK. Pull all my teeth out.' And he went back to training next day with no teeth. Because he figured if he has no teeth he's not going to have any toothaches getting into the way of his training. He's so crazy but I love him."

Ironically Sayama, who had quit the company over Shinma's handling of New Japan's business practices, joined his former rival in this new venture. Sayama went all in, telling the newspapers that he had quit New Japan because Inoki had been taking advantage of the other wrestlers, and even lashing out at wrestling in general by revealing in his book *Kayfabe* that wrestling was not on the level. This would have posed a problem for UWF, but the company, which started as a standard wrestling promotion using American and Mexican wrestlers up and down the cards, soon shifted styles, proclaiming their bouts to be real shoots.

The matches were innovative and very tightly worked, featuring real submission holds, throws, and powerful kicks. There was serious interest in the major metropolitan centers in Japan, but without a television deal, business faltered. The wrestlers, for their part, did all they could to promote the events, breaking all the unwritten rules by not only acknowledging opposing groups in their interviews, but running them down as fakes and phonies. Dave Meltzer explained, "Maeda himself was the most outspoken, mincing no words about traditional pro wrestling offices having worked matches, and insinuating that the UWF was the real thing. Many fans believed it. However, outside of Tokyo where the matches would overflow Korakuen Hall to a scary degree, the first UWF never caught on as more than a cult thing."

With business in the dumps, Sayama and Maeda feuded behind the scenes. When Shinma took Maeda's side, Sayama demanded his old rival Shinma be removed from the company. The bad feelings festered. Maeda preferred a style that featured submissions heavily while Sayama wanted to see a heavier emphasis on kickboxing. The two ended up taking their disagreement into the ring on September 2, 1985. Maeda kicked Sayama in the groin several times and the match disintegrated into a real struggle. Maeda was eventually disqualified and nine days later, the company called it quits. Sayama left to found Shooto, a promotion that would eventually feature real shooting matches but never caught on with Japanese fans. Maeda and the others returned to New Japan.

AKIRA MAEDA

Despite the UWF's struggles, Maeda and the UWF refugees were much bigger stars upon their return to New Japan. The teenagers and 20-something male fans embraced Maeda and his bad boy persona. He was neck and neck with Inoki as the top star in the promotion. It was the natural match to make after Maeda's return, and at one point a bout was even scheduled — but instead it was changed to a 10-man tag team match at the last minute. Maeda refused to lose to Inoki. As the top star of Japan's biggest wrestling promotion, Inoki certainly wasn't going to do any favors for the loser of a promotional war. Wrestling historian Chris Zavisa believes ego got in the way of good business: "The match would have been a classic. In one corner, Inoki, the charismatic star of the '70s and '80s. The rock around which a successful promotion was built. A living legend in Japan who himself was something of a young rebel at one time. In the other corner, Akira Maeda. The James Dean of Japanese wrestling and the acknowledged heir to Inoki as the superstar of the New Japan promotion. The only thing that separated the two was the calendar. Inoki wanted to keep postponing the day when he handed the reins over to new blood . . . Maeda wanted the top spot at once, or at least within a very short period of time. Neither was willing to sacrifice or even compromise their legend for the other or for the promotion."

Maeda, who had made his name by calling out other wrestlers for being fake, carried himself like his mostly fictional tough guy status was real. He refused to lose to anyone he didn't feel was "legitimate" and made a lot of enemies in the New Japan locker room, both among the other Japanese stars and the Americans who toured with the company. In April 1986, someone convinced the 6'10" 500-pound Andre the Giant to do something about it in a bizarre match that would immediately become part of pro wrestling folklore:

> *The Giant refused to sell for Maeda, shrugging off his shooter gimmick by no-selling submission holds and even going for his opponent's eyes. It wasn't long before the match spiraled out of control, with neither man willing to lose.*
>
> *Maeda attempted to take out Andre's increasingly weak knee, shoot-kicking, then immediately backing away. After 15 minutes, he finally toppled the Giant with a single-leg takedown. . . .*
>
> *In the midst of this chaos, NJPW promoter Antonio Inoki ran down to the ring and called for the bell, not even bothering to explain why. The abrupt ending infuriated Andre, who complained that he wanted to go back in the ring and continue the match.*

The match solidified Maeda's reputation with the fans. He had beaten the Giant, knocking him down, brutalizing his legs, and even asking promoters ringside if he could finish him off. As 1986 rolled on Maeda was quickly becoming the hottest wrestler in the industry. On October 9, 1986, Inoki main-evented a card against boxer Leon Spinks at Tokyo's Sumo Hall that drew 11,000 to the building. The event was also broadcast live nationwide on TV Asahi, attracting an amazing 28.9 ratings share and millions of viewers. The biggest audience for pro wrestling since Inoki's ill-fated bout with Ali saw a dull and plodding main event. But they also saw Maeda steal the show in the semi-main-event slot, wowing the crowd with his "wrestler versus boxer" match with Don Nakaya Neilson. The writing was on the wall for Inoki; only one thing was preventing Maeda from wrestling control of New Japan away from him — television ratings.

While Maeda controlled the hardcore wrestling fans, the UWF style he brought with him to the mainstream was harder for casual fans to support and understand. The over-the-top presentation and style of wrestling they had grown accustomed to had disappeared — and in turn, these fans just stopped watching. The UWF wrestlers were doing gangbusters at the live gate, all while television ratings were plummeting. Eventually, New Japan lost its Saturday night prime-time slot. Something had to change.

In 1987, New Japan brought Riki Chōshū back into the fold. A former Olympic wrestler for South Korea, Chōshū had ridden his amazing charisma and go-go-go style of wrestling to great success. He had shocked everyone when he left New Japan for Giant Baba's All Japan Pro Wrestling in 1984, leading to Baba's best year of the decade at the gate. But Baba was set on his own Olympian, "Jumbo" Tsuruta, as his heir and top wrestler. Chōshū had run into a glass ceiling just like he had in New Japan. He wanted a fresh start in a comfortable old home.

Chōshū's return sparked public interest in New Japan; it sparked anger in Maeda. Now the young wrestler was another step removed from the top spot as Chōshū assumed his role as heir apparent. This boiling tempest of ego and testosterone exploded on November 19, 1987, with a kick heard around the world. As Chōshū held Osamu Kido in a scorpion deathlock, both hands busy applying the hold, Maeda entered the ring. Instead of delivering a safe kick to break the hold, Maeda unleashed a full force kick from Chōshū's blindside right to the face. The tough Chōshū staggered but refused to go down. The "tough" Maeda bailed out of the ring. But not even Chōshū could ignore a broken orbital bone for long. As Dave Meltzer explained, New Japan was stuck between a rock and a hard place: "New Japan was faced with one major predicament. What Maeda did was shoot a kick in the same style worked kicks were regularly thrown in. To make a big deal about it publicly would be basically a public admittance wrestling was a work . . . To ignore it would be even worse for business, because anarchy could take over."

New Japan attempted to punish Maeda with a suspension, followed by paying penance with a tour of Mexico. Maeda, who treasured realism, hated nothing more than the flamboyant Mexican style of wrestling and refused. He had his own plans and a vision of what Japanese wrestling could become.

UWF REBORN

With financial backers in tow, Maeda restarted the UWF in May of 1988. This time the Japanese public was ready for it. Fans had grown accustomed to the style on television and understood the submissions wrestlers used in the ring. And Maeda's hype had worked. According to reporter Alex Marvez, many Japanese fans believed the second UWF was real: "The public in Japan believes UWF matches are 100 percent legitimate. They are, and they're not. UWF wrestlers are told to protect themselves at all times, because keeping the public convinced the style is legitimate is more important than someone getting a broken nose for putting their guard down. Wrestlers are also told not to sell any holds unless they really hurt. One UWF wrestler described the style as 75 percent shooting. [Nobuhiko]

Takada even places a piece of paper with a prayer written on it in his trunks before his matches."

Maeda's success was like nothing the sport of wrestling had ever seen before. The first show at Korakuen Hall sold out in just 15 minutes. By 1989 they were breaking wrestling attendance records starting with a sellout of Budokan Hall as well as an overflowing crowd at three closed circuit television venues to watch Maeda submit Takada, who had become his archrival. In November 1989, more than 50,000 packed the Tokyo Dome to watch Maeda take on Willie Wilhelm. The opponent was just incidental. The crowd was there for Maeda in a mixed match they believed to be a shoot. They had sold out ringside tickets in just five minutes. By the end of the first day tickets had gone on sale, more than 40,000 had been sold. The final gate numbers of $2.9 million set a Japanese record and more than doubled the best live gate in U.S. wrestling history.

A huge part of the credit for the promotion's success has to go to Maeda, who despite his fearsome reputation was actually very giving. Perhaps because he had so much trouble getting to the top spot, he was very generous once he was there. His predecessors like Inoki, Baba, and Tsuruta almost never allowed their shoulders to be pinned to the mat. It would have been easy for Maeda to demand to win every match too. Instead, he realized losing would only help boost interest in the shows.

He was knocked out by rising star Takada in 1988, leading to a huge box office return for a 1989 match in Tokyo. He lost additional matches to Takada and Yoshiaki Fujiwara in 1990. But by then, like the first UWF, internal problems were tearing the company apart. President Shinji Jin and the leading wrestlers had different ideas about where the future lay.

Jin wanted some of the UWF's top talent to work together with Super World Sports, a traditional pro wrestling company that was owned by Hachiro Tanaka. As owner of a major Japanese company, Tanaka had been an important sponsor of the UWF just a year prior. But Maeda was aghast at the idea, refusing to take a step backwards and do a show with "fake" wrestlers.

The battle escalated when Maeda demanded access to the company books and was suspended for his public comments about the SWS deal. When the wrestlers supported Maeda, Jin fired everyone and declared the company closed and the Tokyo Dome show scheduled for December 29, 1990, was canceled.

In 1991 each of the promotion's top stars created their own vanity promotion. Maeda started Rings, a promotion so closely associated with his own star power that the television network would only agree to pay for their shows if Maeda appeared in each. Takada formed the UWF International, working a flashier and more popular style with traditional pro wrestling stalwarts like Big Van Vader (Leon White). But the most memorable spin-off group came from the unheralded Yoshiaki Fujiwara.

Fujiwara took three young prospects with him: Masakatsu Funaki, Minoru Suzuki, and Ken Shamrock. When he tried to follow Jin's lead with a series of appearances on more traditional pro wrestling shows, the three quit. No longer constrained by their elders, they went forward with a truly revolutionary idea. On September 21, 1993, the first legitimate wrestling promotion in Japan's history was born. Pancrase brought back real wrestling after decades of show and spectacle.

The UWF was dead. In the wake of its destruction came three promotions that would make a tremendous impact on professional wrestling. Nobuhiko Takada, long the Robin to Akira Maeda's Batman, finally took the lead role in the UWF International. The group was an instant success. Taking a more over-the-top approach than that employed by the UWF, Takada and his compatriots amped up the pro wrestling theatrics and created a hybrid style that was realistic while also being comfortable for traditional pro wrestling fans. Antonio Inoki's newest American star, Big Van Vader, was recruited to play Takada's top rival, and the group immediately became one of the hottest promotions in the world.

19 THE NEXT LEVEL: The Shoot-style Revolution

Maeda went the opposite direction with Rings, wanting to avoid the specter of pro wrestling entirely. Almost no one associated with the wrestling business had anything to do with Rings. He used sambo specialist Chris Doleman to recruit fighters out of Europe and made strong connections in Russia where he found one of the most amazing pure workers the world of wrestling had ever seen — submission specialist Volk Han. Rings bouts looked more legitimate, even compared to the revolutionary UWF matches. On the undercard they often were real contests, but in the main events, it was an illusion. In reality the bouts looked less smoothly choreographed because the competitors, besides Maeda, weren't experienced pro wrestlers. Their awkwardness was sometimes mistaken for being more "real," when fans were actually just watching poorly performed matches.

The smallest of the three UWF offshoots was Pro Wrestling Fujiwara Gumi. Yoshiaki Fujiwara, the top pupil of Karl Gotch, was the headliner, but at the age of 42 was well past his prime. Fujiwara had been an undercard wrestler for most of his New Japan Pro-Wrestling career and just didn't have the charisma needed to carry a promotion on his back. While Takada took most of the UWF's roster of wrestlers, Fujiwara did manage to score several significant coups. Masakatsu Funaki, once thought to be the strongest prospect in the entire industry, was the biggest. But with him came Minoru Suzuki, a collegiate wrestling standout who was an Olympic alternate in 1984, and rising American star Ken "Wayne" Shamrock.

Megane Super Optical, an eyeglasses chain that also supported the more traditional SWS wrestling outfit, backed Fujiwara, who even sent his young stars to work for the SWS and the ultra-violent W*ING promotion on several occasions. Fujiwara was from the old school. Sure he was an accomplished shooter, but in his mind real contests were for the gym. Professional wrestling was an entertainment business, and he had real doubts about how well shoots would be received by the audience. His young stars balked and soon went in their own direction, leaving Fujiwara to form their own promotion. Pancrase, a name devised by Gotch himself, was an ode to the ancient Greeks who had competed in brutal grappling contests very similar to modern mixed martial arts.

MASAKATSU FUNAKI

While the other shoot-style promotions all claimed to be the real thing, Pancrase wanted to take things a step further than big talk and slightly more realistic work — led by Funaki, the Pancrase fighters intended to provide real shoots up and down the card. The promotion held its first card on September 21, 1993, in the beautiful Tokyo Bay NK Hall. Seven thousand fans packed the building to see a show promoted as "Hybrid Wrestling." The rules were the same as traditional pro wrestling — making it to the ring ropes would cause the referee to break a submission hold and no closed-fist punching to the head was allowed. The difference between these bouts and the thousands that had been held in the building before Pancrase was simple — these matches were real.

The atmosphere was electric, especially when the fighters greeted the crowd prior to the bouts and revealed they'd each lost more than 10 pounds. They were lean and ripped, a product of training for competition rather than physique. After the show was over, no one in the crowd could quite believe what they had seen.

It didn't go exactly as promoters hoped. It turns out that real fights don't last long, especially when only one of the combatants is schooled in submission. These certainly weren't the marathon matches shoot-style fans were used to. The six fights that night lasted a total of 13 minutes and five seconds.

The solution was simple. Experienced fighters like Funaki and Shamrock would take their time with opponents, extending the fights long enough to give the crowd their money's worth before finishing their opponent.

Incorporating worked spots into their bouts was a double-edged sword. It was necessary to make sure the crowd got their money's worth. After all, they were charging fans up to $135 for ringside tickets, a pretty pricey seat in 1993. But that opened up the promotion to all kinds of questions. The fighters were mostly pro wrestlers, so the fans were naturally skeptical. Seeing "spots" they were familiar with from the UWF and other "worked shoots" made them even more suspicious.

Former King of Pancrase Bas Rutten explained, "With Pancrase there was always that suspicion. Because you had the other organization Rings that was 90 percent fake. And Pancrase had the same rules and Funaki and Suzuki had come from pro wrestling. So there were always those questions. Some of the fights I would think, 'That looks a little too good.' But it was always between two of the Japanese guys. I said from the get go, there was no way on earth that I would do this. If they are going to ask me to work a fight it won't happen. I will do it in pro wrestling where everyone knows it's fake. But never when it is supposed to be real."

While still refusing publicly to talk much about what happened behind closed doors in Pancrase, top stars like Shamrock confirmed that they did their best to make the shows more entertaining by allowing less talented fighters to survive more than a few minutes in the ring with them. It was a shadowy world, one where even the participants didn't always know what was real and what was fake.

"It's hard to say. You don't always know what's going on there behind the scenes," Shamrock admits. "I know you go out there and do your best to win, but a lot of times guys came in there and didn't have any experience whatsoever. You didn't want to go out there and just destroy them. You want to go out there and maybe give some encouragement to try harder next time. . . . I can't really talk about those things because of agreements and things that were set down by the organization. I can't really comment on that. I went into the UFC trying to be the best. I wanted people to recognize me as the best and I did accomplish that. Set my mind to do it and I did the same thing in Pancrase. I wanted to be the best there and I did that also."

Former Pancrase fighter Scott Bessac, a behind-the-scenes confidant of Shamrock, was privy to many of the promotion's secrets. "A lot of the fans who knew what was going on would say it was rigged. So, of course all the fighters would say, 'It's not rigged.' But the bottom line is it was mostly shoots but they had works. It would be a fight up until the predetermined ending. And you knew what time it would be. There were works. That's just the way it was. They would come to you personally and ask for a work and you'd get paid a little bit more."

THE WORLD'S MOST DANGEROUS MAN

The early Pancrase standout was Ken Shamrock, a rags-to-riches success story who had come from nothing to become a star in Japan. Shamrock was trouble walking as a kid. Born Ken Kilpatrick in Savannah, Georgia, he knew nothing but violence. Growing up in a primarily African American neighborhood, the youngest of three Kilpatrick boys remembers little from his childhood except constant fights and struggle. He left home early, just 10 the first time he ran away, escaping a disciplinarian stepfather.

No one could handle Ken. He was exiled from his own home, spent time in Juvenile Hall, and brawled his way out of group and foster homes. He was on a path to prison or an early grave when at age 14 he first met Bob Shamrock. Shamrock had worked with hundreds of angry young men and had the perfect remedy, combining two things Ken had been sorely lacking in his life — high expectations and love. It didn't hurt that to Ken, Shamrock's ranch looked like paradise on Earth.

"Ken's eyes got really big. Because he had never seen any place like this and this was my home, his new home," Ken's adopted father Bob Shamrock remembered. "We had a big house, well-decorated with antique furniture. We had a swimming pool. I think it was a lot different than the other group homes he had been in."

Bob Shamrock believed strongly that young people could find redemption in his home. He pushed the kids in his home to find an area they enjoyed and excel. With Ken it was athletics — he ended up as a standout football player and wrestler at local Lassen High School.

"If the kid was an artist, we'd send him to the local community college for lessons. If he liked music we'd give him a guitar and encourage him that way. We had a grand piano and my wife Dee Dee and I both sang and played," Bob said. "But Ken was like a lot of the boys. He was a fighter. And we had outlets for those kids too. We had a rule that allowed kids to fight — but it had to be in the ring with boxing gloves on. And I had to be there. Ken was the house champion, in both boxing and wrestling."

After high school Shamrock drifted. He was an undersized nose guard at Shasta Community College, but school just wasn't for him. He was bouncing, stripping, and competing in toughman contests when he eventually found his way into pro wrestling, working as Vinnie Torrelli for South Atlantic Pro Wrestling. Performing at National Guard Armories all over the Southeast, Shamrock was just learning his trade when his friend Dean Malenko suggested he audition for an opportunity with the new UWF, a wrestling promotion that needed tough guys just like him.

After a tryout in Florida, Shamrock made his way to Japan, where he joined other aspiring wrestlers in the UWF's dojo. His initial tryout was a disaster. Suzuki made him tap to a knee bar and Funaki choked him out, twisted his ankle, and caught him in an arm bar in rapid succession. Shamrock may have felt bigger and stronger than either of the Japanese, but he didn't have the tools to win. When it was all over he was dejected, expecting to be sent home. Instead, impressed by his raw tools and heart, the promotion offered him a place in their training program.

As a "young boy," he served the older fighters by cooking, cleaning, and running errands. He was also learning how to fight — and not just in the ring. Professional wrestling dojos in Japan were notoriously brutal places, filled with mental and physical abuse. But for Shamrock, that was just par for the course.

Bas Rutten recalls, "They would beat the crap out of the young guys. They would hold a kid down and turn his face black with a marker. Or twist his ears with rubber bands to make sure he had cauliflower ears. That was just part of the game. The young boys. They had to do everything, cook, wash the laundry, clean the gym. And they become angry. And the idea is to use that anger to motivate them in their training. It all has a purpose."

Shamrock weathered all of that to become a submission expert. Under the watchful eye of Funaki, already an established shooter, and sometimes Gotch himself, Shamrock learned the basics of hooking. "[Gotch would] sit in the office, drink wine, and occasionally he would come out there and work us until we couldn't walk anymore," Shamrock remembers. It was grueling, but by the time it was all over, Shamrock had learned how to make men squeal in pain.

By the time Funaki told him they were breaking free from Fujiwara to attempt to do what hadn't been done in a century, Shamrock was ready. Not only was he ready to compete, he was busy building his own team of fighters to compete with the Japanese stars already signed up to fight. In 1992, back in California, he started the Lion's Den, which was designed both to help Shamrock prepare for fights and to train new fighters for Pancrase.

KEN SHAMROCK WITH HIS 1996 NWA BELT

"We started training, Ken and I, in his garage, at a local racquetball court, at his dad's house on the living room floor. Anywhere we could because there was no place to train like that. There wasn't even a sport yet. We did that for awhile before Ken finally decided he wanted to open up a dojo. We opened it up on Cherokee Road in Lodi," Bessac said. "It was basically Ken just beating the hell out of us. He had gotten trained by the Japanese in submissions and they worked him hard. They destroyed him over there, with submissions

THE NEXT LEVEL: THE SHOOT-STYLE REVOLUTION

until he was black and blue. That's the only way he knew how to pass it on so that's what he did to me. So that's what I did to everybody else. When Vernon White came in that's what he did with Vernon. So that's what Vernon did to everyone else. It all rolled downhill."

Even as he was building his own training program, Shamrock hadn't lost focus on Pancrase. He beat Funaki in the main event of the first show in September 1993 and became the promotion's first world champion in 1994, winning a tournament to crown the "King of Pancrase." He was also playing a key roll behind the scenes. Shamrock was the official North American talent scout and booker, bringing in fighters he thought were ready for the big show. Jason DeLucia, Guy Mezger, and his adopted brother Frank Shamrock all became top Pancrase fighters under Ken's leadership.

"In Pancrase, I had eight of my fighters in the top 10 at one point," Ken Shamrock remembers. "I was the world champion and Masakatsu Funaki was the top contender. All of the rest were Lion's Den fighters or guys I brought in."

EL GUAPO EMERGES

The Americans, of course, weren't Pancrase's only foreign imports. Like Maeda's Rings, the promotion found plenty of talent in Europe as well, most prominently Bas Rutten, a charismatic Dutch kickboxer with a sculpted physique and great stage presence. Rutten, whose sledgehammer kicks and aggressive style made him stand out in an organization that mostly featured slick ground fighters, was a pet project of Pancrase's promoters.

"[Rings fighter] Chris Doleman was the one who discovered me," Rutten said. "He was watching a martial arts show, one of these comedy shows you might see on YouTube. I would do backflips and a cartwheel. My opponent would grab my foot and flip me back in a somersault. It all looked really cool. And Chris Doleman said, 'Man, genetically you've got something. Maybe you should come to our gym and train with us.'"

"It was called free fight. Rings might not have been real, but the training was of course. I got so blown up the first night I called my wife on the way home and said, 'I am pulling the car over. I am going to take a nap right here.' I was done," Rutten remembered. "I couldn't eat for a couple of days, I could only drink liquid. Because my throat was all messed up because I thought I could tough out chokes. Obviously I couldn't. My wife was laughing. She said, 'So that's it.' I said, 'No, that's not it. I'll be back and within three or four months I'll tap everyone there.' So I started working and training hard."

For all his standup prowess, Rutten had limited skills on the ground. Funaki and Suzuki did their best to teach him the basics, and it was rumored they encouraged some of the other Japanese fighters to put Bas over to help build him up as a star. But according to Rutten, they never asked him to lose a fight.

"Suzuki was always very nice to me, but he was a little shy. So was Funaki. Once you broke the ice with Funaki he was a really good guy," Rutten said. "They actually, after my second fight, invited me to have dinner with the both of them. I thought that was going to be it. Because Chris Doleman had told me, 'Bas, they're probably going to ask you to work the fights.' I was totally prepared to say 'F-U.' We went to dinner and we ate and had a good time. They gave me a book from Fujiwara about submissions. And I said, 'Man, you are actually trying to make me stronger.' They laughed and that was it. So when I walked to get in the cab, I turned around and said, 'I thought you guys were going to ask me to throw a fight.' And Funaki told me right to my face, 'I would never ask you a thing like that.'"

Rutten is adamant that he didn't work any bouts for the promotion. He wasn't opposed to doing pro wrestling, and would actually try it later in his career. But losing a bout marketed as a real fight wasn't pro wrestling — it was throwing a fight. Many of Rutten's training partners worked for Maeda and put over the Rings star and some of the other Japanese fighters regularly. Discussions of their time in Japan created tension among the fighters from different promotions.

"I hated those guys in Rings who would claim they were a champion," Rutten admitted. "The worst part was, they would come to the gym and I'd say, 'How did you do?' And they'd say, 'Well I lost. But you know, Bas, they made me lose.' Okay. But when they came back and said, 'I won,' it wasn't the same story. They never said, 'Oh, they just let me win.' I hated that. I never wanted to look in the mirror and think, 'You know what? You're a fake.'"

THE DARKER SIDE OF PANCRASE

While Rutten may not have engaged in any chicanery, it was all around him. In the early days, multiple fights were worked, often with the intention of creating a new star. Sometimes the fighter who benefited from a work wasn't even involved in the decision-making. One case in point was Lion's Den fighter Jason DeLucia. The Pancrase newcomer shocked fans at Amagasaki Gym, making Funaki tap out to a knee bar in just over a minute. Pancrase had a new rising star to go along with Funaki, Suzuki, and Shamrock.

"From what I understand," DeLucia said, "he was supposed to carry me three rope escapes into the match and miscalculated his distance upon the first rope escape [and had to tap] — it happens. The promoters were very unhappy, needless to say."

For Pancrase fighters, matches like that were just part of the business. It was taboo to discuss, even among friends later in the evening at the wrestler's bar of choice, the Gas Panic in the Roppongi district of Tokyo.

"None of us ever said, 'Hey, Jason, was that a work? You submitted Funaki in like one minute. I think that was a work, dude.' It was between you and them," Bessac said. "We never talked about it, but you knew what the deal was."

It was commonplace for established fighters in Pancrase to make opponents look good. Without new stars, the matches would quickly grow stale, so it was important for Pancrase to create the kind of stars who could draw fans to the arena. Sometimes that meant the fighting arts gave way to the fight business.

"When fight companies are small there is work, it is necessary. For example, in those days a fighter like Matt Hume would not be able to fight Bas Rutten unless it was worked or they didn't care about Bas losing," DeLucia said. "Because if they fought, Matt could go to the ground game, mount, and pound Rutten out in a UFC-style fight. It's just a fact that Matt was schooled as a wrestler and Bas as a Thai boxer. So that's why you never saw Bas fight Matt Hume or Todd Bjornethun. It's a matter of securing business objectives."

Hume agrees. Now a respected fight trainer, Hume was involved in one of Pancrase's most obvious works, a match with Ken Shamrock that included amazing pro wrestling–style suplexes and grappling exchanges a little too smooth to be real. Like most Pancrase veterans, he will only talk about worked fights in the broadest of terms.

"There were pros and cons with the Pancrase organization and fighting in Japan, but overall, it was a good experience and helped shape me into the successful fighter and coach that I would later become. The entire experience in Japan is incomparable to anywhere else in the world. The events have the best organization and showmanship and the fans are the best. Jason DeLucia is correct about many of the fights in Pancrase not being on the level. I can only speak for the time I was there, however," says Hume.

NOBUHIKO TAKADA

Funaki was Pancrase's mastermind, carefully moving the pieces to create contenders and the most interesting matchups. Often he chose himself to take the fall. He was, by all accounts, the most skilled grappler in the promotion. He could have beaten most of Pancrase's neophyte fighters in a legitimate contest — but he was also the best known and most popular wrestler in the promotion. A win over Funaki was a star maker, and as one of the owners of the company he had a lot invested in making new stars, leading to some questionable results.

Sometimes business considerations meant losing to fighters he should have (and could have) beaten like Jason DeLucia, Yuki Kondo, and Rutten. Funaki's wrestling pedigree, good looks, and personal charisma allowed him to lose without losing his fan base. Funaki had a pro wrestling mentality and he didn't think twice about throwing fights. He was also a good worker, able to convincingly build up a handful of fighters that could main-event cards without raising many eyebrows or casting suspicion on the legitimacy of the matches.

Pancrase stood alone as the premiere mixed martial arts league in the world for only two months. In November 1993 the Ultimate Fighting Championship (UFC) joined the brawl, running their first show in McNichols Arena in Denver, Colorado. Shamrock was a breakthrough star there as well, but the style of fighting couldn't have been more different. The UFC was a collection of bar brawlers and traditional martial artists. Many were out of shape and, frankly, embarrassing. The fighting in Pancrase was more technical, the fighters in superb condition, and the presentation more professional.

But the rules, created with sport in mind and to minimize unchecked aggression and violence, favored a certain type of fighter. The gentleman's agreement, in which Pancrase fighters agreed to further restrict the rules and not allow any striking on the ground, led to very interesting and dynamic mat work and also helped extend the length of fights that might have ended very quickly if striking on the ground was allowed. The fighters also wore mandatory boots, complete with shin padding, to lessen the impact of kicks. All this combined to favor grappling experts like the Japanese. Rutten doesn't believe that was a coincidence.

"In my third fight, when Funaki took me in a toehold, ow-wee. I couldn't wear shoes," Rutten said. "My ankle was swollen so badly. I didn't even know what a toehold was at that time. That was the whole reason for the boots, let's face it. The Japanese guys were very good on the ground. And they were less good with striking. So what did they do? They said, 'Let's not wear gloves, let's open our hands. It's good for grappling and chokes but not much good for anything else. And we'll wear shin protection so the impact of the kicks will be a lot less.' Plus the shoes were perfect for leglocks. Everything was adapted for their fighting style."

UWFi

While Pancrase was a hot ticket in Tokyo, no promotion was hotter than Nobuhiko Takada's Union of Wrestling Forces International (UWFi). The promotion started slowly, in smaller arenas throughout Japan, building to a December 1991 show in front of 11,000 at Sumo Hall in Tokyo. Taking a page from Inoki's book, the top two bouts featured UWFi wrestlers taking on American boxers. It was an idea that was just as successful for Takada as it had been for Inoki — in other words, it was an unmitigated disaster.

In the semi–main event Billy Scott went to a 10-round decision with boxer James Warring. Scott struggled to take Warring down, but the boxer was scared enough of the ground game that he never really opened up. It was a monotonous affair, with dozens of rope breaks halting any action in its tracks.

In the main event Takada took on former heavyweight champion Trevor Berbick. The match, scheduled for 10 rounds, didn't make it out of the first. Berbick had held the promotion up for more money at the last minute and Takada went out to teach him a lesson. When the first leg kick landed, Berbick's eyes grew wide. Historian Mike Lorefice says the boxer felt misled by the rules, unaware that leg kicks were allowed:

> *This wasn't intended to be comedy, but I can't think of many funnier matches. Berbick just had no idea what he was getting himself into and came off as one of the great wusses of all-time. Takada started with a low kick and Berbick complained it was below the belt. Takada threw another and Berbick stopped fighting altogether, complaining to everyone. . . . In any case, Takada kept throwing low kicks because they were really rattling Berbick, who was totally clueless to why the ref wasn't warning Takada or deducting points for these "illegal" tactics. Berbick told Takada "no more" and pointed to his knee, but Takada kicked it again and again anyway. Finally, Takada kicked Berbick in the knee when he was in the corner and Berbick said, "What the fuck is this? What the fuck is this?" and hopped out of the ring never to return. Outside, he swore up a storm claiming Takada changed the rules. I don't know how to rate this, but it gets huge marks for perverse entertainment.*

By 1992, UWFi was hitting its stride. With Takada in the main event, the company built to a major show at the Yokohama Arena in May. Fourteen thousand people saw Takada lose for the first time in company history, demolished by 300-pound former University of Nebraska All-American Gary Albright.

The doughy Albright, exactly the kind of legitimate wrestler who would have never stood a chance in the body conscious American professional wrestling scene, had been built as a monster. A legitimate amateur, Albright executed picture perfect suplexes, often tossing the smaller Japanese several feet in the air across the ring. He was undefeated in the UWFi when he met Takada in a rematch that September to crown the promotion's first ever world champion.

Takada beat Albright by arm bar, winning a world title belt that looked somewhat dainty compared to the monstrosities carried around by champions in other wrestling promotions. What it lacked in bulk, the belt more than made up for in legitimacy. It had been the belt Lou Thesz wore in the 1950s, and the great champion himself presented the title to Takada in the middle of the ring.

Thesz told *Pro Wrestling Torch* in a 1993 interview, "The UWFi people knew I have a reasonable amount of credibility over there as you can imagine because I beat their champ. . . . They asked me if I would come over and assist them in getting away from the choreographed tumbling that they have over in this country and also in Japan. . . . I said, 'Sure, I'd like to participate, but I want to come over and talk about and know what we're doing before we get into this thing.' I made a trip over and talked with them and we had a meeting of the minds."

Thesz was just one of the wrestling legends the group used to bolster their legitimacy. Billy Robinson and Danny Hodge, both noted shooters themselves, were UWFi commissioners and their names still carried great weight in Japanese wrestling. It was important to the promotion, despite doing what were obviously worked matches, to present a legitimate face to the public.

"Anybody they used in their promotion was a shooter," UWFi wrestler Mark Fleming said. "Iron Sheik, he was a shooter even though he was old and beat up. Gary Albright. Dan Severn. Dennis Koslowski, an Olympic silver medalist. Billy Robinson, who they brought over to help train us. We had to go to that dojo every day man, and we trained there five hours a day. . . . Lou said, 'Go out there, pummel with them, tie them up and throw them.' He said, 'Hurt the sons of bitches. Hurt them, man.' I'd go out there and throw them but them guys were good. They were smaller but tough guys. And very dedicated."

In 1993, Albright was replaced as Takada's top foil by traditional pro wrestling superstar Big Van Vader. Vader had been a star in Inoki's New Japan and was one of the top heels for Ted Turner's World Championship Wrestling in America. He was the world champion for WCW and still signed to New Japan when he agreed to an eight-match deal with the UWFi. Thesz, alongside one of the UWFi's leading power brokers, wrestler Yoji Anjo, was instrumental in getting Vader to sign the dotted line. At the time it was one of the biggest per appearance deals in wrestling history — the American super heavyweight would take home $200,000 for his eight matches with a $50,000 signing bonus, and an unprecedented $31,250 a match, as well as legal support to escape his deal with Inoki.

Vader was the first big-name foreigner who came into the UWFi without legitimate credentials. A former football player at the University of Colorado, Vader was big, quick, and strong, but he had no martial arts or amateur wrestling training. To the crowd, it didn't matter. Vader hit hard, developing a well deserved reputation in WCW for taking advantage of the enhancement talent (men known in the business as "jobbers"), who he tossed around like 220-pound sacks of potatoes. He once actually paralyzed wrestler Joe Thurman with a hard power-bomb. Former manager Harley Race may have put it best: "Personality-wise, he was a big asshole."

Personality aside, Vader's style, the same style that made him one of the most hated wrestlers on the American scene amongst his coworkers, was a perfect fit for the UWFi. He could beat on the young Japanese wrestlers as hard as he possibly could, and they would simply smile and come back for more. It was supposed to be as close to legitimate as you could get. His Japanese employers wanted it stiff and his opponents would dish it out as well as they took it, making Vader's propensity to draw blood and cause bruises nothing out of the ordinary.

"You could bust their mouth open," Fleming remembered. "And after it was all over with they didn't care. They shook your hand, bowed, they didn't care."

With Vader in the lead heel role, the UWFi graduated from smaller buildings to some of Japan's biggest arenas. Two of his first three events sold out Budokan Hall. The arena seated 16,500 for wrestling, each seat with perfect sight lines. It was a venue created for judo at the 1964 Tokyo Olympic Games, but is probably best known in the West for concert appearances by the Beatles, KISS, and Cheap Trick.

The Budokan shows followed the exact same pattern the promotion had used the previous year with Albright. Vader dominated the younger wrestlers and even Takada's contemporary Kazuo Yamazaki, building to a match with Takada himself. Buoyed by the immediate success with the Vader-led sellouts, the UWFi took the next step in their plan for world domination. Many had questioned the Vader signing — the company had been doing well without him and his high-cost contract sent shockwaves through a dressing room already obsessed with who was being paid what.

But the pieces to the puzzle all came together when the company announced their debut on American PPV in October 1993. Vader was meant to be the star attraction, a well-known commodity Americans could recognize and embrace. But WCW's attorneys put an end to that dream quickly. Vader was allowed to work the shows in Japan but was prohibited from appearing on the PPV broadcasts, a significant problem for a promotion that intended the 300-pounder to be its top star.

Despite leaving Vader's match on the cutting room floor, the PPV broadcast was a stunning success. American fans were ready for something new. Traditional wrestling had moved too far towards kids programing. Fans yearned for something a little more action packed and sports oriented, and the UWFi hoped to fill the gap. Their debut scored almost 100,000 pay-per-view buys.

In his fourth UWFi match, Vader and Takada packed the Jingu baseball stadium with a capacity crowd of more than 46,000 faithful to see their hero beat the giant American. The political implications within the wrestling business were staggering. Before the match Thesz declared the bout was to determine the real world wrestling champion. While Vader's WCW world title was not on the line, the crowd couldn't fail to notice the symbolism. Takada wasn't just vanquishing Vader, he was defeating traditional pro wrestling. In a brutal match the Japanese hero and the American heel battered each other, Takada with his powerful kicks and Vader with his clubbing forearms.

"There was nothing worked about those kicks or those punches," Vader said. "I'm not trying to insult anyone's intelligence, it was a worked shoot. But there's no way that man could have kicked me any harder. After those matches I couldn't work. I couldn't walk for two or three days."

The match was marred by some awkward, business-exposing moments. At one point the two miscommunicated and Vader went over for a Takada hip toss a good five seconds after the Japanese star had already tried and seemingly failed to pull it off. Takada finished the fight with his trademark arm bar, causing Vader to scream out in pain despite the move never quite being applied completely. Still, the battle had a big match feel, and the crowd was ecstatic to see their champion triumph.

Success for both Pancrase and the UWFi continued into 1994. Pancrase had established three major stars in Shamrock, Funaki, and Suzuki. And with Takada, Vader, and Albright leading the way, the UWFi averaged 15,000 fans for their monthly shows. But change was coming for both groups — and it had the same name. The Gracie family was already leaving their mark on the world of wrestling.

While Pancrase had shown the world what a real shoot might look like, it was more of a contest than a fight. Its wrestlers considered themselves sportsmen, competing in an athletic competition. Two months after Pancrase's launch, the Ultimate Fighting Championship made its debut in Denver, Colorado, and the product they featured was something different entirely. Conceptualized by the Gracie family, the event was closer to a street fight than a collegiate wrestling match or a judo bout. These were no-holds-barred slugfests, a test not just of the athlete but of his martial arts style.

The UFC was the product of several fertile imaginations. It took a real team effort

20 UFC: No Holds Barred

to transport an updated version of the old Gracie Challenge from Rorion Gracie's family scrapbooks to America's television screens. Movie director John Milius thought of the Octagon-shaped cage. Art Davie and Campbell McClaren combined on a brilliant marketing plan to launch the promotion. And Bob Meyrowitz at Semaphore Entertainment Group had the courage to fund a risky venture that had been turned down by every other pay-per-view company in the industry.

Gracie had a clear mission in mind: spreading his family's martial art, a judo variant they called Gracie Jiu-Jitsu. In a bold move, Rorion Gracie's brother Royce was selected to represent the family art of Gracie Jiu-Jitsu. Royce was not considered the family's top fighter — that honor belonged to his older brother Rickson, who was a finely sculpted and vicious alpha male. Royce was different. Skinny, quiet, and unassuming, he looked more like an accountant than a cage fighter. Barely over 170 pounds, he was the odd man out amongst a collection of burly kickboxers and gigantic sumo wrestlers. But that was exactly what Rorion wanted. If Royce Gracie won the UFC, it would clearly be because of the superiority of his martial art — the idea that he was a superior athlete would never even be considered.

Royce Gracie's toughest challenge at the first UFC event would be Ken Shamrock. The Pancrase star had heard about the new show from his training partner Scott Bessac. Shamrock and his support team were skeptical it would be real, skeptical that it would even happen. Four days earlier he even competed in his third Pancrase fight, taking the long flight back from Japan with mentor Masakatsu Funaki in tow, waiting for word that these would actually be worked wrestling matches.

"Right up until the day of the event we were waiting for them to let us in on the secret," Shamrock's father and business manager Bob said. "Ken thought it was likely just a pro wrestling event in disguise. But they never did ask anyone to do a work and suddenly it was time to fight."

After beating Pat Smith in the first round, Shamrock was sure he was on his way to victory. He figured Smith was the toughest customer in the whole competition besides Shamrock himself, a muscular kickboxer with an excess of testosterone and hard punches and kicks. He hadn't been impressed with Gracie in the first round, and with more than 30 pounds on the smaller man, assumed he was going to steamroll him. Shamrock was confident in his abilities on the mat, in retrospect too much so.

Royce looked to take Shamrock down, but the Pancrase star easily blocked his feeble double-leg attempt. It made little difference to Gracie — he just wanted Ken on the ground and was just as happy on the bottom in the famous Gracie guard as he was on the top. Royce was a predator from the guard, waiting for a Shamrock mistake. He didn't need to wait long.

When Shamrock grabbed hold of Gracie's leg and went for a leglock, the Brazilian grappler pounced. Using Ken's own momentum, Gracie landed on top of the stunned wrestler. In the scramble that followed, Royce was able to snake his arm under Shamrock's throat. Shamrock tapped the mat — three times, as the announcers famously pointed out.

Unfortunately, the referee appeared to have missed Shamrock's concession. As officials looked to restart the fight, Ken's sense of fair play overrode his desire to win. Royce whispered in Ken's ear, "You know you tapped." Ken was a man of honor. "I tapped the mat and the referee didn't see it. He was going to let it go, but I tapped the mat. I'm not going to lie. Otherwise the referee was going to let it go. He let go of his hold already. It wouldn't be fair for me to say, 'Keep going.' He'd already let go of the hold."

Ken had no answer for Royce's gi or his strategy. He was used to the Pancrase style. In Japan, you could afford to be patient on the mat. If you made a mistake, the ropes were there to save you, forcing a break in the action. It was a style that worked very well — in Pancrase.

Shamrock explained, "There was definitely a different strategy, because when I was first fighting in the UFC, there were no time limits and no rules. If you made a mistake, it could be a long and serious problem. There were no rounds to save you. No referees to save you. You didn't want to be on the ground because they could kick you in the head, kick you when you were down. It was pretty much anything goes. There was a big-time difference in strategy going into the fight. Pancrase was, in the standup, open hand palm strikes.... In the UFC it was closed fist, bare knuckle. And no rules. It was a huge difference from Pancrase where you could grab a rope and escape and start over again standing up. But you lost points when you did that. You lost five points and the fight's over. That's a whole lot of chances to escape out of a submission hold. It was a lot more strategic and you had to be a lot more skilled in your submission game. The UFC was less skilled, but a lot more dangerous than Pancrase."

The Gracie win propelled the show into the mainstream. If Shamrock had triumphed it might have been dismissed as a toughman clone. Gracie prevailing opened people's minds to what fighting really is.

"When I fought Shamrock," Royce Gracie said, "everyone said, 'Wow, look at this little guy beat this big muscular guy. Can you believe this?' I showed that Gracie Jiu-Jitsu can really work. If I can beat Ken Shamrock, anyone can with the right skills."

"Our intention was to create a conflict of styles," Royce's brother Rickson explains. "Because it was our belief that jiu-jitsu was superior. When my brother dominated so many other styles it really shocked the martial arts world."

Some of Shamrock's fellow Pancrase standouts loved the idea of the UFC. Bas Rutten wasn't sure what to think at first, afraid that the lack of referee intervention could lead to serious harm. "Then I saw the first UFC in Holland on an illegal tape and a friend of ours, Gerard Gordeau, was fighting and he kicked a sumo in the face," Rutten recalls. "Teeth go flying out and I say, 'Okay. This is good stuff.' It was wild, man."

Dave Meltzer, editor of *Wrestling Observer* newsletter, says not everyone in the organization was as pleased as Rutten with what they saw that night. Funaki and the Pancrase leadership disliked the UFC, considering the bare-knuckle spectacle barbaric: "UFC and Pancrase were very different. Pancrase was considered by its combatants as a civilized 'game,' which was physically far harder, particularly on the joints, because it was submission experts constantly ripping on the body, than the less skilled UFC brawls.... UFC was considered more unruly and brutal, like a legalized street fight. At first, Funaki hated UFC, even though he was in Ken Shamrock's corner for his early matches. Shamrock even waved a Pancrase flag at early UFC events."

Pancrase wasn't the only promotion struggling with the Gracies. Desperate to capitalize on the family's sudden prominence, the UWFi was looking to sign Royce for a match with their headliner Nobuhiko Takada. When Royce rejected their offer, they turned to his brother Rickson instead. Business had been at record highs in 1993 and 1994, but hard times were ahead. The promotion had taken a step back towards traditional professional wrestling when they signed Vader and claims to legitimacy had been further exposed by Pancrase, UFC, and Satoru Sayama's Vale Tudo Japan 1994, an organization that swooped in and signed Rickson for a no-holds-barred tournament.

Sayama had disappeared from the scene back in 1984 when the original UWF fell apart. He spent the bulk of his time creating "shooting," a new sport he was trying valiantly to get off the ground, but one that had completely flown under the radar in Japan. Although he is commonly credited with forming Shooto, an early Japanese MMA promotion that existed years before Pancrase, Sayama was mostly creating training centers and developing a new sport. The few early events he did promote looked more like shootboxing, a combination of kickboxing and throws, certainly nothing like modern MMA. The fighters in actual combat wore padded gear, including head protection. Events would also include grappling demonstrations, but the actual amateur contests seemed more focused on standing exchanges than ground work.

"His version of Shooto was all about conceptually creating a gym system for shooting," Japanese wrestling expert Zach Arnold said. "It was more or less an extension of the UWF, the same techniques taught to the newcomer wrestlers in the dojos when the guys in New Japan would often shoot on each other during training sessions to show who was tougher."

MMA website Sherdog's Japan correspondent Tony Loiseleur says this "proto Shooto" didn't hold any professional events until 1989. Even then, he says, they were a far cry from what fans would come to expect in a post-Gracie world.

"The first few years of Shooto competition consisted exclusively of amateur events, held with the intent of giving professional wrestlers and martial artists experience in real prizefighting, since at that time, none of these guys in Japan had much experience in fighting real cross–martial arts free fights," Loiseleur said. "As such, Sayama and the Japan Pro Shooting crew's concept of real free fighting at the time was quite rudimentary, and that's what you're seeing in the protective gear and otherwise awkward looking Shoot-style wrestling matches. It wasn't until the introduction of BJJ and vale tudo that things started to evolve more toward the look and feel of modern MMA."

Signing Rickson Gracie was a huge coup for Sayama. When he decimated the competition, beating three opponents in just over six minutes combined, Rickson became priority one for the UWFi office duo of Yoji Anjo and Yuki Miyato. The UWFi offered what some insiders say was the single biggest two-match money guarantee in wrestling history, a deal that would have him split a pair of matches with Takada, but the proud Brazilian balked. His uncle George had turned to professional wrestling in Brazil, capitalizing on the family name, and Rickson's father, Helio, and the rest of the family had essentially disowned him. Rickson wanted nothing to do with pro wrestling, so Miyato came up with another plan to take advantage of the Gracie name.

After failing to sign Rickson to a pro wrestling match, he sent one of his toughest guys, midcarder Yoji Anjo, to challenge Rickson to a fight on December 7, 1994 — Pearl Harbor Day. They expected that Rickson would decline the impromptu fight, or that Anjo would beat him, and that they would return to Japan with a public relations victory. Gracie had other plans.

At home with his family, he got the call that a Japanese wrestler was at his Los Angeles dojo with the media in tow. While UWFi official Ted Pelc says Anjo intended to stay in Los Angeles for two weeks getting acclimated and into shape before challenging Gracie, the media's presence escalated things. "Jet lagged, right after Anjo gets off the plane, the press takes him on the bus and they go directly to Gracie's dojo," Pelc said. Worse still, the company didn't get any of the publicity footage they wanted. "When the fight took place, Gracie shut the cameras out. The only photos available are after the fight."

Anjo called Rickson a coward in front of his entire family and his students, and it was on. Asked if he needed time to get ready, Rickson replied, "I was born ready, motherfucker." Gracie brutalized Anjo. Witnesses say Gracie got the mount position and rained down punch after punch on the helpless wrestler's face. The Japanese papers ran pictures of Anjo looking like he had been in a gang initiation, his face turned to hamburger by Gracie's vicious assault.

Anjo had brought the press along with him to record what he expected to be a triumph. "[He] followed the media rather than taking control of the situation as originally planned," Pelc said. "A regrettable mistake, but it happened."

"Anjo got embarrassed by Rickson," Arnold said. "It haunted Takada until the end of UWF-Inter because fans kept asking, when is this guy going to defend UWF-Inter's honor?"

For his part, Gracie thought the man he was facing was actually Takada himself. And as the senior man, Japanese culture dictated that Takada should have stepped in to challenge Rickson where his protégé had failed. Instead, the promotion continued forward as if nothing had happened. Takada took the UWFi title back from Vader in April 1995, freeing the WCW star to lose his WCW title to Hulk Hogan. The American star had been handcuffed by wrestling politics — he couldn't do a clean job in WCW for fear that it would hurt the UWFi's cache with hardcore fans. Those fans truly believed the UWFi champion stood head and shoulders above everyone else in the industry. Losing to a "fake" wrestler like Hogan, so synonymous in Japan with Inoki and his promotion, would have been disastrous.

STRUGGLES WITH SHAMROCK

Funaki was also having trouble with his top gaijin, Shamrock, whose attention was focused like a laser on Royce Gracie and the UFC. Shamrock's loss in the first event had spooked Funaki and the other Pancrase leaders. Ken had lost badly and it had hurt the promotion — their top fighter being dismantled by Gracie made Pancrase look weak.

The promotion wasn't going to tell Ken he couldn't do the UFC events, but before he left he had to do something to make the group look strong.

Said Lion's Den trainer Scott Bessac, "Ken told me a lot, but it was mostly on the personal tip. . . . I know the fight with Suzuki, where he hurt Ken's knee — that was a work. And the one where Funaki submitted Ken in a couple of minutes with a rear naked choke? That was because Ken was about to go back to the UFC."

The first job Bessac describes was in January 1994 for Minoru Suzuki, prior to the UFC's second event. Shamrock faked a knee injury for the Japanese press; ironically a misplaced Vernon White kick actually prevented him from competing, breaking his arm just a few weeks later.

The second work Bessac describes came just a week before the third UFC, a much-hyped tournament with Ken and Royce in opposite brackets, Ken did another job, this time a loss to Funaki in just 2:30. Again, it ended up being for naught. Gracie had to leave the competition early after a grueling fight with Kimo, and Shamrock pulled out in despair.

With Shamrock's attention elsewhere, the promotion turned its energies to other fighters. Rutten was a Funaki favorite and the company had high hopes for the charismatic Dutchman. He was a bundle of energy, attacking life with the same infectious joy he took into the ring. Rutten had lost to Shamrock early in his career and got a second chance, a shot at Ken's King of Pancrase title, in March 1995. Funaki, intent on building his new star, looked to have Shamrock drop the title in a worked match.

"Ken was like, 'No way, I'm not losing to Bas.' Bas and Ken got along fine," Bessac said. "But that was a no go."

With Shamrock refusing to cooperate, Funaki concentrated on helping Rutten take the title from Ken the hard way. It was to no avail. Shamrock caught Rutten in a knee bar just a minute into the fight. Captured beautifully on video, it is an amazing snapshot that incapsulates an era.

"That overhead camera shot they used was one of the best shots ever in all of MMA," former UFC champion and pro wrestling star Josh Barnett said. "It was just so perfect, the way he swung into that knee bar. It was picture perfect."

Rutten, who was dramatically better than everyone else in the promotion on his feet, was crushed that the extra work with the Japanese experts hadn't helped.

"[Funaki] was a great guy," Rutten said. "And he tried to help me with my fight with Ken. But when he tried to show me how to defend the knee bar, he should have told me, 'Listen, don't let him step over your hip.' There are many ways to get in the right position for it. But Funaki only showed me one way to defend. And we worked on it for three weeks. Then when I fought Ken Shamrock he threw his leg over my head. He did it a different way and I thought, 'Hmm.' After that I didn't listen to anybody. I would listen, but I would check later to see if it was actually true. And I'm going to see if I can make it better than what Funaki is doing and try different setups. It's what made me really good at the submissions."

"It was the loss against Ken," he continued. "I really had it. I'm a very sore loser and I knew what the problem was. It was because I didn't train any ground. That decided it for me. Forget about striking, nobody's going to strike with me anyway, even Maurice Smith took me down in a fight. So I start concentrating on grappling two times a day, seven days a week. I really took it to the next level in training. I always told Ken, 'Thank you for that, buddy, because that actually made me very good.' I never lost again."

Pancrase's other new star was Ken's adopted brother Frank Shamrock. Like Ken, Frank Juarez had been a lost boy when Bob Shamrock rescued him and gave him his name. He was dropped off, fresh from prison, to learn the fight game at Ken's gym where the elder brother gave him his first beating, pounding him until he couldn't move and choking him unconscious.

"It was nuts. And I didn't really have a comparison except for being in jail. They were similar type activities. I had never played sports so I didn't really get the whole machismo thing. I didn't understand any of it. And clearly I didn't know how to fight," Frank Shamrock said with a laugh, remembering the early days of hazing at the famed Lion's Den. "It was like that for months. Because I didn't really know anything. Everybody was a tough guy and I was a young kid. It was tough. It was wild. I'm surprised I made it, because it wasn't a welcoming atmosphere where they wanted you to be successful. It was certainly not that. . . . Ken was the king of the cavemen and we were all underneath him. We learned that way."

When the younger Shamrock made his Pancrase debut he was already a star by virtue of his last name. His early success was shocking. Despite just six months' worth of training, Frank came shooting out of the gates with big wins over some of the sport's biggest stars. Some called him a prodigy, but Scott Bessac disagrees: "Frank was a work. He used the Shamrock last name and was worked right up the ladder. Frank was just work."

DAN "THE BEAST" SEVERN

Like with most things associated with Pancrase, no one can say for certain. Frank doesn't deny the charge — there were times things seemed off to him too. Although he would later become the best fighter in the world, he wasn't a world-beater yet in 1995, and yet there he was beating Suzuki and Funaki by submission.

"I know that it went on. I don't know if I was just too young, or didn't need to know, but no one ever shared anything with me. I had a feeling . . . there were always secret meetings and whatnot, but I never knew anything about it," Frank said. "No one ever asked me to end it a certain way. I do know that it went on, but I was never approached or had any experience with it. I believe some of the fights that I fought with the upper-echelon guys, they may have let me win or had some sort of ending in mind. But I always fought my heart out and fought as hard as I could and gave as much as I could."

THE ROAD TO UFC 6

By UFC 5, an event that would finally feature a Ken Shamrock–Royce Gracie rematch, the Gracie name was big enough in Japan that Pancrase could allow Ken to risk loss without first making him put over one of their own stars. It was a calculated risk — they hoped a Shamrock win would make him an even bigger star in Japan and didn't want to devalue him by having a loss so fresh in fans' memories.

His match with Dan Severn at UFC 6 was a different story. Like Shamrock, Severn was a wrestler in Japan, working the midcard for the UWFi. This put him on a lower tier than Shamrock in Pancrase's view, and a loss would be a major embarrassment. Worse, Severn was a traditional pro wrestler too. In a last-ditch effort by promoters to reestablish some credibility, he was the latest NWA world champion. Dave Meltzer had suggested the move, thinking that Severn's Ultimate Fighting success would help give the title some much needed attention and respect. Severn was a throwback to an era when it mattered whether or not the champion could actually wrestle a lick. In his gray athletic shirt, covered in sweat even before he made it to the ring, Severn made amateur wrestling his gimmick.

"I only wish I had been brought into the professional wrestling business at another time," Severn said. "The first time I met Lou Thesz in Japan, he really was watching a great deal. He really was watching the scientific, mechanical way I did things and created leverage. It was actually quite a honor that it was Lou Thesz who presented me with my very own NWA title belt at one of the Cauliflower Alley banquets for all I did for the organization and bringing a lot of recognition to professional wrestling. Because I was kinda like that first professional wrestler who crossed back over from no-holds-barred to professional wrestling. Before your Brock Lesnar and Bobby Lashley and that kinda stuff."

Thesz's respect for Severn's work made him one of the wrestlers Thesz encouraged the UWFi to push hard. Severn was a repeat national champion and would have represented the United States in the 1980 Olympics if the country hadn't boycotted the Moscow location. In 1935, Severn would have probably been a big star in pro wrestling. Unfortunately, in 1995, the fans were indifferent in America, and in Japan it took some time for Severn to catch on to the shoot style.

Thesz's protégé Mark Fleming said, "[Thesz] thought Dan Severn was great. Dan Severn was a hell of a wrestler. . . . He's probably the best wrestler, I think, in my era, in my age group, best ever. He was the best. He could do it all. He could do Greco, he could do freestyle, he could do folkstyle, he could do submission style. Then he could do the street fighting. He could do it all. . . . He's a super guy, and Lou respected him."

In the UFC, the mild-mannered Severn had become a star as "The Beast." He took Royce Gracie to the limit and then dominated the competition on his way to winning the tournament championship at UFC 5. His superfight with Shamrock was to be the first shooting match between two pro wrestling champions in decades — until Pancrase pulled the plug. The group's founders still had a pro wrestling mentality and their priority was protecting the championship. Most favored Severn in the match and the idea of Shamrock losing to a fake NWA world champion who was also way beneath him in the Japanese wrestling hierachy was more than Pancrase could tolerate. They asked Shamrock to drop his title to Suzuki before the Severn fight, which he did, again falling to a knee bar in just a few minutes.

Suzuki, Pancrase's biggest native Japanese star besides Funaki, was the real deal. He had been an Olympic contender in 1984 before taking the plunge into pro wrestling. With his slicked-back hair and all-black attire, he played the gangster to a tee. Like Funaki, he was being groomed for a major role in New Japan Pro-Wrestling, but preferred the "cool factor" of the more progressive shoot style. He was one of the most aggressive wrestlers in Japan, often calling out performers in other companies.

When wrestlers from outside came into Pro Wrestling Fujiwara Gumi, before the transition to Pancrase, Suzuki would explain away their poor performances. "They're just rusty," he would say. "They haven't wrestled a real match in years." The seemingly benign comments from Suzuki were really a clever way of suggesting other wrestling promotions weren't nearly as real as his own. Funaki had a similar attitude, once giving a bad beating to former WWF champion Bob Backlund in a UWF match because he didn't think Backlund's showier style had any place in a realistic wrestling promotion. The two men could talk the talk because they could walk the walk. Suzuki was a dazzlingly good wrestler and could lock on a hold from any position. Super heavyweight Olympic gold medalist David Gobezhishvili learned that the hard way. The two were working out together before their match in 1992 and the nearly 300-pound Russian wrestler was tossing Suzuki around the ring like a sack of potatoes. But when the sparring hit the floor, Suzuki tapped the monstrous Russian out repeatedly.

"I remember Suzuki being super, super fast," Rutten said. "That's what he was known for. He was flying around people and putting them in crazy positions. He would tap guys out with inverted neck cranks, but he would use his legs! He would crank the head between his knees. He made the guy tap and in the moment he tapped, Suzuki took him with a straight arm bar because he was in a perfect position for it. He made the guy tap twice. I thought that was really cool.

"He fought Remco Pardoel, who was famous for his knockout of Orlando Weit at UFC

2," Rutten continued. "When Suzuki fought him in Pancrase, Pardoel was on his knees and turtled up. Suzuki looks at the audience and you can tell he's very annoyed by this. Because Pardoel doesn't want to do anything. So he puts his foot in front of Pardoel's face. He's waving his foot in Pardoel's face and Pardoel looks up because he sees peripheral movement. And the moment he looks up, Suzuki slaps a rear naked choke on him."

Like Funaki, Suzuki spent time honing the skills of the men he would end up facing in the ring. That was just the way business was done in Pancrase. It was his responsibility to make the promotion a success and if that meant building a fighter who would one day be able to beat him, so be it. He had been training in submissions for years and was one of Fujiwara and Gotch's best students.

"Suzuki was the guy who told me how to beat Bas Rutten in my first fight. He said, 'Bas knows nothing about wrestling.' And I said, 'But I know nothing about wrestling either,'" recalled Frank Shamrock, breaking into laughter. "But he said, 'You've trained with Ken, you at least know how to take someone down.' And he was right. I didn't know how to strike or do much of anything. But I knew how to take people down."

Things were rarely fun and games at the Pancrase dojo. The training was serious and sometimes the fighters got a reminder of how dangerous their profession could be.

Rutten said, "I heard a rumor that Suzuki actually killed someone by accident, one of the young boys. . . . Something went wrong and he broke his neck. I don't know what happened . . . That was a wild story. I think it changed his fighting style. And from what I've heard those parents are still at the Pancrase shows."

With Suzuki installed as champion, Ken Shamrock was free to take on Severn without the honor of Pancrase being on the line as well. Heated words flew before the men even entered the Octagon. Severn walked out of the prefight press conference, infuriating Shamrock, who warned Severn's manager Phyllis Lee, "I was just going to beat him. Now I'm going to hurt him." Once the fight began, Shamrock was a man of his word, making short work of Severn. Shamrock was thought to have a wrestling disadvantage, but he shrugged off the more experienced wrestler's first takedown and choked him out with a front facelock in just over two minutes.

Less than a year later, in May 1996, the two were scheduled for a rematch. By then the battles outside the cage were as fierce as anything inside it. Michigan's attorney general sought an injunction to stop the show, citing an 1883 law that banned all unregulated prize fighting. United States District Court Judge Avern Cohn called the law antiquated saying, "This is entertainment the same way football and hockey are entertainment." Lawmakers considered passing a law specifically banning mixed martial arts bouts but it wouldn't have been signed into law in time to stop the event.

It was another in a series of close calls for the UFC. The courts established some modified rules for the fights, barring closed fist punches. The UFC was happy to play along — they would agree that closed fist punches were illegal and agree to fine any violators $50. It was a clever way around the letter of the law, which satisfied all the competitors — all of them except Ken Shamrock. Months earlier, a group of fighters was arrested after a show in Canada. Ken was worried that could happen to him and almost dropped out of the fight with Severn.

David Isaacs, the UFC President at the time, said, "I remember Ken Shamrock screaming in the hotel room. Bob Shamrock told me, 'Once Ken thinks he's right, there's nothing you can do to change his mind.' And it can be about anything. I don't think he's a lunatic, but when he gets convinced that this is the way things should be, you just can't change his way of thinking. With Ken it was just hard. Once he kind of settled on a position on anything he was not flexible. He seemed to have a lot of rage at times. In Detroit, when the courts told us what the rules would be for his fight with Dan, Ken was just fucking furious. I just said, 'What are we going to do, Ken? What do you want to do? That's what the court said.'"

Shamrock went through with the fight, but seemed disinterested. Today he shrugs with embarrassment when asked about it. Not Severn. To him, it's still a crowning moment, the night he became UFC champion.

"A lot of people did not like that match. I think it was even chronicled in different books as one of the worst matches in UFC history," Severn said. "At that time, for being the marquee match, it did not produce. But in my own personal opinion, it was the most well thought out, psychological match ever in UFC . . . the crowd was not liking this match, and they start booing. They start doing everything I hoped they would do. Because Shamrock at that point in time was a counter fighter. As you attack he counter attacks you. And I thought if I do the exact same thing and circle and basically do what he is doing, nothing. The crowd is going to get rather restless, and they would start to boo and they end up booing and even throw garbage in the cage."

Severn was hoping the angry crowd would prompt Shamrock into action. But that night nothing could. Fans called it "The Dance in Detroit," and it's gone down as the worst fight in UFC history. To this day, UFC officials are furious about both men's performances. It was a deadly dull affair, one that many believed hurt the UFC long term. For Shamrock and Severn it was the beginning of the end for their first runs in the UFC.

"There were a lot of problems and Bob Meyrowitz, the UFC owner at the time, was facing going into court constantly, and it cost him a lot of money and eventually ran him dry. Everywhere we went we were getting a lot of political pressure," Shamrock said. "Even the cities where we held the events were getting pressured not to hold the fights there. I remember one time we were in New York and they shut the event down. We had to pack up and load everybody up on a big old 747 and move to Dothan, Alabama, set up in a 24-hour period, and still have the show. It's the kind of thing that happened in Detroit, where they put in rules at the last minute where we couldn't punch, couldn't hit a downed opponent, and really changed the dynamics of the UFC."

Shamrock had left Pancrase in the dust earlier in the year, replaced by Severn's manager Phyllis Lee as the North American talent scout. By the end of the year he was out of MMA entirely, moving on to the greener pastures of the WWF.

In the UFC Ken Shamrock and Royce Gracie had both come and gone. There was a changing of the guard coming in Japan too. Pancrase and the UWFi had gotten the ball rolling, but in 1997 Pride burst on the scene to take MMA in Japan to new heights.

Although Rickson Gracie's December 1994 demolition of Yoji Anjo didn't have immediate repercussions at the box office (in fact the UWFi sold out Budokan Hall that January for a Gary Albright versus Big Van Vader title match) the company saw business slowly slide. By April they had to cancel an event in Kobe and the much anticipated rubber match between Vader and Nobuhiko Takada failed to sell out the Rainbow Hall in Nagoya, something that would have been unthinkable just a year before.

Takada, their leading man, was looking like damaged goods. His inability to get Gracie in the ring hurt him, but so did his flighty personality and lack of discipline. People who

21 FIGHTING for PRIDE

worked with the star described him as "whimsical." He would come to a rash decision, like retirement, and announce it publicly, only to recant the next week. A run for public office — in typical Takada style, one that was aborted midway only to be resumed days later at the zero hour — also placed a heavy burden on the UWFi coffers.

"Takada ran for political office and cash went out the door," Zach Arnold explained. He lost his bid for a seat on the House of Councilors in embarrassing fashion, but was soon on to his next adventure. The wrestler's stoic and serious hero image was a media creation. In real life he was a bit of a goofball: charismatic, ostentatious, and way over the top. "Takada is more like the Hustle character (his bombastic general manager alter ego in the new-wave comedy wrestling promotion in the 2000s) in real life than the wrestler he was all those years," Arnold remembered.

His win over Vader was the American's last match with the promotion. Vader went back to WCW, escaping what would have been inevitable demands for a real shooting match. Instead he found a fight in the WCW locker room, taking a poke at mostly retired wrestler Paul Orndorff. But his tough guy image shattered as Orndorff stomped him.

"Before I knew it, he's sucker punched me," Orndorff said. "He made a mistake and I got up and the rest is history."

Orndorff, despite having an arm shriveled by nerve damage courtesy of an old wrestling injury, despite wearing sandals, despite being nearly 50 years old, had beaten Vader easily:

> Vader had showed up late for the Center Stage tapings and Orndorff started yelling at him to hurry up and do his promos. There had been previous heat between the two. Both got face to face and Orndorff begged Vader, who outweighed him by 200 pounds, to start something. Vader shoved him down with a palm blow and Orndorff came back fighting, flooring Vader and knocking him for a loop with a punch from his bad left arm. Orndorff proceeded to kick at Vader's face with his sandaled feet until all the wrestlers broke it up. Amazingly, everyone just left Vader on the floor in a fetal position and went back to doing their thing, so when Vader recovered he walked right into Orndorff's office and they got into another fight. After this fight was broken up, Vader was sent home with the belief that he'd instigated it, and Orndorff ended up working a match later that night with a busted up face against Barry Houston. WCW ended up firing Vader, who immediately jumped to the WWF.

Orndorff notes, "It was one of those unfortunate things that happened. The only thing that I am thankful for is that if my body wasn't hurt. If I didn't have all of that nerve damage on my right, God knows I might be in jail for killing him. I am not taking anything from anybody."

Most fans never knew about the incident, but Vader's locker room reputation was never the same — and neither was his career. He went from being the tough "shooter" to being a fat clown, mocked by WWF announcers just a few years later for being overweight. Wrestling wasn't a shoot in the ring, but in the back, the boys played for keeps.

While Vader escaped back to America and a $500,000 a year job, fellow American import Gary Albright struggled to make a living in the UWFi. As his place on the card slipped, so did his temper. Albright was a nice man with a soft voice, the kind of guy who played fantasy hockey, not a big partier. But frustration was taking its toll. Drinking and fighting in the Tokyo clubs soon followed.

"Gary Albright and I would go to get a few beers when we were off duty at the local bars and we'd have some of the American style wrestlers join us when they happened to be in the same town," UWFi insider Ted Pelc remembered. "Naturally, some muscle-heads from one of the military bases, people who claimed to be boxers, karateka, judoka, martial artists, what have you, would start trouble and feel that they had to test us just because we were hanging out with some 'show' wrestlers, despite the fact that we were just minding our own business and keeping to ourselves. None of those 'challengers' even came close to going the distance with them. It goes without saying, but Gary would always do just as well and I've never seen him break a sweat in a straight bar room brawl. It was always quick, if you blinked you generally missed the whole thing. We really didn't get into fights, it was more like a five-year-old attempting to fight an adult."

Some of Gary's aggression was also taken out on his opponents in the ring. Angry at having to put over Kiyoshi Tamura in a bout just a month after losing to Masahito Kakihara to set up a Kakihara title challenge, Albright refused to play along and let the rising star look good. At just 175 pounds, there was little Tamura could do on the mat with the 300-plus-pound NCAA All-American. The match was a mess with Albright clearly refusing to cooperate. "Break, Gary, break," the official had to shout at one point when Albright wouldn't let up on a hold in the ropes.

In the end, Albright lost the match. But Tamura knew it had been a debacle, confusing for the fans, and hard on the eyes. It was to have been the greatest moment of his young career and when it was over, despite his hand being raised, he broke down in real tears.

"Tamura was in the wrong place at the wrong time," Arnold said. "Gary wanted financial security and just didn't get it. This is why he ended up with All Japan, but it took a while (as all things do in Japan for various political reasons)."

By October 1995 the UWFi was nearly broke and in desperate straights. The group had no choice but to do the same thing the original UWF had done a decade before — look to New Japan Pro-Wrestling for a lifeline. Soon, with a record-breaking crowd of 67,000 watching closely inside the massive Tokyo Dome, Takada and the other UWFi wrestlers sold out.

For years they had challenged the legitimacy of the "fake" New Japan wrestlers. But, in the end, money is the most real thing in the fantasy land of professional wrestling. New Japan had it and Takada's crew didn't. According to *Wrestling Observer*, this gave New Japan booker Riki Chōshū the power to call all the shots. And Chōshū, with a definite axe to grind against the "shooters" dating back to the infamous Maeda kick in 1987, made the UWFi wrestlers look second rate, even if doing so may not have been the best move for business. Even Takada lost his first match, submitting in embarrassing fashion by figure four leglock to Keiji "the Great Muta" Mutoh in the center of the ring: "Fans left the show with the distinct impression that the UWFi so-called shooters and style were second rate in comparison to New Japan. If this was a one shot deal, New Japan did the right thing for its status as the top company in the Japan (and the world) and its business. But with the interest and money this drew and had the potential of doing in the future, Takada needed to win the first match to give the underdog promotion credibility for a long-term feud."

The crowd was on fire for the matches, which mostly ended quickly and decisively in favor of the New Japan stars. Chōshū himself destroyed UWFi heel Yoji Anjo and the feud between the two groups was mostly dead on arrival. The other wrestlers became afterthoughts with only Takada himself remaining a viable competitor.

Like Ric Flair in America, Takada's power tower at the box office was untouchable. His rematch with Mutoh and subsequent match with Shinya Hashimoto both drew more than 60,000 fans to the Tokyo Dome, and he followed up his New Japan run with a pair of tremendous matches with Genichiro Tenryu on the independent scene. But options for Takada, it seemed, were limited. Fans were demanding one match, a bout with Rickson Gracie to settle the score.

"It haunted Takada," Arnold said. Finally, with the financial backing of mobster Hiromichi Momose, Pride Fighting Championship was born in 1997. With Nobuyuki Sakakibara helping on the TV end and Naoto Morishita providing some marketing hustle, the promotion lasted a decade, producing some of the best fights and fighters in MMA history. But, originally, it was a promotion created to showcase this single fight.

There is a lot we don't know about the financial backers behind the earliest events that would later be known as Pride FC, and given the yakuza scandal and intrigue that ultimately crippled Pride and forced its sale to Dana White and the Fertitta brothers of UFC fame, that might very well be for the best.

But one thing we can say with relative certainty is that these backers were betting on the viability of Japan's wrestling heroes as legitimate fighters when they put up the money for the first Tokyo Dome spectacular — or, at the very least, they were betting on the Japanese ticket-buying public's belief in the legitimacy of their wrestling heroes. It's possible that some among the thousands in attendance were there out of nothing more than morbid curiosity, secure in the knowledge that these professional wrestling performers were just that, performers, and would quickly be exposed by serious and rigorously trained no-holds-barred martial artists. But from the way those crowds roared, the way the cheered and chanted, it's hard to hear anything like cynicism in that incredible din.

No, it was with genuine adoration and a willingness to believe that the Tokyo crowd cheered Nobuhiko Takada, the first of their great wrestling heroes to enter the world of mixed martial arts. The Japanese fans had seen Takada, a veteran of countless shoot-style wrestling classics, combine his submission skills and stiff kicks with an indomitable will to win as he emerged the victor in performances against the likes of Keiji Mutoh and Big Van Vader. Even if those contests were not exactly on the up and up, it didn't seem *completely* unreasonable to expect that at least some of those attributes might translate from the notoriously tough world of shoot-style exhibition to the even tougher world of real athletic competition.

This is not, however, how thing played out before a live audience of 47,860. Super Vader had been scary. But Rickson Gracie — by all accounts the greatest exponent of his family's art, distilled and honed, as it was, from the fundamentals of grappling the traveling Mitsuyo Maeda had taught his uncle Carlos decades before — was much, much scarier.

Their October 11, 1997, bout opened with Takada coming out cautiously in a deep, defensive stance as Rickson stalked him with the strange upright posture characteristic of the Gracie family in the early days of mixed martial arts. Once the fighters tied up in the corner, it was clear that Takada was not just cautious, he was frightened: terrified of the legendary grappler's submission skills, Takada clung to the ropes rather than risk being taken down. But that only delayed the inevitable. Once the fighters were restarted, Rickson attempted another takedown, and, after a brief scramble, dramatically slammed Takada to the canvas with a solid double-leg. The rest was academic. Gracie slipped effortlessly from side control to mount as Takada could do nothing more than hang on for dear life. Less than three minutes after the bout had begun amid the rapturous cheers of tens of thousands of puroresu fans, it ended with their hero Takada tapping out to the vastly, effortlessly superior submission fighter. Rickson by arm bar.

It was, to say the least, an inauspicious beginning for the heroes of Japanese professional wrestling on the biggest stage in mixed martial arts. And that is without question what Pride was from its inception: the number one show in the world. While the Ultimate Fighting Championship was struggling against regulators and widespread public scorn to put on shows for a few thousand rough-and-tumble fans in out-of-the-way places like Bay St. Louis, Mississippi, Pride was almost immediately part of the Japanese sporting mainstream. How could it not be when it came out of virtually nowhere to draw an audience of nearly 50,000 to the Tokyo Dome? The public demand was enormous; the professional wrestling and sporting media simply followed the dollars.

When the fight finally happened on October 11, 1997, Takada's poor performance shocked fans. He had been built for years as the toughest man in professional wrestling. Where were his kicks that allegedly struck blows more powerful than a man swinging a baseball bat? Where were his vaunted submissions? Takada's reputation died that night at the Tokyo Dome.

Pride paid Takada $180,000 and Rickson a rumored $1 million for the fight. It could have easily been the end of the road for major league MMA in Japan. But the passionate fans of the UWF refused to let a dream die.

Despite Takada being clearly outclassed, UWF fans were undaunted. The biggest roar from the crowd that night was for a non-combatant shown briefly on the big screen in the Dome. When the camera panned to Akira Maeda the Tokyo Dome was alive. Takada had lost and let them down, but surely Maeda could beat Rickson and restore the UWF to glory?

"Everyone in the Big Egg knew that there were only two left. The two who still carried, at the time, what I would call an 'Illusion of UWF.' Masakatsu Funaki and Akira Maeda,"

Japanese MMA writer Shu Hirata wrote at BoutReviewUSA.com. "The fans wanted to believe their hero could be the best in the world so they pinned their hopes on Maeda, the oldest member of the club and the most charismatic out of the three. That's why fans went crazy when they saw Maeda's close-up displayed on that gigantic monitor."

The buzz was like nothing else. Takada was always the better athlete, and was in better shape too, as a series of injuries had left Maeda unable to train and overweight. But to the fans, Maeda better represented the Budo ethos of the Japanese warrior. Unlike Takada, who had avoided Rickson for three years, Maeda wasted little time trying to put the match together and responded to the fans' calls right away.

Maeda tried hard to bring in Rickson to Rings for his retirement bout. He thought he had the deal wrapped up and was surprised to see an announcement that there would be a rematch with Takada instead. Maeda would finish his career against wrestling legend Alexander Karelin rather than Rickson and would never get the chance to set things right with the Gracies.

A year to the day after Takada's defeat, the two had a rematch, again at the famed Tokyo Dome. Again, Takada could mount little resistance. The second loss to Gracie left Takada's reputation badly damaged. He had recovered easily from losses in the pro wrestling world — after all, many fans were able to tell themselves that if the bout had been real Takada would have surely triumphed. Now, exposed as a charlatan, his star was dimming, and Takada's losses were soul crushing for the hardcore fans that made up Pride's audience.

The promotion, built on the Japanese wrestler's popularity, was faltering as well. They attempted to rehabilitate Takada, bringing in former UFC champion Mark Coleman to put him over in a worked match. Dave Meltzer was consulted on the finish, as a purported sporting event was headlined by what was really a pro wrestling match.

"It was what it was," Coleman said. "I needed to support my family. They guaranteed me another fight after that and I needed that security. It was what it was. I'm going to leave it at that."

Many fans in America were disgusted. This was supposed to be a sport, and they didn't understand that the promotion was the creation of pro wrestling fans with the sole purpose of promoting a pro wrestling star. To these diehards, adding in the occasional worked match muddied the waters. They didn't want ambiguity, the kind of perpetual questions that linger over Pancrase bouts to this day. They wanted definitive answers about who the best fighters in the world were. While many fighters also disagreed with Coleman's move, it was an era before big money existed for anyone not named Gracie. Coleman had to do what he could to survive.

"I don't agree with it, but I can't fault him for it," fellow Pride star Mark Kerr said. "It paid dividends for him. He sacrificed a little but it gained him so much. I made it perfectly clear that it was my reputation and my integrity on the line. I made it clear to them that there was no way I would ever compromise it for financial gain. It would be too hard for me to carry that to bed every night."

Kerr was approached about his own fight with Takada at Pride 6. "This is the way the Japanese do business," he explained. "They pulled me aside and said, 'Hey, Mark, we want to talk to you about something you maybe don't understand. The Japanese fans, they love technique. They really know this sport and are familiar with it and the techniques.' That being said to me, well, you can kind of fill in the lines. Meaning, they don't want to see me get on top of him and pound the crap out of him. That's what I took out of the conversation. It was a whole conversation with the promoters talking about how they appreciated technical things. And they just left it at that. I left the meeting kind of chuckling. If I needed to go out there and punch him in the face until his nose fell I would have done it. But he gave up the submission, and that was easier for me."

Kerr would become the company's standard-bearer. He was considered by most to be the best fighter in the world and the Japanese fans were awed by his bodybuilder's physique and aggressive fighting style. Unfortunately, the kind of fights that could have made Kerr a legend never seemed to transpire.

"They marketed me to the nth degree," Kerr said. "I did their TV, their radio, their version of Johnny Carson, their Japanese game shows. I dressed up in a sumo suit on national television. . . . I wish things had gone as originally planned. To get me to agree to go over there, they offered me what was then the ridiculous sum of $150,000 and a chance to fight Royce Gracie. I actually signed a fight poster with me and Royce Gracie and it said Pride 2. That would have been awesome and might have changed how people view me."

The Gracie match fell through and Kerr ended up fighting a succession of uninspiring opponents like kickboxing champion Branko Cikatic and Luta Livre ace Hugo Duarte. Eventually, drug abuse got the best of him and his once fearsome fighting spirit seemed to have withered on the vine. Pride was dying without a Japanese star to replace Takada or a foreign import who could draw money, until a young fighter, fresh from the UWFi undercard was able to make his mark. Pride was built on the foundation of a Takada versus Gracie feud, and fittingly, it was Takada's understudy Kazushi Sakuraba who made the promotion a sustainable venture, bringing hope to pro wrestling fans everywhere who were afraid that the art form simply couldn't compete with its jiu-jitsu counterpart.

Professional wrestling has never seemed like a more viable and effective martial art than it did during the Pride years. When Pride Fighting Championships was a legitimate popular phenomenon in the Japan, routinely drawing television audiences in the tens of millions and reaching a level of media saturation that makes even the post–*Ultimate Fighter* success of the UFC seem almost culturally insignificant, there was really only one man at the center of that maelstrom.

Kazushi Sakuraba, a former collegiate wrestling captain schooled in the submission wrestling handed down to him by his seniors in the UWFi ranks, was not just the

22 SAKU

undisputed top draw for one of the hottest wrestling or fighting promotions the world had ever seen; he transcended his sport, however briefly, to become a Japanese national icon. And everything he did, he did with a showman's flair. From his elaborate and comic ring entrances to his often bizarre fighting techniques, nearly every movement he made on camera was in tribute to the professional wrestling stars that had captured his imagination as young fan. He would walk down the massive Pride ramp like "The Great Muta," like a Road Warrior, like Vader, or the incomparable "Tiger Mask." And once he'd entered the ring, the homage would continue.

Who knew we would ever see the Mongolian chop used in a legitimate fight? And not by some marginal figure in a sideshow match, but by the best mixed martial artist of his generation, arguably the greatest in the young history of the sport? Seemingly against all odds, throwing all we'd thought we'd learned about the martial arts on its head, it turned out that the most technically adept, celebrated, and respected mixed martial artist on the planet was a professional wrestler.

It wasn't that Sakuraba was the first wrestler to assert himself in mixed martial arts competition. Far from it: by the time Kazushi Sakuraba appeared on the scene, we'd already seen Ken Shamrock, professional wrestler and Pancrase star, emerge from the chaos of the earliest UFC events as the promotion's top draw and first Superfight champion before ultimately losing that latter title to another man with strong ties to the world of professional wrestling, Dan Severn. Amateur wrestling, represented by Severn, Mark Coleman, Mark Kerr, and Randy Couture, had already emerged as a force to be reckoned with in the cage. There could be no doubt of the effectiveness of the fundamentals of wrestling as martial arts techniques, or of highly trained and well-conditioned wrestlers as potentially first-rate mixed martial artists. But the ineffable Kazushi Sakuraba was something else entirely.

The Kazushi Sakuraba story can, and has, been told many ways. But it has never been told better than by the man himself. Sakuraba has penned three volumes of autobiography, the first published in 2000 and the most recent in 2007. While none of them are likely to ever receive official English-language publication, the first and third volumes have, however, been made available in English through a user-supported online project called MMA Translations. These very readable editions, both entitled *Me*, reveal Sakuraba to be a charming and candid prose stylist with a dry, ironic sense of humour. The first volume charts Sakuraba's long road to the top; the third, his seemingly even longer road to physical ruin.

Sakuraba insists that "besides pooping and larceny, I really was a good, polite, and humble kid." He lived a quiet life in a remote corner of rural northern Japan until a fateful day in his first year of middle school, when a *Tiger Mask* manga caught his eye as he walked the aisles of a small bookshop. Amazingly, this was the first time the young Sakuraba had encountered the Tiger Mask craze that saw Satoru Sayama don the guise of the manga and anime hero to the delight of children across Japan. That's because, for children growing up in Akita prefecture, it was different: "Pro wrestling broadcasts were put on in a late-night timeslot, which made it difficult for kids to ever even see it. That's the boonies. It sounds like I'm joking, but I only learned very recently that at that time, pro-wrestling was broadcast all over Japan during primetime, 8 p.m. on Friday evenings. But, that was for everywhere except Akita." Because of this "painful circumstance," Sakuraba had been completely oblivious to the world of professional wrestling. But he would quickly make up for lost time.

A week later, Sakuraba saw the words "Pro Wresting — Tiger Mask" listed in the TV guide describing New Japan Pro-Wrestling's horrible late-night television slot, and, after struggling to stay awake, Sakuraba was moved. "Seeing Tiger Mask for the first time as a kid had an amazing impact on my heart," he recalls. "Jumping and flying, all of his movements were so beautiful . . . I was completely blown away. That this kind of interesting sport existed in the world." From that moment on, Sakuraba's focus was singular — well, *almost* singular: "It was at this time that I decided what I wanted to be when I grew up — a pro-wrestler (or if that was no good, a pilot)." Inspired by the example of Masakatsu Funaki, who had entered the world of professional wrestling directly upon graduation from middle school, Sakuraba announced his intention to do exactly the same. Understandably, his parents were horrified, and insisted that their son at least complete high school before even entertaining any such notion. And so, as a dutiful son, Sakuraba turned his energies towards wrestling of a slightly different kind — that is, amateur wrestling at Akita Shougyou High School — with the long-term goal of one day joining the professional ranks.

Years later, at the height of his powers in the Pride FC ring, Sakuraba's techniques often appeared as effortless as they were stylish. It would be easy to mistake Sakuraba for a natural. But nothing could be further from the truth. Despite his undeniable enthusiasm for wrestling, Sakuraba was completely unprepared for the athletic and technical demands of the sport. His only previous sports experience had been in basketball, a sport he hated, but hated slightly less than baseball, which had been his other option as a mandatory sport until high school. He came to the wrestling mats in passable physical condition, but immediately found that "the level of practice was quite high." He elaborates, "For the guys that joined in the same year as me, there were kids that had become Tohoku [regional] judo champions when they were in middle school or kids that had shown superiority in their results in sports, mostly kids like that. As for kids who had voluntarily joined the wrestling department, it was just me and one other boy. The rest were all basically a group pulled in there on sports recommendations. In my first year in high school, I was rag-dolled by even the tiny judo kids."

An inauspicious beginning for the finest mixed martial artist of his generation, to be sure. The sparring was a brutal grind, and the conditioning even harder. But Sakuraba was not just undeterred; he was elated. With visions of Tiger Mask still firmly in his mind, Sakuraba was exactly where he wanted to be, whatever the hardships. "I was doing what I loved, wrestling," he explains. "Even when other guys around me were grumbling, I was laughing, having fun doing it."

All the while, his focus on the world of professional wrestling never wavered. This was the time of shoot-style splinter group UWF's return to New Japan Pro-Wrestling, a brilliant angle that pitted feared outsiders against the familiar heroes of NJPW, the same program that would later inspire the WCW vs. nWo feud that helped vault professional wrestling to its late 1990s North American business peak. Sakuraba was completely engrossed. "I borrowed videotapes of the original UWF from my friend and watched religiously," he recalls. "As I filled the days and hours in high school with wrestling practice, I came to really understand the flow of pro wrestling. I watched the matches on TV, and during my time off, I did nothing but read *Shuukan Puroresu*. I had to read every single nook and corner of every page or I wouldn't be satisfied, so a single issue would always take me about two weeks to finish."

Despite being enthralled by one of the greatest angles in professional wrestling history, Sakuraba's desire to jump to the pro ranks at the earliest opportunity, a desire that had horrified his parents only few short years before, had almost completely left him. "Where'd my dream gone of being a pro-wrestler . . . I realized that even more than being a pro-wrestler, I had come to love amateur wrestling. I wanted to do more wrestling." To his parents' great relief, this meant college, specifically Chuo University. Chuo was no wrestling powerhouse, but hardly a slouch: a blessing penned by Chuo alumnus and super heavyweight Greco-Roman wrestling Olympian Tomomi Tsuruta, better known in his professional days as the fearsome "Jumbo," hung on the wrestling room wall as a concrete symbol of the opportunities available to the young men assembled on those mats, to those among them with the dedication and ability to make the most of their time there.

Sakuraba threw himself completely into his training, and took every opportunity to spar with those senior students gracious enough to offer tips and encouragement to an enthusiastic freshman. "Losing when you spar against the really good guys is a matter of course," Sakuraba says. "It's not a match. Training is training. So, I never felt real humiliation in training. Of course, if I lost I'd first get pissed. But just getting pissed isn't enough. It's important to use the energy of that anger and put it back into training. If you lose in sparring, just get back to training and get stronger."

This is clearly the attitude of an athlete committed to genuine self-improvement. Japanese society, especially in athletics, was divided into a strict hierarchy made up of senior men (senpai) and junior men (kouhai). Sakuraba was battling this system as much as opponents or his own body. It was about temporarily putting aside the demands of the ego, turning off that inhibiting part of the mind that compels the weak senpai to either bully their kouhai or avoid sparring entirely for fear of embarrassment, and embrace the routine defeats that come in training as opportunities to learn. "On the other hand," Sakuraba adds, "losing in a real match is wretched, that's all that can be said about it."

The high point of Sakuraba's competitive collegiate career came early, in the summer following his first year, when he faced Tokuya Ota, who would eventually claim the bronze medal in freestyle at the 1996 Olympics in Atlanta. There is no real accounting for Sakuraba, an enthusiastic but uncredentialed wrestler, taking a win over an athlete the calibre of Ota, and years later, Sakuraba can offer very little by way of explanation. "Dumbfounded," he writes, "I found myself scoring against him, and I suddenly realized I'd won." Sakuraba was as surprised as anyone. "It didn't feel real to me, but I thought, 'In the end, I trained my ass off, so that's probably why I won.'"

Whatever great expectations were visited upon Sakuraba in the wake of this stunning win over one of Japan's most promising wrestlers were short-lived, however, as Ota did his homework in the wake of his loss, and discovered Sakuraba's dark secret: "Yeah, I'm not good with throws," Sakuraba was forced to admit once again. "I get ragdolled even in training. Shit, I hate losing." They would face each other three more times, without Sakuraba mounting so much as a fraction of the offense that had seen him somehow emerge the victor in their first encounter.

In the end, Sakuraba was outclassed by Ota. He was also badly outworked. The enthusiasm that had carried Sakuraba through that grueling first year of not just wrestling training itself, but the difficult life of a kouhai, had begun to flag. "The fun training had suddenly become boring," he writes, and his willingness to put the necessary work in dropped off almost immediately. Despite temporary bursts of fanaticism, Sakuraba's commitment to training throughout his career wasn't always what it could or perhaps should have been. As early as his second year of high school, Sakuraba admits to figuring out which corners he could cut in training. "I'd gotten the feel for where I could cheat," he says, and whether that took the form of lackluster burpees and pushups whenever a trainer's back was turned, or assigning a lookout and goofing off if the coach had to step out for a meeting, Sakuraba figured out all the angles. He didn't want to run. He didn't want to do squats. All he wanted to do was wrestle.

Despite this drop in interest and application, and a stormy relationship with his coach, Sakuraba was named captain of the wrestling team after his third year. Rather than reignite a fading passion for the sport, the burden of being captain only heightened his overall displeasure with his situation: the upperclassmen he'd most liked to train with had moved on; "picking on the kouhai" who remained didn't suit him; rumors swirled that his coach had, oddly, run him down verbally to the rest of the team despite naming him captain; and training had become nothing more than a tedious grind. "The captain who fucking hated being captain" is how Sakuraba describes his agitated condition. And so he got out. Sakuraba "made up a lie" and quit, and spent a fifth, aimless year nominally fulfilling final requirements at Chuo while in fact spending as much time as possible playing pachinko and drinking, and deferring, as much as possible, any serious thoughts about his future. Think Dustin Hoffman in *The Graduate*, only rather than Mrs. Robinson showing up and suddenly making things a lot more interesting, it was Yoshiki Takahashi.

THE BUSINESS

A night of heavy drinking and attendant soul-searching led Sakuraba to the conclusion that all that awaited him after college were limited and decidedly unthrilling employment prospects. "I really didn't have anything but wrestling," he said. With his modest amateur career at an end, that could mean really only one thing. "There's nothing I can do," he decided, "but become a pro wrestler." Sakuraba had become accustomed to having this idea laughed off by whomever he shared it with, but on yet another night out, emboldened once again by drink, he couldn't help himself: "I bravely said, 'I'm going to be a pro wrestler!' but really I had no idea how to become one." In an incredible stroke of luck, that night's drinking buddy didn't laugh, but instead told Sakuraba that he had Takahashi's phone number, if he wanted it. "You bastard," Sakuraba replied, "you have Takahashi's phone number!? You shoulda said something earlier!"

Takahashi was a name from Sakuraba's past, a familiar figure from the high school wrestling tournaments of years gone by, though the two had never properly met. Still, it was a connection, however tenuous, to the world of professional wrestling: Takahashi was now working for Pro Wrestling Fujiwara Gumi, one of the shoot-style groups to emerge from the disorder that followed the second UWF's 1990 disintegration. This, Sakuraba decided, was his in. He made the call, and learned from Takahashi that he could try out whenever he felt he was ready. Both nothing and everything came out of this chance contact with Takahashi: in the end, Sakuraba never tried out for Fujiwara Gumi, but inspired by that conversation, Sakuraba rededicated himself to his middle-school dream of becoming a professional wrestler. When, only a few days later, he learned from the pages of *Shuukan Puroresu* that UWF International, another shoot-style group, was looking for new talent, Sakuraba enthusiastically applied, and found himself taking the entrance exam shortly after his 23rd birthday. UWF-Inter, as he most often calls it, had been very clear that they were looking for recruits no older than 22, but Sakuraba, whose application had been sent in mere days before his birthday, wasn't going to let that technicality get in the way.

Much to his surprise, Sakuraba was the lone candidate set to be examined by six UWFi regulars. For a young man who had gotten by since his second year of high school by dropping his knees on push-ups when the coach wasn't looking, "This was a really awful situation. I died doing the hill dash," he writes. "I died doing squats. I died doing push-ups. I died five or six times from this test." But he passed and was told that if he quit school almost imediately, he would be taken on as a shindeshi — a new recruit, a disciple. To the understandable dismay of his parents, Sakuraba did exactly that, and entered the world of professional wrestling September 1, 1992, just as he'd first dreamed of that late night in Akita years before when he'd seen Tiger Mask fly through the air in an inspiring display of athleticism and physical grace. And what was Sakuraba's first duty, after having his head ceremonially shaved as he entered the dojo? "Weed the lawn," Hiromitsu Kanehara told him. Not an inspiring start. But the next day, Sakuraba found himself enjoying barbecue on the beach with Kanehara, Yoshihiro Takayama, and the great Nobuhiko Takada. There was still a definite senpai/kouhai dynamic at work, but this wasn't going to be like the Chuo University wrestling team at all.

This is not to say that life as a UWFi trainee was a walk in the park. "I was doing endless squats and push-ups," he remembers. "As pros, we were expected to do repetitions with numbers that were virtually astronomical. I was made to do squats until my knees sounded like a skeleton laughing." Sakuraba, true to form, thought this kind of unending, mindless repetition was "pointless." He certainly wasn't alone in that assessment: new recruits, and even people slightly higher up the ladder, routinely disappeared from the dojo without a trace. "Night flight is a standard part of this world," Sakuraba tell us. When one of the UWFi regulars who had helped administer Sakuraba's entrance exam slipped off in the middle of the night, Sakuraba felt the loss acutely. "I became completely lonely." After only a month, he was made a special assistant to Nobuhiko Takada, which meant he sparred almost exclusively with Takada and Yoji Anjo, both of whom outweighed Sakuraba by more than 50 pounds. Against significantly bigger men with much greater knowledge of and experience with submissions, Sakuraba was routinely overmatched. "It wasn't until about two or three years had passed that I could start to not get owned," he tells us. Worse than the sparring, though, were the meals. Sakuraba had entered the dojo at 154 pounds, which was seen as far too slight for a professional wrestler. Eating to the point of serious discomfort was understood to be part of the job. Substantial weight gain proved elusive, however, since sleep was at a premium: Sakuraba's duties as a kouhai kept him busy cooking, cleaning, and laundering during hours that he dearly wished he could spend quietly alone, recovering from the rigours of training and the suffering of constant overeating, "always feelings close to death."

But the new frontiers of striking and submissions that were opened up to him each day in sparring made it all completely worthwhile. Sakuraba was so fascinated by what he was learning in the dojo for its own sake that when he was informed that he would make his professional debut August 13, 1993, at the Budokan against Steve Nelson, the news didn't bring with it any sense of reward or relief. "When I was told, 'You're next, going to make your debut,'" Sakuraba remembers, "I just said, 'Oh, really,' or something like that." It was, if anything, a hassle, a distraction from the sparring in the dojo that was the real reason Sakuraba cooly endured life as a UWF-Inter kouhai. "It was a pain in the ass," he says flatly, "so I didn't even shave." It was "a rather emotionless pro debut fight," and ended in a loss. (Sakuraba refers to both pro wrestling matches and mixed martial arts contests as "fights," and at no point concedes that there was anything prearranged about the in-ring action in UWF-International or any other professional wrestling organization.)

Nelson remembers his own opposite emotions. While Sakuraba wasn't keen on the match, others in the company took note of his potential. "There were 17,000 people there and I was real excited. The bosses told me it was a good match and I would be back to wrestle again . . . I had no idea he would become the real deal. I was 28 and he was around 23 so I just looked at him as a new wrestler. We were both just kids. My first three matches in the UWFi were against Sakuraba. The company considered us a great match up for the fans."

Freed from the hassle of his pro debut, Sakuraba was able to direct his attention back to the dojo, where he soon found himself sparring not just Takada and Anjo, but some notable foreigners too. Dan Severn, former Olympic team alternate and future UFC tournament and Superfight champion, failed to make much of an impression, however. Sakuraba acknowledges that Severn was "really good at using his weight and at throwing," but beyond that, he has nothing but a kind of amused derision towards Severn's skills. "I didn't get the feeling that he was really strong. He didn't know the ground game. I was a beginner, but I thought, 'If it's submissions, then I'm better.'" That verdict won't surprise anyone who later watched Severn steamroll his way into the finals of the UFC 4 tournament only to fall victim to a Royce Gracie triangle choke. But Sakuraba's harshest words are reserved for Severn's striking, which he calls "half-assed and weak." Sakuraba says, "I actually laughed. He faced off against the heavy bag, windmilling bitchslaps at it. I think he was aiming for palm strikes, but from what I saw, they were girly slaps." Sakuraba isn't talking about the kind of jarring palm strikes that would become the hallmark of the Pancrase organization, used with stunning force and precision by the likes of Bas Rutten, among others. "It wasn't with the hard part in the palm," Sakuraba takes pains to specify, "but with just his fingers really cutely tapping the heavy bag. 'Pechi pechi pechi pechi . . .' Whenever Severn was training striking, the gym was always filled with that insubstantial little hitting sound. But maybe Severn was aiming to do that, who knows. His opponent wouldn't expect him to come flying in with windmilling bitchslaps. Maybe he had it all planned out." Severn might have been brought in to square off against the top names in the UWFi ring, but for Sakuraba, what happened in the ring was insubstantial. What happened in the dojo is what counted, and in the dojo, as far as Sakuraba was concerned, Severn simply didn't measure up.

Sakuraba's slightly strange lack of interest in his own early professional matches melted away entirely when, to his surprise, Nobuhiko Takada announced that the UWFi wrestlers would be participating in a series of challenge matches against the brightest stars of New Japan Pro-Wrestling. Sakuraba's cynicism about his own nascent career melted away in a rush of childlike enthusiasm: "NJPW, the one I had been watching all through my childhood, that one? Whoa, I'm going to be able to fight a guy I've seen on TV?! Yes, I'll do it, I'll go." Sakuraba was elated. But those around him who understood the business a little better — Masahiko Kakihara, Hiromitsu Kanehara, and Kiyoshi Tamura, among them — could see the writing on the wall. "Ehh, the only happy one is me?" Sakuraba asked. "I couldn't read the signs of the situation at all." UWFi was at death's door, but it was not about to go quietly into that good night.

The October 9, 1995, Tokyo Dome NJPW vs. UWFi event headlined by a clash between Keiji Mutoh and Nobuhiko Takada drew a monstrous crowd of 67,000 and yielded the highest gate in the history of Japanese professional wrestling. Sakuraba found himself opening the show, paired with Kanehara in a tag team bout against Tokimitsu Ishizawa and Yuji Nagata, acquaintances from Sakuraba's collegiate and even high school wrestling days. This was Sakuraba's position throughout the massive NJPW vs. UWFi feud: at or near the bottom of the card, but being exposed to the biggest crowds imaginable, and "already thinking about how to please the audience while fighting." Further, "in that way," despite his lowly position in the grand scheme of that legendary feud, "the challenges against NJPW made for good homework." On top of that, Sakuraba had a brief conversation with Riki Chōshū in the bathroom, which, for him, made it all worthwhile.

SHOOT STYLE'S LINGERING DEATH

By the end of 1996, UWFi closed its doors for good. In its wake came Kingdom, made up mostly of UWFi refugees, it was a now largely forgotten shoot-style promotion that, to say the very least, failed to reach the dizzying heights the UWFi enjoyed. "Thinking back on it," Sakuraba wrote more than a decade later, "I have no idea what the hell kind of organization Kingdom was." He was not alone. The earliest shows, which falsely advertised Nobuhiko Takada, drew well enough at Yoyogi National Gymnasium, but soon Kingdom was confined to the much more modest Korakuen Hall for its particular brand of shoot-style, a style that was quickly fading as audiences became more exposed to the real thing. Takada, who could tell which way the wind was blowing, was already making preparations for a potentially huge money match with Rickson Gracie. Money was tight; pay was cut in half; and the workload for the few wrestlers left on the roster doubled. The Kingdom years, Sakuraba writes, were "proof of entropy."

But even as the product in the ring suffered and drifted into irrelevance, Sakuraba again took refuge in the dojo. A new friend of Kanehara's had started turning up to

KAZUSHI SAKURABA WITH NOBUHIKO TAKADA IN HIS CORNER

train: Enson Inoue, a Hawaiian-born, Japanese-American, Brazilian Jiu-Jitsu black belt, a Shooto and vale tudo Japan veteran. "Enson's BJJ system was completely different from what we were doing," Sakuraba writes. "Our whole thing was to get the takedown and get on top. Working like this, we could see the opponent's movements and start to understand how they fight. Sparring with Enson, I really came to understand, 'Ahh, this is the way BJJ guys move.'" Unlike his usual sparring partners, who would do their all to secure the top position and grind their opponent down, Inoue was a different animal entirely: "If I'd shoot, he'd at first try to stuff the takedown but if it didn't immediately work, he would just accept the bottom. And from there he'd work for an arm bar or a triangle." This early experience with the strategy and tactics of Brazilian Jiu-Jitsu would prove invaluable to Sakuraba as he embarked on his mixed martial arts career, which, much to his surprise, was just around the corner.

Shoot-style was clearly dying. Takada understood this, and brought top coaches, including Barcelona Olympian Takumi Adachi, into the well-appointed Kingdom dojo to help ready him for the transition to mixed martial arts. Kanehara understood this too and decided that the only way to bolster interest in their fading promotion was to prove that their wrestlers were, without question, legitimate fighters, capable of handling themselves against the no-holds-barred upstarts, and what better opportunity than the upcoming UFC Ultimate Japan event in Yokohama Arena? Yoji Anjo was chosen as the first Kingdom representative. After Kanehara withdrew with an injury, Sakuraba was chosen as the second. Unfortunately, nobody told Sakuraba anything about his role in any of this until the evening of December 17, 1997, when he emerged on the wrong side of a two-day bender. Ultimate Japan was scheduled for December 21. To make matters worse, it was a heavyweight tournament, and despite the bogus figure of 203 pounds Sakuraba presented in order to compete that night, he was no heavyweight. His opponent, Marcus "Conan" Silveira, a 243-pound Brazilian Jiu-Jitsu black belt under Carlson Gracie, most assuredly was. This was not an opponent to be taken lightly, in any sense of the word. "The pro wrestling world was in the midst of the 'Rickson Shock' after the October Pride 1 event just some weeks earlier," Sakuraba reminds us. "It was the era where just saying the name 'Gracie' had people pooping their pants." But Sakuraba, as we've already seen, is a man more comfortable in that situation than most.

The other side of the tournament bracket saw the brawler Tank Abbott best Yoji Anjo by decision. "If I lose next," Sakuraba thought, "Kingdom is over." This anxiety didn't stop him from attempting to take the massive BJJ expert to the ground almost immediately, as Sakuraba shot in for Silveira's ankle off of a feinted punch. Sakuraba's first few attempts fell short, and Silveira let his hands go. "Conan's punches hit the hardest part of my head," Sakuraba remembers, "so it didn't hurt at all. If he punches like this, there's no way I'm going to get KO'd. I was a little relieved." Still, though, no takedown, despite Sakuraba's best efforts. Until: "I got a great hold on Conan's leg. If I get him down from here, I can finish him and win. That is, it was my big chance. But, at that instant, I felt a huge crash into my internal organs. Bam! Owww. Who the hell, who came in and hit me? Going for the shoot, I realized that I had been blown off by someone else that had shot in on me. The perpetrator's name was John McCarthy."

There are few people in mixed martial arts with a track record as reliable as Big John McCarthy's. In a sport where virtually every referee's call is scrutinized and hotly debated by media and fans alike, the list of calls John McCarthy has clearly blown is short indeed. But he blew this call. Sakuraba wasn't out, nor was he necessarily in any real danger. He'd dropped low to secure the takedown just as Silveira's blows fell upon him but you can see, even now, how McCarthy could have had the impression that Sakuraba needed out, and fast.

"In the replay, plain as day, Sakuraba took the punch and then dropped levels for a single-leg takedown," McCarthy wrote in his autobiography *Let's Get It On*. "There was no debate at all. I turned to commentator Jeff Blatnick and said, 'I screwed up.'"

"There was no way I could accept the decision," the famously easygoing Sakuraba says. "Directed by Kanehara, I took the mic and screamed, 'I didn't lose.' And then everyone from Kingdom came into the Octagon." Their nearly 30-minute sit-in was effective: it was decided that yes, McCarthy's decision had been an error, and since Tank Abbott had broken his hand during his bout with Anjo, Silveira and Sakuraba would fight again later that night, this time for the tournament title. At this point, fatigue became a legitimate concern for Sakuraba and his camp, as he had stayed up until 3 a.m. the night before playing *Pokémon*. Seriously. "Don't worry about it," Kanehara said. "Your fighting spirit!" Laughing, "I really don't think this is gonna be good" is all Sakuraba could manage in reply.

But it *was* good: Sakuraba finished the Brazilian Jiu-Jitsu black belt by arm bar in only three minutes and 45 seconds, which was never, ever supposed to happen. A professional wrestler beating a BJJ black belt at his own game? Only weeks after Rickson Gracie embarrassed the great Nobuhiko Takada in front of tens of thousands at the Tokyo Dome? Inconceivable. As the Kingdom contingent poured into the Octagon and raised Sakuraba onto their shoulders, the martial arts world had quite simply been turned on its head in a reversal on par with the shock first felt when the unheralded Gracie family proved the merits of their art at the inaugural UFC. In response to a magazine headline that appeared in the wake of the Takada disaster, "Japanese Pro-Wrestlers Are Weak," Sakuraba turned the tables: "In fact, professional wrestling is strong," he said to the delight of the many who had always wanted this to be true but had come to fear that it quite simply was not.

Professional wrestling was indeed strong — here was incontrovertible evidence — but it was also broke. Sakuraba was understandably growing tired of Kingdom's inability to pay their wrestlers properly, or even at all, and followed Naoki Sano and Daijiro Matsui to Nobuhiko Takada's newly formed Takada Dojo, to make the best of the new opportunities available to them in the world of kakutougi, the fighting arts, leaving behind the fading world of puroresu. Here, the new directions in training that Sakuraba had experienced only by chance in his UWFi and Kingdom days could be actively pursued. He could seek out fighters like Tsuyoshi Kohsaka, whose unique blend of Brazilian Jiu-Jitsu and judo gave Sakuraba fits. "Every day at Takada Dojo was perfect training," he says. "Even sparring with the members that had joined the classes was great training for me." Released from the demands of regular pro wrestling appearances, the members of Takada Dojo were free to travel for training too: Sakuraba recounts an early trip to Marcus Ruas's Beverly Hills Jiu-Jitsu Club, where unfortunately Sakuraba found the attitudes of Ruas's students

— though not of Ruas himself — to be disappointingly overbearing and condescending, at least until he was able to prove himself in sparring. "I don't really know," he says, trying to find the right words to describe the personalities there, "kind of self-important or proud. Some guys would even just come up to me like, 'So, here's what jiu-jitsu's about' . . . The guy that came to me trying to tell me what jiu-jitsu was about, when we'd spar, I'd tap him out and he would bow ridiculously deeply and thank me in Japanese." Eventually, Sakuraba managed to earn the respect of his new training partners, but it didn't come easy. "I threw one guy with seoi nage [shoulder throw]," he says. "That guy was a representative of America in Greco-Roman wrestling. After that moment, everyone looked at me like they were seeing 'the mystery of the Orient.'" His initial reception might not have been what he'd hoped, but unlike the rigid senpai/kouhai training environment he'd come up in at home, at Ruas's gym, respect could be earned quickly through performance.

And performance, of course, was never a problem for Kazushi Sakuraba. Indeed, the performances Sakuraba would soon put on in the Pride ring have become the stuff of legend. First, there was the veteran Vernon "Tiger" White, who Sakuraba bested by arm bar after a grueling 30-minute bout. "What a pain in the ass," Sakuraba says. "Tiresome." Then Carlos Newton, the elegant young grappler with whom Sakuraba would trade hold after hold in one of the finest submission battles in the history of the sport. "A great fight," Sakuraba says simply, and there can be no argument to the contrary.

Newton recalls a young fighter who was clearly going places: "When I was in Japan and sitting at the same table as Sakuraba, seeing the way the other Japanese around him conducted themselves around him, I knew they had a lot of respect and reverence for the guy. His attitude very much typifies the great Japanese fighters — soft spoken, but carrying a very big stick. He had a very intuitive way about him in the ring. He wasn't all over the place and scrappy like some of the other Japanese fighters. He had very good composure."

An uninspiring draw against Allan Goes was followed by a winning effort against Vitor Belfort, handing the young standout only his second career loss. "The first time I used face-stomping," Sakuraba recalls fondly. "It was Kanehara's idea." Dynamic submission wins over Luta Livre stylist Ebenezer Fontes Braga and the journeyman Anthony Macias — a fight most notable for Sakuraba's famous Mongolian Chop ("Maybe I was playing too much," he concedes) — set the stage for the the confrontations that would define Sakuraba's career.

"GRACIE HUNTER"

Sakuraba's feud with the Gracie family — which would earn him the nickname "Gracie Hunter," cement his status as one of the sport's true greats, and make him the brightest star in both Japanese mixed martial arts and professional wrestling — didn't begin the way he wanted it to. Sakuraba didn't get the Gracie he wanted, at least not right away. He wanted to fight Renzo. "Renzo's a great guy," he says. "He's got a good personality and he's got good technique. He really has the heart of a warrior." The two would eventually meet in a classic at Pride 10 that would not be decided until Renzo, unwilling to quit but unable to continue with a spectacularly broken arm, had to be saved from himself.

But instead of the respected and beloved Renzo, Sakuraba's first encounter with the Gracies was with Royler, who Sakuraba takes pains to belittle. "I didn't want to fight the little guy," he insists, saying he had no time for this "tiny pup" of the Gracie clan, whose "selfishness" in first demanding the fight and then insisting on special rules and considerations is symptomatic of "the comedic selfishness of the whole family (excluding Renzo)." Such was his disdain for Royler that even as the fight seemed well in hand, with Royler showing little ability to contend with anything Sakuraba had to offer, there wasn't so much as a shred of pity: "I ended up wanting to bully the weak." He remembers "bending his tiny little arm" in a Kimura, telling one of the ringside judges, "If I go for it, his arm is gonna break." The referee stopped the fight. Royler was incensed, insisting, quite rightly, that he'd never tapped. But Sakuraba would have none of it: "What could he do to escape from that? No matter how much you proclaim, 'I didn't tap,' the fact is Royler didn't have a single good thing going for him. Whatever is said, I won the fight."

To Sakuraba's disappointment, the fight failed to turn Royler into "a respectable and proper person." His hope from the beginning was that a win over Royler would bring about a match against older brother Rickson, a chance to avenge Nobuhiko Takada's two decisive losses to the great champion of the Gracie family. But it would never come to pass. "I have a slight feeling like he ducked me, but I personally don't have any interest in Rickson anymore," Sakuraba said only a few months after the Royler fight. It had already become clear that a bout with Rickson would never come to pass. "He's a quitter. And I think rather than fighting an old guy, fighting someone younger and with energy makes for a more interesting fight."

And that was always Sakuraba's primary objective, even if it came at the expense of a winning game plan. "Even in the case where I lose," he says, "I want them to think, 'Sakuraba's fight was really interesting.' I want to give the fans an interesting fight that makes a lasting impression on them. That's the kind of fighter I'm aiming at being." The show is everything. Professional wrestling and mixed martial arts aren't identical, in his mind, but are much more closely related than pure sports fans might like to admit. "It's like, the different schools of karate," he explains. "It's all karate, but each of the different schools has different rules. It's like that."

Judged against those standards, his fight against Guy Mezger in opening stage of the Pride Grand Prix was a complete disaster. First of all, Sakuraba had no interest fighting against a field of significantly larger competitors. Given his track record, fans could be forgiven for thinking that Sakuraba was unconcerned with the size of his opposition, but that's not the case. "There was an unnecessarily big weight difference among all the competitors," he admits. "In a GP with people all around my weight, it would be no problem, but with this kind of weight difference, it's asking too goddamn much." The bigger, stronger Mezger took the fight on only two weeks notice, and had been clearly contracted to fight only one 15-minute round, at which time a decision was to be rendered. When the often questionable Pride judges declared that single, tepid round a draw and ordered the fight to continue, Mezger's cornerman Ken Shamrock balked and ordered his fighter to leave the ring and take the forfeit loss.

"Pride has their own agenda," Mezger said. "They brought me in there to lose to Sakuraba and then he'd enter the tournament to fight Royce Gracie. I was a fly in the ointment, because I beat him, and the best they could do was make a draw out of it."

However unjust this decision may have been, every mixed martial arts fan should be thankful for it: it set the stage for the greatest marathon the sport is likely to ever see, an epic contest between the rising Sakuraba and the first hero of the Ultimate Fighting Championship, the legendary Royce Gracie.

Sakuraba's first volume of autobiography was written in the run-up to his Pride GP bout against Royce Gracie, and, ever the professional wrestler, he does all he can to build the fight and create the impression of real antagonism. How real that emotion is, we'll perhaps never know, but the words themselves are remarkable. "The Gracies really are fools," he begins. "Fools, idiots, retards, jackasses, buffoons . . . No matter how many bad words I line up, I can't express my feelings for them. I'll take you on, with your own rules." Those rules were certainly a matter of contention. Royler had asked for special rules, and still found himself on the wrong end of what the Gracies considered to be an unjust referee's decision. This time, they left no room for error, as they saw it: unlike every other tournament bout, Sakuraba vs. Gracie would not be subject to referee stoppage, and it would go on for as many 15-minute rounds as it took to decide a winner. "If he comes like an adult and fights me," Sakuraba said, "No one will have any problem. But of course they ask for rule changes and, as a special bonus, threaten to pull out if Pride doesn't accept the changes. What social status they must have." Sakuraba acknowledges that "it is due to expressionless Royce and his relative Rorion . . . that we have this no-rules fighting," but suggests that "when they started to not be able to win, Royce and Rorion made some excuse and ran from the Ultimate," and derides them both for being "that kind of weakling."

However much of that antagonism was real, none of it seems to have survived their 90-minute Tokyo Dome struggle. As the two embraced in the ring amidst the cheers of tens of thousands of fans in awe of the singular contest they'd just witnessed, there was no sign of animosity, only mutual respect. It would be wrong to say their match was thrilling, exactly. How could it be, for 90 minutes? This was not a match defined by its incredible pace or dazzling exchanges of blows, positions, or submission attempts. Yes, Sakuraba came seemingly very close indeed to ending the match in the first round with a knee bar, and yes, Gracie had his chances with a guillotine choke, and yes, Sakuraba dazzled at times with his leaping, cartwheeling style. But this was, on the whole, a contest defined by attrition, by Sakuraba's slow, steady dismantling of the great grappler with a series of leg kicks that Gracie had no answer for.

"In the sixth round he kicked my left instep twice in exactly the same place," Gracie remembered. "I told [my family] about the pain. I wanted to make them understand that my leg was in so much pain that I couldn't move as they demanded."

When Gracie's corner wisely threw in the towel after the sixth 15-minute round, there could be no doubt: Kazushi Sakuraba stood alone at the top of the mixed martial arts world. When he came out again later that night, and, at a mere 173 pounds, lasted a competitive 10-minute round against Igor Vovchanchyn, then the most feared heavyweight striker in the sport, it was almost too much to be believed. This time, it was Sakuraba's corner that threw in the towel, but their man left that night in triumph, regardless of the official result.

The Gracie hunting wasn't finished. The long-awaited contest against Renzo ultimately materialized at Pride 10 and was a classic. Caught in a Kimura, Gracie let his elbow be dislocated rather than tap out. "I believed I could win the fight without it," he simply said. After the loss, Renzo refused to complain. "Many people make excuses when they lose," he told the joyous Japanese crowd. "I have only one. He was better than me tonight."

Although most expected a bout with Rickson to follow, Sakuraba had to settle for the fiery and troubled young Ryan, who fought bravely but came no closer to besting Sakuraba than his elders. That match ended with Sakuraba literally spanking the Gracie bad boy in front of the martial arts world.

Then, as with any great rise, came the great fall. By the time we rejoin Sakuraba in his 2007 volume of autobiography, again titled *Me*, we find a battered and baffled fighter trying to deal with the sudden revelation of his own in-ring fallibility. First, there was an upset loss to the terrifying Wanderlei Silva, who Sakuraba bravely traded with before being battered to a finish in less than two minutes, and then a better effort but another loss to the same great fighter that left Sakuraba with a grotesquely broken collarbone. Sandwiched between those two stunning losses was a spectacular win over future UFC Light Heavyweight Champion Quinton Jackson, but the tide had clearly turned: Sakuraba was no longer able to do exactly what he wanted to do, whenever he wanted to do it, against whomever he chose to do it to. The long, painful decline had begun. Before a crowd of 71,000 at Tokyo National Stadium, Sakuraba took on devastating heavyweight kickboxer Mirko Cro Cop, and, unsurprisingly, emerged from that contest with another loss on his record and, this time, a fractured orbital bone for his trouble. "Why this card was put together," he says, "I have literally no idea."

In the blink of an eye, Sakuraba has gone from fighting and finishing the best in the world to battling against a knee injury while struggling to finish the utterly inconsequential Gilles Arsene. He did so with some inspiration from the example of Ric Flair. "More than being strong," he recalled, "Ric was a 'never lose' champion. Sometimes he would get his opponent in a cobra twist and grab the ropes, with his opponent folded up like a shrimp, he would put both legs on the ropes and increase his weight to get the three-count, or he would weave some crafty cheating into the bout while he fought." There was nothing untoward or illegal about the unique way Sakuraba used the ropes to finally secure the arm bar that half-rescued an otherwise atrocious showing against the novice Arsene, but there was definitely a craftiness to it that would have done the Nature Boy proud. But his continued fascination with the pro wrestling of his youth would hurt him as much as it helped him: against the feisty journeyman Nino Schembri, whom Sakuraba should have handled easily, a foolhardy Mongolian Chop led to an inadvertent head butt and a TKO loss in a swirl of soccer kicks.

It's one thing for the great Sakuraba to lose, even three times, to a fighter of Wanderlei Silva's caliber, or to come up short against a Mirko Cro Cop, but it's quite another to be violently pounded out by Nino Schembri. Although he went on to uninspiringly avenge that loss, calls for Sakuraba's retirement began to be heard not long thereafter, following a savage beating at the hands of Ricardo Arona that left the once great fighter battered almost beyond recognition.

All the while, Sakuraba's passion for alcohol and cigarettes continued unabated, which surely didn't help. There were some major changes to his training regimen, including a trip to seriously, properly study striking with his former foes at the Chute Boxe Academy in Curitiba, Brazil, under Rudimar Fedrigo, "Lovely Fedimar," as he calls him. This paid immediate dividends with a flash knockout against an equally tragically diminished legend of the sport, Ken Shamrock, but it was too little to late. It was all clearly coming to an end for Sakuraba. As it was, shockingly, for the seemingly unstoppable Pride FC, rocked by a yakuza scandal that cost the promotion its lucrative Fuji Network television deal. Sakuraba, no stranger to failing promotions, jumped ship to the rival K-1 Hero's promotion, where the fading star took center stage one final time, playing a key role in an extraordinary drama.

Yoshihiro Akiyama was the hottest star of Hero's, their new light heavyweight champion after defeating the ferocious Melvin Manhoef in a spectacular tournament final. Born Choo Sung-hoon, a fourth-generation ethnic Korean raised in Japan, Akiyama had the potential to be a top draw in two countries, and possessed both the in-ring skills and the natural charisma needed to reach the pinnacle of the sport. Hero's, no stranger to pro wrestling–style promotional tactics, worked hard to position Akiyama as a babyface, going so far as to incorporate dozens of children into his elaborate, stylized ring entrance. To those that remembered the credible allegations of cheating that dogged Akiyama throughout his successful judo career — he was accused in both national and international competition of doctoring his judo gi to make it slippery to the touch and thus difficult to properly grasp and throw — this reconstructed, inspirational friend-of-children-everywhere version of Akiyama was a little hard to take. But that was inconsequential. The Hero's promotional machine had found their new champion, and any vague memories of alleged impropriety were not about to get in the way of potentially huge business. Akiyama was booked in a New Year's Eve contest against Sakuraba in which the only reasonable expectation was that Sakuraba would be pummeled, and symbolically pass the torch to Akiyama as the new face of Japanese mixed martial arts. This wasn't supposed to be a competitive fight; it was the once great Kazushi Sakuraba being used as nothing more than a prop, a device, a means of getting Akiyama over.

There was, however, just enough left of the Sakuraba mystique to worry Akiyama. The younger, stronger, faster, better fighter shouldn't have had anything to worry about. But what if Sakuraba was able to pull off one more incredible win, one more submission out of nowhere? What if, like the "never-lose" NWA champion Ric Flair he so admired, Sakuraba could snatch victory from the jaws of defeat one more time? There was just enough menace left in the veteran fighter to plant that seed of doubt in Akiyama's mind, just enough to bring old habits to the surface. After the elaborate entrances, the lights, the children, the screaming fans, the two locked up in the center of the Kyocera Dome Osaka ring. Something wasn't right.

"The fight had just started," Sakuraba says. "Neither of us had been moving so much as to cause a lot of sweat. And does sweat cause this much slipperiness?" Sakuraba had spent a life on the mats and in the ring, but this was something he'd never encountered before. "It left a strange feeling in my hand, like after having grabbed an eel, adding credibility to the rumors I had heard about his earlier judo days." Sakuraba protested to the referee as Akiyama escaped his grasp again and again. Fight on, the referee instructed. Akiyama showed no mercy for the floundering legend, and forced a first-round TKO stoppage with a relentless barrage of blows, as he escaped not just every attempted takedown but every attempted grip. The result would later be overturned, and Akiyama's reputation utterly ruined when video evidence compelled him to confess to the illegal application of body lotion in a deliberate act of cheating.

Sakuraba, retelling this tale, can't bring himself even to refer to Akiyama by name: for Sakuraba, Akiyama is never Akiyama; he is only a despised and unnameable "him." "So after all, the first world really is a shady world," Sakuraba is forced to conclude. "The MMA genre is in danger," he worries. Sakuraba of course had every reason to be irate and disillusioned. But there was a larger significance to what had transpired. The revelation that Akiyama had cheated one of mixed martial arts' great legends — perhaps its greatest legend — was nothing short of scandalous.

In the world of professional wrestling that gave Sakuraba his start and formed his sensibility, this was a heel turn, one that manipulated the audience's love for their fading hero into hatred for the villain who had the audacity to cheat him, and rocketed the newly loathed Akiyama to top-draw status. Sakuraba was rightly furious: there was no question he'd been wronged, and he couldn't be expected to see any upside in anything that had transpired. Akiyama has since reinvented himself stateside as the irresistible "Sexiyama," and against all sense and good judgment, Kazushi Sakuraba continues to fight on, despite serious health concerns and admissions of memory loss. But that night in Osaka was, in a sense, the end — of relevance, at least — for the man who once fought to prove that "in fact, pro wrestling is strong."

Sakuraba showed pro wrestling at its best, as a glorious art created by legitimately tough and focused men. On the other side of the world, Vince McMahon also wanted to show the world how tough wrestlers were — but to a very different response.

Professional wrestling in America made a startling return to the world of the legitimate contests on June 29, 1998, in Cleveland, Ohio. The Brawl for All competition started that night on the WWF's flagship television program, *Monday Night Raw*. And in a change of pace for wrestling fans in the newsletter era, the tournament was a complete surprise.

By the 1990s it was hard to keep a secret in the world of professional wrestling. The days of being "underground" were long gone. Dave Meltzer's *Wrestling Observer* and Wade Keller's *Pro Wrestling Torch* had official contacts in the WWF's office in Stamford, Connecticut, and heard whispers from the competing factions in WCW's Atlanta

23 BRAWL for ALL

headquarters on a daily basis. Little escaped their notice. But neither man had any idea what the WWF had in mind with this remarkable shift in focus.

Of course actual mat wrestling on a professional wrestling program was a thing of the distant past. Brawl for All wasn't a plan to bring it back either. Instead, it was busy work for the WWF's extra talent, guys kind of milling around in the back that the bookers had no plans for. They didn't want to let anyone go; after all, their competitor down south could scoop them up and potentially make something out of them. WWF had taken a WCW castoff, "Stunning" Steve Austin, and made him the biggest star in the industry. Something similar happening would be mortifying for the proud WWF owner Vince McMahon.

Like most bad ideas coming out of Stamford in those days, the blame for the Brawl for All has been placed squarely on the shoulders of head writer Vince Russo. It doesn't feel much like a Russo idea, as the writer's modus operandi was to eliminate the sporting element of wrestling shows all together, preferring to focus on sexy women and raunchy trash talk. But he makes a handy scapegoat for others in the company, including Vice President of Talent Relations Jim Ross and McMahon himself, both men obsessed with double tough hombres and the kind of oversized behemoths who made up the tournament.

The matches themselves were unique spectacles. Brawl for All was a mixture of boxing and wrestling. The wrestlers wore comically oversized 20-ounce gloves and scored 10 points for a knockdown. A takedown was worth five points. In the case of a decision, landing more punches than your opponent was also worth five points. Once on the mat, the fighters were quickly stood up. Submission holds weren't allowed and a pinfall, the signature method of ending a professional or amateur bout, was not in effect. It was a glorified toughman contest, featuring athletes who hadn't competed in years, or in some cases, ever. To then–WWF writer Jim Cornette, it was a concept with obvious flaws.

"They were actually telling the guys to get in the ring and try to beat each other up for real," Cornette said. "And to make sure they tried, they were giving the winner of each fight $5,000 and the chance to continue on for a big prize. . . . There were a lot of great athletes and tough guys in the WWF, but they had not been in training for competition. They had been in training for performance . . . the unathletic people who structured this had no fucking clue that's a recipe for disaster."

The first shoot in a major pro wrestling promotion in decades involved two of the most hyped "real" fighters in the company. Marc Mero may have played the role of a makeup wearing, bedazzled Little Richard clone named Johnny B. Badd in WCW, but in real life he was a tough former New York Golden Gloves boxing champion. Steve Blackman's gimmick was more true to life — the soft-spoken Pennsylvanian sported black karate pants and called himself "The Lethal Weapon." With years of martial arts training in his past, many thought it a suitable sobriquet.

But the toughest man in the ring wasn't either participant. The legendary Danny Hodge was brought in to officiate the bout, and even at 66 could have likely done plenty of damage. While Ross attempted to put him over strong on television, no one in the building had any idea who Hodge was. The crowd, confused and unprepared for this kind of contest, voiced their displeasure loudly, chanting, "We Want Wrestling."

Blackman gave them what they asked for, taking Mero down over and over again. Of course, amateur wrestling takedowns weren't what the crowd had in mind. Blackman won the fight 25–5 on the unofficial scorecard, scoring five takedowns in three one-minute rounds. Although the audience wasn't won over by the one-sided fight, it was a thing of beauty compared to the second bout.

John "Bradshaw" Layfield was one of McMahon's locker room enforcers, a 300-pound former football player who'd tried out for the Los Angeles Raiders. Bradshaw was noted for being a tough guy, but intimidating smaller wrestlers in the shower, allegedly a Bradshaw trademark, wasn't going to be enough in the Brawl for All. It would require holding up your hands and throwing hard punches with giant gloves — easier said than done.

"Rowdy" Roddy Piper and Mr. T had learned that lesson the hard way at *WrestleMania 2* back in 1985. The two stars had a fixed boxing match, but could barely lift their arms after a few minutes in the ring. Boxing was hard stuff and used a set of muscles that are dormant in most people, even athletes like the great WWF performers who were used to tough physical activity.

Layfield's opponent was Mark Cantebury, another giant wrestler who was playing a farmer called Henry Godwin. It was a role that required him to wrestle in the mud and get dumped in pig swill and suffer various livestock-related indignities. The two went toe to toe, at least for a matter of moments. Then they started heaving for breath. In the *Observer*, Meltzer was less than impressed: "Bradshaw was awarded the decision over Cantebury, although if you kept score, it should have been a draw, as Bradshaw won two of the three rounds, giving him a 10–5 edge, but Cantebury did take him down once. There was a period in the second round where Bradshaw rocked Cantebury, although he never knocked him down. That was more like watching a low level toughman contest as two big guys banged away with no form or skill, and even with the short one minute rounds, both were noticeably gassing 40 seconds into it."

Meltzer's *Pro Wrestling Torch* counterpart, Wade Keller, was immediately excited by the prospects, not just for the company, but for the wrestlers who were stuck on the undercard with seemingly no escape: "The fans reacted to the Mero-Blackman shootfight Brawl for All with boos in part because they didn't know it was a shoot. Once it is established that the matches are shoots, fans will probably be much more receptive, even if the wrestlers involved aren't over. Some, though, will remain upset because they just want to see acrobatic style pro wrestling. I really like the concept of shoot fights for a number of reasons. One, it is novel and intriguing to watch. Two, it will inspire some mid-card wrestlers to get into better shape. Three, someone languishing on the undercard could get over after a few impressive fights. Will the WWF have to become regulated again in the states where they have fought so hard to be deregulated? Or will they claim the real fights are fake, too?"

As reporters began to dig, the real reason for the Brawl for All came to light. It wasn't just a tournament to keep wrestlers on the undercard busy, or even a scheme to draw all important television ratings. The idea was to catapult one man to stardom: recent import "Dr. Death" Steve Williams.

THE DOCTOR

In the 1980s, two men stood out in the American wrestling scene, both revered by their peers as the toughest guys in the business. Williams was a legendary figure in the industry. A former football star at the University of Oklahoma, and a four-time wrestling All-American in his spare time between football seasons, he was considered unbeatable. The only one in his class was Tonga Fifita, who wrestled in the WWF as Haku.

Haku was a mild-mannered guy — unless you insulted the wrestling business. That was his trigger. Unfortunately for loudmouths across the country, wrestlers hanging out at a bar tended to attract notice and jealous catcalls. Haku had his own way of dealing with the debate about whether wrestling was real or fake.

"When I walk in and you tell me it's fake, I'll show you how fake the business is," Haku said. "Whether I take your teeth out or take your eyeballs off or whatever it was in those days. Maybe they're going to kick my butt around, but watch it — I'm coming back and finding you. But those were those days. I'm glad nobody picked up a gun and shot my ass. But in those days, that's how it was."

Haku's most legendary battle didn't happen in the ring or battling his way through a throng of angry fans to get back to the locker room. His legend was born at a hotel near the Baltimore Airport. That's where he introduced a hapless opponent to the Tongan version of "got your nose."

"When they were ready to close, we had a few drinks, and on our way out there were five guys just sitting there," Haku remembered. "Of course, the same thing came out. The 'fake' stuff. 'Hey, are you guys with those guys — wrestlers? The fake wrestlers on TV?' You know. I said, 'Yeah. I'll show you.' And I reached over without thinking . . . grabbed his face, and bit his nose off. Then the fight started. Me and Silva kind of cleaned house there and left. I'll never forget it."

Williams didn't have a fight quite that insane in his wrestling scrapbook. But he had more than 20 years of strongman feats and bar brawls to sustain his reputation. His legend started all the way back at Lakewood High School, where he broke his nose in a match but finished the season wearing a hockey mask, earning his Dr. Death nickname. Williams may have been the best heavyweight wrestler of his generation. Wrestling only part time in college, and having joined the team with the season already in progress, he competed against men who were wrestling full time. Despite the tremendous disadvantages, Williams pinned top stars like Dan Severn and took future Olympic champion Bruce Baumgartner to the limit in the 1982 NCAA Finals, falling 4–2 in the final match. Meltzer says the heavyweight limit in college wrestling was created with Williams in mind: "The top coaches were wanting to impose a weight limit on the heavyweight division, because the feeling was the 400-pound heavyweights who couldn't really move but also couldn't be moved easily, were leading to dull matches and making the heavyweight division appear to not be athletic. They decided to come up with an upper weight limit, and few know this, but it was Steve Williams, the 285-pound weight limit in the heavyweight division, which still exists to this day, came from. Williams entered the tournament that year at 285 pounds. Most of the real athletic heavyweights were around 240, but there was no denying Williams was quick, powerful, and conditioned at 285, so the feeling at the time was that was the heaviest weight you could maintain still being a great athlete at."

Williams came up in Bill Watts' Mid-South Wrestling. It was a hard gig, one with long miles and violent audiences. When the oil riggers and other crusty men who made their living in Oklahoma, Mississippi, and Louisiana got riled up, the action outside the ring was often more violent than anything that happened in the squared circle. The heels needed police escorts just to make it to the back alive. Unless you were Williams and partner Hercules Hernandez, who together once took on 10 fans at one time — and battered them all on their way to the back for a beer.

Williams recalled, "I told [opponent] Ricky Morton he better hurry up and beat me. Because those raging cajuns were coming over the barricade. We got to the back and someone had locked the door to the heels' dressing room. When you're a heel down in the south, a lot of crazy stuff can happen. We were fighting to survive. That's just how the business was back then, when we had the people."

Watts liked his performers tough, and Williams was his favorite. He saw something of himself in the young star. Both were Oklahoma graduates and big strong guys. But that hardly made Williams unique in that territory. "It was all tough guys," Williams remembered. "Ex football players, former wrestlers, bouncers." Like most pro wrestlers, the boys liked to relax after the matches at the nearest bar, but the locals had other ideas, often wanting to try their luck with the big wrestlers. Watts had no problem with the wrestlers handling their business — as long as they came out on top. Said Watts, "If you got into a fight at a bar, I didn't care, but if you lost I fired you. It was that simple — if you were going to go out and make an ass of yourself, you'd better win."

Williams was built like a fireplug. He was solid muscle, the functional kind that could do real damage. His was not the lean and cut figure that would end up defining the wrestling industry in the post–Hulk Hogan generation. He was simply *big* and his strength was put on display for the world to see. Fellow wrestlers were marks for the strongman act every bit as much as the fans. Williams would take a huge wrestler like Ray "Big Bubba" Rogers and press him over his head five or six times, never even changing the expression on his face.

Williams was a rough-and-tumble performer, what other wrestlers called "stiff." When you finished a match with "Dr. Death" you felt it. Combined with an interview style that didn't fit into the more flamboyant "sports entertainment" McMahon created in the 1980s, Williams was lucky to find the perfect home for a man of his talents in Japan. Wrestling for Shohei "Giant" Baba's All Japan Pro Wrestling, Williams became one of the most popular foreign attractions in a country that loved its professional wrestling.

Williams and tag team partner Terry Gordy were dubbed the Miracle Violence Combination. While some of the Japanese nicknames for American wrestlers sounded goofy in English, this one was spot-on. Williams and Gordy were indeed a particularly brutal team, perfect for a promotion that was upping the ante on extreme stunts and ultra-violent matches. Williams became the promotion's champion in 1994, beating the top Japanese star Mitsuharu Misawa in a fantastic match in Tokyo.

Drugs plagued both Gordy and Williams throughout their careers. Williams was arrested multiple times at airports with steroids and other pills, but those arrests came in the United States. He was busted with pot at the Narita Airport in Japan, a serious crime in that country that often involves major prison time and would usually prevent a foreigner from ever returning to the country.

"It was a bad mistake. I was involved in a lot of drugs and a lot of alcohol back then," Williams admitted. "It almost cost me my career with that company and it ended up taking Terry's life."

Williams served a one-year suspension and Baba was able to pull strings to get him back into Japan the next year. But the damage was done — his career as a Japanese headliner was effectively over.

In 1998, Ross was able to talk Williams into joining him in the WWF. Once Watts' right hand man, Ross now served in the same capacity for McMahon. He was in a position of power and could promise Williams he would get a fair shake in an organization stocked top to bottom with fiercely political stars who would lobby hard to keep their positions as the WWF's top stars.

"Ross was a University of Oklahoma football mark. He loved everyone that came out of that program, me included," Williams said. "He loved all that stuff."

The Brawl for All was supposed to be Williams' ticket to the main event for a promised program with "Stone Cold" Steve Austin. His reputation was so huge, his legend so large, that it seemed like a given he would win, despite being 38 with almost 20 years of hard wear on his big body. Williams wasn't sure about the concept, but the lure of big money was calling his name. He says he was promised $100,000 to take the tournament. Meltzer reported $75,000. Either sum was a pretty figure for a man whose career seemed on its last legs.

Originally Williams was the one ringer in the tournament. Neither Dan Severn nor Ken Shamrock, two UFC veterans, were considered. Shamrock was too big a star and Severn was thought to have too much of an advantage. Williams had actually beaten Severn in the past in amateur contests but was years removed from his glory days.

"I was pressured to do it by who I am in the business," explained Williams. "Because I was the strongest guy in wrestling and the toughest man in the business for so many years. I was worried about hurting one of their guys. In a shoot you can go for a takedown and take out a guy's knee like that. Instead, that happened to me."

THE BEST LAID PLANS

By the time Williams made his first appearance in the tournament, fans had seen three weeks' worth of fights. It wasn't a huge success, but it wasn't a failure either. It maintained ratings, keeping the status quo, but that was deceiving. It was maintaining those ratings with what was considered second-rate talent, guys who would normally have hundreds of thousands of viewers clicking over to WCW's competing program *Monday Nitro*.

Puerto Rican star Savio Vega was the most impressive of the first round competitors in the early going, battering the overly muscular Brakus and bloodying his nose. It was an instructive moment for wrestling fans. Brakus was muscle-bound and shredded, 300 pounds with almost no body fat. Vega seemed doughy in comparison, one of the few WWF wrestlers who competed with his shirt on to protect the world from his jiggling chest. But none of that muscle could help Brakus defend a punch or a takedown, and Vega dominated.

Vega recalled, "We all sat down before and they told us, 'This is okay, this is not okay.' One of the things they said was no kicks. I was like, 'What? Come on.' Because the only guy who knew how to kick was me . . . Brakus, he was a nice person. He thought it was going to be a work. I told him, 'No, brother.' After that he was mad at me."

Fans were starting to become intrigued by the Brawl for All concept, but two names dominated the conversations — Severn and Shamrock. Originally prohibited from throwing their hats in the competition, both were invited to participate. Shamrock, who was rising up the ranks and already a star, declined. He was a professional fighter and knew that he hadn't trained for a fight. Severn, whose calm and laid-back persona wasn't getting over with WWF fans, jumped at the opportunity.

"When they first announced the concept they said, 'Ken and Dan, you're not going to be a part of this.' A few weeks later they gave me a call and said, 'Do you want to be in the Brawl for All? I asked, 'How much?' They gave me a figure and I said, 'Sure.' It was that easy. A no-brainer," explained Severn.

His fight with the "Godfather" Charles Wright showed that it wasn't just wrestling fans who had lost touch with their amateur wrestling roots — the announcers had too. Even Ross, who had been such a fan of Hodge, Jack Brisco, and Williams, didn't seem to recognize what he was watching. Severn took the Godfather down twice in the first round, even going so far as to turn him over and pin him, clearly not understanding the rules didn't allow for much actual wrestling.

Ross and announcing partners Jerry Lawler and Shawn Michaels seemed clueless. Because Severn was using simple takedowns, and not outrageous suplexes or high amplitude throws, the threesome seemed unsure whether they were takedowns at all. Despite what should have been a dominant win, the announce crew called the bout like it was a Godfather win. When the former UFC champion Severn had his hand raised in the end, the crowd seemed more perplexed than impressed. When the tournament moved into the next round, the Godfather was the one moving forward despite a loss. Severn watched from the sidelines.

"It was pretty lackluster. You couldn't really do much with those giant 20-ounce gloves," Severn admits. "I did the one match and then I was pulled out of it. I would just be speculating if I told you I knew why. Maybe because he was just a street brawler and would go out there and give them the kind of brawl they wanted. It was just cheap entertainment so maybe they just wanted a couple of chuckos to entertain them. The guys in the back were loving it."

Williams agreed. "The office loved seeing the boys beat on each other. Severn, I wrestled him in the amateurs, he was a pinning artist out there. He would take him down and hold them there. The WWF, they didn't like that."

While it took years for wrestling to devolve into fixed matches back in the 1800s, it took only weeks in the zany world of the WWF Brawl for All. Tag team partners and friends Bob Holly and Bart Gunn had Brawl for All's first worked match, following Severn's snoozefest with the Godfather. Gunn was a slugger with toughman experience. Holly just wanted to get through unscathed. It would turn out to be the only match where Gunn went the distance. Holly was his only opponent to make it to the final bell.

The next week Williams made his highly anticipated debut. He wrecked Pierre Ouellet, a French Canadian wrestler who was no match for Williams standing or on the mat. The fight raised some important questions about the entire tournament. For years the WWF had protested the heavy hand of state athletic commissions who insisted on regulating professional wrestling even though it was clearly performance art. They had succeeded in removing that regulation by admitting to the world that wrestling was merely entertainment and not sport. But now that they were promoting combat sports, it became clear some guiding hand was needed. Ouellet had lost his right eye in a firearms accident when he was just 12 years old. He had no business in the ring in a competitive situation. Not only could he have been blinded if something had happened to his left eye, but a boxer without proper depth perception couldn't possibly see punches coming. Ouellet was not alone. Vega had entered the tournament with a serious neck injury that was exacerbated by the tough competition. Dr. Death was also a physical mess. At his 20-year high school reunion he was in so much pain standing he couldn't even spend an hour with old friends. Williams and Ouellet both survived without serious injury, but despite a dominant win, Williams didn't feel comfortable with the rules or where this could be heading.

"I was an amateur wrestler. I was never a boxer," Williams said. "When you wear those gloves, when you cover up your palms, the wrestler can't do nothing. I mean, I'll fight you, but I'm no boxer. And with the gloves I couldn't hook onto the guy, couldn't grab him."

In the second round of the tournament, Williams was dethroned as wrestling's toughest man by the unheralded Bart Gunn. Gunn hadn't turned heads in his first-round performance and was thought to be an easy mark for Williams. The loss sent a shockwave through the entire promotion and Meltzer called it one of the most shocking moments in recent wrestling history: "Gunn, who has won toughman contests in the past, fought a much smarter fight in beating the tourney favorite. The plan was for Williams to win this tourney to set him up as a challenger for Austin and as UFC has learned, nobody can predict shoots, especially with the strange rules this has."

"DR. DEATH" STEVE WILLIAMS

Williams was ahead 15–0 in the second round when disaster struck. "He faked a punch and then dropped down to take me down. Half my body went out of the ring, but he still had a hold of my legs. I could feel my hamstring tear and my knee pop," Williams remembered. "No matter what though, I wasn't going to quit. I don't know how to quit. I knew I was hurt. Everyone did. You could see it."

BRAWL FOR ALL 241

Dr. Death was saved by the bell and came out fighting in the third round. Essentially immobile, Gunn tore him to shreds, landing a left hook that knocked the All-American out, dislocating his jaw and ending his chance to be a top player in the WWF.

"I immediately got hit and knocked right back down. I didn't even realize I had been knocked out," Williams said. "I was just worried about my leg. When I talked to my wife that night she told me I had been knocked out. I didn't believe her. Not Dr. Death. Tough guy Steve Williams? I'd never been knocked out in my life and I've been hit with some heavy stuff. I said, 'Nah.' She said, 'Oh yeah. Your eyes were rolling around in the back of your head. Are you sure you're okay?'"

It wasn't what anyone in the office wanted, one of the perils of real sports. Without the ability to pick and choose winners, the unexpected becomes the expected, the unusual the usual. It also divided the locker room. WWF stars may have been fierce competitors behind the scenes, but in the ring they were teammates. As WWF manager the Jackyl wrote in the *Winnipeg Sun*, this changed the dynamic:

> *There was also the philosophical issue of pitting the guys against each other in a way that seemed to suggest that the tension backstage could be upped in a dangerous way. We wondered how the fans would react, and what message were we sending them about the traditional pro wrestling that was our livelihood? At the end of all the backstage debate, the bottom line was that nobody knew what was going to take place on live television once that bell rang. Due to the very realistic nature of this concept, there was a "sellout at the monitors" in the back as everyone from Austin to the ring crew guys crowded to get a look at what would happen. As most of us saw, Bart Gunn possesses a left hook and a calm assassin's demeanor, which perfectly suited the competition, as perhaps it hadn't suited him in the normal WWF environment.*
>
> *Gunn may have been the only one not surprised by his win. He had been nervous about participating from the get-go, making sure that the front office wouldn't be upset if he disrupted their plans for Williams. Bruce Prichard, the WWF employee tasked with putting the tournament brackets together, assured him that the company would be behind him even if he beat Williams.*

"I asked if I was going to get any heat," Gunn recalled. "Obviously you want Steve to win this, based on the vignettes you're doing. You aren't paying any attention to the other guys. If you want, why not save me and him until the end, we'll work it, and I'll let him beat me. He said, 'Ah, that won't be necessary.'"

Gunn was steamed by the perceived lack of respect. Williams paid the price. "Nobody liked it," Williams said. "The fans didn't like it. It was the stupidest thing I've ever done.

I was able to make a star out of it, but it wasn't me. Bart Gunn — God bless the kid. He knocked out a legend."

The WWF deserves credit for plowing forward with the concept even as their carefully laid plans were thrown awry. "Jim Ross was steaming," Gunn said. "Jerry Lawler and all these guys were needling him because that's all Ross had been talking about for weeks: 'Steve, Steve, Steve.'" Instead of Williams, they seized the moment and pulled Gunn from obscurity. Wade Keller mused over the implications of this unforeseen upset: "WWF fans didn't care about him a month ago and now he's probably going to be too over with fans to be held back in the Midnight Express tag team. The goal of the concept was to create something different that made for compelling viewing and to create some new stars from the muddy undercard. Bart is the first to rise above . . . Ross, who is a big proponent of Dr. Death, worked hard to establish that Doc is out of his element with boxing gloves on. He said he's had his bell rung before and he doesn't win every fight, but he'll be back. The WWF had big plans for Doc. I wonder if that will change now? It showed that main-eventers do have something to lose by participating in the shoot fights."

It wouldn't have been wrestling if they didn't try to spice things up a bit though. Gunn did a pull-apart brawl with his semi-final opponent the Godfather just a week before their fight. He also engaged in a war of words with Ross, accusing the announcer of downplaying his win to protect the Oklahoman's old friend Williams.

"I knocked out Dr. Death Steve Williams with a good left hook," Gunn said. "And when I go home and watch television, all I hear is you and everybody else making excuses for him."

On the other side of the bracket, confusion reigned. Darren Drozdov, an unexceptional former football player best known for an uncanny ability to puke on command, advanced despite going to a draw with the 40-something Road Warrior Hawk in the first round. In the commentary Jim Ross explained that Hawk had suffered a broken nose so Droz was selected to continue. He snuck by Savio Vega, who was in no condition to compete, but Droz looked like he'd never even seen a fight before in his life, let alone participated in one.

Marc Mero was also back, despite losing his first round matchup against Steve Blackman. A legitimate martial artist, Blackman was actually serious enough about the contest to train for his second fight. But his preparation backfired when his knee wasn't up to the strain of training and he was unable to continue. Of course, no one bothered to tell the crowd though, so Mero moved forward with no explanation. Mero, the former boxer, expected to make the most of his second chance, but his opponent Bradshaw was having none of it. The Texan bent the rules, unclear in the first place, to the breaking point, angering wrestling critic Christopher Robin Zimmerman: "Bradshaw's blatantly cheating, putting Mero in a headlock and rabbit-punching him. Bradshaw gets a takedown for five and Mero again looks to get the five for the most punches. This seems to make Bradshaw look like a damn wuss who wants to take the shortcut to get the win — much like Blackman destroyed Mero pointswise with takedowns and not bothering with punches . . . Bradshaw is announced the winner. What bullshit. It's completely obvious they WANTED Bradshaw to move on and they made sure he won — it was a fix."

By the semifinals, critics on the fence initially, like Meltzer, were calling the experiment a success. The ratings were proof that it worked, even though fans in the arenas still weren't responding positively to the bouts. The human cost, however, was staggering. Drozdov tore a bicep, Vega's neck never recovered and he was gone from the WWF for good, Williams was out of action for months, and the Godfather suffered a hairline fracture of his ankle after falling awkwardly when Gunn knocked him out in the semifinals. In the other bracket's semifinals, Bradshaw continued to flout the rules, hitting Drozdov with rabbit punches on his way to winning a razor tight fight.

Bradshaw had made it to the finals by the skin of his teeth. All of his wins were super close, foul plagued, and often controversial. That all came to an end against Gunn in the tournament finale. Bradshaw was competitive in the staredown, as intense as any we'd seen in the competition. Once the bell rang, it was immediately clear he was outclassed. Gunn knocked him down quickly, but he made it to his feet to face the referee's standing eight count. Bradshaw's eyes were glazed, but the fight was allowed to continue, albeit not for long. Bradshaw had trouble getting his bearings and was dropped by two more hard punches. It took smelling salts to revive him, and Gunn was suddenly king of the wrestling tough guys.

Gunn won $75,000 for taking the tournament. Bradshaw's series of tainted wins helped him to the $25,000 prize for second place. But the following months proved Gunn's fears were warranted after all. There was no big push to the top of the cards after his win. Instead he disappeared from the WWF.

"I'm going, 'Hey, where's my run? Where's my run?'" Gunn said. "And they're saying, 'Hey, we don't know what to do with you. We don't know how to use you. We're working on it.' Meanwhile I'm sitting at home."

To be fair to Ross and other decision makers, Gunn had never been considered a hot commodity. At the end of the day, his ability to beat up novice wrestlers in a modified toughman contest could only take him so far. His work in the ring and his interviews were lifeless and uninspired. Almost anyone else could have been propelled to stardom. Bart Gunn, however, just didn't have it in him.

The company sent him to Japan, the one place besides the WWF back office that beating Williams really meant something. Teaming with Johnny Ace, Gunn finished near the top of All Japan Pro Wrestling's Real World Tag League, an annual tournament featuring some of the world's best wrestlers. Gunn looked out of place, several notches below amazing Japanese wrestlers like Kenta Kobashi and veteran Americans like Stan Hansen and Vader.

On the homefront, the WWF's creative team couldn't think of a single idea for Gunn. They brought him back for a brief feud with his former partner Holly, even getting a returning Williams to interfere in the match. Now wearing a mask, which apparently made the distinctive Dr. Death unrecognizable to the announce team, Williams was managed by Jim Ross himself. The WWF, especially lead writer Vince Russo, was looking to push Ross out as the lead announcer in favor of Michael Cole. This was his fallback position, and his heart wasn't in it. Fans were confused by the babyface Ross siding with a masked man who seemed to be a villain. Williams was failing and failing fast. "He was supposed to be my manager and I was supposed to be a heel," Williams said. "But Jim didn't like hearing the boos. So we were kind of going nowhere."

Gunn fared little better. His angle with Holly was scrapped. It was decided Brawl for All was what Gunn did best, so they'd give him one more shot at it — but they wanted to take things up a notch. Instead of pitting Gunn against other wrestlers, the WWF looked to bring in a major combat sports star to take on Gunn at *WrestleMania XV*. Former UFC sensation David "Tank" Abbott was considered, but the promotion ended up settling on rotund boxer "Butterbean" Eric Esch.

Packing 400 pounds on his 5'11" frame, Butterbean was a gimmick boxer, usually featured in four-round bouts as a TV novelty act before the serious fights started. But appearances can be deceiving — he was a skilled fighter who had once gone to the limit with former champion Larry Holmes. Sure, Holmes was 52 years old at the time, but Butterbean had a lifetime of boxing experience. Gunn had just a few months training with Marc Mero's old coach in New York.

Incredibly, many fans and wrestlers were picking Gunn to win. At least the ones who believed it would be a real contest. Most thought it would be a worked bout. So did boxing star Vinny "The Pazmanian Devil" Pazienza, who was brought in to referee the fight. Wrestling historian Basil Devito Jr. explains, "Not until shortly before the Brawl for All actually began was Pazienza convinced that Butterbean and Bart Gunn were going to be involved in a legitimate fight; this was not a predetermined event, and I think that surprised Pazienza — he hadn't come to Philadelphia expecting to handle the responsibilities of a true referee."

Pazienza didn't have to work long for his paycheck. Butterbean knocked Gunn down in the first few seconds and them knocked him cold with a huge right hand. It was this knockout, not the tepid live crowd response to the tournament, that killed the Brawl for All. Gunn hadn't just made himself look bad by losing in a devastating fashion in just 35 seconds. He had made the company, the business, and the boys look bad too. If a joke boxer like Butterbean could beat him, and he beat the other wrestlers so easily, what did that say about the wrestling industry?

The WWF needed a new shot of credibility. Gunn's had been killed dead by Butterbean's massive punching power. The disgraced Gunn was shipped off to Japan — permanently — and Dr. Death wasn't far behind. But the WWF office had a new idea to bring legitimacy to their show. In the months between the beginning of the Brawl for All and the ill-fated *WrestleMania* showdown, the company signed a wrestler that would turn the business upside down. An Olympic hero, 1996 gold medalist Kurt Angle, was coming to *Raw*.

The boos rang down from the rafters, quite a change of pace for the man in the middle of the ring. Just four years earlier the 1996 Olympian had been cheered in this very city, winning the gold medal and impressing the world with his grit and determination. None of that mattered in 2000, not to these wrestling fans. Less than a year into his WWF career, Kurt Angle already had the people right where he wanted them, as he told the crowd in Atlanta's Georgia Dome how much better he was than their hometown sports heroes like John Rocker or Isaiah Rider.

Angle was the virtuous babyface. Too virtuous. He preached the three I's (intensity,

24 YOUR OLYMPIC HERO: Kurt Angle

integrity, and intelligence) and later became an advocate for abstinence. This might have made him a huge babyface in the 1970s. In a wrestling boom spawned by the antihero "Stone Cold" Steve Austin, it made him a heel. Big time.

Angle told Fox Sports, "I was the Olympic hero that saved the nation. Then the fans started booing me because I was coming off like a square. So I started feeding off of that and started to act like more of a square and started preaching to people about my three I's and they didn't want to hear it. So I started grinding them about their town and how bad their athletic team sucked and I wasn't lying. That's how I came up with the line 'It's true.' I would say, 'Your team stinks,' and they would boo, and I'd say, 'No it's true, it's true.' Before I knew it, I was one of the biggest heels in the business, whereas 15 years ago I would have been a huge babyface. The business has been changing, and you have to change with it."

Angle adapted to pro wrestling as well as anyone before or since. From the very beginning, the WWF knew it had a star on the rise. Former world champion and WWF trainer Dory Funk Jr. remembers meeting Angle for the first time. "My first opportunity to meet Kurt Angle came in the gym at Titan Tower. I was excited at the opportunity to meet him . . . Our routine was weights in the morning followed by in-ring performance at the WWF studio in the afternoon. Kurt couldn't wait to get to the ring. He was happy to be there and loved training," Funk wrote on his blog. "The first thing I told Kurt was that anything he did in amateur wrestling he could work into his professional wrestling career. Kurt executes the best pro fireman's carriage in wrestling. Kurt is an exceptional athlete. I was a fan and coach of Kurt Angle and respected him for his accomplishments in amateur wrestling, so you can imagine how good I felt after our first practice session when Kurt looked and me and said, 'Hey, Coach, this sport is hard work, and I love it.'"

He was a natural, an amazing wrestler in the ring who also understood how to capture the fans with his interviews and innate acting talent. Before his first year in the WWF was complete he was already the world champion, taking the title from Dwayne "the Rock" Johnson in October 2000. In just four years with the WWF he was put through the ringer, through indescribable physical pain; through endless political manipulations backstage; through every goofy storyline imaginable. But no story could ever match the story of his life. If you made a Kurt Angle movie, no one would believe it. The tales of his heroism and toughness would seem too impossible, too outlandish to believe.

A Pittsburgh native, Angle attended nearby Clarion University. His heart had been set on football, but too small and a step too slow for major powerhouses like Penn State, he turned his attention to wrestling. In his final three years he finished an amazing 87–2–1. He won an NCAA title in 1990 and finished second in 1991, despite blowing out both knees and being outweighed virtually every time he hit the mat. That just set the stage for his greatest collegiate accomplishment.

Going into the NCAA tournament in 1992, Angle was 26–0. Across the bracket lurked the monstrous Sylvester Terkay. Terkay pushed the 275-pound limit to the breaking point. Angle barely broke 200 pounds most of the season and weighed in at 199 pounds for nationals. While Angle relied on speed and finesse, Terkay was a bruiser. Angle won a series of close matches while Terkay pinned every wrestler he faced, all in the first three-minute period, an unprecedented achievement.

Terkay was one of the best heavyweights of his generation and ended his amateur career with 64 pins and went 122–14 in his time at N.C. State. In 1993 he would prove unstoppable, finishing 41–0 and winning the 1993 NCAA title, but on a single March afternoon in 1992 he met his match in Kurt Angle, who remembers the contest vividly: "In the final period, the match was tied 1–1. With 18 seconds remaining, I slicked him. I faked one way, ducking under his left armpit, and he sprawled, thinking I was going that way. Instead I went all the way across, under his right armpit, and ducked behind him. I burned him badly with that move. . . . It blew everybody's mind because it was so quick, and I held on for the final seconds. That quickly, I'd done it. I dropped to my knees and cried that day, the same as I would in the Olympics."

THE LONG ROAD TO ATLANTA

His college career complete, Angle turned his attention to learning the freestyle game. A cousin of the folkstyle wrestling he had excelled in at college, it took Angle a little time to get the hang of the new rules and methods. Even in a sport known for its hard workers and insane workouts, Angle's intensity was legendary. There would be stronger wrestlers. Better wrestlers. But no one would outwork him. Every day for two years leading into the 1996 Olympic trials was like a scene from *Rocky IV*.

To prepare for his Olympic dreams he traveled the globe competing — Siberia, Bulgaria, Turkey, he was everywhere. In 1995 he shocked the wrestling world by winning the World Championship. Accusations of drug use soon followed. Angle's workout routine had added 10 pounds of solid muscle to his frame and some were suspicious that steroids were behind the change in appearance. He was tested monthly and passed with flying colors. Compared to what would come, it was only a minor inconvenience on the road to Olympic glory.

On January 26, 1996, Angle and the whole wrestling community were shocked by the murder of his coach Dave Schultz. John du Pont, the eccentric billionaire who had sponsored Schultz and his Team Foxcatcher protégés like Angle, had snapped and shot the 1984 Olympic gold medalist to death, firing three bullets from his black Lincoln Town Car. In the tense standoff with police that followed, du Pont would demand to be addressed as "his holiness" as he locked himself in his library. Police captured him after they shut off the boilers heating his giant mansion in the cold Pennsylvania winter and he journeyed outside to attempt to fix them. Eventually diagnosed as a paranoid schizophrenic, du Pont died in prison in 2010.

Schultz was one of America's most important wrestlers, not just for his achievements on the mat, but for his role as an ambassador of the sport, bringing home technical knowledge from Russia and other wrestling hot spots. Mixing exotic judo techniques with the staples every American collegiate learns, Schultz was a technical wizard and his students counted on his expertise heavily.

Angle was devastated. While some wrestlers like 1996 gold medalist Tom Brands stayed at du Pont's world-class facility and kept cashing his checks even after the murder, Angle and others couldn't bring themselves to do it. In the middle of his final preparations for the Olympic Games he had lost his coach and mentor and his training facility. Just two months before the Olympic Trials, he lost his good health as well.

At the U.S. Nationals, Angle was caught off guard with an arm throw by Greco-Roman specialist and Army soldier Jason Loukides. Trying to avoid the loss of the three points that were automatically docked when you were taken from your feet to your back, Angle tried to block his opponent's arm throw with his own face. In his memoir, Angle recalls, "I felt everything crack, crunch, and pull in my neck. And the force of the throw still carried me onto my back, so almost immediately I heard the ref say, 'Three,' and that sickened me more than the sound effects my neck was making."

Angle would later find out he had herniated two disks, cracked vertebrae, and pulled four muscles in his neck. The doctor on the scene was concerned about his long-term health — Angle was more concerned with his match in the finals six hours later. Instead of the hospital, he went to a chiropractor and an acupuncturist and came back to beat Kerry McCoy, a talented wrestler who was still in college and would later go on to represent the United States in two Olympic Games.

Almost unable to move, and giving up almost 40 pounds to the larger McCoy, Angle held on, keeping the match, and winning on a judge's decision. It was an important win. As the national champion he wouldn't have to compete at the Olympic Trials later a mere two months away. Instead, he would meet the winner to decide who would represent America in Atlanta that summer.

Doctors told Angle it would take six months for his neck to heal enough to give wrestling another shot. The problem? He had less than three before he would have to face the winner of the Olympic Trials for a spot on the team. Instead of giving up on his Olympic dreams, Angle decided to do whatever was necessary to perform. He got injections of mepivacaine, a local anesthetic, in his neck and soldiered on.

Angle and most wrestling fans expected he would meet future UFC champion Mark Kerr in a rematch of their close World Team Trials matchup the year before. The two were evenly matched and Angle had escaped by the skin of his teeth. But Kerr was eliminated early and Angle instead faced Dan Chaid, a 1985 NCAA champion at the tail end of his wrestling career. Like Angle, Chaid was a Schultz protégé. He was a rugged wrestler who tried to grind opponents down, a wrestler Angle knew would target his injured neck.

DANNY HODGE GIVING HIS APPROVAL TO KURT ANGLE

The neck didn't end up being an issue for Angle but was a problem for Chaid. He attacked Angle's injury relentlessly but at the expense of smart strategy or any sense of caution. In a best of three matchup, Angle won two in a row. Chaid never scored a point.

GOLDEN BOY

In the Atlanta Games, Angle was awestruck to be among the world's best wrestlers. Although he had been the world champion the year before he wasn't favored to win the gold medal. He had never been in the Olympics before and jitters were common. Besides, his win in the World Championships had been a surprise, and no one was quite sure if he had what it took to take home amateur wrestling's top prize.

Angle nearly proved the doubters right when he almost didn't make it past the quarter-finals. Ukrainian Sagid Murtazaliev took him down early with a fireman's carry, pocketing three points. Three points is an almost insurmountable lead among world class competitors but Angle rallied to win 4–3. In the semifinals he cruised to a win over Kyrgyzstan's Konstantin Aleksandrov, but suffered a hip flexor injury. It never bothered him during that match, but in the hours between the semi-finals and the finals, the muscle got tighter and tighter. So did a wound-up Angle, who nearly lost control minutes before the biggest match of his life. Angle writes, "I got a little panicked, with tears in my eyes right there in front of all these other guys. I think I was reflecting back to my childhood, how my fear used to overcome me. I started breathing quickly, almost hyperventilating. My coach, Bruce Burnett, came over to me and said, 'What the hell is wrong with you?'. . . I couldn't even look at him, but Bruce slapped me in the face and made me look him in the eye."

His coach sent him out to the mat with fire in his eyes. Angle had conquered his fears, but there was still an Iranian champion to overcome. Abbas Jadidi had been the world champion in 1993 — at least for several months before his drug test came back. He tested positive for the steroid nandrolone, the same drug that would later plague Barry Bonds, UFC champion Royce Gracie, and athletes throughout the sports world. Jadidi forfeited his medal and sat out a two-year suspension. He returned in 1995 to finish third in the World Championships.

At the top of his game, Jadidi took the early lead on Angle, but the American came back immediately to even the score. At the end of overtime it was deadlocked. The score was tied 1–1 and both men had two stalling warnings. The officials met with the referee to discuss who would be awarded the gold medal. The Iranian entered the discussion, adamant that he should be the champion despite nearly passing out from exhaustion in the overtime period. Rick Reilly gave the match national play in *Sports Illustrated*:

> At first it appeared that the referee was raising Jadidi's arm, but it was only Jadidi trying to force it up. "That scared the heck out of me," said Angle. Then suddenly the referee raised Angle's arm, and the American fell to his knees in jubilation, tears flowing down his perfectly square jaw and chiseled body. Angle gave the gold to his mother, who raised him alone after her husband died in a

construction accident 11 years ago. Then Angle said, *"If I died right now, I'd still be happy."*

The Iranian, though, could not accept the decision. At the medal ceremony, he stood off to the side glaring at the international wrestling officials, gesturing and cursing until he was pushed to the podium by his coach.

Following his win, Angle told reporters he was considering becoming an actor. When Vince McMahon came offering a $250,000 a year multi-year contract, Angle didn't even consider it. "Immediately after I won, they flew me out and offered me a very nice, very sweet contract," Angle told Fox Sports. "I never took it seriously because I was always told not to watch it and not to do it, since I was doing the legit wrestling, the amateur wrestling. I was told to turn my back on pro wrestling."

Instead, after a brief flirtation with Hollywood, Angle tried his hand at local news, becoming the weekend sports anchor at Pittsburgh's Fox affiliate. But his heart just wasn't in it and he didn't have a real affinity for the news business. He was downgraded from anchor to reporter and eventually left all together.

At a loss for what to do next, Angle decided to give wrestling another try. This time there would be no giant contract offer. He would be just another guy trying his hand at the wrestling game, albeit a guy with an Olympic pedigree and great look. Success seemed inevitable from day one.

GOING PRO

"The first day of training was a Monday," Angle remembered. "By Friday they had me do a wrestling match in front of a live crowd. No one's ever done that. For some reason they thought I could."

Like he had with his amateur career, he put his heart and soul into it. Despite already operating on two bum knees and a busted neck, Angle was willing to do whatever it took. Not just to make it: to be the best in a competitive industry.

At first, he wasn't quite cut out for the Machiavellian games that went on backstage at wrestling events. Before his first major match, a loss to ECW mainstay Taz at the 2000 Royal Rumble, Angle talked to Mick Foley about what to do if the match became a shoot — something that essentially never happened. Someone had gotten in Angle's head about Taz, who worked a shooter gimmick, with work being the operative word. Foley remembered, "He goes, 'What do I do if Taz tries to test me out there?' I looked at him and said, 'Kurt are you serious?' He said, 'Yeah.' I said, 'Kurt, you're kind of an Olympic champion aren't you?' He said, 'Yeah.' I said, 'First of all, I don't think that's what this match is about. Second of all, I don't think you have to worry about that.'"

It didn't take long for Angle to find his way. Brand new to the sport, Angle was able to work intricate and dynamic matches with the best wrestlers in the business like Chris Benoit and Eddie Guerrero. From an aesthetic standpoint, the matches were fantastic. Fast-paced and hard-hitting, the bouts made it clear these were elite athletes in a dangerous game of high-stakes stunt work, But for his career's longevity and his long-term health, he couldn't have picked two worse role models.

Guerrero and Benoit were the professional versions of Angle: obsessed to the point it wasn't healthy. Both were smaller men, jacked to the gills on steroids to make it in a big man's game. Both had resulting insecurities. Being in the ring with Angle, a man being immediately given what it took them a decade to earn, was only fuel to the fire that drove both men.

Benoit, especially, became Angle's most noted rival. The two were magic in the ring and WWE booker Paul Heyman almost never failed to put them together in the kind of long matches fans loved and the wrestlers prided themselves in. Dave Meltzer compared them to Ric Flair and Ricky Steamboat, who'd created one of wrestling's most legendary feuds. It was a lot to live up to. Benoit, his neck hurting him to the point he could barely function, never let injuries stop him. Angle's health was little better, but as Matthew Randazzo V explained in *Ring of Hell*, nothing would prevent either man from putting it all on the line, even in an essentially meaningless match of WWE's *SmackDown* television show: "Standing in the ring with an athlete of Angle's quality made Benoit insecure and encouraged him to play a game of in-ring chicken with the Olympian, as if both men had a death wish. Like Benoit, Angle was a suplex specialist; these throws strained the neck of both the wrestler performing the move and the wrestler taking the move. Not to be upstaged, Benoit insisted on topping Angle by performing a German suplex from the second rope. . . . When Angle backflipped from the top of the cage all the way down to the mat, the audience knew that Benoit could never let such a daredevil feat go unanswered. Benoit prepared his tour de force: a diving head butt from the top of the cage, or basically a face-first belly flop onto hard canvas from 12 or 13 feet in the air."

Eventually those grueling matches took their toll on Angle. His neck was already in bad shape before he ever started wrestling for the WWE. The hard style he preferred in the ring only wore him down further. He got the bad news about his neck at the worst possible time — weeks before his *WrestleMania XIX* headliner with the WWE's new hot amateur wrestling prospect: "The Next Big Thing" Brock Lesnar.

Brock Lesnar walked into the arena, muscles bulging, wild eyes daring anyone to take a step towards him, dancing around the spectators and his opposition. He raised his arms into the air, exhorting the crowd to cheer: commonplace for the WWE, the modern home of professional wrestling hijinks. Less so for the staid NCAA tournament, home of tradition-loving, corn-fed athletes, men fearless on the mats and humble off them.

Lesnar was different. It wasn't just his cocky attitude and natural charisma. The first thing you noticed was his sheer size. Standing 6'4" and weighing 270 lbs. with less than 10 percent body fat, Brock was a once-in-a-lifetime specimen. His chest was 56 inches,

25 THE NEXT BIG THING

his biceps 21. Even the great Dan Gable, America's most legendary wrestler and coach, couldn't help but be impressed. Calling Lesnar's matches on TV for the Iowa Public Broadcasting Company, Gable quipped, "When Brock Lesnar strips off his warm-ups, he turns more heads than Cindy Crawford in a thong."

Even in the age of steroids, Lesnar's freaky musculature did not go unnoticed. He hadn't even been a heavyweight until his senior year of high school, putting on 20 pounds almost overnight and eventually outweighing almost anyone who stood across from him on the mats by the time he reached his peak at the 2000 NCAA Championships.

"All I wanted to do was get big and strong," says Lesnar. "I was amazed by guys like Arnold Schwarzenegger, and I'd always be doing push-ups and pull-ups at home. On the farm I tried to be a workhorse because I knew if I could cut it on the farm, I could cut it anywhere."

When he first arrived at the University of Minnesota, coach J Robinson had him drug tested immediately. There had been whispers of steroid use and Robinson wanted to clear the air. Lesnar passed the test, and every test he would subsequently take in his athletic and wrestling careers, with flying colors.

Lesnar was just big—but he didn't wrestle that way. He came up in the sport as a skinny kid, so he had a quickness and skill set rare for a bruiser of his size. He learned to wrestle in his home state of South Dakota. His main opponents were the Madsen brothers, Dan and Jon. The three waged fierce battles for supremacy, attracting throngs of fans to gymnasiums his senior year to watch Brock and Jon Madsen (a future training partner) go at it.

"For a small town there were 2,000 people in the gym," Dan Madsen remembered. "One side of the gym was yelling for Brock, and the other was yelling, 'Go Mad Dog' for Jon. They were intense matches, snot flying . . . I think wrestling Jon helped Brock develop his skills."

Brock never won a high school title, a failure that drove him to continue wrestling. When he arrived at Bismarck State, Lesnar weighed just 210 pounds, making him a very small heavyweight. By the time he left junior college, Brock was enormous, thanks to a new obsession with bodybuilding. But he hadn't lost the quickness that had made him such a tough competitor in high school. The combination was deadly. Lesnar could shoot in quickly on his opponents, then literally scoop them into the air to win a succession of easy matches.

A junior national championship at Bismarck State opened the door to almost any NCAA program in the country. One school, however, already had an "in" with the future NCAA champion. Lesnar had impressed Robinson, the long-time Minnesota coach, at the Bison Open, a wrestling tournament that mixed wrestlers from different levels of competition. Lesnar had won the tournament's heavyweight title, the only non–University of Minnesota wrestler to do so. Robinson immediately introduced himself to Lesnar. He was looking to replace his own heavyweight Shelton Benjamin, who would be graduating that spring, and like everyone else who had witnessed Lesnar wrestle live, Robinson saw tons of potential in the agile bruiser.

"I've been in this 25 years," Robinson told the *Minneapolis Star Tribune*. "And I've never seen a guy built as big and strong and powerful as he is."

After sitting out a semester, Lesnar made quite a debut for a team that had finished second in the nation in 1998. At the National Duals in January, he didn't just beat, he pinned Iowa's Wes Hand on the Hawkeye's home turf. Hand was just one of four wrestlers Lesnar pinned that weekend, catapulting him to the number two ranking in the country.

Lesnar breezed through the season and into the NCAA tournament. Minnesota did well in the competition, and on the final day pulled within two points of Iowa. The NCAA title was within their grasp. They just needed a single victory to take home the title — Brock Lesnar had to beat Stephen Neal to win the heavyweight championship.

Neal was in the midst of one of the most dominant runs in modern NCAA history. He had capped an undefeated 1998 with an NCAA title and had yet to taste defeat in 1999. Still, Lesnar gave him all he could handle. A single takedown was the difference. Neal scored one early in the first period and Lesnar couldn't recover, losing 3–2 in a dull affair. It was a very cautious match, but Neal says that was for good reason.

"He was just this big, strong, powerful man the wrestling world hadn't seen," Neal said. "He was so big and strong, you didn't want to make a mistake against him."

The next season, the legend of Lesnar spread. Fans came out to see him in droves and he became a celebrity in the Twin Cities. The "Minnesota Wrestling Weekly" was a hit on KFAN with Brock as a regular guest on the show. The athletic department even went so far as to release a Brock Lesnar poster called the "Brockfast of Champions" that they gave out at wrestling meets.

Brock started the season with 22 straight wins, but it was the lone loss that stung the most. A record-setting 13,128 fans packed the Williams Arena to see Lesnar's Gophers take on the top-ranked Iowa Hawkeyes. The winning team would be the top team in all of college wrestling, and the head-to-head matchup between Lesnar and Hand had its own high stakes. Hand, despite losing twice to Lesnar the previous season, was telling the world he had the big man's number. Tensions were high as the two set to square off. The action was intense even before the two ever touched as the school's *Minnesota Daily* wrote:

BROCK LESNAR WITH THE NJPW GRAND PRIX WORLD TITLE

During pregame introductions, Hand walked over to Minnesota's side of the mat waiting to shake Lesnar's hand.

Lesnar emerged from behind his teammates and ran past Hand, making his way to center circle while indicating to Hand that center circle was where the two should meet. Hand went to center circle, acting like he would wish Lesnar good luck there and shake his hand.

But Hand fooled all, running to center circle and right past Lesnar. The Gophers heavyweight simply waved good-bye.

Hand was as good as his word, putting Lesnar on his back early with a whip-over for four points and then holding on for a 5–3 win. Minnesota, up on the Hawkeyes going into Lesnar's bout, never recovered, losing the Big 10 title. Lesnar took the defeat in stride

256 SHOOTERS: THE TOUGHEST MEN IN PROFESSIONAL WRESTLING

— he was focused on the Big 10 and NCAA tournaments coming up in the next month. "Better to lose now," he said, "than then."

Prophetic words indeed; Lesnar beat Hand 2–1 to take his second straight Big 10 Championship and then outlasted him in overtime to win the NCAA Championship 3–2. Lesnar became Minnesota's first heavyweight wrestling champion since Verne Gagne back in 1949.

"That night I felt like a weight was lifted off of me," Lesnar remembered. "Waking up the next day though, I felt empty. I had been wrestling for so long, I didn't know what to do next."

What was next was obvious to most watching closely. Lesnar would do what it appeared he was born to do — entertain as a professional wrestler. The Olympics were a possibility. The National Football League was also a challenge that would linger in his mind for years, and Minnesota football coach Glen Mason made him an offer to play for the Gophers the next year.

But buoyed by the success of Angle in the WWE ring, there was never a better time to be a big, muscular, charismatic amateur wrestler: Lesnar would command quite a price from the WWE. They were definitely interested and not alone. Offers also poured in from New Japan Pro-Wrestling and World Championship Wrestling. Everyone wanted the next Angle — and with his sheer size, Lesnar had the chance to be an even bigger star in the image-obsessed wrestling business.

Said former WWE Vice President of Talent Relations Jim Ross, "I recruited him out of Minnesota for WWE when I was executive vice president of the company, in charge of talent. He wrestled for J Robinson, and J was roommates with Jerry Brisco, one of the guys I worked with . . . Jerry was a great recruiter and really helped us a lot. I think we met Brock as a junior at Minnesota. And how could you not be attracted by the look of this guy? . . . We saw Brock, and we saw a guy that was an amazing athlete with a phenomenal look. He was a natural 285-pound guy with freakish quickness, agility, and balance. He was pretty sure that he wasn't interested in pursuing wrestling internationally when he finished college. I didn't have any conversations with him regarding MMA, because he wanted to make some money right away. Of all the guys that I signed, and I signed some intriguing guys like Steve Austin, Dwayne "The Rock" Johnson and others, he made it to the seven figure level faster than anyone we'd ever signed. I don't think there's been anyone in the history of the business who made that much money, and as quickly, as Brock Lesnar did."

"When I got out of college, after I won my NCAA title, I didn't have a lot of options. There aren't a lot of options for an amateur wrestler. You can go to the Olympics or you can become a coach," Lesnar said. "The bottom line was Vince [McMahon] had $250,000 waiting for me and a contract on the table, and I was 21 years old and didn't have a pot to piss in. Come on. You make the decision."

In August 2000, Lesnar joined the WWF's Ohio Valley Wrestling developmental program in Louisville, Kentucky. In a warehouse across the Ohio River in Indiana, Lesnar learned the basics of the wrestling business from Jim Cornette and former wrestler "Dangerous" Danny Davis.

"We used to call him Block Lesnar here in OVW for block-head," Cornette said. "Not in front of him now, behind his back everybody did. . . . I always thought that Brock was holding back in developmental; I didn't think he gave his best effort even though he was getting paid 250 grand a year to train. I didn't think Brock had a lot of personality — I was wrong about that. I was right in the context of pro wrestling but I was wrong [saying] he didn't have personality. I always thought Brock Lesnar had a number of character flaws, one of which being you know he's the big farm boy, right? The big, meat-headed farm boy."

He may not have impressed with his brains, but Lesnar was a quick study in the ring, teaming with his predecessor at Minnesota, Shelton Benjamin. Benjamin was a two-time All-American and continued on with the program after he graduated as an assistant, spending plenty of time on the mat with Lesnar. Possessed with natural athleticism and rare physical presence, the two both seemed like future stars.

In March 2002, Lesnar made his television debut on *Raw*. Accompanied by manager Paul Heyman, who dubbed Lesnar "The Next Big Thing," Brock was an immediate hit. WWE officials had been worried about a lack of personality, "no sizzle," as Jim Ross put it to the *Minnesota Star Tribune*, to go along with his steak. It was a concern they had expressed about Angle as well. Both men, it seemed, were better when the bright lights were shining than they were on the practice stage.

Lesnar skyrocketed to success faster than anyone in WWE history. Borrowing a page from WCW's playbook, Lesnar received a push similar to that of wrestling's previous breakout star Bill Goldberg. Demolishing everything in sight, Lesnar became a star by winning, winning, and then winning some more. Just six months into his professional career, Brock beat the company's brightest star the Rock at SummerSlam 2002 for the WWE heavyweight title, at 25 becoming the promotion's youngest-ever world champion. As Dave Meltzer wrote in the *Wrestling Observer*, it was an attempt to make a new star for the first time in years: "The idea was that to get Lesnar over as a fresh money draw, the guy he needed to beat was the Rock, and that Rock would do it the right way. The fact that he was untarnished, in that fans never saw him lose . . . for all the talk of winning and losing not meaning anything, was part of the reason this worked. And they went full steam ahead in that direction, with the great finishing touches being the training videos for both that aired on many different shows. Rock, to his credit, put Lesnar over in the middle with the F-5, and whatever Lesnar's career does from here can't be blamed on the Rock not giving him the proper sendoff."

The big push continued with a huge win over the Undertaker in a Hell in a Cell match, a rare honor and a clear sign that the company was behind him 100 percent. He lost his title to the Big Show at Survivor Series that year, his first televised pinfall loss since starting with the WWE that spring. Heyman turned on him and suddenly the odds were stacked against him — an attempt to turn Lesnar babyface. The WWE liked long-term champions to be good guys — after all, the good guys sold the merchandise and this was a multi-pronged business. There was, it was thought, money in Brock Lesnar.

CLASH OF THE TITANS

Behind the scenes, Lesnar struggled with the road schedule and the industry's cutthroat politics. Competing now for wrestling's top spot, he was an amateur in a professional game for high stakes. His traveling partner was Kurt Angle, and the two went back and forth, two alpha males sparring verbally and physically about who was best. Eventually it came down to testing each other on the mat.

"Brock and I mixed it up — we used to train and wrestle and spar," Angle said. "I used to win a lot because I was a much better wrestler than him. We'd go at it and I'd beat him. A lot of people made a big deal out of it but this was not MMA, it was Olympic-style wrestling."

"I was in there with him when he was jacked up at 315. He said I was too small and every week I would get on him," Angle told radio shock jock Bubba the Love Sponge. "Finally, him and Big Show were in the ring wrestling. He was throwing Big Show around pretty good. I was like, 'Wow. Big Show's 520 pounds and Brock is throwing him. This kid's strong.' I told Big Show, 'Get out.' I walked in behind him and tapped on Brock's shoulder. He turned around and gave me a look like 'Oh no.' We went at it and I took him down eight or nine times. It was a humbling experience for Brock. There were so many people there watching."

The two eventually made their feud public in front of a paying audience and television cameras. It was the first matchup of NCAA champions in decades, and the two had amazing chemistry both in and out of the ring. Both natural heels, Lesnar started their program as the babyface, with Angle cutting promos trashing local sports heroes and plotting and scheming with dastardly manager Paul Heyman and Team Angle, his own stable of heels. It had the look of a classic feud, but just as things got heated up for their first singles bout headlining *WrestleMania XIX*, Angle could no longer keep a secret that had been tormenting him for some time — his neck was in constant agony.

Lesnar blames himself. "When me and Kurt Angle got in the squared circle, there were a lot of real things going on. We pushed each other to the limit. That's one of those guys I felt he and I could go out and not only tear the house down but execute things that looked real. And they were very real. Some nights they were very real. One night, Kurt had neck problems going way back, but I threw him into the turnbuckle and hit him very hard. I believe his refracture in the wrestling business came from me. I broke his neck that night. I wasn't the first to break his neck, but it was hard. Me and Kurt went at it. He hit me hard and I hit him back harder."

Most in the industry thought the *WrestleMania* main event would be off. Angle was clearly in no shape to wrestle and was risking serious and permanent injury by even considering it. It was expected he would drop the title in a quick television match and have immediate surgery. Instead, he decided to do what he always does — give it his all. Angle had been planning on doing what a star of his caliber rarely did in the cutthroat wrestling culture of the early 2000s — he was going to make a star of Brock Lesnar if it killed him. Unfortunately, in this case, that was more than just a turn of phrase. Angle was intent on putting on a great show, regardless of the consequences. Of course, he didn't make that decision in a vacuum. Vince McMahon helped him find his path.

"The worst thing I ever experienced in the WWE was at *WrestleMania XIX* when Kurt Angle faced Brock Lesnar in the main event," former WWE writer Dominick Pagliaro recalled. "Angle was suffering from really severe neck and spinal cord problems — he needed surgery immediately. His doctor told him that if he wrestled that match against Lesnar, he probably wouldn't be able to stand up and walk out of the ring; he'd be paralyzed. So Kurt goes to McMahon and tells him this, and I watch Vince. Vince just looks at him and is like, 'Yes, you could not wrestle the match, or you could wrestle the match,' in this way that was very Vince, very subtly letting him know that, even knowing he might be paralyzed, he expected him to wrestle that match."

Before the match, the normally fearless Angle was petrified. His daughter had been born shortly before *WrestleMania* and the consequences of his actions were suddenly seeming pretty important. He might have been willing to cripple himself for his art, but was he willing to risk being able to play with his kid when he got older?

"The first and only thing I was thinking about was 'God, I hope I make it through this.' At this point I only had 20 percent strength in my left arm," Angle told *Off the Record*'s Michael Landsberg in 2004. "My arm could have fell off because I had no strength in it. And the thing I was most nervous about was Brock Lesnar. Here's this guy, he's a rookie who doesn't know how to let up in the ring. This is his first *WrestleMania*. So he's nervous as hell. I have a 300-pound man who can bench 700 pounds getting ready to face me at *WrestleMania*, his first, and he doesn't really know how to work yet. He's basically a loose cannon and I have the injuries to my neck. Man, that is not a good mixture."

The match was a classic, of course. When firing on all cylinders, Angle was as good as anyone. Even with his physical shortcomings, he was able to perform at a level few would ever reach. Fans and media critics, who knew of Angle's real life injuries, watched with a sense of foreboding and doom hanging over the match. Angle, despite his physical state, refused to adjust his style in the ring. In the *Observer*, Dave Meltzer was aghast: "Even in his condition, except for the fact that he had a concerned look on his face, he didn't shy away from any moves. He took bumps on his neck, and a hard clothesline. There's a line between guts and bad judgement and most of your top wrestlers at times cross it, but he was all the way into another state."

The two were on their way to an amazing bout when Lesnar decided he wanted the match to be a thing of legend, not just another main event. For the finish, he decided to climb to the top rope and do a reverse somersault off it, a move called the shooting star press.

This was a pretty difficult bit of acrobatics. Much smaller men had tried and failed time and time again. WWE star Chris Jericho had broken his arm in an attempt and Billy Kidman, who specialized in using the move, was hurting himself or opponents on what seemed like a nearly constant basis. Lesnar had used the move during his training days in Ohio Valley but hadn't debuted it in the WWE yet. It would have been the perfect end to a great match — the culmination of what *Pro Wrestling Torch* columnist Bruce Mitchell called "one of the great wrestling events of the modern era." Instead, Lesnar slipped and landed right on his head.

"When he landed on his head, I didn't even think he was going to be able to finish the match," Angle said. "I figured, 'Oh man, I'm going to have to hold my title another month and put off my surgery.' The good thing is, thank God, he was able to come out of it and able to hit his finish. I thought it helped the match that he didn't hit it. The fact that he landed on his head — a lot of people remember that."

A glassy-eyed Lesnar was able to get to his feet and pick Angle up for his F-5 finisher. He had suffered a major concussion. Backstage, it looked like a war zone.

"I watched Kurt after that match, and he was laid out on the floor spasming out of control and foaming at the mouth and just in unimaginable pain and fear for his life," Pagliaro remembers. "They had to call in the medics — you can watch and you'll see that Kurt was never the same."

After the match, Angle shocked onlookers again, choosing not to use famed surgeon Lloyd Youngblood who had done wonders with WWE stars like Steve Austin and Chris Benoit, instead going with the experimental treatment offered by Dr. Hae-Dong Jho. Jho's treatment intrigued Angle because it would put him out of action for just six weeks instead of a calendar year. Long term, the decision would have major repercussions, but in the short term it was a huge success. By June, Angle was back in the ring and he and Lesnar picked up right where they left off.

Their feud reached an apex with a 60-minute iron man match on live television that September. It was the first televised match of its kind in the United States since Curt Hennig and Nick Bockwinkel had wrestled 60 minutes on ESPN in 1986 for the AWA. The two would wrestle a full hour — whoever had the most pinfalls or submissions at the end of the time limit would be declared the winner. Angle and Lesnar were so good a pairing that they necessitated a culture shift in the promotion. A year earlier, no one would have considered a 60-minute match on television. Wrestling matches were seen almost as filler between interviews and skits. Angle and Lesnar helped change all that.

The match itself was a cathartic experience. Angle lost his older sister to a heart attack the day before the bout. Lesnar sprained his knee the day prior to that in a tune-up match, an injury initially feared to be an MCL tear, but continued wrestling despite the pain. Lesnar won the WWE title, outlasting Angle 5–4 while refusing to tap to a last-second heel hook that would have evened the score. The match was met with rave reviews in the wrestling press, with *Pro Wrestling Torch* editor Wade Keller giving it a coveted five star rating:

> *It was a risky decision by WWE and a gutsy challenge to undertake by Angle and Lesnar. It was a show of faith in Brock and Angle as athletes and perhaps just as much an experiment to see how such a match would hold up in the ratings.*
>
> *Plus, Angle shouldn't have even been wrestling today considering he was reluctantly resigning himself to forced retirement just before* WrestleMania *this year due to his bad neck. Brock Lesnar is so early in his pro career, he really has no business being this good, this fast, even with a phenomenal performer such as Angle (perhaps the best all-around and most consistent worker of the last ten years) in the ring as his opponent.*

Soon after, however, the decision to go with the less invasive neck surgery came back to haunt him. He needed corrective surgery and then suffered issues with a blood clot. As Angle struggled with his health, Lesnar faced his own battles with the wrestling industry. The travel schedule was wearing him down. He bought a private plane to ease some of the strain, angering his WWE colleagues who thought he was getting a little big for his britches, but the schedule was still grueling. *Pro Wrestling Torch*'s Jason Powell wrote that problems in his personal life were making a bad situation worse: "Lesnar started voicing his frustration with the hectic WWE travel schedule. It's no coincidence that he encountered problems with his romantic life around this same time. The pressure of juggling his long-time girlfriend (who is the mother of his child) and his on-the-road girlfriend Rena Mero started catching up with him. The word from Lesnar's Minnesota pals is that his long-time girlfriend, for whatever reason, decided to move a few hours away from Lesnar's home with the couple's daughter."

Suddenly, Lesnar's travel schedule became even more hectic. In addition to making his WWE commitments Saturday through Tuesday each week, friends say Lesnar also spent countless hours making the long road trip from the Twin Cities to pick up his daughter. A typical Wednesday "off day" for Lesnar involved flying home from wherever the *SmackDown* tapings were held the night before, driving a couple hours to pick up his daughter, and then making the return trip home with her. Lesnar usually repeated his road trek at some point before he headed back to work on Saturday morning.

He was also, for the first time, not the focal point of WWE's plans going forward. Eddie Guerrero had assumed the mantle of champion and was doing good business. When he beat Lesnar for the title, there were no plans to put Brock back on top. He was also scheduled to lose a series of matches to the Undertaker, something Lesnar still wasn't quite comfortable with despite years in the wrestling business. He decided, instead of weathering the storm and enjoying his unprecedented seven-year, $1-million-a-year guaranteed contract, to quit the business. *WrestleMania XX* would be his last match with the company.

When word leaked, fans were furious. His opponent, Bill Goldberg, was also leaving the company and the fans let both men hear it. Chanting, "You sold out," and "This match sucks," wrestling fans spoke for many in the industry who weren't happy with the two stars who had been given everything so quickly and appreciated nothing. Guest referee "Stone Cold" Steve Austin closed the book on both men's WWE careers with his signature stunner in the middle of the ring.

Lesnar remembers looking out over the locker room, seeing the wrestlers in a pain- and drug-induced haze. He didn't want to be them in 10 years. And he was already suffering the effects of the wrestling lifestyle after just a few years in the business.

"I had three broken ribs and a bad knee," Lesnar told *Maxim*. "During that period I would take a couple Vicodin and wash 'em down with a few slugs of vodka. That's what got me through. The ribs didn't heal for another eight months, because there's no off-season in pro wrestling ... You get so brainwashed. You're on the road 300 days a year, and that's why guys get so messed up. This life becomes a part of them. It's not real, but some guys who are still in the business think it is."

TOUGH ENOUGH

Lesnar left to pursue an NFL career and eventually fell into a career in mixed martial arts, but Angle was a lifer. Despite his injuries he soldiered on. Soon he couldn't wrestle, but his personality and star power were big enough to merit a regular spot on television. That's how he ended up in the ring for what Dave Meltzer called "one of the more famous one-minute periods in modern pro wrestling history" on November 2, 2004.

Angle was hazing contestants from *Tough Enough*, the WWE's ill-fated attempt at a reality show, bullying the wrestling wannabes and challenging them to a real match. Angle pinned his first challenger, Chris Nawrocki, in just 26 seconds. And then he asked for another challenger. Daniel Puder stepped forward.

Puder was a budding MMA prospect who'd trained training for years with the famous

American Kickboxing Academy in California, and even helped Frank Shamrock train for Tito Ortiz before their famous fight at UFC 22. Puder had also had wrestling training with Danny Chaid, a top amateur who had taken Angle to the limit in the 1996 Olympic trials. And, most importantly, Puder didn't have a neck that limited his movement and strength like Angle did.

It was a bad spot for Angle to be put in. He was in no shape to perform in the WWE and certainly in no shape for a contest with a real shooter. Despite the wear and tear, and a hand gone numb after the short match with Nawrocki, Angle was able to get Puder to the mat. But there, the tables turned as Puder caught the former WWE champion in a Kimura lock and had him in a very bad position. Puder was on his back, a bad spot in amateur wrestling, but right where he wanted to be to submit Angle with his arm lock.

Gerald Brisco, a former Oklahoma State amateur, immediately recognized the danger and told the referee to quickly count Puder down. In amateur rules his shoulders were down for a one second count, all that is required. In a pro match, his shoulders were clearly up, but referee Jimmy Korderas quickly counted to three anyway. Angle was furious afterwards, refusing to shake Puder's hand and telling him, "Don't you know any better? It's not a fucking UFC match, it's an amateur wrestling contest."

The actual rules of the bout are anything but clear. Before the two squared up, Angle asked Puder if he had ever fought an Olympic champion, insinuating this was more than a wrestling contest. Puder told Bubba the Love Sponge that he specifically asked about whether submission holds were legal.

"It wasn't an amateur wrestling match," Puder said. "The refs told me, 'No striking.' That's it. Anything else goes."

According to Dave Meltzer, WWE officials believed they had dodged a bullet: "A lot of people thought if Angle tapped, it would have killed his career and made WWE look bad because an unknown fighter tapped their big star."

Others believed the promotion should have taken advantage of the unscripted moment they were handed. You couldn't have written a better script to propel a new star to the top of the WWE — but instead of using it and making magic, the WWE ran from opportunity simply because it hadn't been part of their master plan. In the end, nothing became of Puder at all. He won the reality television show but was never pushed prominently on WWE television.

While Angle continued the pro wrestling grind, Lesnar was trying and failing to make it in the NFL. Lesnar was an amazing athlete, strong and fast. He had the physical tools to play professional football, but there was one small wrinkle keeping him from his dream — he hadn't played football since high school and even then wasn't good enough to attract any real interest from a college powerhouse. Lesnar was bounced from the Vikings' training camp roster with scant delay, his most memorable moment coming during a pre-season brawl with the Kansas City Chiefs when Lesnar hit quarterback Damon Huard in violation of a no-contact agreement and then got into a scrap with lineman Johnathan Ingram.

Football now a distant memory, Lesnar was back doing the only thing he knew how to do. He renegotiated with the WWE to return, before joining New Japan Pro-Wrestling in October 2005, following a long line of superstar foreigners that included Stan Hansen, Hulk Hogan, and the Road Warriors. Lesnar was immediately pushed hard, winning the IWGP title in his first match, but the business was in such disarray in Japan that he didn't have much impact.

Soon he was battling the WWE in court. In order to get his release from the promotion, Lesnar had signed a no-compete deal that prevented him from fighting or wrestling elsewhere through 2010. As the two went to war in a messy court battle that included the WWE claiming Lesnar had threatened to commit suicide if he wasn't released from his contract with the company, Lesnar continued wrestling in Japan. The two sides reached an agreement and settled their differences in April 2006. Days later Lesnar was ringside at a K-1 show in Las Vegas announcing his intention to give MMA a try and training for his MMA debut with Pat Miletich in Iowa, eventually landing at Greg Nelson's Minnesota Martial Arts Academy closer to home. On August 12, Lesnar officially signed a contract with K-1 to fight the giant Korean Hong-Man Choi. Less than two weeks later, Angle had his own announcement — he and the WWE were parting ways. Although the split was said to be mutual, with Angle and manager Dave Hawk quoted in the WWE release announcing the news, in the *Figure Four Weekly* newsletter, Bryan Alvarez reported otherwise:

> *The reality is that this was not a mutual agreement. According to WWE sources, Angle and Hawk met with WWE on Friday and Angle, who just returned from a 30-day suspension for pain pill issues, was basically told he needed to get help immediately. He refused and was subsequently fired. The decision was made, for whatever reason, to publish all the WWE.com articles in an attempt to help him save face in the situation.*
>
> *According to sources in WWE, Angle is heavily addicted to painkillers and a walking wreck. While he has serious neck and back issues dating back to the Olympics and exasperated by his intense pro style, I'm told the recent claims that he pulled his groin and tore an ab muscle are a work. It is said that he has showed up at events messed up worse than Shawn Michaels or Brian Pillman at their peaks. Others have said he's the worst anyone has ever seen. Worse than the physical issues are the mental issues. Besides dealing with a body that won't do what he wants it to do anymore, he's also going through a divorce with his wife, Karen, mother of his three-year-old daughter, Kira, and currently pregnant with his first son.*

Pro Wrestling Torch columnist Bruce Mitchell agreed Angle was a mess in the days and months before he was fired: "Kurt Angle was fired from WWE because he was in terrible shape, physically, mentally, and emotionally. He has a torn groin, a bad back, and a broken neck. He has an admitted pain pill problem that he has apparently done nothing about. He was impossible to communicate with by the end of his WWE tenure and was driving everyone in the locker room crazy."

Angle admitted as much in subsequent interviews, facing down his problems admirably. To battle his perpetual neck problems he had become addicted to pain pills, walking around in a perpetual fog like a zombie.

"It tore my soul apart. I missed the first two years of my daughter's life," Angle told the *Pittsburgh Tribune-Review*. "Painkillers are like heroin. When you get caught up in it, you start taking 10 or 20. I was up to 65 a day. I had to take 18 to get out of bed. I went to the pharmacy every other day. I found a way to get 10 different doctors to get my prescriptions. It worked out perfectly; every other day I got 120 pills. My first priority was to get to the pharmacy."

Angle's time on the national stage was over. He would go on to join Total Nonstop Action, but it was a promotion struggling to survive. The rest of his career would be featured in backwoods arenas and in front of thousands rather than millions. Lesnar, meanwhile, was nowhere near the height of his fame. Soon Lesnar would become the first man to earn an amazing trifecta: NCAA, pro wrestling, and MMA world champion.

In June 2007 K-1, the groundbreaking Japanese kickboxing promotion, was looking to make a major splash in a new market. The UFC's success had emboldened a slew of competitors, all looking to cash in on what looked like an enormously profitable new sport. Eventually it would become clear that UFC owner Lorenzo Fertitta was right when he said, "There isn't an MMA boom. There's a UFC boom." But in the middle of 2007, K-1 was thinking big. Really big. They booked the mammoth Los Angeles Coliseum, looking to put more than 100,000 fans in the building to break all American records.

The show was a debacle of epic proportions. If you wanted to write a book about how

26 WRESTLING INVASION

not to promote a fight show, this would be your template. K-1, it turns out, had no promoter's license. It had no plan on how to entice 100,000 people into the L.A. Coliseum. It didn't have the first clue about how to ensure its athletes were able to compete under athletic commission guidelines. But K-1 did do something right — they signed Brock Lesnar to fight in their main event.

The former WWE champion had been preparing for this moment for a long time. K-1 had been teasing his debut for nearly a year, with each announcement pushing his first match, further and further back. Fans had seen it before. The promotion had promised Mike Tyson so many times, once even having him stage a scene with Bob Sapp at a fight in Las Vegas, but had never delivered. Lesnar, though, eventually did get in the ring, preparing for his first fight in the comfort of his Minnesota stomping grounds.

Lesnar started his MMA training at Pat Miletich's camp in Iowa. A former UFC champion, Pat was known for grooming champions — Jens Pulver, Matt Hughes, and Tim Sylvia had all won gold under Pat's watch. But things had changed at Team Miletich. The training wasn't as organized as it had been and Pat's focus was spread thin on a number of different projects and fighters. Lesnar wanted the single-minded and focused approach he had experienced at the University of Minnesota. Instead of searching for a camp that could meet his expectations, he created it.

The first step was hiring a man he thought had been integral to his amateur success. Lesnar said, "I went back to my grassroots . . . Marty Morgan is an assistant coach at the University of Minnesota where I won my national title. He coached me to be a champion. And that's why I wanted him on my team."

Lesnar was supposed to be fighting the giant Korean Hong-Man Choi, but a brain scan had revelealed a tumor on Choi's pituitary gland. The tumor is typical of those with acromelagy, also know as gigantism, and Choi was aware of the issue. "The MRI test on Choi Hong-Man didn't go well," K-1's Korean CEO Jeong Yeno-soo said. "There was no MRI equipment that fit the size of his head, so he had to do an external MRI." The less accurate external test caused doctors' concern and Choi was nixed from fighting in California, perhaps the first fighter scratched for being too large for the medical equipment.

Lesnar ended up fighting Min-Soo Kim, a 1996 Olympic silver medalist in judo at 209 pounds. Kim had blown up in weight and was a glorified punching bag for K-1's Hero's promotion. They were taking no chances with their meal ticket. Lesnar went on last, a main-eventer in his very first match. He ran over Kim in just over a minute.

K-1 printed 75,332 tickets to the event. More than 40,000 people were in the building according to the California athletic commission. Unfortunately for the promotion, only 3,674 tickets were actually sold to paying fans. K-1 likely lost millions, but at least they lost them in style. *Figure Four Weekly*'s Bryan Alvarez was on the scene to describe the spectacle:

> *They had a gigantic fireworks display, and for those that didn't see it, this wasn't a WWE pyro display or anything like that. This was the Fourth of July in a major city. As this gigantic display was going on, as things blew up in the skies above the L.A. Memorial Coliseum, dudes shot off guns of confetti, gun after gun, and the air was utterly filled with it. Asians were everywhere, smiling and laughing and pointing, and it was like a giant New Year's party in the middle of Tokyo. That was the magic of this show. Like with Pride in Las Vegas, K-1 didn't come to America to run a show. This was like they took a K-1 show in all its glory in the Tokyo National Stadium, uprooted the entire thing, and took it to America. Sure, they spent $5 million to do it and probably only made a half million at the gate (and zero dollars on merchandise), but by God they did it . . . But I really wasn't thinking much about business at the time. I just stood there watching fireworks in a snowstorm of confetti and reveled in it like a little kid. Everyone else was trying to get the hell out, so I took one last look, which I'll never forget, and grabbed a piece of confetti to take home with me.*

Lesnar was just happy to have his debut behind him. He had wanted to work on his striking, confident already in his ability to take almost anyone on the planet down, but his wrestling mindset took over and he, in turn, took Kim to the mat at the first opportunity. "I was prepared to strike with him this evening," Lesnar said. "But he gave me his leg. It just happened like that. . . . It was instinct."

The MMA media descended on Los Angeles in force. Lesnar took questions, and though he'd moved on from WWE, the media hadn't. Pro wrestling was *the* story and essentially the only topic they wanted to cover.

"I'm an amateur wrestler first of all, a pro wrestler second. . . . My amateur wrestling is who I am, and I'm going to evolve as a fighter," Lesnar said. "Unfortunately I have a black cloud over my head because I was a pro wrestler. . . . I had a point to prove tonight. That I am a fighter. I have a very big heart for this fight game and I'm going to be around for a while."

Lesnar wasn't content to be in the minor leagues for long. The top promotion in the world was the UFC and Brock set his sights on getting the organization's attention. It wasn't easy. Kurt Angle had made plenty of noise about fighting, and UFC President Dana White had wasted valuable time negotiating with a wrestler who was never actually going to fight. They weren't going to make the same mistake on Lesnar.

Lesnar made a splash by showing up at UFC 74 in August 2007 to watch Randy Couture defend his heavyweight title. He bought front row tickets, but the UFC kept cameras far away from him. When a montage of celebrities was shown, Lesnar was notable by his absence. The UFC was ignoring Lesnar and he didn't like it:

> *I jumped down to the main floor, pushed my way through the crowd, and walked right past security. When I got near the Octagon I found myself directly behind Dana White, so I tapped him on the shoulder and introduced myself.*
>
> *We found an empty room in the back of the arena, and Dana sat down with me and my lawyers. I'll give him credit; Dana didn't pull any punches . . . "What makes you think you can do this, Brock? What makes you think you can be in the UFC with the best fighters in the world?"*

"Brock's record was 1–0, but when I started talking to Brock he thought he was ready and this was where he wanted to be," UFC President Dana White said. "We told him, 'There's no easy fights here in the UFC.' And he said, 'I don't want easy fights. I didn't like the way the last show went, I wasn't happy with it. I want to be in the UFC. I want to compete at that level.' So he comes right into the UFC taking on former world champion Frank Mir."

Mir was the perfect opponent for Lesnar. A former world champion, he had a respectable enough pedigree that no one could accuse the UFC of giving Lesnar a tomato can. At the same time, Mir was still struggling with the after-effects of a motorcycle crash that had cost him his title and almost his career.

"I went from being one of the top martial artists in the world to being a guy who might never be able to fight again," Mir said. "It took me four years to get back to where I was because of one car wreck. There were several times I was in the UFC head office begging not to be cut. I was one decision, one breath, away from never having my career ever again."

Lesnar, for his part, was ready. The fight was given the full court press by the UFC — posters, billboards, advertising, the works. Lesnar had a name and if they were going to use him, the UFC wanted to make sure the world knew about it. The former WWE champ wasn't about to be intimidated by the promotional bombast: "There's a little pressure, but I'm not going to piss my pants or anything like that. . . . This is nothing new to me. I've been in front of thousands of people for eight, ten years now."

In the Octagon for the first time, Brock looked like he belonged. Lesnar exploded like a caged animal, knocking Mir down with a punch and nearly ending him on the ground. With Lesnar dominating the action, referee Steve Mazzagatti jumped between the two fighters. Lesnar, like many in attendance, thought the fight was over. Instead, Lesnar had a point deducted for hitting to the back of the head and Mir was given precious time to recover his senses. With a new lease on life, Mir was able to pull off a miracle. Lesnar took him right back down and proceeded punching him in the face, but the former champion had the wherewithal to catch the rookie in a fight-ending knee bar.

Lesnar's submission wrestling coach Erik Paulson gave his ringside perspective. "I think that Mazzagatti thought that maybe it was too early of a call so that when he stopped it, he was like, 'Now what?' When he raised Brock's arm up I thought the fight was over. Then all of a sudden he goes, 'Point,' and all of us in Brock's corner were like, what? I think he knew he made a mistake since he stopped and paused and then he wasn't quite sure what to do. We all thought the fight was over. You don't raise a fighter's arm up in the air and then say, 'Point.' Dana [White] came into the locker room after the fight and said that it was a *bullshit* call. He said that we should file a grievance with the commission."

"He doesn't deserve to watch one of our fights, let alone referee it," White said, lambasting the embattled referee after the fight in front of the gathered media.

Lesnar conceded he'd made a few mistakes of his own. "I understand that I've got 15 minutes to try to win a bout. I really rushed that fight, and I made a foolish mistake. I had Frank in a dominant position, and I stood up and fed him a foolish amateur mistake, and it was something that we worked on a million times," Lesnar said. "Just to be a more controlled fighter and a little more relaxed in there. We've been working on that. It has to do with just putting time in the gym, and that's exactly what I've been doing. Just trying to polish every aspect of the fight game and try to better myself every day."

In the immediate aftermath, UFC officials were ecstatic. They knew they had at least one solid pay-per-view buy riding the broad back of Brock Lesnar. After his display in the Octagon, it seemed Brock wouldn't just be a flash in the pan after all. White and his team started planning for the future — one it looked like Lesnar would play a big part in.

White, never shy about sharing an opinion, was willing to admit he'd been wrong about Lesnar. "All the guys came up to me — [Matt] Hughes, [Quinton] Rampage [Jackson], [UFC's flagship star Chuck] Liddell — and said, 'This guy's going to be scary in a couple of years.' He needs time. . . . I'll be honest: I didn't think he could come in here with no fights and compete on this level. He proved me wrong."

Next in line for Lesnar was supposed to be former UFC champion and wrestling Olympian Mark Coleman. A bulked up Coleman, who wrestled in college at 190 pounds, was one of the sport's legends. He had essentially provided a template for wrestlers everywhere by dominating opponents with his ground and pound style. Coleman wasn't a slick submission artist and never tried anything clever. Coleman would put his prey on the mat and proceed to demolish him with head butts, elbows, and punches.

Coleman had excelled in the no-holds-barred early days of the sport. When rule changes were implemented to civilize the fight game, he suddenly found himself struggling. He had been content to coast on the skills he had, refusing to add to his arsenal. As the game changed, Coleman had a hard time keeping up.

"I was content with the weapons that I had," Coleman said. "I didn't feel I needed to add any weapons, but all of the sudden when they did eliminate the head butt, I was way behind in the game. I had a lot of catching up to do. I hadn't improved my game at all because I felt what I had was enough to win just about any fight. When the head butt was gone, it became a completely different sport. I definitely prefer the older rules and feel I am a better fighter with no rules. But I'm glad they added them or the sport wouldn't even be around today."

Coleman, truth be told, wanted no part of Lesnar. Brock was the bigger man and just as good a wrestler. Early in his career Coleman had smashed an older wrestler, the great Dan Severn. Fueled by youth and anger, he had taken the skill set Severn introduced to the UFC and upped the ante. Severn was cautious and careful. Coleman was rage personified. He didn't want to be Severn, humbled by a new and improved version of himself. Mark bowed out of the fight. In his place stepped Pride star Heath Herring. In his memoir, *Death Clutch*, Lesnar explains, "I don't think Heath took me seriously, and that rubbed me the wrong way. He looked at me like I was a greenhorn, a WWE wrestler who didn't belong in the Octagon with an experienced veteran like him. He acted as if it was beneath him to fight me, and I was determined to make him eat his own words."

Lesnar was under significant pressure to win. His first show had drawn 600,000 pay-per-view buys, half of them coming from first-time buyers. But winning was the name of the game, and the UFC wasn't likely to stick with a main-eventer who failed time and again. Fan interest would plummet too. For Lesnar to make it, he needed to win big fights. He had purposely asked for the best, eschewing the more typical route that sees a fighter prove himself against progressively harder competition. Lesnar started at the top and didn't intend to reinvent himself as a midcarder. He was either going to make it as a champion or move on with his life.

Against Herring, Brock was fighting in his adopted home of Minneapolis, Minnesota. Unlike in his Las Vegas debut, Lesnar would be the crowd favorite. Maybe the more familiar environment relaxed the big man, because he opened the fight with a thunderous punch that sent Herring to the mat. The Pride star rarely got up again; he looked helpless, but survived a three-round drubbing.

"When he hit him with that right hand," White said, "Heath's face — it was unbelievable when he came back to the corner. One of our guys said, 'It looks like he's hitting him with lunch boxes out there.' That's how big Brock's hands are." In fact, Brock's hands are so big the UFC had to create a new glove size just to house them.

After the fight a riled up Lesnar pretended to lasso Herring, nicknamed "The Texas Crazy Horse," and pretended to ride him like a bucking bronco. UFC fans, used to a mutual display of respect after the fights, didn't quite know what to think.

"I got really excited after I won and I had every right to be," Lesnar said. "I was coming off a loss and it was tough. I don't like to lose. . . . I had been in front of a lot of crowds but the one thing I hadn't been is in the Octagon. I had a lot of pressure for that first fight, more pressure than this fight. I wasn't coming out of there without my hand being raised. That wasn't a possibility."

"This is his first win," White laughed. "He's only had a couple of fights. He's got a lot to learn. . . . I'm telling you, I'm blown away by his performance."

Next for Lesnar was supposed to be French striker Cheick Kongo, but it turned out bigger things awaited the UFC's new star. Randy Couture, a bona fide Octagon legend and champion as both a light heavyweight and a heavyweight, was the reigning UFC heavyweight champion. Couture had been away from the Octagon for almost a year, caught in a brutal contract dispute with the UFC that featured dueling press conferences, leaked contract terms, and plenty of bad blood. Many expected Couture to challenge the UFC in court to get out of his contract, but already 45 years old, the two-time Olympian saw his window of opportunity closing quickly.

Although White had claimed Lesnar wasn't ready for a title shot, money and Couture both said otherwise. Couture asked for Lesnar specifically, knowing the big man would lead to a big payday. Yet the event wasn't promoted as hard as some inside the company would have liked. The UFC didn't quite know what to do with a star of Lesnar's magnitude yet. Up until this point White had been pushed harder than any individual fighter, a foul-mouthed, bald headed everyman in tight-fitting T-shirts. With a natural charisma that connected with reporters and viewers alike, White had a knack for promoting his events and fighters.

The sports world was abuzz over this fight, like it had never been for a UFC fight before, and it had nothing to do with White's considerable talents. Lesnar was clearly on another level, possessed of the kind of charisma that draws every eyeball in the room. Couture represented Lesnar's polar opposite. While Lesnar was seen as brash and cocky, the consumate pro wrestler, Couture represented the humble and respectful fighting culture. But the UFC had gotten used to presenting a fight a certain way and didn't make the most of these contrasts. Lesnar's reluctance to come out of the Minnesota hills certainly didn't help things.

Falling just short of a million pay-per-view buys, UFC 91 didn't become the best-selling event in company history. It didn't even beat out the UFC's very next event, a supercard with Mir taking on Antônio Rodrigo Nogueira for an interim heavyweight title that was automatically rendered moot by Couture's return. But it was still an enormous success, in the cage as well as at the box office. Lesnar had the opportunity to become just the third pro wrestler (joining Ken Shamrock and Dan Severn) to win the UFC title and did just that. He knocked Randy down with a right hand that grazed the 45-year-old Couture's ear, before finishing the fight with a barrage of punches on the ground.

"I don't remember the punch [that knocked Couture down]. The only thing I remember is hitting him about 40 times on the ground. I was wondering when the ref would stop it," Brock said. The difference maker in this fight was pure size. Lesnar reportedly had to cut 12 pounds on the day of the weigh-ins, coming down from 277 pounds to the heavyweight limit of 265. Couture weighed in at a slim 220, actually smaller than the typical light heavyweight on fight night. Lesnar used his bulk to block Couture's numerous takedown attempts, but it ended up being his long reach more than his weight advantage that ended the night for Couture.

"Those are some big ass hamhocks coming at you," Couture said with a grin.

Lesnar won the heavyweight title in just his fourth professional fight, silencing critics who thought he was moved into the title picture early. The brash Lesnar, who was heavily booed by the partisan Couture crowd, defended his pre-fight proclamations that he had no weaknesses: "I may come across as a cocky SOB, but I'm just confident. It's what the Lord gave me, my body and my mind. I want to thank Dana White, the UFC, and I want to thank this guy: Randy Couture. It takes a lot of balls to take a year off and come back and fight a young buck like me."

A rematch with Mir was next on the agenda. Originally scheduled for UFC 98, it was delayed until UFC 100 while Mir recovered from arthroscopic knee surgery. It was one time a hurdle in the UFC's path was actually a fortuitous event. Putting Lesnar in the

100th UFC event was a marketer's dream. The sport's biggest star was headlining a show that the UFC put all its promotional muscle behind — and the result was record-setting PPV dollars.

Lesnar was still the outsider, but no longer one people expected to be overwhelmed. Lesnar had been the favorite against Couture and would be again against Mir. His fans saw a man destined to be an all-time great. His critics saw a pro wrestler who didn't understand their sport, didn't embrace its unwritten rules of civility and respect, and, worse than being lucky, was actually good. Tens of thousands wanted to see him fight and win. Thousands more wanted to see him humbled. He was a polarizing figure, but the one thing fans on both sides of the Lesnar divide could agree on was simple — they wanted to see him fight.

Mir was better equipped to do his part of the pre-fight promotion this time around too. Well spoken, quick, and funny, Mir had a natural confidence that came across to many as cockiness. Against most fighters, that made him the bad guy. Against Lesnar, it was just what many fans wanted to hear. His win over Lesnar had helped make him a star. An impressive performance as a coach on *The Ultimate Fighter* and a win over former Pride champion Nogueira solidified his spot as one of the UFC's best. And for this second fight with Lesnar, Mir was pulling no punches in the press.

Said Mir, "If Brock Lesnar was never in the WWE, he would have never gotten a title shot. And he knows that. . . . All I remember from last time is him whimpering and wincing as I was tapping him."

Mir was pushing all the right buttons and Lesnar was infuriated by the time the bell rang starting the bout. He overwhelmed Mir, using size, speed, and science to dominate the smaller man on the mat. His control of his opponent's hips was breathtaking. He wasn't just bigger than Mir — he was more technical as well, on this night anyway. He completely shut down Mir's half guard, using a variety of techniques including an old catch wrestling stockade to keep Mir pinned on his back where Lesnar could do him the most harm.

"I think nobody has been really able to understand since I've been training with Brock," Erik Paulson explained. "His transitions, controlling and riding people are unbelievable. He was really good at riding people in college wrestling."

Lesnar stopped Mir with punches on the ground in the second round. After the bout was stopped, Lesnar went wild. With spittle flying, he got in Mir's face while the former champion was still obviously dazed. The taunts drew boos from the crowd, prompting Lesnar to flip them off and egg them on during his post-fight interview with announcer Joe Rogan.

"Frank Mir had a horseshoe up his ass. I told him that a year ago. I pulled the sumbitch out and beat him over the head with it," Lesnar yelled, pulling out his mouthpiece to better let America and the Mir family know how he felt. He told the world, while standing in a cage adorned with the Bud Light logo, that he was going to go to the back and drink a Coors instead. "A Coors Light, not a Bud Light, because they won't pay me anything. . . . And hell, I may even get on top of my wife. See you later."

After the fight, Dana White tracked Lesnar down in his locker room and read him the riot act. To White, the behavior was inexcusable. The UFC had worked hard to build relationships with corporate sponsors like Budweiser, and Brock had done serious damage to the relationship. In his defense, Lesnar had a lot on his mind that night, money near the top of the list. A month before the fight White and UFC owner Lorenzo Fertitta had flown in to sign him to a new contract. They had discussed the possibility of some major endorsement deals to go along with his pay for the fights. In the end, it didn't happen. Lesnar writes, "I'm not the easiest guy in the world to get along with. I'm also not someone who likes to be played, so the Bud Light thing was somewhere in the back of my mind during the fight with Frank Mir, and when I saw that logo on the Octagon floor, the trigger was tripped. Hey, I was on top of the world looking down. And when I looked down, I saw that big Bud Light logo, and all that went through my mind was how much money the UFC was making on that sponsorship, and how much I wasn't."

White demanded an apology and Lesnar acquiesced, saying he would carry a Bud Light keg into the room when he went to meet the media. That seemed like overkill. But when the new undisputed champion came out for the post-fight press conference he was drinking a Bud Light to make amends.

"I think it was a heat of the moment thing," former WWE Vice President Jim Ross said. "He went on his instincts and how he felt at that time. He got a little carried away. He's an emotional guy, a very spirited and proud guy. When you look at it in total, here's a guy who has been training on a mat in a combat sport since he was a young kid. He paid the price to be a star from high school all the way to college, the WWE, and now the UFC. He comes into the cage and he's in great shape. He's got the right demeanor and he's got the right look. He's got the right skill set. And he's getting booed? He wondered what he could have done to piss off all these fans. It can be frustrating when you've worked so hard to get there. Brock just got caught up in the emotion of the moment."

Despite all of his experience in the world of pro wrestling, essentially spending years learning how to manipulate emotions with masters of the craft like Vince McMahon and his close confidante Paul Heyman, Lesnar had allowed Mir to get under his skin. An online video, with the son of Mir's manager Dean Albrecht playing Lesnar as a musclebound imbecile, particularly bothered the fighter. In the end, Mir had to pay a physical price.

"It was a revenge match 17 months in the making," Lesnar told ESPN's Jon Anik after the fight. "I'm a sore loser, I'll admit that. The world has been lifted off my chest and I am the true heavyweight champion of the world. . . . It's not that I disliked Frank. He beat me.

That burns deeper than anything else. And to have to wait 17 months to get revenge on this man. And to have to listen to him talk about what he's going to do to me. The icing on the cake was having to be pulled off by the referee."

For fighters and many of the sport's media, the display was an uncomfortable reminder that Lesnar came from another world. While trash talk was common before a fight, afterwards fighters almost always embraced and shared a few words. The fact that the fight was over when the bell rang was one of the most sacred precepts of mixed martial arts — it was one of the facts defenders of cage fighting used to distinguish the bouts from street fights and the fighters from thugs.

Heavyweight Shane Carwin was one of the most offended, speaking out against Lesnar's post-fight conduct. Before his uncharacteristic and outspoken verbal assault on Lesnar, Carwin had mostly flown under the radar. He had won all of his fights, but was often on the undercard, out of the limelight. His trash talk bumped Carwin up from a title elimination fight with Cain Velasquez directly into a bout with Lesnar, scheduled for November 2009 at UFC 106.

"The flipping off of the fans that just lined your pocket with millions of dollars is just lame," Carwin said. "He may be a champion, but he has a long ways to go before he earns the respect of a champion. The fans are why we do this, Brock. This sport is not about fat paychecks and drama. It is about hard work and sacrifice for a shot to do what you did [that] night. It doesn't matter how much money you make if you can't earn your peers' respect and the respect and love of the greatest sporting fans in the world."

Carwin would have to wait nearly a year to get his hands on Lesnar, as the champion found himself ill. Initially diagnosed with mononucleosis, Lesnar figured he was in the clear after taking it easy for several weeks. He missed his scheduled fight with Shane Carwin at UFC 106, but hoped to relax a little with a hunting trip into the Candadian wilderness, and then return to training. It was in Canada that things took a turn for the worse. He woke up in a sweat with a fever of 104 degrees and a stabbing pain in his gut.

"I didn't know where I was and realized I had to seek medical help," Lesnar said. "I'm out in the boondocks. It was about two and a half, three hours from what I thought would be a good medical facility."

Unable to find the medical care he needed in the Canadian woods, Lesnar's wife, Rena, drove like a bat out of hell to get him back to the States, to North Dakota where the champion spent 11 days eating from a tube and losing almost 50 pounds. Things started to look desperate. Facing a potentially career-ending surgery to combat diverticulitis, a digestive disease, Lesnar prayed for a cure. Luckily for the UFC champion, and Dana White, who had gotten used to collecting multi-million dollar checks every time Lesnar fought, there was a cure within. When Lesnar returned to the doctor to check on his progress and decide whether or not to have a surgery that could end his career, he found his miracle.

"They found absolutely nothing," Lesnar said. "The doctors came in and their whole panel at the Mayo Clinic just said, 'You just got a winning lottery ticket. We don't need to do surgery on you.'"

The culprit, it turns out, was a diet heavy on meat and potatoes and light on anything green. Within weeks Lesnar, a self-described carnivore, had a new diet and a new outlook on life. "When you think you're doing all of the right things and all of a sudden something like this happens, obviously you're not. I had to make some changes," Lesnar said in January 2010. "I'm getting ready for anybody and everybody. I know the heavyweight division is definitely back on its toes again because Brock Lesnar is back."

BLACK LESNAR

While Lesnar prepared for his return, others tried to follow in his very large footsteps. Fellow WWE superstar Bobby Lashley came from a similar background, starting his wrestling career as an amateur star, even making a run at the Olympic Games in 2004 before injuries to his leg stopped him in his tracks. Like Lesnar and Kurt Angle, Lashley was discovered by WWE executives when they saw him at an amateur meet. Like Lesnar, he had the look of a star.

"Kurt Angle was in the WWE at the time and he came to Colorado Springs to the Olympic Training Center," Lashley remembered, "He was doing a little vignette, a promo, and they were talking about his amateur days. That was the first time I met Kurt. And Kurt said, 'Have you thought about it? You have a great look for the WWE.' At the time I was still wrestling, but I had watched it as a kid. I enjoyed it, but I had never seen myself doing it. We exchanged numbers and talked from time to time. Then I got a call from [WWE Executive] Gerald Brisco because they were discussing me again. This time when they said, 'Come out and we'll have a look at you,' and I did."

Lashley, who wrestled in college at just 177 pounds and in the Army at 211 pounds, was soon up towards 275 pounds of pure ripped muscle. It was no surprise to long-time WWE fans when Lashley, despite a lack of experience and "it" factor, got a serious push. He had the look that Vince McMahon loved and was given every opportunity to succeed. Lashley even main-evented *WrestleMania 23*, beating Umaga in a hair versus hair match that allowed Donald Trump to shave McMahon's head.

"It's no secret Vince has this mindset that you have to be a big, juiced up steroid monster if you wanted to get pushed," former WWE writer Dominick Pagliaro said in *Ring of Hell*. "It was strongly implied. You were either on it or you weren't a star."

The similar background and newly muscle-bound physique earned Lashley the sobriquet "Black Lesnar," but he never quite lived up to those high standards. Lashley had all the tools, but was missing that certain something that makes a wrestler a star instead of

BOBBY LASHLEY
© WREALANO@AOL.COM

just another jobber. He worked and worked, but the fans never embraced him. Neither did some members of the locker room who resented Lashley's fast rise to fame. For his part, Lashley was enjoying the ride.

"It was probably the most fun I've had in my whole life," Lashley said. "Professional wrestlers aren't actors, so we can't really play a character. Very, very few are good enough actors to play a character. Vince would say, 'We just want you to be yourself, but with the volume turned up. Think about who you are, and then turn the volume up.' It was actually a fun transition, because you get to find out who you are."

After four years of the WWE grind, Lashley was wearing down: "At first you're in your honeymoon period. You don't realize the toll you are putting on your body because you are just so happy to be there and are having so much fun. But as the years go on, man. We're doing four shows a week. That's every week, because there is no down time. Your body is going to suffer because of it, but when it breaks down you can't quit. Because the show must go on."

It wasn't just the grueling road schedule or constant wear on his body. Locker room politics were also a drain on his mental reserves. WWE booker Michael Hayes, a former wrestler who used to come to the ring draped in the Confederate flag, was fired for directing racial slurs at black wrestler Mark Henry. Sources say he had run-ins with Lashley as well. A combination of the mental and physical stress made Lashley say goodbye to WWE.

He once again followed the path laid out by Lesnar, joining the MMA world and looking for his shot at either the UFC or a big money match in Strikeforce. He started training out of his adopted Colorado home, working with established UFC stars like Carwin and Nate Marquardt. Marquardt, not impressed with Lashley's dedication to the team, sent him packing and he landed in Florida, working out part time with American Top Team while continuing his wrestling career with Total Nonstop Action, a promotion that held weekly shows in the Sunshine State.

Lashley fought four times in the first six months of his career, the most significant bout a win over Bob Sapp in Biloxi, Mississippi. The competition was nothing to write home about; despite winning four of his first five by TKO or submission in the first round, Lashley seemed to be constantly disappointing MMA fans. Like Lesnar, he came with the taint of pro wrestling. Unlike the UFC star, he didn't challenge himself against the best or earn fans' respect. Explains BloodyElbow.com,

> *In a lot of ways Bobby Lashley owes his career to Brock Lesnar. . . .*
> *That's both a good and a bad thing. Lesnar has paved the way, but he's also created enormous expectations. Unrealistic expectations. Few will ever be able to match Brock's rocket like rise to the top of the MMA business. He fought former champion Frank Mir in his second fight. By his fourth fight he was*

WRESTLING INVASION 279

vanquishing the legendary Randy Couture. Lashley couldn't match that. No one could.

"It's hard when you have your first fight. And that first fight is on TV," Lashley told Bloody Elbow Radio in an exclusive interview. "You have a lot of publicity around you. It's kind of hard. Other guys, they get a handful of fights before they ever see any competition or are even on TV or anything like that. My first fight was on a major card and I've been on TV my whole career. Everybody was like, 'Who are you going to fight next? Are you going to fight Fedor [Emelianenko, a MMA legend]?' And man, I've only got one fight under my belt!"

Fans wanted to see Lashley in with the best heavyweights in the sport. He wanted to build slowly. The reality is most fighters aren't Lesnar. They can't jump immediately into the deep end and swim with the sharks. Lashley was criticized for taking a bout with part-time fighter Chad Griggs, a firefighter who was moonlighting as a professional. It turns out, it was a fight at exactly the right level for a prospect like Lashley with lots of flaws. Griggs stopped him in the first round, a loss Lashley blames on illness.

"I'm not giving up. I know what I'm capable of. . . . There's going to be a lot less pressure. Because I'm not undefeated anymore," Lashley said. "That's going to alleviate a lot of pressure for me. I don't have to worry about keeping this undefeated streak or anything like that. I can just go out there and be more comfortable. I think you're going to see a much better fighter, because I think they're going to let me fight every couple of months. I'm just going to get better and better and better."

THE NEW BROCK

While Lashley faded from the sport, only fighting once in the year after the Griggs loss, Lesnar made a triumphant return to face Carwin at UFC 116 on July 3, 2010. Off for almost an entire year, Lesnar carried more than his title belt into the cage. He carried a year's worth of anxiety and worry, all the questions about his future, and a burning desire to be the best.

It was an epic fight that saw Lesnar put to the mental test for the first time in his MMA career. Lesnar admits to being nervous of Carwin's heavy hands, and reacted poorly when he was hit hard for the first time, stunned by a left uppercut. Backed into the cage, Lesnar meekly covered up as Carwin knocked him to the ground. Lesnar would later compare Carwin's assault to Hurricane Katrina, and the fight looked like it would be stopped as Carwin landed blow after blow to Lesnar's head and arms. But Brock never gave up: "With every punch he threw, I could tell Carwin was shooting his wad. Each punch was a little lighter than the previous one. . . . I just wanted to survive that first round. It would sum up what I had been through the past eight months. I'd be able to regroup, but it would destroy Shane's confidence. He hit me with everything he had and couldn't put me away."

Referee Josh Rosenthal had told both fighters he would give them plenty of leeway since it was a title fight. He was true to his word. Many fights have been stopped for much less, but to Rosenthal's credit, Lesnar had continued to defend himself throughout and the ref let the fight go on. In the second round an exhausted Carwin was like a spectator at his own execution. Lesnar took him down with ease, submitting him with an arm triangle. Just like that Brock had done what had looked like an impossible task just a few minutes earlier. He had not only survived, he had beaten Shane Carwin.

"[It] nearly gave me a heart attack," White said. "I went to the back. I walked right out of the Octagon into my back room back there and sat down. I thought they were going to have to bring a defibrillator back there. Seriously, that's how messed up I was after the show. I was blown away. I needed a nap."

Up next for Lesnar was Cain Velasquez, a Mexican American heavyweight who had become legendary in MMA circles for his work ethic and potential before he ever set foot in the Octagon. It got so bad that Velasquez's management wasn't able to bring him along slowly in the sport's minor leagues the way they had intended. Cain's reputation had grown so quickly that no one would fight him. Manager and trainer Bob Cook had to take him right to the UFC after just two fights.

"Ideally you want guys to have a lot more fights than that before they go, but I struggled to get him fights on the smaller shows," Cook said. "We were really struggling to get him in the cage. I had four shows booked and not one fight came out of those shows. We went through seven or eight opponents in that process. Because they know he comes from a wrestling background and they know he's working at AKA on his standup and the rest of his game. They would Google him, see the wrestling, and take a look at him, and he's pretty intimidating looking. So they decided not to fight him."

"That time was tough," Velasquez said. "There were probably eight weeks straight where we went to fights and they'd say they'd have somebody for me. Then right before the weigh-ins the fight would get called off or we'd hear the show wasn't going to happen. That time was tough. We just decided to get a training session with Dana so he could see what I had to offer. And he signed me right away."

Velasquez earned his shot at Brock with a first round knockout of Antônio Rodrigo Nogueira in February 2010. Cain had stopped all but one of his six UFC opponents, quickly mastering the striking part of the fight game to compliment his All-American level wrestling. But Lesnar had two secret weapons in his training camp — coach Marty Morgan and teammate Cole Konrad. Morgan had coached Konrad to a series of wins over Velasquez when both were still in college. If anyone knew what Velasquez was capable of, it was Morgan. He and Konrad were confident Brock would be too much for Cain. His athleticism was something tough to prepare for — there are no "Brock Lesnar types" you can bring into your training camp.

"If you haven't worked out with him and felt that athleticism and explosion, it's hard to comprehend. As big and strong as he looks, he actually feels more powerful and more explosive," Konrad confided. "It's hard to believe. You get so used to going with a guy that big, that explosive, that powerful, that when you step back and get in with someone who isn't on that level you think, 'Well, wait a minute here.' Because he isn't in the same league as what you are used to seeing."

Velasquez, it turned out, was ready for everything Brock had to offer and then some. Lesnar took him down off the bat, but Cain was back to his feet in a matter of seconds. Once again, Brock seemingly panicked the first time he ate a punch from Velasquez, stumbling around the cage in a manner that can best be described as undignified. Unlike Carwin, who attacked a hurt Lesnar with reckless abandon, Velasquez picked his shots and finished the fight. It was a truly a masterful performance.

Looking back on the fight, Lesnar sees a game of inches that he lost. Physically, he says, he felt fine. But mentally he was exhausted. If he could take it back, if he could delay the Velasquez fight, he would. It was too much too soon.

Lesnar explained, "I experienced a lot last year, so from a fighting standpoint it probably wasn't great timing. . . . But from the business side of things when me and my team sat down to accept the fight, we discussed positives versus the negatives, and the positives outweighed the negatives for fighting in October. So, at the end of the day, this is prize fighting and I answered the call. But I fell short."

Lesnar ended the year as the biggest star in UFC history. In 2010 he became just the third man in combat sports to draw more than two million pay-per-view buys in a single year. But, in many ways, he was also a fighter on the edge of oblivion. He had looked bad against Carwin before his miraclulous comeback. Against Velasquez, he was simply outclassed. Another bad performance would leave fans wondering just how much the illness had taken out of him. He would likely have the same questions himself.

His return to the public eye, months after his Velasquez loss, shocked everyone, even those close to him. The notoriously private Lesnar had accepted Dana White's offer to coach *The Ultimate Fighter*, uprooting his family from Minnesota for a six-week stint on the Vegas strip as a reality television star. The opposing coach was Brazilian Junior dos Santos, a boxer who was next in line for a title shot. When Velasquez was forced to undergo shoulder surgery, dos Santos was more than pleased to face Lesnar instead: "I got very happy when I heard the news I'd be coaching alongside Brock on *TUF* and Brock is a guy that's bringing a lot of fans into MMA, he's a guy that's very well known in the U.S., and I'm a guy who's starting to come up right now and this is a great opportunity for all of my fans to be able to see me."

Dos Santos has learned what the UFC discovered years ago — Brock Lesnar is a steam engine capable of carrying a fighter (or a promotion) to wealth beyond imagination. A fight with Velasquez may have been for the title, but a fight with Lesnar is for the spotlight, something the two men shared on the 13th season of *The Ultimate Fighter*.

Said dos Santos, "Being in front of the cameras for that long and being in the house and the show was a new experience for me, I really enjoyed it and being on the show with Brock was great because Brock is so used to the media spotlight and being in front of the cameras. I'm a professional guy, a serious guy, so it was a great experience for me, and I feel that both of us really did their best in the show. . . . Prior to the show I'd never actually met Brock, so I was a little bit surprised of how professional and how easy to deal with Brock was, even though we weren't able to be together all that much. In the end it was great to be able to meet my next opponent and the experience overall was phenomenal."

Lesnar was expected to battle neck and neck with YouTube sensation Kimbo Slice as a *TUF* ratings draw. Slice had invigorated the reality show during his tenure as a fighter, providing quite a punch for a rumored $500,000 price tag. Lesnar would command much more than that; the UFC's contract with Spike TV was up at the end of 2011 and the Lesnar move was a power play by the UFC to show just how big their show could be. Instead, Lesnar and the show fizzled. The show with Brock as the star failed to meet the promotion's lofty expectations. It barely kept up with the program's average rating.

Things went from bad to worse when Lesnar's diverticulitis flared up in the midst of training for his fight with dos Santos. Now the reality show wasn't just a ratings disappointment — it was a ratings disappointment advertising a blockbuster main event that wasn't going to happen. More importantly, Lesnar's career might never be the same. He had 12 inches removed from his lower intestine at the Mayo Clinic, but was adamant that the surgery wouldn't stop him for good.

Lesnar told Mauro Ranallo on *The Fight Show*, "No, it's not over. It's not a career-ending surgery by any means, so I've just got to weigh out all my options at this time and see if that is the right thing to do or if there's any other medication that I can be on or any other thing. I don't know how I can change my diet any more than I have but we're looking down all avenues right now and I foresee in the near future that I'll be able to step back in the Octagon." It was actually about seven months before Lesnar would make a return to the cage. When asked how long it took him to feel like his old self after the surgery, Lesnar jokingly responded, "About six hours." But when he finally returned to action against enormous Dutch kickboxer Alistair Overeem at UFC 141, he didn't quite seem himself.

Overeem was a MMA veteran, in another lifetime a promising prospect at light heavyweight who never delivered when it mattered most. Bulking up to heavyweight changed everything. With the extra power, Overeem thrived, not only in mixed martial arts, but in kickboxing as well. He won the K-1 Grand Prix and became one of the heavyweight division's most fearsome fighters. Lesnar's equal in size, Overeem believed his experience would give him an advantage.

"Do I have an experience advantage? I believe I do. About ten times as much," the former Strikeforce champion said. "I'm going to tear this guy apart — piece by piece."

Overeem was true to his word, decimating Brock's tender insides with hard kicks to the body. "I predicted it the night before to my fiancée . . . I said, 'First I'm going to do this, then I'm going to do that. And I'm going to finish it with a liver kick," Overeem said after the fight. "I don't know if it's luck or it's strategy. But it turned out that way, and I'm happy that it did."

After the fight, Lesnar stood in the center of the Octagon and announced his retirement from the sport. "I've had a really difficult couple of years with my disease, and I'm going to officially say tonight is the last time you'll see me in the Octagon," Lesnar said. "I promised my wife and my kids if I won this fight, I would get a title shot, and that would be my last fight. But if I lost tonight . . . you've been great."

For the 34-year-old Lesnar, it had been a tumultuous four-and-a-half years in the sport. He competed almost from the start with the best of the best. In the end, it was his own failing body that did him in. In those four plus years, he accomplished more than most fighters do in a lifetime, winning the UFC title and becoming the sport's biggest box-office draw. "Brock Lesnar has made a lot of money in his career and has achieved a lot of things. He brought a lot of excitement to the heavyweight division," said UFC President Dana White. "What he accomplished in a short amount of time is amazing."

Outside of Sakuraba and the Pancrase veterans, catch wrestling has rarely been represented at the highest level of mixed martial arts. But there's one notable exception: "The Babyfaced Assassin" Josh Barnett, a former UFC champion and one of the sport's most controversial figures. Now a grizzled warrior in his mid-30s, the "Babyface" nickname seems out of place — but in 1999, at the age of 21, he still had the baby fat to go with his babyface. Barnett wasn't just out of shape or dumpy. He was legitimately fat. But inside that layer of lard lurked a hell of a fighter.

At SuperBrawl XIII he rampaged through an eight-man heavyweight tournament

27 THE FUTURE

— kind of a major deal because the T. Jay Thompson–promoted show was still seen as a ticket to the bigtime. In the field were six future UFC veterans including Heath Herring and Bobby Hoffman and future UFC heavyweight champion Ricco Rodriguez. When the dust settled, Barnett was crowned king.

His ticket to the UFC, however, still hadn't been punched — not quite yet. UFC matchmaker John Perretti didn't like Barnett's doughy look: gaining entry to the Octagon wouldn't be easy. He needed one more big win to secure his spot. Beating Bobby Hoffman was one thing. Dan Severn was another kind of test all together.

The "Beast" had been an early UFC standout and was still wreaking havoc on the independent scene all over the world. He had three losses on his record — to Royce Gracie, Ken Shamrock, and Mark Coleman, all cream of the crop athletes. Since his loss to Coleman, he had gone 21–0–3 over the next three years. In short, Dan Severn was still a force to be reckoned with.

"Dan was one of my favorite fighters from the early UFCs," Barnett remembered. "He was a pro wrestler, of course, and when you rolling German suplex a guy, you tend to leave an impression on people's minds, especially mine. Besides me, Dan is the only person to pull it off in an MMA match. But he did it first. When I had a chance to fight him, he had already beaten Lance Gibson and Doug Murphy, two guys from my gym. So him being an idol wasn't on my mind. The only thing on my mind was to kick the living crap out of him. At the time he hadn't lost in years. And it was my chance to show everybody that I'm one of the best in the world."

In typical Severn fashion, it wasn't pretty. The two men spent most of the first three rounds clinching against the ropes or charging each other like two bull elephants. Severn managed a takedown in each round and was likely ahead on the cards as they entered the fourth and final round. But when the tide turned, it turned quickly.

"He thought he was going to ride it out. But come that fourth round, [trainer] Matt [Hume] slapped the shit out of me and it really woke me up," Barnett said. "I just went out there berserk, swinging on him. He tried to lateral drop me and I blocked him. That was the end of the fight."

Barnett's dismantling of Severn, finishing the legend with a mounted arm bar, launched a career that would take a kid from Seattle, Washington, all over the world. He announced his presence early, losing a fight to perennial contender Pedro Rizzo, but doing it in style, standing and trading with the powerful kickboxer.

"I try never to be in a boring fight. In an exciting fight, win or lose, if people like what they see you're going to have a fanbase," Barnett said. "People are going to want to watch you fight. I think some of these promoters get that all mixed up and get too caught up on who's won what. That certainly does matter. But does this guy bring what I want to see? Or is he just somebody who happens to win?"

As his overall game improved under the guidance of former Pancrase fighter Matt Hume, Barnett lived a dream, winning the UFC title from the great Randy Couture in 2002.

Hume outlined Barnett's training: "When he started training with me he was just out of high school and still a kid; he spent many years training under me and became a world champion before going on his own. I trained Josh the same as I train everyone else. I attempt to develop all areas. Technically: striking, takedowns, and ground equally. Conditioning and strength to [fight] at a pace that the opponent can't handle. Strategy: to understand the fight game and your opponent's strengths and weaknesses. Mental preparation: To have no fear and keep your mind focused on what you are going to do to your opponent, concentrating on your strength and ability and not on your opponent's."

"I trained Josh as I would train anyone in any weight class," he continues. "At heavyweight, the fighters tend to focus less on the things that I mentioned and more on power, which I feel is a mistake and contributes to incomplete skills in the heavyweights. I believe that Josh had an advantage over heavyweights because of the understanding that I gave him in those areas."

When Barnett was at his absolute peak, with a dominant win over Couture in the record books and the UFC belt around his waist, things went horribly awry. He was busted for steroids, and then made matters worse by suggesting the test was doctored and that

UFC President Dana White was using the publicity as a negotiating tactic as the two discussed a new contract.

His UFC career ended with that positive test for performance enhancing drugs, but Barnett landed on his feet. He moved on to Japan, joining his idols in New Japan Pro-Wrestling and main-evening in the mammoth Tokyo Dome. Barnett was even able to claim the title belt that meant the most to him — the King of Pancrase.

"It was probably the highest point of my career, the thing that is most memorable to me. Winning that title meant so much," Barnett said. "It means more than anything else I've done in MMA. My coach Matt Hume competed for the original King of Pancrase. He didn't win it, but I got the chance 10 years later to go back and do it. It really made me proud to come home with that belt. And it really but the belt, in the eyes of people, at the level it should be treated."

Later Barnett joined the Pride promotion and he beat some of the best, including becoming one of the few men to defeat Antônio Rodrigo Nogueira. Along the way Barnett's path diverged from most mixed martial artists — his preferred style on the mat was catch wrestling, an art he learned from Billy Robinson in Japan and Hume in Seattle.

Barnett told Jake Shannon at ScientificWrestling.com, "One of the reasons I got into MMA was because of pro wrestling. I always knew that pro wrestling was a sport of real tough men and that most people only knew the surface of pro wrestling. I get upset to see that something like catch, that used to be known and popular all throughout the world, is being ignored. Catch was here before BJJ and BJJ is not the end all, be all of submissions. I will bring catch wrestling back to the forefront and in the limelight again and I'll do it by beating my opponents."

Now 33, Barnett is writing the final chapters of his story. It's unclear what the future holds — several drug test failures have made it hard for him to get licensed to fight in many states and the market for MMA in Japan has withered. In the United States, only the UFC's parent company Zuffa remains as a major player, and bad blood with Dana White may prevent him from ever returning to the Octagon. But Barnett, ever an optimist, believes he may get another chance in the UFC.

"You don't burn bridges with Dana," Barnett told MMA journalist Sam Caplan.

> *If you can make him money, he puts you in there. If he thinks he's going to get rich, he uses you or in some instances he has his guys that he calls his "boys," or whatever. He knows where his bread is buttered and if he sees green — it's a go. Randy got an instant title shot coming out of retirement. You know why? Because he saw green.*
>
> *I'm not the only person to ever have issues with Dana and I'm sure — in fact I know for a fact — that there are fighters that are in the Ultimate Fighting*

Championship right now that have a problem with Dana White. But this is a completely different scenario. If he wants to have personal issues with fighters then there's nothing I can do to help that guy.

In terms of business, I make promoters money and promoters make me money and that's what it comes down to and when it comes to calling somebody unbeatable you better make sure next time that the guy that beat him for the heavyweight title before isn't in the same room.

NEW GENERATION

While Barnett's best days may be behind him, a new generation of catch-based fighters is on the horizon. The lead grappling trainer at Randy Couture's Xtreme Couture gym in Las Vegas is a catch aficionado named Neil Melanson — a former student of Gene LeBell disciple Gokor Chivichyan. Melanson became Couture's grappling instructor prior to the UFC legend's fight with Nogueira and the techniques and strategies he's showing Couture — and other fighters around the country who flock to Randy's gym — is resonating with wrestling-based fighters.

"I'm moving away from a jiu-jitsu mentality," Couture said before his fight with Mark Coleman at UFC 109. Working with Melanson had opened his eyes about what was possible on the ground. "With Neil, I'm looking more with a wrestler's eyes. Instead of jiu-jitsu positions, Neil is showing me catch wrestling and submissions as they come from wrestling positions. It's really a lot of fun for me."

But Melanson, the man reviving catch wrestling, insists it's still a rare skill set. "Its original form is almost dead — there's a few guys out there that can really do it. I consider myself a catch wrestler but when it comes down to true catch wrestling, I'm really not. That particular form, it's so hard to find guys that know that style well. It had a lot to do with the application of what I call 'mat wrestling.' People associate takedowns with wrestling and don't realize there's a lot of mat work in wrestling."

Besides Couture and other MMA stalwarts like Chael Sonnen, Melanson has also trained extensively with Bryan Danielson, the independent wrestling star now making a name in the WWE as Daniel Bryan.

"He's getting good," says Menalson of Danielson. "The problem is, now that he's doing pro wrestling, he's hardly getting a chance to train. He's a tough bastard, he's a legit grappler. He's rolled with Randy, he's rolled with those guys. . . . He's a strong, strong guy. You know when you meet people and they're like, 'This guy's a good guy?' He is by far one of the best quality human beings I've met in my entire life. I hope he continues to be successful in what he does."

Danielson, who once considered making a career out of fighting, is starting to catch on in wrestling's last remaining major league — but he hasn't left his catch roots behind entirely. He's using the LeBell Lock as a submission finisher, keeping another wrestling legend alive on national television.

"It's actually an omoplata with a cross face, but I've mostly just called it the LeBell Lock," Danielson wrote. "Neil Melanson, my friend and one of the best grappling coaches in the country, taught me the move and he learned it from the legendary 'Judo' Gene LeBell. I've never met Mr. LeBell, but he is one of the grappling greats."

The future looks bright for catch wrestling. In addition to Melanson, Billy Robinson is still active training young wrestlers with the help of Scientific Wrestling's Jake Shannon. There are teams of young fighters competing in grappling tournaments worldwide, flying the flag for catch wrestling. Professional fighters like Matt Hughes are implementing catch techniques into their bouts.

For decades tough men spent their lives on the mat, refining the sport until it was nearly perfect — equal parts art and science. Its secrets were passed on from one generation to the next in wrestling rooms, dojos, carnival tents, and even in the Octagon. Its appeal is universal — the catch wrestling web was spun all over the world, from dingy gyms in Wigan, England, to Tokyo, and even to the jiu-jitsu artists in Brazil.

The art is still being passed on today, and in MMA has a proving ground to show its efficacy. Submission wrestling, once thought to be dead, may be approaching a new renaissance. As long as men struggle for physical supremacy, there will always be a place for wrestling and its ultimate expression — catch-as-catch-can.

SOURCES

1. MULDOON AND THE DAWN OF AMERICAN WRESTLING

Baker, William Joseph, *Sport and Society* (University of Illinois Press, 1988).

———, *Sports in the Western World* (University of Illinois Press, 1988).

Griffin, Marcus, *Fall Guys: The Barnums of Bounce* (The Reilly and Lee Co., 1937).

Hauser, Thomas, *Muhammad Ali and Company* (Hastingshouse/Daytrips, 1998).

Lang, Arne K., *Prizefighting: An American History* (McFarland, 2008).

Morgan, Jaret, "In the Shadow of John L. Sullivan," EastSideBoxing.com, January 2003.

Morton, Gerald W. and George M. O'Brien, *Wrestling to Rasslin: Ancient Sport to American Spectacle* (Popular Press, 1985).

Mott, Frank Luther, *A History of American Magazines, 1850–1865 Volume II* (The Belknap Press of Harvard University Press, 1968).

Shannon, William V., *The American Irish: A Political and Social Portrait* (University of Massachusetts Press, 1990).

Somer, Dale A., *The Rise of Sports in New Orleans: 1850–1900* (Louisiana State University Press, 1972).

Sugar, Bert, *Bert Sugar on Boxing: The Best of the Sport's Most Notable Writer* (The Lyon Press, 2005).

Van Every, Edward, *Muldoon: The Solid Man of Sport* (Frederick A. Stokes Company, 1929).

SELECT NEWSPAPERS:

Brooklyn NY Daily Eagle, November 14, 1877

New York Times, March 23, 1878

Reno Evening Gazette, March 8, 1919

2. THE UNCIVILIZED IMPORT: CATCH-AS-CATCH-CAN

Adelman, Melvin L., "The First Modern Sport in America: Harness Racing in New York City 1825–1870," *Journal of Sport History*, Volume 8, Number 1 (Spring 1981).

Armstrong, Walter, *Wrestling* (F.A. Stokes, 1890).

Beafort, K.G. and Alfred Watson, *The Badminton Library of Sports and Pastimes: Fencing, Boxing, and Wrestling* (Longmans, Green, and Co., 1893).

Beekman, Scott M., *Ringside* (Praeger, 2006).

Bothner, George, *Scientific Wrestling* (Richard K. Fox Publishing, 1912).

Carew, Richard, *The Survey of Cornwall 1602* (Printed for B. Law, 1769).

Casebolt, Lee, "From Sidebets to Sideshow — The Influence of Gambling on the Development of Professional Wrestling in America, 1870–1920" (Masters dissertation, University of Iowa, 2007).

Connors, Tom, *The Modern Athlete* (E. Bulfin, 1890).

Fleischer, Nat, *From Milo to Londos* (The Ring Athletic Library, 1936).

Hewitt, Mark, *Catch Wrestling Round 2* (Paladin Press, 2009).

Svinth, Joseph, "Japanese Professional Wrestling Pioneer: Sorakichi Matsuda," *INYO: Journal of Alternate Perspectives* (November 2000).

Zarnowski, Frank, *All Around Men: Heroes of a Forgotten Sport* (Scarecrow Press, 2005).

SELECT NEWSPAPERS:
Bismarck ND Daily Tribune, September 16, 1891
Chicago Tribune, October 12, 1888
Des Moines Register, March 4, 1918
Inter Ocean, October 12, 1895
Madison Democrat, August 21, 1885
Madison Magazine, December 1991
Milwaukee Sentinel, March 8, 1886
New York Times, December 22, 1880; July 27, 1884
Ogden Standard, March 1, 1891
Pittsburgh Dispatch, June 14, 1887
Wisconsin State Journal, February 15, 1886; January 30, 1886

3. "FARMER" BURNS

Chapman, Mike, *The Life and Legacy of Frank Gotch* (Paladin Press, 2008).

Gilbey, John, *Western Boxing and World Wrestling* (North Atlantic Books, 1986).

Hewitt, Mark, *Catch Wrestling* (Paladin Press, 2005).

Hornbaker, Tim, "Farmer Burns Wrestling History," LegacyofWrestling.com.
———, "Frank Gotch Wrestling History," LegacyofWrestling.com.
Nash, John, "The Forgotten Golden Age of Mixed Martial Arts: The Golden Age of Wrestling and the Lost Art of American Catch-as-Catch-Can," BloodyElbow.com.
Robbins, George S., *Frank A. Gotch, World's Champion Wrestler: His Life, Mat Battles and Instructions on How to Wrestle* (Joseph B. Bowles, 1913).
Teal, Scott, "Farmer Burns," *Whatever Happened To . . . ?*, Volume 6.
Wallace, Eugene and Halm, John, *The Lifework of "Farmer" Burns* (A.J. Kuhlman, 1911).

SELECT NEWSPAPERS:
Semi-Weekly Klondike Nugget, September 18, 1901

4. JENKINS, THE TURK, AND THE AMERICAN TITLE

Burke, Tom, "The History of Wrestling Managers — Part 1," *Ring Wrestling*. May 1979.
Chapman, Mike, *The Life and Legacy of Frank Gotch* (Paladin Press, 2008).
Duncan, Royal and Gary Will, *Wrestling Title Histories* (Archeus Communications, 2000).
Fleischer, Nat, *From Milo to Londos* (The Ring Athletic Library, 1936).
Gilbey, John, *Western Boxing and World Wrestling* (North Atlantic Books, 1986).
Gotch, Frank and George Robbins, *How to Wrestle* (Max Stein Publishing House, 1934).
Hewitt, Mark, *Catch Wrestling Round 2* (Paladin Press, 2009).
———, "Tom Jenkins: Tough as Barbed Wire," 1WrestlingLegends.com.
Noble, Graham, "The Life and Death of the Terrible Turk," *Eurozine*, May 2003.
Rauer, John E., "'Rough Tom' Jenkins," PWHF.org.
Reeder, Rex, "You Don't Have to Be as Big as the Other Man: The Tom Jenkins Story," *The Authoritative Encyclopedia of Scientific Wrestling Volume III* (Scientific Wrestling, 2005).
Robbins, George S., *Frank A. Gotch, World's Champion Wrestler: His Life, Mat Battles and Instructions on How to Wrestle* (Joseph B. Bowles, 1913).
Shannon, Jake, *The Authoritative Encyclopedia of Scientific Wrestling Volume III* (Scientific Wrestling, 2005).
Shepherd, Barron, "Tom Jenkins," CatchWrestling-Coach.blogspot.com, July 26, 2009.
Yohe, Steve, "A Review of the Nine Frank Gotch/Tom Jenkins Matches," WrestlingClassics.com, June 16, 2007.

SELECT NEWSPAPERS:
Baltimore Sun, November 8, 1901
Chicago Tribune, December 26, 1902
Cincinnati Enquirer, May 6, 1898
Cleveland Plain Dealer, May 6, 1898
Dubuque Sunday Herald, July 1, 1900
New York Times, March 27, 1898; May 1, 1898
New York World, April 30, 1898

5. THE RUSSIAN LION ROARS

Chapman, David, *Sandow the Magnificent* (University of Illinois Press, 1994).
Fleischer, Nat, *From Milo to Londos* (The Ring Athletic Library, 1936).
Gentle, David, "George Hackenschmidt: The Russian Lion," SandowPlus.co.uk.
"George Hackenscmidt — The Russian Lion," WrestlingHeritage.co.uk.
Gotch, Frank and George Robbins, *How to Wrestle* (Max Stein Publishing House, 1934).
Hackenschmidt, George, *The Way to Live* (Strength and Health Publishing, 1908).
Lurich, George, personal letter, from the Mark Hewitt Collection.
MacKaye, Milton, "On the Hoof," *Saturday Evening Post*, December 14, 1935.

SELECT NEWSPAPERS:
Cleveland Plain Dealer, January 29, 1904
Marshfield Times, December 1, 1905
New York Times, April 16, 1905; May 5, 1905
Oakland Tribune, March 28, 1905
United Press Association, January 31, 1904
Washington Post, December 19, 1906

6. OLD WORLD VS. NEW WORLD: GOTCH VS. HACKENSCHMIDT

Beekman, Scott M., *Ringside* (Praeger, 2006).
Chapman, Mike, *Gotch: An American Hero* (Culture House Books, 1999).
———, *The Life and Legacy of Frank Gotch* (Paladin Press, 2008).
Gotch, Frank and George Robbins, *How to Wrestle* (Max Stein Publishing House, 1934).
MacKaye, Milton, "On the Hoof," *Saturday Evening Post*, December 14, 1935.
Robbins, George S., *Frank A. Gotch, World's Champion Wrestler: His Life, Mat Battles*

    and Instructions on How to Wrestle (Joseph B. Bowles, 1913).
Smith, Ed Wallace, *Professional Wrestling* (American Sports Publishing Company, 1912).
Ward, Geoffrey, *Unforgivable Blackness* (Vintage, 2004).
Yohe, Steve, "A Review of the Nine Frank Gotch/Tom Jenkins Matches," WrestlingClassics.com, June 7, 2007.

SELECT MAGAZINES AND NEWSPAPERS:
Chicago Daily Tribune, April 4, 1908
Health & Strength Magazine, March 7, 1931
Evansville Press, October 21, 1915
Lowell Sun & Citizen Leader, 1942
Reno Evening Gazette, November 18, 1914
Seattle Times, March 10, 1910; November 29, 1910; January 1, 1911
Stevens Point Journal, September 3, 1910
Washington Post, April 6, 1908; December 6, 1931

7. FROM THE KODOKAN TO THE COUNT OF COMBAT: MITSUYO MAEDA

Bunasawa, Nori and John Murray, *Mitsuyo Maeda: The Toughest Man Who Ever Lived* (Judo Journal and Innovations, 2007).
Gracie, Renzo and John Danaher, *Mastering Jujitsu* (Human Kinetics, 2003).
Green, Thomas and Joseph Svinth, *Martial Arts in the Modern World* (Praeger Publishers, 2003).
Hewitt, Mark, *Catch Wrestling* (Paladin Press, 2005).
"History of Jiu Jitsu," CrosleyGracie.com.
Kano, Jigoro, "Conversation with Gunki Koizumi," *Budokwai Bulletin*, April 1947.
Svinth, Joseph, "Tokugoro Ito," *Electronic Journal of Martial Arts and Sciences*, July 2006.
Virgilio, Stanlei, *Conde Koma* (Editora Átomo, 2002).

8. A WORLD WITHOUT HEROES

Beekman, Scott M., *Ringside* (Praeger, 2006).
Davis, Mac, *100 Greatest Sports Heroes* (Grosset & Dunlop, 1958).
Duncan, Royal and Gary Will, *Wrestling Title Histories* (Archeus Communications, 2000).
Fleischer, Nat, *From Milo to Londos* (The Ring Athletic Library, 1936).

Gilbey, John, *Western Boxing and World Wrestling* (North Atlantic Books, 1986).
Griffin, Marcus, *Fall Guys: The Barnums of Bounce* (The Reilly and Lee Co, 1937).
Hewitt, Mark, *Catch Wrestling* (Paladin Press, 2005).
Mucken, Lynn, "The Strangler and the Mauler," *Sports Illustrated*, August 3, 1970.
Yohe, Steve, *Ed Lewis Biography* (WrestlingClassics.com, 2011).
——— and John D. Williams, "Joe Stecher Bio," WrestlingClassics.com.
———, "Wladek Zbyszko Bio," WrestlingClassics.com.

SELECT NEWSPAPERS:
Associated Press, November 27, 1922
Des Moines Register, January 23, 1918
Japan Times, March 3, 1921
Los Angeles Times, February 1, 1917
New York Times, December 14, 1920; January 31, 1920; April 5, 1921, November 9, 1921
Nashville Banner, March 16, 1922
Rochester American, December 10, 1922

9. POLICEMEN, TRUSTBUSTERS, AND THE DOUBLE CROSS

Beekman, Scott M., *Ringside* (Praeger, 2006).
Campbell, Jason, "Pro Wrestling Supercards: Chicago," ProWrestlingHistory.com.
Duncan, Royal and Gary Will, *Wrestling Title Histories* (Archeus Communications, 2000).
Fleischer, Nat, *From Milo to Londos* (The Ring Athletic Library, 1936).
Griffin, Marcus, *Fall Guys: The Barnums of Bounce* (The Reilly and Lee Co, 1937).
Haynes, Richard, "The Joe Stecher Ring Record."
Hewitt, Mark, *Catch Wrestling* (Paladin Press, 2005).
———, *Catch Wrestling Round 2* (Paladin Press, 2009).
Hornbaker, Tim, "Tom Packs Wrestling Biography," LegacyofWrestling.com.
Oberthaler, Joan, "King of the Ring: Gus Sonnenberg: Lawyer, Football Star, Heavyweight." *Marquette Monthly*.
"Sport: Baba & Behemoths," *Time*, May 18, 1936.
"Sport: Lewis vs. Munn," *Time*, January 19, 1925.
"Sport: Steele vs. Strangler," *Time*, December 12, 1932.
Thesz, Lou and Kit Bauman, *Hooker: An Authentic Wrestler's Adventures Inside the Bizarre World of Professional Wrestling* (Lou Thesz Books, 1995).
Wrestling Champion of the World," *Marquette Monthly*, October 2000.
Yohe, Steve, *Ed Lewis Biography* (WrestlingClassics.com, 2011).

SELECT NEWSPAPERS:
- *Boston Globe*, June 28, 1935
- *East St. Louis Journal*, June 20, 1934
- *Ironwood Daily Globe*, July 13, 1929,
- *Los Angeles Examiner*, October 10, 1934
- *New York Times*, March 1, 1921; November 14, 1921; November 15, 1921; November 16, 1921; July 10, 1929
- *Schenectady Gazette*, June 28, 1935
- *Vancouver Sun*, December 6, 1932
- *Washington Reporter*, July 31, 1935

10. THESZ

Benaka, Lee, "Lou Thesz," DeathValleyDriver.com.
Gordienko, George, "George Gordienko Autobiography," HouseofDeception.com.
Hallinan, Mike, "No Angel of Islington," WrestlingHeritage.co.uk.
Hartley, Jeremy, "Lou Thesz Interview," TWConline.com.
Hornbaker, Tim, *National Wrestling Alliance: The Untold Story of the Monopoly that Strangled Pro Wrestling* (ECW Press, 2007).
Meltzer, Dave, *Tributes II* (Sports Publishing LLC, 2004).
Murdock, Bill, "Dick Hutton: A True Legend," MikeMooneyham.com.
Oliver, Greg, "Nephew aims to boost Gordienko's legacy," Slam.Canoe.ca.
Phantom of the Ring, "Life and Times of a Hooker," *Wrestling Perspective*, Volume 13, Issue 100.
Skolnick, David, "The Bruno Sammartino Interview," *Wrestling Perspective*, Volume 11, Issue 71.
Shannon, Jake, *Say Uncle* (ECW Press, 2011).
Teal, Scott, "Wrestle in Peace: Lou Thesz," *Whatever Happened To . . ?*, Volume 52.
Thesz, Lou, interview with author.
────── and Kit Bauman, *Hooker: An Authentic Wrestler's Adventures Inside the Bizarre World of Professional Wrestling* (Lou Thesz Books, 1995).

11. THE REVOLUTION WILL BE TELEVISED

Abramson, Albert, *The History of Television: 1942–2000* (McFarland, 2003).
Baughman, James L., *Same Time, Same Station: Creating American Television, 1948–1961* (JHU Press, 2007).
Brooks, Tim and Earle Marsh, *The Complete Directory to Prime-Time Network and*

Cable TV Shows, 1946–Present, 6th Edition (Ballantine Books, 2007).
Dolin, John, director, Wrestling with the Past, 1999.
Gilbey, John, Western Boxing and World Wrestling (North Atlantic Books, 1986).
Hall, Ward, "Sideshow World," SideShowWorld.com.
Hogan, Hulk, Hollywood Hulk Hogan (Simon and Schuster, 2002).
"It's a Gaudy Show," Sports Illustrated, April 11, 1955.
Kisseloff, Jeff, The Box: An Oral History of Television (Viking, 1995).
Mooneyham, Mike, "Matsuda very influential in pro wrestling," Post and Courier, December 5, 1999.
Oliver, Greg, "Classic AWA to air on Viewer's Choice," SlamWrestling.com.
———, "Mad Dog gets top CAC honor," SlamWrestling.com, 2003.
Presley, Jeff, "Interview with Billy Wicks," Catch.20m.com.
Race, Harley and Gerry Tritz, King of the Ring: The Harley Race Story (Sports Publishing LLC, 2006).
Shagawat, Robert, "Television Recording — The Origins and Earliest Surviving Live TV Broadcasts Recordings," EarlyTelevision.org, October 2004.

12. THE GREAT DANNY HODGE

Baker, Ox, "$10,000 Wasted," 1WrestlingLegend.com.
Botter, Jeremy, "Exclusive: Legendary Announcer Jim Ross Validates Folklore," Heavy.com.
"Dan Hodge's Progress," Sports Illustrated, April 7, 1958.
Duncan, Royal and Gary Will, Wrestling Title Histories (Archeus Communications, 2000).
Funk, Terry and Scott Williams, Terry Funk: More Than Just Hardcore (Sports Publishing LLC, 2006).
Hodge, Dan, interview with author.
Hornbaker, Tim, National Wrestling Alliance: The Untold Story of the Monopoly that Strangled Pro Wrestling (ECW Press, 2007).
In Your Head Wrestling, "Danny Hodge Interview," July 16, 2010.
Meltzer, Dave, "Danny Hodge: What might've been?" Yahoo.com.
Molinaro, John, "Danny Hodge: The Giant Jr. Heavyweight," SlamWrestling.com.
———, Top 100 Pro Wrestlers of All Time (Winding Star Press, 2002).
Parker, Don, "Dan the Puncher," Sports Illustrated, March 17, 1958.
———, "The Man to Beat," Sports Illustrated, April 1, 1957.
"Sugar Ray's Manager Hired by White Pro," Jet, May 29, 1958.
Watts, Bill and Scott Williams, The Cowboy and the Cross (ECW Press, 2006).

Wrestling 411, "Mike Chapman & Dan Hodge talk about the new book, *Oklahoma Shooter: The Dan Hodge Story*." Wrestling411.com.

13. NO ONE BEFORE KIMURA, AND NO ONE AFTER

Chen, Jim, "The Man Who Defeated Helio Gracie," JudoInfo.com.
Kimura, Masahiko, *My Judo* (Budo Videos, 1985).
Marshall, Gavin. "Death of a Hero," *Wrestling Revue*, April 1964.
Meltzer, Dave, "MMA to return to Brazilian roots for UFC 134," Yahoo.com
———, "Remembering Helio Gracie," Yahoo.com.
Nishi, Yoshinori, "Helio Gracie Interviewed," *Kakuto Striking Spirit*, May 1, 2002.
Thesz, Lou and Kit Bauman, *Hooker: An Authentic Wrestler's Adventures Inside the Bizarre World of Professional Wrestling* (Lou Thesz Books, 1995).
Whiting, Robert, *Tokyo Underworld* (Random House Digital, 2000).

14. WIGAN

Duncan, Royal and Gary Will, *Wrestling Title Histories* (Archeus Communications, 2000).
Flair, Ric and Keith Greenberg, *Ric Flair: To Be the Man* (Simon and Schuster, 2004).
Graham, Billy, interview with author.
Kleinberg, Adam and Adam Nudelman, *Mysteries of Wrestling: Solved* (ECW Press, 2005).
Martin, Todd, "The Overlooked History of Mixed Martial Arts," CBSsports.com, 2007.
Malenko, Joe, interview with author.
Mooneyham, Mike, "'God of Wrestling' Gotch Dead," MikeMooneyham.com, 2007.
Robinson, Billy, interview with author.
Shannon, Jake, interview with author.
———, *Say Uncle* (ECW Press, 2011).
Snowden, Jonathan, *Total MMA: Inside Ultimate Fighting* (ECW Press, 2008).
Todd, Mike and Ian Bennett, directors, *Catch: The Hold Not Taken*, 2005.
Wrestling Observer Radio, "Billy Robinson Interview," October 28, 2009.

15. JUDO GENE AND BAD NEWS

Billington, Tom, *Pure Dynamite* (Sw Publishing, 1999).

Cater, Dave, "Legend in His Own Time," InsideKung-fu.com.
Coage, Allen, interview with author.
Falcone, Dewey, "Judo vs. Boxing," *Black Belt*, May/June 1964.
Harris, Jeff, "This Mall Cop Is Real Bad News," SlamWrestling.com.
Hillhouse, Dave, "Messing Around with 'Judo' Gene LeBell," SlamWrestling.com.
Jacobs, Mark, "Tough Guys Wear Pink," *Sports Illustrated*, April 3, 1995.
Kram, Mark, "The Lady Is a Champ," *Sports Illustrated*, November 6, 1967.
LeBell, Gene, "Bruce Lee — Student, Friend and Teacher," GeneLeBell.com.
——— and Bob Calhoun, *The Godfather of Grappling* (Gene LeBell, 2005).
———, interview with author.
McCoy, Heath, *Pain and Passion: The History of Stampede Wrestling* (CanWest Books, 2005).
McGee, John, "Allen Coage: Would You Send This Boy to College?" *Black Belt*, January 1969.
Miller, Davis, *Tao of Bruce Lee* (Random House, 2001).
Nilsson, Thomas, "A Conversation with the Toughest Man Alive," *Black Belt*, April 1994.
O'Brien, Jess, *Nei Jia Quan: Internal Martial Arts* (North Atlantic Books, 2004).
People v. Lebell (1979) 89 Cal.App.3d 772 [152 Cal.Rptr. 840].
Smash Wrestling, "Bad News Brown Interview," March 2001.
The Joe Rogan Experience, February 9, 2011.
Wertheim, L. Jon, *Blood in the Cage* (Houghton Mifflin Harcourt, 2008).
Zemen, Ned, "Seagal Under Siege," *Vanity Fair*, October 2002.
Zimmerman, Richard, "Allen Coage: Judo Player of the Year," *Black Belt*, January 1978.

SELECT NEWSPAPERS:
Los Angeles Times, September 12, 1976; June 14, 1979

16. THE INOKI LEGEND BORN

"Ali, Inoki, Pick and Roll to Standoff in Sleeper," *Jet*, July 15, 1976.
Cashill, Jack, *Suckerpunch* (Thomas Nelson, 2006).
"Catch as Ali Can," *Sports Illustrated*, April 19, 1976.
Draeger, Donn, "Muhammad Ali versus Antonio Inoki," *Journal of Combative Sport*, 2000.
Duncan, Royal and Gary Will, *Wrestling Title Histories* (Archeus Communications, 2000).

Hauser, Thomas, *Muhammad Ali: His Life and Times* (Simon and Schuster, 1992).
Heenan, Bobby and Steve Anderson, *Bobby the Brain: Wrestling's Bad Boy Tells All* (Triumph Books, 2002).
Kram, Mark, "... But Only a Farce in Tokyo," *Sports Illustrated*, July 5, 1976.
Molinaro, John, *Top 100 Pro Wrestlers of All Time* (Winding Star Press, 2002).
"The Nation: A Glittering Courtesy Call," *Time*, July 19, 1976.
Thesz, Lou and Kit Bauman, *Hooker: An Authentic Wrestler's Adventures Inside the Bizarre World of Professional Wrestling* (Lou Thesz Books, 1995).
Whiting, Robert, *Tokyo Underworld* (Random House Digital, 2000).

SELECT NEWSPAPERS AND NEWSLETTERS:
New York Times, May 21, 1976; May 19, 1976; June 25, 1976; June 27, 1976; July 2, 1976; July 4, 1976; February 23, 1977
Wrestling Observer Newsletter, August 14, 1996; April 1, 2009

17. BRISCO: THE LAST OF HIS KIND

Brisco, Jack, interview with author.
——— and William Murdock, *Brisco* (Culture House Books, 2004).
Duncan, Royal and Gary Will, *Wrestling Title Histories* (Archeus Communications, 2000).
Dunn, Kevin, director, *The Most Powerful Families in Wrestling*, 2007.
Funk, Terry and Scott Williams, *Terry Funk: More Than Just Hardcore* (Sports Publishing LLC, 2006).
Hornbaker, Tim, *National Wrestling Alliance: The Untold Story of the Monopoly that Strangled Pro Wrestling* (ECW Press, 2007).
MacArthur, Paul, "The Jack Brisco Interview," *Wrestling Perspective*, Volume VII, Number 60, April 2, 1996.
Nulty, Mark, director, *Jack Brisco Shoot Interview*, 2002.
Watts, Bill and Scott Williams, *The Cowboy and the Cross* (ECW Press, 2006).
Wilson, Jim, *Chokehold: Pro Wrestling's Real Mayhem Outside the Ring* (Xlibris Corporation, 2003).
Wrestling Observer Live, "Jack Brisco Interview," March 29, 2004.

SELECT NEWSLETTERS:
Wrestling Observer Newsletter, February 17, 2010.

18. THE UWF AND SHOOT STYLE

Krugman, Michael, *Andre the Giant: A Legendary Life* (Simon and Schuster, 2009).

Marvez, Alex, "Inside the Universal Wrestling Federation," *Wrestling Observer 1989 Yearbook*.

Meltzer, Dave, *Who's Who in Pro Wrestling* (Wrestling Observer, 1986).

Molinaro, John, *Top 100 Pro Wrestlers of All Time* (Winding Star Press, 2002).

"Shootstyle," ProwrestlingHiostory.com.

Snowden, Jonathan, *Total MMA: Inside Ultimate Fighting* (ECW Press, 2008).

SELECT NEWSLETTERS:

Wrestling Observer, August 14, 1996; July 27, 1998

19. THE NEXT LEVEL: THE SHOOT-STYLE REVOLUTION

Bessac, Scott, interview with author.

DeLucia, Jason, interview with author.

Feinstein, Rob, director, *Shoot with Vader*, 1998.

Foley, Mick, *Have a Nice Day* (Avon Books, 2000).

Hume, Matt, interview with author.

Martin, Todd, "The overlooked origins of mixed martial arts," CBSSports.com, 2007.

Meltzer, Dave, interview with author.

Mezger, Guy, interview with author.

Oliver, Greg and Steve Johnson, *Pro Wrestling Hall of Fame: The Heels* (ECW Press, 2007).

Rutten, Bas, interview with author.

Shamrock, Bob, interview with author.

Shamrock, Ken and Richard Hanner, *Inside the Lion's Den* (Tuttle Publishing, 1997).

———, interview with author.

Shamrock, Frank, interview with author.

Shannon, Jake, "Mark Fleming Interview," ScientificWrestling.com.

Snowden, Jonathan and Kendall Shields, *The MMA Encyclopedia* (ECW Press, 2010).

———, *Total MMA: Inside Ultimate Fighting* (ECW Press, 2008).

White, Vernon, interview with author.

SELECT NEWSLETTERS:
Pro Wrestling Torch #248, October 16, 1993
Wrestling Observer Newsletter, February 22, 1993

20. UFC: NO HOLDS BARRED

Arnold, Zach, interview with author.
Barnett, Josh, interview with author.
Bessac, Scott, interview with author.
Gracie, Rickson, interview with author.
Gracie, Royce, interview with author.
Isaacs, David, interview with author.
Loiseleur, Tony, interview with author.
Malenko, Joe, interview with author.
Nelson, Steve, interview with author.
Pelc, Gene, interview with author.
Pelc, Ted, interview with author.
Rodgers, Victor, "The Dan Severn Interview," CagesideSeats.com.
Rutten, Bas, interview with author.
Severn, Dan, interview with author.
Shamrock, Bob, interview with author.
Shamrock, Frank, interview with author.
Shamrock, Ken, interview with author.
Shannon, Jake, *Say Uncle* (ECW Press, 2011).
Snowden, Jonathan and Kendall Shields, *The MMA Encyclopedia* (ECW Press, 2010).
Snowden, Jonathan, *Total MMA: Inside Ultimate Fighting* (ECW Press, 2008).

SELECT NEWSLETTERS:
Wrestling Observer Newsletter, September 8, 2003
Pro Wrestling Torch #387, May 11, 1996.

21. FIGHTING FOR PRIDE

Arnold, Zach, interview with author.
Coleman, Mark, interview with author.
Gracie, Rickson, interview with author.
Kerr, Mark, interview with author.

Meltzer, Dave, interview with author.
"The Paul Orndorff Interview," *Wrestling Perspective* #111.
Pelc, Ted, interview with author.
Quadros, Stephen, interview with author.
Rutten, Bas, interview with author.
Snowden, Jonathan, *Total MMA: Inside Ultimate Fighting* (ECW Press, 2008).

SELECTED NEWSLETTERS:
Figure Four Wrestling #288, January 1, 2001
Wrestling Observer Newsletter, October 16, 1995

22. SAKU

Gracie, Royce, interview with author.
Isaacs, David, interview with author.
"Royce and Rorion Gracie," *Kakutogi Tsushin* (translated by Yoko Kondo), June 11, 2000.
McCarthy, John and Hunt, Loretta, *Let's Get It On!* (Medallion Press, 2011).
Mezger, Guy, interview with author.
Nelson, Steve, interview with author.
Newton, Carlos, interview with author.
Sakuraba, Kazushi, *Me* (MMA Translations, 2001).
———, *Me* (MMA Translations, 2007).

23. BRAWL FOR ALL

Club WWI, "Haku/Meng," October 2011.
Devito Jr., Basil, *Wrestlemania: The Official Insider's Story* (Regan Books, 2001).
Duncan, Royal and Gary Will, *Wrestling Title Histories* (Archeus Communications, 2000).
Feinstein, Rob, director, *Shoot with Bart Gunn*, 2007.
———, *Shoot with Savio Vega*, 2010.
———, *Shoot with Steve Williams*, 2002.
"Pierre Carl Oullet," SlamWrestling.com.
Rodgers, Victor, "The Dan Severn Interview," CagesideSeats.com.
Ross, Jim, interview with author.
Severn, Dan, interview with author.
Shamrock, Ken, interview with author.

Watts, Bill and Scott Williams, *The Cowboy and the Cross* (ECW Press, 2006).
"Who's Slamming Who?," Cornette's Commentary with Jim Cornette, March 16, 2009.
Williams, Steve, interview with author.
Zimmerman, Christopher Robin, "WWF Raw is War, 8/10/1998," SlashWrestling.com.

SELECT NEWSLETTERS:
Pro Wrestling Torch #501, July 4, 1998; #505, August 1, 1998; #509, August 29, 1998
Wrestling Observer, July 6, 1998; August 3, 1998; August 24, 1998; January 11, 2010

24. YOUR OLYMPIC HERO: KURT ANGLE

Angle, Kurt, *It's True, It's True* (Harper Entertainment, 2001).
Curby, Jake, "Drug Testing in Wrestling," CurbyWrestling.com.
Dunn, Kevin, director, *WWE 24/7 Legends of Wrestling: Bad Asses*, 2007.
"DuPont Heir Dies in Prison," UPI.com, December 10, 2010.
Funk Jr., Dory, "In Funk's Corner: Do Your Best and Don't Quit," Dory-Funk.com.
King, Peter, "Gripping Finish," *Sports Illustrated*, August 1, 1996.
Landsberg, Michael, Host, *Off the Record*, April 29, 2004.
Randazzo V, Matthew, *Ring of Hell* (Phoenix Books, 2008).
Reilly, Rick, "Holding Their Own," *Sports Illustrated*, August 12, 1996.
Turkington, Carol, *No Holds Barred: The Strange Life of John E. du Pont* (Turner Pub, 1996).

SELECT NEWSPAPERS AND NEWSLETTERS:
New York Times, February 4, 1996
Wrestling Observer Newsletter, August 23, 2004

25. THE NEXT BIG THING

Botter, Jeremy, "Exclusive: Legendary Announcer Jim Ross Validates Folklore," Heavy.com.
Feinstein, Rob, director, *Shoot with Kurt Angle*, 2008.
Landsberg, Michael, Host, *Off the Record*, April 29, 2004.
Lennon, Patrick, "Fighting Talk: Angle Grinder," *Daily Star*, July 30, 2010.
Lesnar, Brock, interview with author.

Penn, Nate, "Brock Lesnar: "I Like to Punish People," *Maxim*, May 2009.

Randazzo V, Matthew, *Ring of Hell* (Phoenix Books, 2008).

Rippel, Joel, *Brock Lesnar: The Making of a Hard-Core Legend* (Triumph Books, 2010).

Schecter, B.J., "Very Big Man on Campus," *Sports Illustrated*, March 6, 2000.

Smith, Michael David, "Patriots' Stephen Neal Recalls Wrestling UFC Heavyweight Champ Brock Lesnar," AOLNews.com.

"Who's Slamming Who?," Cornette's Commentary, July 20, 2009.

SELECT NEWSPAPERS AND NEWSLETTERS:

Figure Four Weekly #584, September 4, 2006

Pittsburgh Tribune-Review, November 12, 2006

Pro Wrestling Torch #777, September 27, 2003; #802, March 20, 2004; #934, September 27, 2006

Wrestling Observer Newsletter, September 2, 2002; April 7, 2003; November 15, 2004; December 20, 2004

26. WRESTLING INVASION

Botter, Jeremy, "Exclusive: Jim Ross Talks Becoming an MMA Fan, James Toney, Brock Lesnar and more," Heavy.com.

Carwin, Shane, interview with author.

Coleman, Mark, interview with author.

Cook, Bob, interview with author.

Iole, Kevin, "Lesnar-Carwin a Fitting Finish to a Special Night," Sports.Yahoo.com.

Konrad, Cole, interview with author.

Lashley, Bobby, interview with author.

Lesnar, Brock, interview with author.

——— and Paul Heyman, *Death Clutch: My Story of Determination, Domination, and Survival* (Harper Collins, 2011).

Mir, Frank, interview with author.

Penn, Nate, "Brock Lesnar: 'I Like to Punish People,'" *Maxim*, May 2009.

Randazzo V, Matthew, *Ring of Hell* (Phoenix Books, 2008).

Velasquez, Cain, interview with author.

White, Dana, interview with author.

SELECT NEWSLETTERS:

Figure Four Weekly, June 11, 2007

27. THE FUTURE

Barnett, Josh, interview with author.
Caplan, Sam, "5 Oz. of Pain Exclusive: Josh Barnett Responds to Dana White," FiveOuncesofPain.com.
Hume, Matt, interview with author.
Melanson, Neil, interview with author.
Roth, Matthew, "HKL Exclusive interview with Neil Melanson Pt 1: Catch Wrestling and His Books," HeadKickLegend.com.

I owe a debt of gratitude to Dave Meltzer and Ed "In San Antonio" for this book. *Shooters* was initially conceived as a magazine article, and they helped me flesh out a list of tough guys in the media room at a UFC event. Without their enthusiasm and expertise, I may have never gotten up the nerve to turn this into a book. Thanks, gentlemen.

Thanks as well to Kendall Shields. Although the project didn't go as planned, Kendall's voice and research rings clear throughout. He wrote much of what you see in the Mitsuyo Maeda, Masahiko Kimura, and Kazushi Sakuraba chapters. I hope we work together again sometime down the road.

ACKNOWLEDGMENTS

What can I say about Jake Shannon and J. Michael Kenyon? They lent generously from their huge collections of wrestling history and memorabilia. Don Luce, Mark Hewitt, John Nash, and Steve Yohe also helped with their time and resources. Yohe, in particular, served as my guide when things got confusing. He and Tim Hornbaker are titans in the field of wrestling history. I couldn't have done it without you.

Of course, in the modern era, Dave Meltzer stands alone as our top expert. I relied on him heavily, supplemented by Wade Keller's excellent *Pro Wrestling Torch* and Bryan Alvarez's *Figure Four Weekly*. Thanks, too, to all the wrestlers and fighters who took the time to talk with me. This is your story. I'm proud to tell it.

THEM'S FIGHTING WORDS!

HOT SHOTS AND HIGH SPOTS
George Napolitano's Amazing Pictorial History of Wrestling's Greatest Stars
George Napolitano

THE MMA ENCYCLOPEDIA
Jonathan Snowden
and Kendall Shields

TOTAL MMA
Inside Ultimate Fighting
Jonathan Snowden

PHYSICAL CHESS
My Life in Catch-As-Catch-Can Wrestling
Billy Robinson
with Jake Shannon

SAY UNCLE!
Catch-As-Catch-Can Wrestling and the Roots of
Ultimate Fighting, Pro Wrestling, & Modern Grappling
Jake Shannon

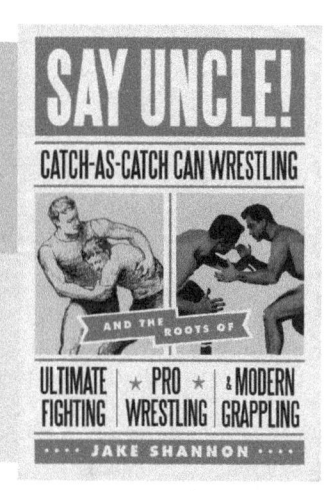

OCTOBER 2012

FEBRUARY 2013

**THE PRO WRESTLING
HALL OF FAME** Heroes & Icons
Steven Johnson and Greg Oliver

**THE 50 GREATEST
PROFESSIONAL WRESTLERS
OF ALL TIME** The Definitive Shoot
Larry Matysik

ECWPRESS.COM/FIGHTINGWORDS

At ECW Press, we want you to enjoy this book in whatever format you like, whenever you like. Leave your print book at home and take the eBook to go! Purchase the print edition and receive the eBook free. Just send an email to ebook@ecwpress.com and include:

- the book title
- the name of the store where you purchased it
- your receipt number
- your preference of file type: PDF or ePub?

A real person will respond to your email with your eBook attached. And thanks for supporting an independently owned Canadian publisher with your purchase!

Get the eBook free!*
*proof of purchase required